THE HUMANITIES
AND THE
CIVIC IMAGINATION

✦ ✦ ✦

The Humanities and the Civic Imagination

Collected Addresses and Essays 1978–1998

by
James F. Veninga

University of North Texas Press
Denton, Texas

5 4 3 2 1

Requests for permission to reproduce material from this work should be sent to:
Permissions
University of North Texas Press
P. O. Box 311336
Denton, TX 76203-1336
940-565-2142

The paper used in this book meets the minimum requirements of the American
National Standard for Permanence of Paper for Printed Library Materials,
Z39.48.1984.

Library of Congress Cataloging-in-Publication Data

Veninga, James F. (James Frank), 1944–
    The Humanities and the Civic Imagination: Collected Addresses and
Essays, 1978–1998 / by James F. Veninga.
        p.   cm.
    "Collection of addresses and essays written during author's tenure as
    executive director of Texas Council for the Humanities" – Pref.
    Includes bibliographical references and index.
    ISBN 1-57441-052-0 (paper : alk. paper)
    1. Education, Humanistic—United States. 2. Humanities—Study and
teaching—United States. 3. Civics—Study and teaching—United States.
4. Education—Aims and objectives—United States. 5. Educational
change—United States. 6. Texas Council for the Humanities. 7. National
Endowment for the Humanities. I. Title.
LC1023.V45 1999   98-42778
370.11'2'0973—dc21   CIP

Design by Angela Schmitt

*To my colleagues on the staff of the
Texas Council for the Humanities,
past and present,
with gratitude for our shared journey.*

. . . there just simply must be no neglect of humanities. The values of our free and compassionate society are as vital to our national success as the skills of our technical and scientific age.

Lyndon B. Johnson
200th Anniversary Convocation at Brown University
September 28, 1964

We all lead the life of the mind. When we teach our children not to hit or steal, we are passing on the great ideas of moral philosophy. When we claim our rights as citizens, we invoke a social contract. When we defend our freedom or our neighbors' freedom, we hearken to one of the most stirring ideas of western thought.

When we decide how to vote, when we pray, when we debate an issue, and when we fall in love, we are participating in the humanities. When we reflect on the changes in our own lives, when we recognize some of the things we love about the world, and when we resist loss and death with all our strength—we are participating in the humanities. All adults think and choose; all adults reflect and wonder. The humanities address our deepest contemporary concerns.

Annie Dillard
Testimony Submitted to the
Appropriations Subcommittee on the Interior
U. S. House of Representatives
March 17, 1988

When you sit . . . as a person spending tax revenues, you always are under the gun. Do not make a damn fool of yourself. Do not spend the money irresponsibly. . . .

Charles Frankel
Philosopher and Former State Department Official
at a 1979 conference on federal policy
on the arts and humanities.
Austin, Texas

Contents

Part Three
The Humanities and Society

Preface

On nearly any given day, somewhere in Texas there is a public event—a conference, a community lecture, a documentary film broadcast on a PBS station, a museum exhibition, a library discussion program, a workshop for school teachers—either funded or sponsored by the Texas Council for the Humanities (TCH). Working in collaboration with the National Endowment for the Humanities (NEH), the TCH connects resources in the humanities, including faculty from the state's colleges and universities, with the needs, interests, and quests of an inquisitive public.

The TCH has been part of a national movement to enhance and expand the civic life of the nation through education in the humanities—the study of history, literature, ethics, languages, philosophy, cultural studies, religious studies, anthropology, sociology, and related fields. While this movement has roots deep in American history—public dialogue at the time of the nation's founding, the chautauqua of the late nineteenth-century, women's reading clubs, education programs of labor unions, the theater and writers projects of the Depression-era Works Progress Administration, the citizenship schools of the civil rights movement, for example—it is intimately tied to the passage in 1965 of the National Foundation on the Arts and Humanities Act. At the insistence of the Congress, the NEH expanded its work in the early 1970s by supporting newly established state humanities councils.

Enough time has passed to begin assessing the impact of this movement, to see what has been accomplished, where and how the state humanities councils have benefited villages, towns, and cities throughout the nation, and its impact on the professional lives of the thousands of college and university teachers who have participated in public programs; on cultural institutions, including libraries, museums, and historical societies; on the many civic organizations that have sponsored programs funded by state councils; and, most importantly, on the millions of Americans who have participated in these programs.

The movement has not been without its critics, those who believe that humanities education is essentially a private affair; those who believe that the locale of the humanities is in institutions of higher learning and not in the community; those who believe in the inappropriateness of federal funding to help support this work; those who distrust the open-endedness of humanistic inquiry.

But these critics have posed only modest challenges compared to the powerful influence of popular culture which all too often demeans the individual, suffocates imagination, and undermines those civic bonds and obligations which are so essential to the well-being of democratic society. The public humanities movement has stood for an alternative culture, one that draws its sustenance from reflection, dialogue, and constructive engagement.

This book, a collection of addresses and essays written during my tenure as executive director of the TCH, is preliminary to the task of assessing the historical import of the public humanities movement. In publishing this collection, my goal is to make available pertinent essays that explore the intellectual underpinnings of the enterprise, that demonstrate engagement with challenges along the way, and that show how one state council has sought to nourish and enhance the nation's civic life. Nearly all of the work published in this volume was connected to various initiatives, emphases, and interests of the TCH. Thus the collection evidences the intellectual engagement of the organization as well as that of the author.

Some of these essays have been previously published, as noted in the introductions to the applicable chapters. I am grateful to the several publishers from whom permission to republish was acquired. One of the essays, "Making Connections: The Humanities, Culture and Community," published by the American Council of Learned Societies, was written jointly with my colleague Jim Quay, executive director of the California Council for the Humanities.

I have resisted as much as possible the temptation to tinker with texts of addresses given and essays published. Only minor changes have been made, and most of these involve correcting typographical mistakes and grammatical errors. One exception to this, however, should be noted. During the course of its twenty-five year history, the TCH has been known by three names: Texas Committee for the Humanities and Public Policy, Texas Committee for the Humanities, and, most recently, Texas Council for the Humanities. For the sake of clarity, I have used only the most recent name—Texas Council for the Humanities—throughout the volume.

I am deeply grateful to the 1997 executive committee of the TCH board of directors, chaired by professor of philosophy and director of medical humanities at Texas A&M University, Herman Saatkamp, Jr., whose members encouraged this publication and who suggested that the collection would benefit from an historical overview of the TCH. Staff members Judith Diaz, Frances Leonard, and Monte Youngs provided data and information that proved helpful in writing this over-view. I express appreciation to the board of directors for its support of this project and its desire to see it completed in time for TCH's twenty-fifth anniversary commemoration in 1999.

The essays are organized into three parts, and each essay includes a brief introduction. I have placed the essays in each part in chrono-logical order, thereby assisting the reader in seeing the evolution of interests and concerns.

Part One includes addresses, essays, and congressional testimony that focus on the experimental nature of state council work, on the issue of public accountability, on the relationship of NEH to the state councils, on the multiple roles of scholars engaged in public programs, and on the civic work of the councils. The reader will grasp the extent to which the TCH has been a part of a new national effort. This effort has come at a difficult time in the cultural life of the country, and thus some of these essays here as well as later in the collection show how the TCH and I responded to the so-called "cultural wars" of the 1980s and 1990s.

Part Two includes addresses and essays that reflect on the impor-tance of the humanities to the education of active, responsible citizens. TCH did not turn its attention to elementary and secondary education until the early 1980s. The essay "Texas: The End of Laissez Faire Educa-tion," written in 1984, may seem dated in light of current debate about the future of Texas's public schools, but this debate has its origins in the reforms launched in the early 1980s, and thus this essay provides useful historical perspective. Several of the essays focus on undergraduate education and the relationship of the university to society.

Part Three demonstrates the public uses of the humanities. Several of the essays reflect on one of the critical issues of our time, that of finding unity in the midst of our increasing pluralism. Other essays explore the relationship of the scholar to society, the role of the hu-manities in building community, and the capacity of the humanities to foster positive values and constructive traditions.

I hope that the reader will discover through these addresses and essays the twenty-five year engagement of the TCH with important issues in American culture. The most fundamental point of the public humanities movement, it seems to me, is this: The humanities provide critical resources for strengthening the moral and intellectual fiber of the country. The humanities help keep the fires of community going. They ignite the civic imagination.

My own reflection on this volume, on the work that I and my colleagues at the TCH have been engaged in during the past quarter century, leads me to three basic points. First, the humanities are for everyone, providing tools for self-understanding, discovery, discernment, and growth. Second, the humanities, while documenting and interpreting the past, are inherently forward-looking, helping us to envision the future. Third, state humanities councils, which evidence the American talent for creating new structures to meet identified needs, are part of a much bigger experiment, that of American democracy itself.

This is indeed what the Texas Council for the Humanities has sought to do: to make the humanities accessible to all, to re-vision the humanities as resources for thinking about the future we wish to create, to put the humanities to work on behalf of the American people and our experiment in self-governance.

Introduction
Giving Wings to Ideas

Hanging on a wall in my office on Main Street in Salado, Texas, is a beautifully framed calligraphed version of the preamble to the National Foundation on the Arts and Humanities Act of 1965, a gift from my colleagues at the Texas Council for the Humanities upon my departure as executive director. These colleagues could not have made me happier, for this preamble to the legislation establishing the National Endowment for the Arts (NEA) and the National Endowment for the Humanities (NEH) has been my constant guide for twenty-five years of public humanities work. That preamble includes, among other statements, the following declarations:

> An advanced civilization must not limit its efforts to science and technology alone but must give full value and support to the other great branches of scholarly and cultural activity in order to achieve a better understanding of the past, a better analysis of the present and a better view of the future.

> Democracy demands wisdom and vision in its citizens. It must therefore foster and support a form of education, and access to the arts and the humanities, designed to make people of all backgrounds and wherever located masters of their technology and not its unthinking servants.

> The practice of art and the study of the humanities requires constant dedication and devotion. While no government can call a great artist or scholar into existence, it is necessary and appropriate for the federal government to help create and sustain not only a climate encouraging freedom of thought, imagination, and inquiry, but also the material conditions facilitating the release of this creative talent.

> The world leadership which has come to the United States cannot rest solely upon superior power, wealth,

and technology, but must be solidly founded upon world-wide respect and admiration for the nation's high qualities as a leader in the realm of ideas and of the spirit.

I have been, for this past quarter of a century, chasing an idea: the idea that the humanities provide indispensable resources for a democratic society. I joined the TCH staff in 1974, after three years of teaching at the University of St. Thomas, Houston, and after completing my Ph.D. degree at Rice University. I was drawn to the magnificent opportunity to help extend the benefits of humanities learning to adult Americans in very public settings. But what really caught my imagination was an even bolder challenge, given by the Congress when it amended in 1970 the original legislation, that of relating the humanities "to the current conditions of national life."

These twin Congressional goals, that of expanding the number of Americans who have access to the humanities and who have deep appreciation for humanistic learning, and that of relating the humanities to the "current conditions of national life," have formed the central mission of the Texas Council for the Humanities. Both goals can be seen in the current mission statement: "The TCH, working in partnership with the NEH, seeks to engage the people of Texas in critical reflection of their individual and collective lives by providing opportunities for lifelong learning in the humanities."

We were responding to a new bipartisan federal initiative to ensure that America would be a leader in the realm of ideas and of the human spirit. Untested waters, to be sure—a new mandate, a new organization, new goals, new tasks. Fortunately, the TCH was not alone. There were councils operating in many other states by the time TCH was founded. NEH, in consultation with the councils, had done well in shaping the early parameters of state humanities council work. Nevertheless, this was a once-in-a-lifetime encounter with the proverbial *tabula rasa*.

This is not the place to provide a history of the TCH, and I am not the one to write that history. But the leadership of the TCH board of directors suggested that the readers of this collection of essays might benefit from an historical sketch of the TCH, a summary of what the Council has done and been about. What follows is just that—a sketch, with some concluding remarks about the future. However, I have included many examples of programs and projects funded or sponsored by the Council, for they are the substance of this work, and for them everything else exists. I admit up front my bias: this is a program that works. I believe the TCH has made a significant contribution to the State of Texas and has enriched the lives of thousands of Texans. I also think it has proved to be a source of encouragement and renewal for many humanities teachers in our schools, colleges, and universities.

The Beginning

Public Law 209, passed by the Eighty-ninth Congress of the United States in 1965, established a National Endowment for the Arts and a National Endowment for the Humanities. In the early years of the NEH, the focus was primarily on support for scholarly endeavors—fellowships, books and journals, teaching. A few years after their founding, the Congress expressed some concern with both NEA and NEH: members said too little money was going to achieve the public dimension of the legislation, ensuring access to the arts and humanities by the American public. Strong encouragement was given to expand public programming. By 1970, the Congress, in order to enhance NEH's public mission, was encouraging the NEH to decentralize a portion of its funding through allocations to entities within each of the states, as NEA had done with considerable success.

The NEH considered various possibilities for achieving this goal, as discussed in the first essay in this collection. By 1972, after several years of experimentation, the NEH decided that non-profit citizen committees afforded the best opportunity for promoting the humanities in the individual states.

The NEH invited four Texans to a two-day conference in Washington in May 1972 to be briefed on the new state humanities program. These individuals were Thomas B. Brewer, vice chancellor of Texas Christian University; Levi A. Olan, Dallas rabbi and former member of the University of Texas Board of Regents; Emmet Field, vice president for academic affairs at the University of Houston; and David M. Vigness, chairman of the department of history at Texas Tech University. Following this meeting, this group held a series of meetings in Dallas to discuss initiating such a program in Texas. Through the leadership of Thomas Brewer, the group, calling itself the Texas Committee for the Humanities, applied for and received a $20,000 planning grant from the NEH, effective January 1, 1973.

The TCH next conducted a series of regional conferences to promote the program and to gain public suggestions regarding the council's work. Since NEH required all state committees—as these organizations were then called—to focus on the relationship between the humanities and public policy issues, the group was renamed the Texas Committee for the Humanities and Public Policy. The first implementation grant request was submitted to the NEH on June 15, 1973, requesting funds for administration, program development, and support of local grant projects. A $170,000, eighteen-month grant was approved, effective October 1, 1973. The TCH board employed a director, Sandra L. Myres, a member of the history faculty at the University of Texas at Arlington. The first TCH grant was awarded in January 1974 to KUT-FM, Austin, for a series of weekly two-hour radio programs focusing on the Texas Constitutional Revision Convention. Articles of Association were signed on March 18, 1976, and remained in effect until September 5, 1985, when the Texas Committee for the Humanities was incorporated under the laws of Texas. The Internal Revenue Service granted tax-exempt status on August 25, 1976.

The first office of the Texas Committee for the Humanities was on the campus of the University of Texas at Arlington, which provided both office space and support services. The University Librarian, the late John Hudson, took special interest in housing the TCH at the University. However, it became clear that the TCH needed to be closer to allied statewide organizations and to state government, and in June 1980 the TCH relocated to Austin. After occupying space at 1604 Nueces Street near the University of Texas at Austin, and then space in a small office building downtown at 100 Neches, TCH moved in 1990 into a four-building condominium office project in south Austin, located at 3809 S. 2nd Street. A 1991 grant from the Meadows Foundation in the amount of $50,000 provided funds for a down payment on the 6,900 square foot building that it was leasing. The mortgage was retired in April 1997. TCH currently leases space in an adjacent building for the workshop of the Texas Humanities Resource Center, where exhibitions for statewide touring are fabricated and maintained.

Board Leadership

Federal law allows the governor of Texas to make five appointments to the board. The other directors—with nearly equal representation between academic and public sectors—are elected by the board as vacancies occur. These vacancies are announced to the public and nominations are actively sought. In accordance with federal law, TCH by-laws require a board that is representative of the state. Non-gubernatorial directors serve terms of office of three years, with the possibility that directors may be reelected to a second three-year term.

The extraordinary men and women who have served on the board for the past twenty-five years have brought much vitality to the TCH. They have come from all walks of life. They have been ranchers, corporate leaders, university teachers and administrators, public school administrators and teachers, labor leaders, poets and novelists, media specialists, librarians, museum administrators, politicians, homemakers, and civic leaders. They have come from all parts of the state, from Nacogoches to El Paso, Edinburg to Amarillo. They have been Republicans and Democrats and Independents. They have been black, brown and white. And with just a few exceptions, they have been persons dedicated to the mission of the organization, serious about their responsibilities, and committed to making a difference in Texas through the TCH. Their contributions over the years have been extensive. Board directors have assisted with outreach, program development, legislative affairs, project evaluation, and financial development, in addition to the required responsibilities of policy-making, financial review, grant review, and long-range planning.

TCH has been well-served by the following chairs: Thomas Brewer (1973–1975); A. J. Carlson, dean of humanities, Austin College (1976–1977); the late Alan Taniguchi, architect (1978–1979); the late Edmund Pincoffs, professor of philosophy, University of Texas at Austin (1980); Betty Anderson, past president, League of Women Voters of Texas (1981); Roy Mersky, professor of law and director of research, University of Texas School of Law (1982); Archie McDonald, professor of history, Stephen F. Austin State University (1983); Bob Bowman, corporate manager of public relations, Delta Drilling Company (1984); Rene D. Zentner, associate dean, University of Houston Law Center (1985); William P. Wright, Jr., chairman, Western Marketing, Inc. (1986–1987), Ellen C. Temple, publisher, Lufkin (1988); Edward V. George, professor of classical languages, Texas Tech University (1989–1990); J. Sam Moore, Jr., attorney, El Paso (1991); Everett L. Fly, architect, San Antonio (1992–1993); Wilkes Berry, associate vice president for academic affairs, Texas Woman's University (1994–1995); Rachel R. Johnson, registrar, Tarrant County Junior College (1996); Herman J. Saatkamp, Jr., professor of philosophy and medical humanities, Texas A&M University (1997); and Barbara Gubbin, director, Houston Public Library (1998). Each person brought to this leadership position his or her own perspective on our work. My task as executive director was to capitalize on those perspectives to ensure that the TCH would move forward through the constant renewal of ideas from the board's leadership.

Three of the TCH chairs served the state humanities councils and the NEH in other capacities. Rene Zenter was elected to a term of office on the board of the Federation of State Humanities Councils. William P. Wright, Jr. was appointed by Ronald Reagan to a term on the National Council on the Humanities, NEH's advisory board. Everett Fly was elected to the Federation's board of directors and then was appointed by Bill Clinton to the President's Committee on the Arts and Humanities. In this latter role, he has been an articulate spokesperson for continued funding of the arts and humanities.

The late Sandra L. Myres served as executive director from 1973 to 1975, laying the organizational groundwork for the humanities program in Texas. I joined the staff as assistant director in late 1974 and was appointed executive director in 1975, after Myres returned to her position in the department of history at the University of Texas at Arlington. She became a leading Texas historian with fresh contributions made to the study of women in Texas and the American West. Roberto Salmón, a historian from the University of Texas—Pan American, and a member of the TCH board of directors, served as acting executive director when I took a leave of absence in 1995 to direct a national project sponsored by the Kettering Foundation, NEH, and the Federation of State Humanities Councils, The Humanities and Public Engagement. Upon my return, I continued to serve until August 31, 1997, at which time Richard T. Hull, a professor of philosophy at the State University of New York at Buffalo, was appointed executive director.

Program Shifts

In its 1976 legislation reauthorizing the NEH, Congress encouraged councils to move beyond the singular, NEH-required focus on public policy issues. It wanted to make sure that the programs conducted reflected the needs and interests of the individual states. Since that time, the TCH has funded a wider-range of projects involving all fields of the humanities. In recognition of this shift, the organization was renamed the Texas Committee for the Humanities in 1978. In 1996, the organization's name was changed to the Texas Council for the Humanities, a belated development that reflected the increasing use of the word "council" rather than "committee" by the Congress and state organizations.

The early focus on public policy left a lasting legacy. Some of the most imaginative work of grantees occurred during the early years as connections were made between the disciplines of the humanities and various contemporary issues—the then "current conditions" of state and national life. Here is how TCH, in its 1974–1975 program announcement, made the case for bringing scholars into public discussion on vital contemporary issues:

> It may be said that the humanities and those who have devoted their professional lives to the study and teaching of the humanities have as their central concern the meaning and purpose of human life and human relationships.
>
> While teaching scholars in the humanities have no monopoly on values or on answers to our critical public questions, they are trained in criticism and reasoned discourse, the comparison of values derived from other cultures and critical thinking based on plausible alternatives. The humanities offer moral and ethical considerations that are among our greatest national shortages. They raise questions about the value and 'humanness' of our actions and decisions. They inspire in us an ongoing respect for the richness of our past, for the ideals and perspectives embodied in literature and debated in philosophy.
>
> In short, professional humanists are custodians of the culture who learn new dimensions of humanity while saving the memories of civilization. And as they share and ponder, they can bring to public forums perspectives beyond the hardest facts.
>
> Humanists are concerned with the nature of justice, the value of human freedom, the purpose and conduct of state and social institutions, the moral and ethical consequences of human action, and other concerns which not so surprisingly are also at the center of most contemporary public policy issues.

Here are a few examples of the kinds of projects funded during these early years.

The Texas Committee on Natural Resources received a grant for a project entitled "Property Rights and Individual Rights: Problems of Public Rivers and Streambeds in Texas." A two-day conference of landowners, canoeists, attorneys, engineers, humanists, and state officials was held to alleviate growing conflict—sometimes evidenced by bullets passing over the heads of carefree and not always responsible canoeists—especially along the Guadalupe River. The Friends of the Classics, Inc., Lubbock, sponsored "The Voice of the People," four lecture and discussion programs, and a one-hour television program, comparing fifth-century Athenian democracy to the political structure and democratic practice in twentieth-century Texas, focusing especially on the role of the individual in the development of public policy. The Southwest Center for Urban Research sponsored a one-day conference on "Privacy, Disclosure and Surveillance in the Electronic Age." Austin Community College received funds for the creation of a video program for local broadcast on the formation of neighborhood organizations as they attempt to influence local land use issues. The Globe of the Great Southwest, Odessa, sponsored a presentation of scenes from the play, *The Night Thoreau Spent in Jail*, followed by a discussion on problems related to the issues of ecology, war, and taxation. The Institute of Religion and Human Development, Texas Medical Center, Houston, sponsored a three-day symposium that brought together health professionals, public policy makers, scholars, and citizens to investigate present health care policies. The Catholic Diocese of Brownsville received funds for a series of ten public forums exploring the effectiveness of recent government programs related to health, social welfare, and community development. The Office of the Attorney General received a grant for four regional conferences to discuss current legislation affecting the rights of the handicapped.

Although the TCH never left behind its interest in relating the humanities to contemporary issues, the 1976 legislation resulted in a broadening of subjects and constituencies served. Some critics thought that the public policy focus required by the NEH was too limiting in terms of subject matter and in terms of people served. In too many projects, some argued, the humanities were peripheral, playing second fiddle to public policy analysis. But the most telling concern came from the Congress: state councils needed to be free to form their own identity separate from the NEH, and an NEH-imposed policy on subject matter prevented such growth.

A special committee of the TCH was appointed in 1977 to consider the legislative changes and to make recommendations concerning the future program. A survey of over 1,000 academicians, public officials, project directors, and interested citizens contributed to the committee's deliberation. The TCH board approved a widening of possible topics for TCH funding, and by 1978 TCH was supporting a broader range of programs, including those dealing with local and state history and culture. Texas A&M University received a grant for a symposium on "The

Czechs in Texas." Texas A&I University received funds for a program on Chicano history and culture. The University of Texas of the Permian Basin received a grant for a project on the folklore and history of the Permian Basin. Public policy programs continued, but a dramatic shift had taken place.

The program announcements of the TCH from 1980 to the present have tended to focus on five general categories for grant projects: local, state, and national history; ethnic/women's history and culture; contemporary issues; foreign cultures and international issues (especially after 1991); and other topics drawn from the disciplines of the humanities. In 1996, TCH added an additional category, "enduring questions," to underscore its commitment to public programs that explore the nature of the good life; freedom and responsibility; social cohesion and disintegration; morality and ethics; the nature and meaning of work and play; good and evil; justice and injustice; and the meaning of life.

Examples of projects funded in more recent years, as well as TCH's creative use of requests for proposals to stimulate interest in particular topics, can be found below.

Funding Shifts

State humanities councils experienced modest increases in annual funding from the federal government from their beginning through the early 1980s. In 1986 TCH revenues were cut by forty percent when federal funding dropped significantly and private sector support —weakened by the collapse of the Texas economy—diminished at the same time. Some initiatives had to be curtailed, postponed, and/or eliminated. Funds lost were gradually restored by the early 1990s, and then held stable through 1995. As a result of the 1994 national elections, many federal programs came under close scrutiny by the new Congress, including the NEA and the NEH. By 1996, the annual budget for the NEH had dropped from $178 to $110 million, only slightly more than the amount appropriated for the NEA. State humanities councils, however, experienced more modest cuts, with the TCH losing approximately six percent of its federal funding. Some of the funds lost were restored through the fiscal year 1997 appropriation. Although federal funding for TCH has remained stable the last few years—about $970,000 annually—the council's purchasing power has dropped dramatically from what it was in the early 1980s.

Continued uncertainty over the future of federal funding for cultural programs has cast a long shadow over state humanities councils. Ensuring continued appropriations at adequate levels has been a matter of deep concern for the TCH since the early 1980s. TCH has worked closely with the Federation of State Humanities Councils to make the case before Congress for continued appropriations for NEH and the state councils.

As an independent non-profit corporation, TCH is able to solicit funds from the private sector. Funds received from the NEH must be matched with either hard dollars or in-kind support. In most years, every federal dollar was matched three to four times by TCH and its grantees. But from the very beginning, board directors and staff members considered ways to expand private sector support. For example, in 1976 the TCH submitted to the NEH a detailed plan to increase such support, focusing especially on the need for more funding for TCH-sponsored projects and the opportunity of stimulating more third-party support for approved grant projects. In 1982 a further plan was developed that focused specifically on expanding the number and quality of TCH sponsored programs through private sector support. In 1986, the Texas Humanities Alliance was established to expand the number of individual and institutional donors who would contribute on an annual basis. Thereafter, in nearly every funding request to the NEH, financial development plans were further developed and refined. In 1997, a new plan emerged, one that could lead to expanded support for TCH-sponsored programs such as the Outstanding Teaching of the Humanities Awards, the speakers bureau, the Texas Humanities Resource Center, reading and discussion programs in public libraries, and summer workshops for teachers, through a new corporate and foundation sponsors program. This initiative was scheduled to begin in 1998.

In regard to these plans, TCH's primary goal has been to augment federal funds to help ensure a growing program. TCH and the Texas Humanities Resource Center have raised approximately $750,000 since 1980 for their own projects. Most of these funds were given for new and fairly large-scale projects. TCH's 1986 sesquicentennial project, "The Texas Experience," garnered $195,500 from Shell Oil Companies Foundation and the Hoblitzelle Foundation. Over $90,000, including $50,000 from the Brown Foundation, was raised to expand TCH's publications efforts, including its magazine, *The Texas Humanist*, in the mid-1980s. The Temple Foundation and the publishing firm, Holt, Rinehart & Winston, provided support for the Outstanding Teaching of the Humanities Awards, begun in 1989. The Jones Foundation in Abilene provided funds to help launch the Texas Humanities Alliance. The Rockefeller Foundation provided $25,000 in 1991 for one of THRC's most successful traveling exhibitions, *Splendors of Mexico*. In 1995 Exxon Corporation provided $25,000 through the State Preservation Board for a traveling THRC exhibition celebrating the sesquicentennial of statehood. Most recently, The Meadows Foundation and the Houston Endowment have provided grants totaling $82,730 for the promising "Humanities Interactive" project of THRC.

Additional funding has also come through competitive programs of the NEH. From 1984 to 1997, $440,000 was raised for various initiatives, from the council's project on "Texas Myths" to the $160,000 award for THRC's Columbian Quincentenary exhibitions. Most recently, NEH has made available $105,000 to THRC for planning and implementing the "Humanities Interactive" project.

The growth of the Texas Humanities Alliance has also played a significant role in financial development efforts. Begun by ten former TCH board directors, the Alliance now numbers over one thousand people from across the state. More than $150,000 has been raised from these members since the Alliance's founding in 1986.

Finally, in terms of private sector support, it should be noted that more than $300,000 has been given annually through 1995 by foundations, corporations, and individuals in support of TCH-approved grant projects, with most of these donations qualifying for matching funds from the NEH.

Yet such giving must be seen as only a beginning, for if the promise of the TCH is to be realized in the years ahead, more support will be needed from foundations, corporations, and individuals.

Our inability to augment federal and private sector funding with state appropriations proved to be my biggest disappointment as TCH's executive director. If TCH is to fully carry out its mandate and achieve its potential, it will need to receive the support of the Texas Legislature. Funding for state humanities councils ought to rest on three reliable sources of funding: federal, private, and state. We worked hard to support legislation that would have secured modest appropriations for summer seminars for secondary school teachers, and for new initiatives to promote foreign language and cultures studies. Although authorizing legislation was passed establishing a Texas Academy of Foreign Languages and Cultures, with TCH designated as the agency to manage specific programs, the program has yet to be funded.

Program Development

Given the size and population of the state, TCH has had an enormous challenge in making sure that its efforts would amount to a statewide program. Members of the board of directors have helped immensely in making known to local cultural and educational organizations the existence of the TCH and its willingness to fund projects in local communities. But TCH had to develop strategies to ensure a statewide presence. For example, each year TCH sponsors three or four workshops, in different areas of the state, to acquaint groups with its grant programs and with services and programs provided by the Texas Humanities Resource Center. TCH staff members have worked cooperatively with allied organizations, such as the Texas Association of Museums, the Texas Library Association, the Texas Historical Commission, to make sure that the constituencies of these statewide agencies are aware of the TCH. In the 1980s, such collaboration took TCH into new arenas as we worked more closely with educational agencies and organizations, including the Texas Higher Education Coordinating Board and the Texas Association of School Boards. TCH also sponsors public meetings designed to obtain suggestions on how the TCH program might better reflect local interests. Finally, TCH has consistently developed various kinds of publications to stimulate local interest in the humanities.

Council-Initiated Projects

Although the funding of local projects through a competitive grant program has been a central feature of the TCH, the organization itself has sponsored numerous projects. A resolution was passed by the TCH board of directors in December 1980, calling for the TCH to assume a more "catalytic, leadership" role in the state, taking on new endeavors while sustaining its commitment to serve as a grant-making organization that responds to good ideas from other institutions. Much of the substantive work of the TCH stemmed from this resolution.

One of the first such projects was the publication in 1982 of the report, *Toward Thoughtful, Active Citizens: Improving the Public School Curriculum*. TCH formed in 1981 a Task Force on the Humanities in the Public Schools of Texas, composed of educators and civic leaders. The Task Force's report offered specific recommendations for strengthening the teaching of history, languages, literature, civics, and related fields.

From 1982 to 1990, TCH sponsored an annual Texas Lecture in the Humanities, often in conjunction with a one-day symposium. TCH launched this series with noted biographer and historian Frank E. Vandiver, who chose as his theme, "Biography as Agent of Humanism." The first lecture, held in the Performing Arts Center at the University of Texas at Austin, was followed with a symposium held at a conference facility in Wimberley. Biographers featured included Jean Strouse, Robert Abzug, Ronald Steel, and Stephen B. Oates. Papers presented were published by Texas A&M University Press, *The Biographer's Gift: Life Histories and Humanism* (1983).

The 1983 program featured poet and legal scholar Charles L. Black, Jr., who spoke on "The Humane Imagination in the Great Society." The lecture and symposium were held at The Woodlands Inn in the Woodlands, Texas, with the symposium featuring Robert Plant Armstrong, Philip Bobbitt, Kay Howe, Bob Eckhardt, and Tomas Rivera.

Noted Texas writer John Graves was selected the 1984 Texas Lecturer, and he spoke in the auditorium of the Law School on the topic "Texas Myths and Texas Writing." The symposium featured Lou Halsell Rodenberger, Rolando Hinojosa-Smith, Patricia A. R. Williams, Gilbert M. Cuthbertson, and William T. Pilkington.

Former University of Texas professor and then president of The New York Public Library, Vartan Gregorian, gave the 1985 Texas Lecture, speaking on "Technology and Society: Promise and Peril." The subsequent symposium featured Admiral Bobby Ray Inman, University of Texas chancellor Hans Mark, and scholars Hubert Dreyfus and Carolyn Marvin.

The 1986 lecture was held in the historic San Fernando Cathedral in San Antonio and featured noted Mexican scholar Miguel León-Portilla, who spoke on "Mexico's Cultural Legacy and Identity." The symposium the following day featured scholars from both Mexico and Texas— including Jorge Bustamante and Rodolfo de la Garza—and was sponsored jointly with The Universidad Nacional Autónoma de México en San Antonio.

Barbara Jordan was selected to give the 1987 Texas Lecture in the Humanities, held in Austin. She selected the topic "Equality, Liberty, and the Pursuit of Community in America." The subsequent symposium featured scholars William F. May, Richard Bernstein, Peter Gomes, Patricia Kruppa, and publisher Brux Austin.

"Texas in the 21st Century" became the overall theme for much of TCH work in the late 1980s, and the final three lectures in this series picked up on this theme. Theologian and Rice University president George Rupp spoke on "Preparing for the 21st Century: Beyond Complacency and Nostalgia," at the 1988 lecture, held on the campus of Hardin-Simmons University and co-sponsored by the Abilene Committee for the Humanities. State Representative Wihelmina Delco, chair of the Higher Education Committee, provided the 1989 lecture, speaking on the topic "Texas in the 21st Century: The Role of Education in Shaping the Future." The 1990 lecture was given by Henry B. Cisneros. His theme, "Understanding the Global Community in the Twenty-first Century," augmented work that TCH was doing in promoting international and foreign language studies, and was published by the TCH.

These annual programs were augmented by other TCH projects. Often TCH would issue requests for proposals on the themes selected for the lectures or on related topics, for example: "Texas Myths" (1984); "Science, Technology, and the Shaping of Texas" (1985); "The Mexican Legacy of Texas" (1986); "The Pursuit of Community in Texas" (1987); "Texas in the 21st Century" (1988–1990); "Encounter of Two Worlds," for the 1992 Columbian Quincentenary; and "Building the New Texas" and "Understanding Other Nations" (1993–1994). Such requests, leading to many local programs in communities throughout the state, provided an opportunity to explore the chosen theme in multiple settings and with many scholars of diverse disciplines. Often TCH would sponsor additional sessions at annual meetings of the Texas State Historical Association on these topics. In some cases the emphases would lead to special publications, such as the booklet *Building the New Texas* which contains essays by philosopher Max Oelschlaeger, medical ethicists Martha Holstein and Ronald A. Carson, and literary critic Steven G. Kellman, offering humanities perspectives on the environment, health care, and literacy in Texas.

The scope of TCH's work in these endeavors has been extensive, as seen, for example, in the 1984 emphasis on "Texas Myths." This theme was selected in response to the growing number of grant applications that the TCH was receiving in the fields of local and state history and ethnic history and culture. These projects reflected the geographic and cultural diversity of the state, but we wanted to press deeper, to explore the diversity of myths in Texas. We defined myth as the stories and heroes embodying the values of the various cultures and ethnic groups. Key to this exploration was the discovery of those myths that conflict as well as those which unite. Our goal was not to perpetuate or debunk Texas myths but to elucidate their meaning and to provide a broader fundamental reference for public understanding of Texas history and culture. TCH sponsored a session at the annual program of the Texas Historical Association on "The Texas Frontier: Formative Myths behind the Nineteenth Century Clash of Cultures," with scholars William Newcomb, Felix Alamaráz, William Goetzmann, and Sterling Stuckey. The TCH funded sixteen projects in response to its request for proposals. In addition to these local projects and the annual Texas Lecture and Symposium, noted above, TCH commissioned essays by leading scholars, many of which were subsequently published in the *Texas Human-*

ist and then in the collection *Texas Myths*, edited by TCH associate director Robert O'Connor. TCH also published at the conclusion of the project a small booklet, *A Guide to Understanding Texas Myths*, which provided information on TCH grant projects and summarized the essays contained in the published volume.

   The most extensive project, however, was "Texas in the 21st Century." This three-year project began with TCH funding seven university-based study groups to explore topics identified by the TCH so that a body of scholarship would be available for subsequent activities. Research groups were established at Texas A&M University, Baylor University, the University of Texas at Austin, the University of Houston, Abilene Christian University, Lamar University/Beaumont, and Texas A&M University at Galveston. Because of its long-standing interest in education, TCH itself sponsored study groups on elementary and secondary education, undergraduate education, and community-based cultural institutions. Over one hundred scholars participated, many offering helpful essays that clarified various issues and topics. Lay citizens also participated in these discussions.

A symposium on public education was held on November 14, 1988, in Austin, drawing a statewide audience of over four hundred. Proceedings of this symposium were published in 1989, *Education for the Future*. TCH funded twelve community projects: conferences, symposia, lectures, and reading and discussion programs. Through these projects, more than two hundred presentations were made by humanities scholars to public audiences on various themes. University of Texas at Austin historian Elspeth Rostow, for example, spoke at the Amarillo Public Library on emerging political realities in the global community. James Billington, director of the Library of Congress, spoke on the future of the printed word at a conference sponsored by the Institute of Texan Cultures in San Antonio. University of North Texas philosopher Pete Gunter explored ethical issues related to the environment in a public lecture sponsored by St. Edward's University, Austin. Rice University sociologist Stephen Klineberg spoke on "Texas as a Changing World" at a conference in Beaumont sponsored by Lamar University. James D. Anderson of the University of Illinois examined the future of black higher education at a conference sponsored by Texas Southern University.

The project precipitated the publication of a five-volume series in April 1990, *Preparing for Texas in the 21st Century: Building a Future for the Children of Texas*. The series drew upon the work of the various study groups. The five volumes, published in an attractive slipcase, included *Building Community in Texas*, by TCH editor Catherine Williams; *Texas History and the Move into the Twenty-First Century* by Texas A&M University professors Walter L. Buenger and Robert A. Calvert; *The Humanities and Public Issues*, by former Baylor University regional studies professor Glen E. Lich; *Global Connections* by University of Texas at Austin professor Gordon Bennett; and *Education for the Twenty-First Century*, a volume that I wrote. Press conferences announcing the series were held in Austin, San Antonio, Lubbock, Houston, and Corpus Christi.

Other activities in this large-scale project included the *Children of Texas* exhibition, sponsored by TCH and the Texas Photographic Society. Forty-five black and white prints from the exhibition were included in the book series. Twenty newspapers in Texas published an eleven-part weekly series summarizing key ideas that had emerged in the course of the project. These articles, along with a summary of the entire project, were published in 1991.

This project dovetailed with TCH's legislative agenda to promote foreign language and culture studies. H.C.R 236, adopted by the Texas Legislature in 1989, requested TCH to develop a report "containing a long-range plan for advancing international studies and for sustained educational and cultural exchange programs between Texas and those nations with whom Texas is likely to have close economic, cultural, and other ties." The report, *Texas in the 21st Century: The International Agenda*, was submitted to the Governor and the Texas Legislature in January 1991.

Many of the grant activities associated with this project resulted in additional publications. Especially noteworthy is a remarkable volume of essays that has had substantial impact on the field of Texas studies, *Texas Through Time: Evolving Interpretations*, edited by Walter L. Buenger and Robert A. Calvert.

Another major project that needs highlighting is "The Texas Experience," TCH's project for the 1986 Texas Sesquicentennial, coordinated by Robert O'Connor with assistance from Sherilyn Brandenstein. TCH began planning this project in 1983. The Board and staff believed that most of the state's efforts would be celebratory in nature, and that the TCH could make a major cultural contribution, adding both breadth and depth to the observance. An advisory committee was formed and fifty Texas scholars, with expertise in particular areas of the state's history, were commissioned to write background papers on seventy-four topics. TCH entered into an agreement with KXAS-TV, NBC affiliate in Dallas-Fort Worth, to produce fifty-two one-minute episodes on Texas history. Once final topics were selected, the papers were turned over to a professional scriptwriter for adaptation to television. As noted, the Hoblitzelle Foundation and the Shell Oil Companies Foundation provided major funding for the series. TCH made the television spots available on an exclusive basis to one television station in each of the markets in Texas. The value of the program was exchanged for the value of the air time. The series, one a week for fifty-two weeks, was broadcast by sixteen network television stations. The statewide viewing audience for the year was in excess of twenty-seven million.

The same papers were used in the development of fifty-two articles for newspapers, distributed by the Associated Press to the thirty-nine daily and one-hundred fifty weekly newspapers that signed on to the project. The combined circulation of these newspapers was in excess of 1.2 million.

The third and final component of the project was a book, *The Texas Experience*, published in September 1986, and edited by historian and former TCH chair Archie McDonald. The original work of the scholars was again transformed for a different purpose. This coffee-table book was designed as a companion to the television series.

Grant Program

The grant program has been at the very center of the TCH. Although particular grant lines have changed over the years, TCH's interest has remained constant: sponsorship of a competitive program that would allow TCH to fund discrete projects in communities across the state. Formats for public programs have included conferences, lectures, seminars, panel discussions, reading-and-discussion programs, exhibits, and radio and television programs. Although the vast majority of projects supported have local audiences as the primary beneficiaries, TCH has historically ensured that a portion of its budget would be earmarked for significant regional and national media programs.

The scope of activity can be seen in the number of grant projects supported and the dollars awarded. Here are some statistics drawn from biennial reports submitted to the NEH.

Biennium	Projects Funded	Amount Awarded
1978–1979	93	756,240
1984–1985	132	807,482
1992–1993	164	710,442

Since 1973, the TCH has supported over 1,600 projects, releasing in excess of $10 million. Although it is impossible, in this historical sketch, to do justice to the content and impact of these projects, some examples of the kinds of endeavors that earned TCH support might prove helpful.

Public Discussion Grants

From August 1975 to March 1976, Colonias Del Valle, Inc., a grass roots community organization located in San Juan, sponsored a series of seven workshops to help residents explore with scholars and public policy officials the historical roots of social and political conflicts between Anglos and Mexican American citizens in public policies affecting the colonias, including policies regulating the supply of water, public schooling, and health care. The project was supported with grants totaling $8,248. The workshops drew nearly seven hundred residents.

On February 21–22, 1977, Austin College, Sherman, sponsored a symposium on "The Free Flow of Information: Government, Media, and the Individual." This program, funded with a $4,514 grant, brought together scholars and leading journalists and media executives to discuss the history of the freedom of the press, government's right to privacy on issues related to national security, the individual's right to privacy, the public's right to know, and the responsibility of the press in a democratic society. Over three hundred persons attended the two-day program.

From April to November 1997 the Rosenberg Library in Galveston, with a grant of $10,812, sponsored a project on the American Indian. The library was responding to the relocation of large numbers of American Indians from reservations to urban areas, including the Houston-Galveston area, as a result of federal policies. A total of thirty-six events took place, including lectures and discussions, exhibits, and film showings. Topics included the history of North American Indian tribes, Indian culture, and the history of government policy toward Indians.

In September 1978, the TCH awarded a small planning grant, $882, to the Texas Foundation for Women's Resources, to explore the possibility of developing a major exhibit on Texas women's history. In March 1979 TCH provided the Foundation with an implementation grant of $40,080 for a major touring exhibit that would tell the untold stories of the women who built Texas' communities, organized its institutions, shaped its culture, and contributed to its social, political, and economic development. The following year, the Foundation received $80,000, making this project the recipient of the largest award ever given by the TCH. This project, directed by an interdisciplinary team of scholars and community leaders led by Mary Beth Rogers, had enormous influence in shaping an entirely new discipline in Texas: women's studies. In addition to the touring exhibit, the sponsor produced a number of significant publications, audiovisual materials, and several public forums. The legacy of this early project can be found in subsequent endeavors of the Foundation. Most recently, some of the early leaders, including Foundation president Cathy Bonner, former University of Texas regent Ellen Temple, and former Texas Governor Ann Richards, along with others, including Senator Kay Bailey Hutchison, announced the establishment of a $25 million national Women's Museum and Institute for the Future in Dallas's Fair Park, projected to open in 2000.

One of TCH's most successful grant lines has been the mini-grant program. With an abbreviated application process, TCH's intent has been to award small grants to ensure that public humanities funding is made available to smaller organizations, especially those in the more remote areas of the state. Many of the organizations taking advantage of this grant program have sponsored exhibits and other programs from the Texas Humanities Resource Center. The Las Viajeres Study Club, not an untypical sponsor, received a grant of $340 to sponsor thirteen programs in the spring of 1978 that used the *Adams Chronicles* PBS series, on loan from the THRC. One episode of these films was shown weekly at the county library with an English teacher from the local high school leading the audience in a discussion of American history after each film was shown. The thirteen programs drew an average audience of seventy-five, and the project director reported that the biggest impact of the project was that the programs spurred new patron interest in American history books.

Another example of creative use of THRC materials can be found in a series of programs in the early 1990s sponsored by the University of Texas–Pan American and the Edinburg Public Library. For example, in 1992, as a result of a $1,495 grant, a series of four THRC exhibits were put on display and lectures were held in conjunction with these exhibits. The exhibits and lectures focused on Theodore Roosevelt, the U.S. Constitution, Plains Indians, and New Spain.

The City of El Paso was awarded $10,150 for spring and fall 1979 symposia, one held in El Paso and the other in Cuidad Juarez, to explore the relationship between the two cities and the proposed project of the Immigration and Naturalization Service to build a new metal fence between these border communities. Scholars and public officials from Texas and Mexico participated in the project.

Throughout the 1980s, TCH supported many diverse projects sponsored by newly established local humanities organizations in a number of Texas communities, including Houston, Dallas, Abilene, Lubbock, and Salado. Some of these groups, such as the Houston Committee for the Humanities, no longer exist, but others have gone on to become very distinguished organizations with long track records in the public humanities, especially the Dallas Institute for the Humanities and the Institute for the Humanities at Salado. One of the early grants supporting this work went to the Salado Institute for a remarkable symposium entitled "Understanding Vietnam," held in October 1982, supported in part by a grant of $17,500, and directed by the Institute's founder and president, psychiatrist Harry A. Wilmer. Over the course of three days, the standing room only audience of two hundred, meeting in the Longhorn Room of the Stagecoach Inn, was taken back to this turbulent period in American history. Outstanding scholars of U.S. foreign policy and the Vietnam War joined former public officials of the Johnson administration and military leaders in discussing the impact of the war on the soldiers who fought it and the nation that was torn apart because of it. Here is what Alan Pusey of the *Dallas Morning News* wrote about the event (November 7, 1982):

> There was a school teacher from Plano, a lawyer from Santa Fe, a psychiatrist from Albany, a United Methodist minister from Killeen and a retired general who led part of the invasion of Cambodia. They were led through the (Vietnam) experience by a history professor, a retired general, a presidential advisor, a television producer, two journalists and a poet, and among them . . . were the Vietnam veterans themselves. . . . With the coolness of a decade's distance, they rekindled their own images of the era. They made judgments. Not all agreed. But the fire could still be seen, burning in the distance; Vietnam has been in remission, but it has not gone away.

With a grant of $7,355, Trinity University, San Antonio, sponsored five public forums in the spring of 1984, on the theme of "Persons, Responsibility, and the Law." The project, which garnered the co-sponsorship of seven community groups in San Antonio, brought together philosophical insight and pressing social concerns. Among the topics explored: capital punishment, the plea of "not guilty by reason of insanity," the application or non-application of U.S. civil rights to illegal aliens, and censorship of pornography. Scholars participating came from Trinity and from Oxford University, the University of California–Santa Barbara, and Harvard Law School. Both San Antonio daily newspapers covered the series and one devoted an editorial to the project, praising Trinity for developing a program that reached out to the wider San Antonio community. Each program drew an audience of approximately two hundred and fifty.

The McAllen International Museum in South Texas was awarded $12,650 for a 1985 exhibit, "Mexican Ceremonial and Festival Dance Masks," one of many projects on Mexican American history and culture supported by TCH over the years.[1] The project was jointly funded by the Meadows Foundation and was at the time the largest project ever undertaken by the museum, with over five hundred masks included in the exhibit. Public lectures were held, and a beautiful catalog, *Changing Faces: Mexican Masks in Transition*, was published. The project traced the history of the mask from its employment by Indian peoples long before the sixteenth-century Spanish conquest, to the super-imposition of Christian meanings onto the native traditions in subsequent centuries. The project provided a great opportunity to explore the synthesis of the indigenous cultures with Spanish-Catholic culture. Over nine thousand South Texans saw the exhibit, which was then taken to several other Texas cities.

TCH has funded many local history projects, helping communities throughout the state gain a more comprehensive understanding of their culture and history. Typical of these efforts was a 1987 project of the Amarillo Public Library with co-sponsorship by the Panhandle Plains Historical Museum, "Newcomers and Survivors: Celebrating Amarillo's First One-hundred Years." The $6,393 grant provided support for a series of public discussions, bus tours, a videotape, and an educational packet on Amarillo's development.

TCH has also funded many projects exploring the work of Texas' leading artists and writers, thereby helping the state claim its artistic and intellectual heritage. Typical of such projects was an April 1987 public conference sponsored by Texas A&M University on the life and work of writer Katherine Anne Porter.

The bicentennial of the U. S. constitution was celebrated in 1987 and TCH funded a number of projects to highlight the two-hundred year history of the constitution. For example, the South Plains Friends of the Humanities in Lubbock sponsored a project entitled "The Intention of the Framers: A Local Perspective." The kickoff event for this project was the local PBS showing of a video program prepared by Project '87, the national organization commemorating the bicentennial. The next day a town hall meeting was held, with over one hundred persons attending. A week later four public meetings in different neigh-borhoods were held, with each meeting focused on a specific subject—English as a second language; rights of free speech, assembly and petition; morality and free expression; and the right of the media to obtain and release information. A final component of the project was the display of the THRC exhibit, *The Blessings of Liberty*.

One of my favorite projects took place in late 1987, a special initia-tive to place books in small Texas public libraries. Sam Moore, an El Paso Attorney and TCH chair, had learned that many public libraries had greatly reduced book-buying budgets as a result of the state's tough economic times. Would it be possible, he wondered, to do something special for interested libraries, to assist those libraries wanting to pur-chase a new sixty-four volume collection called The Library of America, with each volume ranging between 1,000 to 1,500 acid-free pages. This splendid series, which retailed for $1,650, was made available to public libraries for $1,000. But a national program to benefit smaller libraries had been put in place by The Mellon Foundation and The Library of America. The Foundation would provide $500 toward the cost if $500 could be raised at the local level. Our research indicated that among the fifty states, Texas libraries ranked near the bottom in terms of the percentage of public libraries applying for the series. In consultation with the Texas Library Association, we promoted a new initiative. TCH would make available an additional $250 for each qualifying library, with the local library needing to raise only $250 from local sources. The TCH awarded $10,000 to The Library of America so that forty Texas libraries could benefit. But within ninety days of announcing the project, over one hundred libraries had applied for the series. The Mellon Foun-dation allocated more money, as did the TCH. In the end, when the funds ran out, one hundred and twenty Texas libraries benefited from this program, and Texas ranked first among the fifty states in the per-centage of public libraries in each state ordering the series.

TCH has funded many workshops and seminars for elementary and secondary school teachers. Some of these projects have sought to dis-seminate to teachers new scholarship in their fields. Others have brought teachers together to explore ways of strengthening the curriculum. Still others have provided opportunity to focus on emerging academic inter-ests; for example, how best to teach the history and culture of other nations. An example of the latter kind of project was sponsored by the Social Studies Education Center at Southwest Texas State University in cooperation with the Center for Middle Eastern Studies at the University of Texas at Austin. In June 1990, twenty-four social studies teachers of grades six through twelve met for three days to explore the geography, religious cultures, and social changes occurring in the Arab societies of North Africa and the Middle East. The project was supported with a mini-grant of $1,250.

A far more extensive project for educators can be found in a remarkable series of programs sponsored by the Dallas Institute of Humanities and Culture. Through the leadership of Gail Thomas and Donald and Louise Cowan, the Institute has done much to invigorate public schooling in Texas. The Institute recognized a great need and opportunity, to bring together principals and teachers to rediscover their powerful roles as educators involved in a common enterprise. For example, from June 21 to July 5, 1991, sixty principals and sixty teachers attended a joint seminar that used traditional and multicultural literary texts as launching points for reflection on their important work as teachers and educational administrators. For the 1991 program, TCH provided a grant of $7,000.

One public program that was consistently funded by the TCH in the 1980s and through the 1990s was an outreach project of Texas A&I University, Kingsville, coordinated by Evelyn Jenson. This series of programs involved weekly reading and discussion programs, normally held through the spring months, in libraries in small communities throughout South Texas. The grant award for the spring 1991 series, highlighted for the purpose of illustrating this program, focused on Borderland literature, including Rolando Hinojosa's *Partners in Crime*, Rudolfo Anaya's *Bless Me Ultima*, Elmer Kelton's *The Good Old Boys*, Denise Chavez's *The Last of the Menu Girls*, and Carlos Fuentes' *The Old Gringo*. Programs were held in Alice, Falfurrias, Hebbronville, Kingsville, and Zapata. Over the years, the project, featuring different books and authors, has taken programs to numerous South Texas communities. Discussions are led by scholars from the university.

TCH has funded many public programs developed in conjunction with the opening of significant new museum exhibitions throughout the state. For example, the Amon Carter Museum in Fort Worth received a grant of $9,960 to sponsor a fall 1991 symposium and lecture/panel discussion series on the social, cultural, and political influences of photography in America from 1839 to 1900, in conjunction with the exhibit, *Photography in 19th-Century America*. A different kind of example, this one involving the interpretation of an historical site, can be found in the $9,700 grant to the Fort Bend Museum Association, which used the funds in 1994 to strengthen its educational programming at the George Ranch Historical Park. Four new outdoor exhibits were created, a short orientation video was produced, and the "living history" programs were enhanced.

National touring exhibitions that come to Texas often provide additional opportunities for public programming. Sponsors of many such exhibits turn to the TCH to expand outreach and to add interpretive components. From October 1994 to January 1995, Laguna Gloria Art Museum in Austin sponsored the national touring exhibit *The Holocaust Project: From Darkness to Light*. TCH provided $7,500 for a series of lectures and discussions, resource materials for middle and high school teachers, and student field trips.

TCH continues to fund many projects on the history and culture of Texas. For example, through the leadership of English professor Steven Curley, Texas A&M University at Galveston has sponsored a very successful series of public lectures for nearly a decade. In 1995, through a $5,745 grant, the series focused on "The Making of Modern Texas." Topics included war hero and actor Audie Murphy; African American artist John Biggers; Janis Joplin's role in 1960s rock music; the Texas mystique in the writings of J. Frank Dobie and Larry McMurtry; Hector Garcia's G.I. Forum; and the impact of the JFK assassination on Dallas. Texas Southern University in Houston, with a $12,510 grant, sponsored a series of three lectures and two exhibits, from February 26 to April 3, 1995, on the history of African American women in the American South, 1896–1960, as part of the project "Salvaging the Self: Race, Gender and Culture in the Jim Crow South." In West Texas, also in the spring of 1995, the Friends of the Sanderson Public Library put together an outstanding grass roots program that included a bilingual photo exhibit, lectures, and panel discussions, all exploring topics related to the long-term impact of a devastating 1965 flood that swept through Sanderson. The project examined the effects of a natural disaster on a community's social relations and collective psychology.

In light of reductions in federal support, the TCH restructured its grant program in 1996 to help ensure continued funding for smaller-scale projects in towns and cities statewide. Three grant lines were established. Community projects grants provide funds for conferences, symposia, interpretive exhibits, lectures, reading and discussion programs, and related activities. Media grants are provided for the production of significant film, video, and radio products, as well as those using new forms of technology, such as CD-ROM. Packaged programs grants provide up to $1,000 for one or more of five TCH-designed programs. One of these five programs is a speakers bureau, *Explorations*, with twenty-four outstanding Texas scholars participating. Although this later grant program was designed for public libraries, any nonprofit organization may apply for funds. Three of the packaged programs are specifically designed to respond to contemporary public concerns: issues related to American identity and character, issues related to American pluralism (a literature-based program), and various public policy issues selected annually by the National Issues Forums. High quality materials, prepared for the general reader, are given to grantees.

TCH has encouraged grantees to explore the possible production of publications that might provide ongoing legacies of their work. A significant number of public discussion grants and a few media grants have resulted in monographs and books. These publications have made it possible to reach entirely new audiences and to contribute to the scholarship of various fields. By way of example, here are three important books that evolved out of TCH grants.

Facing Evil: Light at the Core of Darkness, edited by Paul Woodruff and Harry A. Wilmer, was published by Open Court Press in 1988. The papers and discussions recorded in the volume were given at the symposium, "Understanding Evil," sponsored by the Institute for the Humanities at Salado in October 1987. The book serves as a companion to the documentary film *Facing Evil*, also derived from the symposium.

Tejano Origins in Eighteenth-Century San Antonio was edited by Gerald E. Poyo and Gilberto M. Hinojosa and published in 1991 by the University of Texas Press. This book was a product of a symposium and exhibition sponsored by the University of Texas Institute of Texan Cultures and funded by the TCH.

Dax's Case: Essays in Medical Ethics and Human Meaning was edited by Lonnie D. Kliever and published in 1989 by Southern Methodist University Press. The collection of essays focuses on one of the most important "cases studies" in the field of medical ethics, that of gas explosion victim Dax Cowart. The Cowart story was documented in the award-winning film *Dax's Case*, produced and distributed by Concern for Dying, Inc., and partially funded by the TCH. The film and the book continue to be important classroom tools as well as resources for the wider public interested in "right to die" issues.

Films and Videos for Television

I asked Monte Youngs, senior program officer and director of the grant program, to highlight those film and video projects that he thought represented the best of TCH-funded projects since he joined the staff in 1990, which are presented here without reference to ranking. TCH funding usually represents a small portion of the overall budgets of these media projects.

LBJ, produced by KERA-TV/North Texas Public Broadcasting, Inc. Dallas. TCH provided a grant toward post-production costs for this four-hour documentary film that was aired nationally on PBS's "The American Experience" in the fall of 1991, examining the political life of Lyndon Baines Johnson. This documentary received glowing reviews and exceptional national press coverage.

Coming Through Hard Times was produced in 1993 by the Houston Preservation Place Association, Houston. TCH provided funds for the scripting phase of this sixty-minute documentary video based on the traveling oral history photo-documentary exhibit, "Colorado County Memories," exploring the lives and community values of the predominantly black and elderly residents of rural Colorado County. It won a Gold Award for best documentary at the 1996 Houston Film Festival and a Texas Award for Best Documentary at the USA Film Festival in Dallas. The film was broadcast several times on KUHT-TV, Houston.

Chicano! History of the Mexican American Civil Rights Movement, produced by the National Latino Communications Center, Los Angeles. TCH funding was allocated for one segment of a five-hour documentary broadcast nationally in 1996 and again in 1997, tracing the history of the Mexican American civil rights movement.

Riding the Rails: Children of the Great Depression, produced by Media Network, New York. Broadcast nationally on PBS in the summer of 1997, the documentary examines the experiences of the one-quarter of a million migrant, homeless adolescents who wandered the United States by riding freight trains during the Depression. The documentary won numerous awards, including a Gold Apple Award from the National Educational Media Foundation.

The Orphan Trains, produced by the New York Foundation for the Arts. This sixty-minute documentary film was broadcast nationally on PBS in 1995. The film examines the first large-scale foster care program in America—the orphan train movement. From 1854 to 1929, east coast charities used commercial railways to relocate over one hundred thousand orphans and other poor city children to rural communities across the U. S. The movement played a key role in the shift from institutional care for dependent children to modern foster-family care. The documentary received an Emmy Award in 1995 for Outstanding Individual Achievement in Writing.

Five Women of the West, produced by the New York Foundation for the Arts. This ninety-minute film for national PBS broadcast explored the lives of five minority women in the American West, 1850–1915: Mexican exile in Texas, Teresa Urrea; Paiute chief's granddaughter, Sarah Winnemucca; Chinese emigrant, Mary Bong; Colorado brothel madam, Laura Evans; and Kentucky freed slave, Clara Brown. The film explores the West as a place of opportunity and cultural encounter for women. It was broadcast nationally on PBS in 1995.

. . . *and the earth did not swallow him*, a dramatic film of Tomás Rivera's novel by that title, produced by KPBS-TV, San Diego. This two-hour film adaptation is a portrait of the life of a Mexican American boy and his migrant farm worker family as they struggle to adapt to life in American society. More than one million Americans viewed this film on PBS's "American Playhouse," 1996.

Divided Highways: The Interstates and the Transformation of American Life, sponsored by Skidmore College, Saratoga Springs, New York. This three-part, three-hour documentary was broadcast on PBS October 22, 1997. The film examines the development of the 42,500-mile U. S. Interstate Highway System and its impact on American culture. It received a 1998 Peabody Award.

The Desert Is No Lady, sponsored by the Southwest Institute for Research on Women, Tucson, Arizona. TCH provided post-production funding of this sixty-minute documentary film that looks at nine contemporary Native American, Chicana, and Anglo women writers and artists of the Southwest. It was awarded the "Best Documentary" at the 1996 San Antonio CineFestival.

People of the Sun: The Tiguas of Ysleta, sponsored by the Institute of Texan Cultures, University of Texas at San Antonio. TCH provided post-production funding of this sixty-minute documentary for national PBS broadcast in 1993 on the history and culture of the Tigua Indians of El Paso.

Rebuilding the Temple: Cambodians in America, sponsored by the Roman Catholic Diocese of Springfield, Massachusetts. This sixty-minute documentary film, aired nationally on PBS in 1993, looks at the Khmer culture of Cambodian refugees living in the United States, including the Dallas Cambodian community, and the changes confronting the community as its members adapt to life in the United States.

The Hunt for Pancho Villa, produced by WGBH-TV, Boston. This sixty-minute film, broadcast on PBS's "The American Experience" in 1993, depicts the circumstances that led to Mexican General Francisco "Pancho" Villa's 1916 attack on Columbus, New Mexico, and the subsequent U. S. Punitive Expedition led by General John J. Pershing. The film explores the complex role these incidents had in shaping relations between the two nations.

If one goes back further into TCH history, one finds an equally impressive list of outstanding videos and films. Here are a few.

Facing Evil, a ninety-minute Bill Moyers documentary based on a symposium sponsored by the Institute for the Humanities at Salado, was broadcast nationally several times on PBS.

KERA-TV, Dallas produced a stunning program, *Katherine Anne Porter: The Eye of Memory*, weaving together biography, dramatization of short stories, and scholarly analysis.

Lions, Parakeets, and Other Prisoners is a thirty-minute film about teaching inmates to understand themselves through writing and reading poetry.

West of Hester Street is an early-TCH funded dramatic film that encourages viewers to look at the history of Jewish settlement in Texas.

Lone Star, an eight-part series of hour-long programs produced by the PBS affiliate in Corpus Christi, for national broadcast over PBS.

Wildcatter, the story broadcast over PBS of a modern independent driller who gambles on striking oil. This story is viewed against the history of Spindletop, dreams of gushers, and such illustrious figures as "Dad" Joiner and H. L. Hunt.

Journey to the Sky, a documentary film on the Alabama-Coushatta Indian tribe of East Texas.

Photographer: Russell Lee explores the life and career of this well-known Depression-era photographer for the Farm Securities Administration.

Goin' On: The Life of J. Mason Brewer, is narrated by John Henry Faulk. The biographical film documents one of the state's great folklorists.

Frontier Boy is a sixty-minute documentary film based on William Owens's autobiography, *This Stubborn Soil*.

Radio

TCH has also used radio to provide programs for the public and to heighten public awareness of the importance of the study of history and culture. Here are a few of the many noteworthy projects.

Lincolnville, Texas, produced by Baylor University's Institute for Oral History, 1987. The program focuses on a primarily black community which flourished between the Civil War and World War II, but now survives mainly in the memories of former residents and in their shared values of family and community.

Lift Every Voice: 50 Years of Texas Black Gospel was produced by the Texas Folklife Resources. These thirteen five-minute radio programs explored the history and culture of black religious traditions, particularly preaching and music.

The Deputy, produced by the Goethe Institute, based on German writer Rolf Hochhuth's play, for NPR broadcast. *The Deputy* was one of the first German artistic works attempting to come to terms with the Holocaust.

Letras Femeninas: The Writings of Hispanic Women, produced by KAMU-FM, Texas A&M University.

The Corpus Christi Chronicles: A Quincentenary Salute to the Americas, was sponsored by the Corpus Christi Quincentenary Commission. This series of two-minute radio spots aired twice daily over one NPR and five commercial stations in South Texas. The spots chronicled the Columbus landing, examined the Spanish heritage of South Texas, and detailed the social, cultural, and political history of the Corpus Christi area.

Legendary Texas, produced by KAMU-FM, Texas A&M University. This series of five-minute radio programs spotlighted ordinary individuals whose lives shaped Texas history.

Texas Country Roots, sponsored by the Texas Folklife Resources. This thirteen-part series of eight and one-half minute radio spots, focusing on early country and western music and the regionally distinctive contributions of Texas and its musicians to the field, was broadcast nationally on NPR.

These and hundreds of other programs funded during the past twenty-five years would not have taken place without the enthusiastic participation of many of the state's humanities scholars. Their record of accomplishment is truly outstanding. The scholars participate because they see involvement in public programs as an extension of their responsibilities as scholars. And the experiences are rewarding—they learn from the community. The scope of activity is impressive. For example, for the two-year period 1990 to 1991, more than seventeen hundred scholars participated in TCH projects. Twenty-two percent of them were historians, sixteen percent taught literature, twelve percent taught art history and criticism, twelve percent were from the fields of anthropology and folklore; ten percent from comparative religion, ten percent taught psychology and sociology, and lesser percentages represented other fields: American studies, archaeology, ethnic studies, and classical and modern languages.

One more point needs to be noted: the conscientious manner in which TCH grantees have fulfilled their fiduciary responsibilities. Each year there are a few projects that are not as successful as one would hope, but the vast majority of projects consistently fulfill and often exceed the objectives for which they were funded. TCH has been fortunate in that out of the sixteen hundred projects funded since its founding, only a handful of sponsors submitted financial reports that raised serious questions on our part or required the intervention of a TCH-designated auditor. Only once in the past twenty-five years did the TCH request a return of funds based on expenditures that were prohibited by the terms of the grant. TCH's director of finances for the past decade, Yvonne Gonzáles, has done a superb job in maintaining financial accountability for the grants awarded. She has also done superb work in ensuring TCH compliance with all rules and regulations governing the receipt and expenditure of federal funds for state humanities councils.

Texas Humanities Resource Center

A key component of the TCH program has been the Texas Humanities Resource Center (THRC). The Center was established in February 1978 as a unit of the University of Texas at Arlington Library. A year earlier, the TCH, responding to a condition attached to its previous NEH award, that TCH needed to increase the number of programs in small towns and more rural areas of the state, had submitted a plan to the NEH that called for the development and circulation of high-quality packaged programs. TCH highlighted two fundamental problems in providing programs for smaller communities. First, the more rural areas of the state often lacked the financial and humanistic resources for the development of competitive grant proposals. Second, there was a lack of awareness in many communities that there was a state humanities council with financial resources to help fund projects. The TCH thus conceived of a Resource Center that would respond to both problems. By making available traveling exhibitions, media products, and educational materials, it would increase the number of programs taking place in the more rural areas of the state while enhancing the profile of the TCH in these communities. It was the first such resource center established for this purpose by a state humanities council.

The Center's first director, whose task it was to lay the conceptual foundation for the Center, was Catherine Williams. Frances Leonard assumed the directorship one year later, a position that she has held since that time. Williams and Leonard, both with Ph.D. degrees in British literature, possessed broad interests in the humanities and thus were able to conceive of a center whose holdings included resources and programs from very diverse subjects drawn from ancient cultures, American history and literature, European history and literature, and Texas history and culture. While assembling initial materials for programs, THRC published *Planning Humanities Programs: A Guide for Project Directors*, a helpful document that is still in print.

After eighteen months of operation, the Center was distributing five programs that would serve as models for all subsequent collections: *The Adams Chronicles*, a film and discussion series; *Albert Einstein: A Centennial Celebration*, a touring photographic exhibition and a film and discussion program; *The American Short Story*, a film and discussion program; *Pompeii, A.D. 79*, a touring photographic exhibition with slide-tape and optional film and discussion units; and *The Treasures of Tutankhamun*, a touring exhibition of posters with slide-tape and film and discussion units.

The Center was also distributing some outstanding films produced through funding from the TCH, including *Rosebud to Dallas*, a documentary on U. S. policy toward American Indians, and *Who Remembers Mama?*, a documentary exploring the rise of displaced homemakers as a result of increased divorce in American families. Such films were often accompanied with print materials for public discussion programs.

Eighteen months after the Center's founding, over one hundred programs had taken place in Texas communities, and more than 340,000 Texans had participated in these programs. Sponsors included small museums, public libraries, historical societies, community colleges, cultural arts centers, youth agencies, city governments, labor organizations, shopping malls, chambers of commerce, and nursing homes. Programs were being sponsored by the Hillsboro Public Library, the Rusk County Memorial Library in Henderson, the Scurry County Museum in Snyder, and the Nuevo Santander Museum in Laredo. Many of the sponsors would submit small funding requests—$500, $700, a $1,000—to the TCH to promote programs and to contract with scholars to lead discussions.

The Center's holdings expanded dramatically through Leonard's ability to garner funds from NEH's Division of Public Programs. For example, the Center received funds to develop small traveling exhibitions based on five large "blockbuster" exhibitions that appeared in Texas and its neighboring states in the early 1980s. The museums were pleased with the opportunities provided for outreach; the THRC and the TCH were pleased with the wealth of materials made available by these museums for outstanding circulating programs.

After seven years of generous support from the University of Texas at Arlington, the Center relocated to Austin, but not without travail, for its preference at the time was to remain in North Texas. Resources had grown tight as appropriations for higher education were squeezed, and University officials felt that for the University to justify continued support at the level of $50,000 a year and free office space, the Center needed to refocus its work by joining the University's media services department, with the consequence that its role would inevitably be more internal than external to the University. This offer proved to be problematic to the TCH and the THRC. But it also was clear that closer proximity to the TCH would prove helpful to the Center and the TCH, and thus the Center moved to Austin, in a building adjacent to the then TCH office on Nueces Street. The loss of financial support, however, hurt deeply. Staff size was reduced and fewer projects could be undertaken.

The Center operated as an independent nonprofit corporation from 1986 to 1992, when it merged with TCH. Functioning as a division of the TCH, the THRC continues to organize and circulate exhibits, audiovisual programs, and print materials, for use by cultural and educational communities in Texas and beyond. It has had to select new projects with care, given limited resources, and more time has had to be spent on fund-raising for specific endeavors. The Center's holdings presently include eighty-three photo-panel exhibits on fifty-three separate topics, one-hundred and fifteen films, nearly four hundred videos, ninety-five slide-tape programs in carousels, and hundreds of print resources to accompany the exhibit and media collections.

Through 1997, the THRC provided resources for over thirty-six hundred programs serving more than 6.9 million citizens of all ages. These programs took place in two hundred and thirty-three towns and cities in Texas, one hundred twenty-seven communities in the four neighboring states, and one hundred thirty-six in forty other states, the District of Columbia, and Mexico. While the Center continues to respond to the needs of cultural and educational institutions and organizations in rural villages and small towns, its clientele has grown over the years and now includes central and branch libraries in major urban areas, colleges and universities, and community centers in our largest cities.

A typical "package" includes a photo-and-text panel exhibit, illustrated brochures, posters, films and video programs with viewing/discussion guides, and a directory of speakers. Many exhibits are accompanied by major exhibition catalogs, books, or other print resources. Sponsors are given a press kit, public-service announcements to publicize their programs, and the *Planning Humanities Programs*, which leads step-by-step through the successful production of a public humanities program.

THRC has operated with a tiny staff, especially since its relocation from Arlington in 1986. In addition to Leonard, present TCH employees assigned to the Resource Center include the very knowledgeable Maryrose Hightower-Coyle, resource coordinator, who also doubles as TCH's technology coordinator, and JIC Club, who brings to his position of exhibitions manager strong credentials in commercial and theatrical design.

In 1996 the THRC launched a four-year initiative involving production, testing, and dissemination of electronic resources to improve teaching of the humanities in Texas schools. This new assignment represents a significant departure for the THRC. To some extent, hammers, screwdrivers, and plexiglass have given way to electronic publishing software, scanners, and service providers. Entirely new skills and means of communication and programming have been learned.

While the Center will continue to develop new physical products for packaged programs, funding permitted, it has taken on one of the most innovative and potentially far-reaching projects of the state humanities councils. THRC will transfer fifty-three photo-panel exhibits for dissemination over the Internet and on CD-ROM. The first "repurposed" exhibit, *Bonfire of Liberties: Censorship of the Humanities*, was made available via the Internet in April 1996, and won several prestigious awards from on-line magazines and Internet providers. The exhibits will be organized into nine distinct collections: *Border Studies*; *Texas History, Texas Cultures*; *American Culture and History*; *Ancient Cultures*; *The Chivalric World*; *Literature and Our Imaginative Heritage*; *The New World*; *Arts and the Humanities*; and *Understanding Other Cultures, at Home and Abroad*. Initial financial support for this project was provided by the Meadows Foundation, The Houston Endowment, and the Division of Education at the NEH. It will need another $250,000 to finish the project. When completed, it will provide one of the largest public humanities resources on the Internet.

Through the Center, the TCH inaugurated in 1997 summer workshops for teachers. Each summer the THRC teams up with three or four colleges or universities to offer one-week professional development opportunities focused on the holdings of the Center and the new transmission and use of those holdings via the new technologies. The 1997 workshops focused on *Border Studies*, a collection of nine exhibitions, and were held in El Paso, Laredo, and Edinburg. The 1998 workshops on *Texas History, Texas Cultures*, took place in Dallas, Snyder, and Temple.

I asked Frances Leonard for a list of her favorite exhibits, noted below. No mention is made of the multitude of print and visual resources that accompany these programs.

Pompeii, A.D. 79, an exhibit in eighteen photo-panels. This exhibit is now nineteen years old and still very much in use. It is based on the major international exhibition that appeared in Dallas in 1979.

Shakespeare, an exhibit in ten panels, featuring thirty-five images, most from the Folger Shakespeare Library. The photographic exhibit premiered at the Southern Methodist University theatre department and was the catalyst for a TCH-funded public forum coordinated by the Resource Center and cosponsored by the University of Texas at Arlington, Southern Methodist University, Texas Christian University, Austin College, and the Dallas Museum of Art, "Politics, Power, and Shakespeare."

Martin Luther King and the Civil Rights Movement and *The Road to the Promised Land: Perspectives of the 1990s* (updated version). These two exhibits total forty panels with extraordinary photographs. Leonard believes that these exhibits are the most significant ones owned by the Center. As Leonard writes, Martin Luther King, Jr. was himself "a walking humanities project, using religion, philosophy, poetry, history, jurisprudence, to urge America toward fairness." In the updated version, *The Road to the Promised Land*, the acuity of King's vision, she says, "continues to impress and touch the heart not made of stone."

Bonfire of Liberties: Censorship of the Humanities, a photo and text exhibit in eighteen panels, each looking at issues of censorship as related to various fields of humanistic inquiry and publication. This packaged program also includes a locked case of censored books. As noted, this exhibit was selected to be the prototype for the "Humanities Interactive" project for the Internet.

Mexico: Splendors of Thirty Centuries, an exhibit in twenty-four panels with approximately one-hundred fifty images. This packaged program has been a catalyst for programs throughout the Southwest, providing an introduction to the three-thousand-year history of Mexico. This was originally developed with a $30,000 grant from the Rockefeller Foundation.

Annexation: Celebrating 150 Years of Texas Statehood, an exhibit in twenty-four panels narrating the story of Texas in relation to Mexico and the United States in the years between 1836 and 1851, based on an original exhibition at the State Capitol. This traveling exhibition first opened at the Texas State Fair. According to Leonard, the exhibit "provides solid lessons in history and citizenship."

The Art of Chivalry, an exhibit in eighteen panels with sixty-seven photographs of arms, armor, and images of real and poetical knights.

New Spain: The Frontiers of Faith, an exhibit in twenty panels featuring sixty photographs of paintings, engravings, and documents from the Gilcrease Museum, Tulsa. The exhibit begins with the discovery of the New World and the Caribbean Islands, then looks at Mexico and the Southwest, finally focusing on the Inquisition.

American Anthem, an exhibit in sixteen panels with sixty-five images tracing American history from 1790 to 1933. According to Leonard, "this is a superb exhibit, since it offers a traditional approach to history (not really Eurocentric, but certainly not contentious) and involves many topics that engage the viewer: founding of the nation, slavery and the civil war, the Indian wars, women's rights, development of technology, traditional and popular music."

I must add to this list one of my own favorites, a more recent exhibit, *Istanbul: Portrait of A City*, the product of collaboration between TCH/THRC and the Center for Middle Eastern Studies at the University of Texas at Austin. The exhibit, created by the THRC with assistance from faculty members in Middle Eastern Studies, features two-hundred photographs, prints, engravings, and maps arranged with quotations and explanatory captions to form a twenty-six panel display. It displays life in Istanbul for two millennia, with special emphasis on the past one hundred years.

This exhibition was made possible through the financial contributions of the U.S. Department of Education, the Bernard and Audre Rapoport Foundation, the College of Liberal Arts at the University of Texas at Austin, and the TCH. Sponsors receive a teacher's guide, viewer's guide, brochures, and two documentary videos developed by scholars Ian Manners and Abraham Marcus, in collaboration with the Department of International Relations, Marmara University, Istanbul, and the University of Texas at Austin.

The Center operates on an annual budget of approximately $160,000. I have often wondered what it could do for smaller public libraries of Texas, for senior citizen centers, and elementary and secondary public schools across the state, if it had a budget equal to its mission and its accomplishments. Someone needs to endow the Center with a $5 million gift.

Texas Humanities Alliance

Another component of the TCH program is the Texas Humanities Alliance, a friends organization. In 1986, ten former members of the TCH board of directors established the Alliance: Austin College professor A. J. Carlson; former Dallas Public Library director Lillian B. Bradshaw; University of Texas at Austin professor Betty Sue Flowers; attorney Paul Leche; historian Al Lowman; University of Texas law professor Roy Mersky; University of Texas–El Paso professor Joan Quarm; Thomson Conference Center director Gene Sherman; publisher Ellen Temple; and businessman William P. Wright, Jr. Lillian Bradshaw served as the first chair of this new organization. The Alliance was incorporated as a 501(c)3 organization. Bob Wallace, a banker from Corpus Christi, also played a prominent role, including service as a subsequent chair. Initial funds to help launch the Alliance were provided by the Jones Foundation of Abilene.

A part-time coordinator was employed, but after one year, when the initial grant expired, and with TCH still accommodating to reduced federal funding, it was decided that responsibility for administering the Alliance should fall to the TCH staff. Judith Diaz, then assistant to the director, working in the areas of administration as well as council-sponsored programs, became the Alliance's coordinator. For the past decade, she has nurtured the Alliance with great skill and commitment, devising and supervising membership recruitment initiatives, overseeing annual renewals, and keeping alive the idea that the TCH is deeply enriched through the demonstrated commitment of hundreds of people across the state. The Alliance has grown to number more than one thousand. Funds received have provided important support for various activities and projects, including publication of TCH's magazine, establishment of the Outstanding Teaching of the Humanities Awards, the creation of new exhibits by the THRC, and payment of the office building mortgage.

Because of the Alliance, TCH has friends in communities large and small throughout the state. Members receive periodic mailings to keep them informed of new programs and opportunities and are often invited to assist the TCH in promoting grant opportunities for their local cultural and educational institutions and in securing programs from the Resource Center.

To keep the Alliance's overhead costs as low as possible, the Alliance was merged with the TCH in 1994, thereby eliminating expenses associated with a separate board and such obligations as IRS reporting.

It now operates as an activity of the TCH with ultimate responsibility resting with the TCH board of directors.

Outstanding Teaching of the Humanities Awards

TCH established in 1990 an awards program to recognize and reward the contributions of exemplary humanities teachers in Texas elementary, middle, and high schools, both public and private. Each May the TCH names six teachers as award winners, with $1,000 given to each teacher and $1,000 to each teacher's school for the purchase of humanities instructional material. In addition, six to eight teachers receive honorable mention plaques. Through 1997 the awards program drew nominations from nearly 1,000 Texas teachers representing more than 700 schools from over two hundred and fifty Texas towns and cities.

The program has been masterfully coordinated from its inception by Monte Youngs. Each year a call for nominations is sent to each of the more than fourteen hundred superintendents of Texas public and private schools, to more than three hundred newspapers, to members of the Texas legislature, to the heads of professional education organizations, the directors of the twenty Regional Education Service Centers, and to other targeted groups. Each year the TCH has an excellent pool of nominees, and even a quick review of the material submitted brings much comfort to those who worry about the quality of teaching in the schools of Texas.

Following selection of the winners and honorable mentions by the board of directors, based on the recommendations of a committee of the board, Youngs promotes widely the winners of the competition. Recognition ceremonies are usually held each fall for the winners, sponsored by their schools or school districts, or sometimes by community organizations. The winners are presented with a plaque, most often by a TCH board director. The fall meeting of the board always includes testimony from those directors who have taken part in these hometown presentations, for they are moved by the power of this recognition bestowed on the teacher. And so are the teachers. Here is what one winner, Cherilen A. Brewer, wrote us in 1994: "I celebrate your organization's mission and encourage you to continue recognizing the exemplary work of teachers who advance the study of the humanities in Texas. This award has definitely given me and Estacado High School an impetus to continue improving our curriculum and methodology in teaching the humanities."

It's doubtful that any other initiative of the TCH has accomplished so much good with so little money. The annual budget for this program in 1998 was $13,600—$12,000 for the awards and $1,600 for printing, postage, and the cost of the award plaques.

Texas Journal of Ideas, History and Culture

One of the biggest challenges facing the TCH from its founding has been that of attaining visibility in a state as geographically large and as heavily populated as Texas. Such visibility has been important, not as an end in itself, but in order to accomplish the mission for which it was created. Among the many efforts designed to assist the TCH in meeting this challenge, TCH's role as a publisher of public humanities materials has been among the most important. During the past twenty-five years, TCH has published newsletters, occasional reports, monographs, booklets, program announcements, promotional brochures, annual and then biennial reports to the people of Texas, books, and a public humanities magazine.

The *Texas Humanist*, renamed in 1985 *Texas Journal of Ideas, History and Culture*, was first published in September 1978 as a twelve-page tabloid designed to promote the TCH, to share with wider audiences the work of our grantees, and to stimulate public interest in the humanities. Over the course of the next four years, Joe Holley, who served as the first editor, reported on dozens of TCH projects. By the time Holley left in November 1982 to assume the editorship of the *Texas Observer*, the publication had begun to take on a life of its own, moving beyond original objectives to become a forum for writers and scholars, a place to voice views on the role of the humanities in contemporary society. The publication provided opportunities to promote the public humanities, drawing on the substance of projects funded, demonstrating the connections that could be made between the humanities and the needs and interests of contemporary Texans. Issues focused on the enduring legacy of the cowboy, on the new urban architecture of Houston, on women and the frontier, on Black folk traditions, and on the perils and promises of modern technology. We also learned that the publication could be used as an educational tool; requests for multiple copies often came from teachers for use in their classrooms. By 1982 the publication was being mailed to seventy-five hundred readers, including the heads of museums and libraries, TCH project directors, scholars participating in TCH programs, public school and university administrators, and citizens with strong interest in the humanities.

Beginning in 1982, TCH took steps to expand the publication. A committee of the Board was formed to oversee this development, and a reader's survey was undertaken. Marise McDermott, city/state editor for the *Austin American-Statesman*, and a former philosophy graduate student, was appointed editor in January 1983. A board of contributing editors was appointed, and this group met in the spring of 1983 to offer advice on the future of the publication. Barbara Paulsen joined the staff as assistant editor. The *Texas Humanist* was redesigned as a magazine and the editorial thrust was expanded so that the publication could take on a new role, that of stimulating scholarship on topics and themes of importance to the TCH.

A five-year business plan, prepared by an outside consultant, was adopted by the board of directors, based on our goal to make the publication self-supporting by 1989. Subscription and advertising programs were launched. To achieve this goal, substantial funds were required, and TCH launched an aggressive program to obtain corporate and foundation support which, with additional funding provided by the NEH, would be sufficient, we believed, until such time as subscription and advertising revenues could cover most of the cost of publishing such an expanded magazine.

During this experimental period, each of the bimonthly issues focused in part on a particular theme, contributing to scholarship on topics of interest to the TCH. Here are subjects pursued during this period:

The Power of Traditional Cultures	September/October 1983
Hollywood Portraits of Texas	November/December 1983
Texas Cities	January/February 1984
Texas/Mexico Border	March/April 1984
Death in the Life of Texas	May/June 1984
The Politics and Culture of Water	July/August 1984
Education and American Culture	September/October 1984
Texas Literature: Past and Present	November/December 1984
Texas Myths: Heroes, Legends, and Archetypes	January/February 1985
Family: Beloved, Battered, and Ever Transformed	March/April 1985
Working: Texas and the American Dream	May/June 1985
Texas Music: Past and Present	July/August 1985

The magazine was well received, winning the interest and good will of the state's leading writers, scholars, and artists. Several prestigious design awards were received. Although the advertising revenue fell below projected levels, TCH was on target in terms of paid subscribers by the fall of 1985—five thousand. But despite everyone's good intentions, TCH was unable to sustain publication of this subscription-based magazine, the first such effort of any state humanities council. We experienced a dramatic loss in federal revenue at the very time that the Texas economy sank into one of its cyclical busts, and private revenue evaporated. We tried to adjust to reduced funding by redesigning the magazine, changing the title to *Texas Journal of Ideas, History and Culture*, and adopting a quarterly publication schedule. The first issue under this new title was published in the fall of 1985 and focused on "Texas Architecture: the Myth and the Making." But even with these major adjustments, it was impossible to continue; TCH ended the year in the red, the first and only time in its twenty-five year history. Staff reductions had to be made and several initiatives and projects, including the magazine, had to be postponed or shelved altogether.

During the following year we focused on the core TCH program, especially our grant projects, while following through with our contribution to the Texas Sesquicentennial, "The Texas Experience," with its television, newspaper, and book components, and with the "Mexican Legacy of Texas" project, combining our work with that of grantees. Funding for both endeavors had been previously secured.

Fortunately, the board and staff did not lose sight of the importance of publishing a high-quality magazine. To help get this project back on track, I patched together a new issue of *Texas Journal* in the fall of 1986, a forty-eight page publication that provided more information than substance, but it marked a new beginning. Technology made this possible: for a fraction of the cost, new computer publishing software provided us with a new opportunity. The first such issue was far less than satisfactory, but a start had been made. The TCH board renewed its commitment to publishing a magazine, on a semi-annual basis, with renewed focus on TCH projects.

The spring/summer 1987 issue was guest-edited by Catherine Williams, TCH assistant director in the mid 1970s, and she set the course for the magazine for the next decade. By the fall of 1987, Williams, then named editor by the board of directors, had begun to refocus the magazine, drawing material from TCH projects. The new *Texas Journal* evolved into a publication that combined the thematic approach of the former *Texas Humanist* with grant projects and sponsored programs of the TCH. Thus each issue used materials derived from projects to elucidate certain subjects. During the past decade, the magazine became a very important vehicle for demonstrating how the humanities are engaged in public life. The magazine represents the continuity of the

TCH, its deepest commitment to expanding opportunities for learning while contributing in important ways to American and Texan public culture. Here are the themes pursued during the past ten years:

Imagination and Culture	Fall/Winter 1987
Community in Contemporary America	Spring/Summer 1988
Religion in America and Art and Gender	Fall/Winter 1988
Multicultural Understanding	Spring/Summer 1989
Culture and Moral Values	Fall/Winter 1989
Women and Culture	Spring/Summer 1990
Educating for Global Understanding	Fall/Winter 1990
Literary Imagination	Spring/Summer 1991
The Humanities and Popular Culture	Fall/Winter 1991
Seeing Ourselves: Museums and Cultural Diversity	Spring/Summer 1992
The Colombian Quincentenary	Fall/Winter 1992
Restoring Trust in Health Care	Spring/Summer 1993
The Humanities and The Environment	Fall/Winter 1993
Literacy and Human Empowerment	Spring/Summer 1994
Latino Literature in the United States	Fall/Winter 1994
American Pluralism and Identity	Spring/Summer 1995
The Arts and Humanities in American Life	Fall/Winter 1995
Reflections on Religion in America	Spring/Summer 1996
Home, Community and the Spirit of Place	Fall/Winter 1996
Writing from their Roots & Literary Voices and Visions	Spring/Summer 1997
The Border: Human Destinies and the Great River	Fall/Winter 1997
Civility	Spring/Summer 1998

The magazine continues to serve as the voice of the TCH, representing the needs, interests, and ideas associated with grant programs and TCH special emphases, the Texas Humanities Resource Center, and the various constituencies represented in the state program—libraries, museums, colleges and universities, historical societies, public radio and television, university presses, and so forth. Particularly gratifying are the large numbers of individuals whose assistance, without cost, makes possible the magazine—project directors, writers, and photographers.

In addition to Williams, the magazine has been served well these past ten years by the indefatigable Judith Diaz who, in addition to her many other duties at the TCH, has for the past decade directed the circulation of the magazine and coordinated the advertising program, a modest but well-focused and effective effort directed primarily at university presses in Texas and beyond. The circulation of the magazine in 1988 was in excess of ten thousand.

Re-visioning

TCH, which has spent much time and many resources the past decade in helping Texans think about the twenty-first century, must now think about itself, about where it has been, what it has valued, what it has sought to do, how it has sought to be, in order to determine where it will go, what it will value, what it will do, and how it will be in the next twenty-five years. An era has come to a close, not so much because of the advent of new board and staff leadership, but because of important changes taking place in American society and culture.

State humanities councils will be in a stronger position to deal with these changes than they would have been just a few years ago, for votes cast in 1997 and again in 1998 indicate that the Congress will continue to fund the NEH. That is good news, for the state councils have been through turbulent times, despite a remarkable and nearly unblemished record of service to the nation since their founding in the early 1970s.

Attacks on the NEA, begun in the early 1980s but heightened dramatically in the late 1980s and early 1990s because of the public controversy over several highly unfortunate projects funded through federal funds, most notably the photographic exhibits of Andres Serrano and Robert Maplethorpe, spilled over to the NEH. As the culture wars intensified, some representatives of the far religious and political right sought to defund both NEA and NEH. By focusing on these sensational projects, it has been easy for some members of the Congress to forget that these projects were just a few of more than one hundred thousand grants awarded by NEA from its beginning in 1965. And it has been just as easy to forget what the NEH has done to further the study of history and literature and languages in our nation's schools, colleges, and universities, what it has done to preserve and publish the papers of America's founders and literary masters, what it has accomplished in bringing the humanities to millions of Americans through outstanding PBS programs and nationally significant museum exhibitions. In this war of words and legislative posturing, it has been all too easy to dismiss the need that any advanced civilization has—or any civilization at all—to care for those whose task it is to preserve history, to remember the pains and pleasures of collective journeys, to express in art and stories the fears and hopes that we all share as human beings.

Perhaps a more conciliatory spirit in the Congress may emerge, a recognition that the United States will not be the only advanced nation to fail to provide public funds for culture. If so, Congressional sentiment will be catching up with that of the public, for polls have consistently shown strong public support for continued federal funding of the arts and humanities. The TCH and its sister state councils might now be looking forward to a measure of federal support which is so critical to their continued existence and to the stimulation of other sources of funding. They will also be able to spend more time doing the work that they were created to do, and less time in defensive actions, drawing up one contingency plan after another in response to dwindling resources. In short, they will be able to get on with their business with renewed confidence in the important and ongoing work that they are doing.

But various changes are taking place in American society and culture that call for a response from the TCH. Among them are: the decline in public space where the public's business can be done; the growing poverty crisis; the quest for more effective elementary and secondary schools; and the cultural transition to an advanced information age.

Decline in public space. A number of the essays in this volume deal with the contemporary problems of civil society, with the apparent loss of public space where the public can do the public's business, on the dramatic loss of public confidence in the major institutions of our society—government, "mainline" churches, corporations, and universities. There is, it would seem, a turning inward on the part of Americans, a lack of engagement in substantive ways with the issues that confront us as a people, a loss of opportunities to think together about complex issues. Instead of engagement, we have radio and television talk shows that focus on the personal, and that demean and divide. Numerous books have been written in the last few years in response to the problems of civil society, such as M. Scott Peck's *A World Waiting to be Born: Civility Rediscovered*, and Stephen Carter's *Civility: Manners, Morals and the Etiquette of Democracy*. Various reports have also been published, such as "A Call to Civil Society," a product of the Institute for American Values and written by a collection of prominent scholars, political leaders, and public intellectuals. The crisis we face in the erosion of civic life, especially as that civic life is connected to politics—to practicing the art of self-government—should be a matter of deep concern to all state humanities councils.

The poverty crisis. While millions of Americans have benefited greatly from the roaring economy of the 1980s and 1990s, our nation seems to be unraveling. The gap between those who have material bounty and those who lack has grown significantly. In many inner cities and rural areas, poverty has increased dramatically, and the long-term consequences of welfare reform remain unknown. Where poverty exists, so do concomitant social ills: homelessness, hunger, drugs, inadequate health care, illiteracy, teenage pregnancy, and bulging prison populations. In a recent article, Jim Wallis, founder of Sojourner's Community in Washington, D.C., argues persuasively that spiritual and civic poverty often accompany material poverty. The despair generated by poverty often leads to disengagement, loss of hope, and violence. America is deeply wounded by its poverty; the long-term future of the nation is threatened by our seeming moral and political inability to find solutions.

Quest for more effective elementary and secondary schools. We are finally recognizing that for Americans to prosper economically in the world of the twenty-first century, we will need better and more effective schools. Public education is finally receiving the attention it deserves, and the quest to ensure that a larger number of Americans pursue post-secondary study is underway. All this is positive, but the danger is that the humanities will be squeezed out of the curriculum in our schools, colleges and universities as these institutions are transformed to meet the demands of the new economy and to promote a consumer culture whose values are often in tension with humanistic values. If our schools are to fulfill their historic role as providers of opportunity, we must ensure that quality education is made available to all—regardless of location, ethnicity, and economic status.

An advanced information age. The new information age holds enormous promise for the humanities. Never before have so many Americans been able to access the histories, cultures, and literatures of the world. From one's home computer, whether in a study or a hallway closet, it is now possible to read the classics, to tour the world's leading museums, to learn about ancient Mayan culture, to study Scandinavian history, to explore one's own or another's religious heritage and faith. State humanities councils, as agencies that promote adult learning through public programs, must form creative and wholesome responses to this new form of self-education. TCH should promote such learning, and it should help ensure an abundance of useful materials on the Internet, especially materials that relate directly to its mission. But at the same time, state councils will be called upon to articulate in new ways the value of communal learning, of public dialogue, of give and take, of arriving at shared truth. There may be some ominous connections between the new information age and the problems of civil society. Further, we know that accessing information is only the first step in the pursuit of meaningful knowledge. How to put this new information to use in constructive ways in our personal and collective lives is a matter that will need continual addressing.

What do these cultural and societal developments say about the future mission of a state humanities council? If that mission is framed by past goals, those of increasing public understanding of and appreciation for the humanities, and relating the humanities to the "current conditions of national life," some important discoveries might be made.

First, TCH may need to focus more money and time on elementary and secondary education to help ensure a citizenry in touch with history and culture, a citizenry that possesses understanding of and appreciation for the humanities. Perhaps the focus ought to be more evenly balanced between adult learning programs and efforts to improve learning for today's children and youth, including those who are considered to be at risk for dropping out of school. A higher percentage of resources may need to be directed toward after-school programs and summer programs.

Second, TCH may need to expand present avenues or find new ways of illuminating contemporary public issues through the humanities, and new ways of bringing the public into dialogue on those issues. It may need to address more extensively the loss of civic space, the erosion of confidence in the political process, the growing gap between people and the powerful issues that confront the U. S. and the global community. More of its resources may need to be directed toward public forums and to the engagement of scholars in the humanities with these issues and with the public, as well as toward using older (publications) as well as newer (the Internet) avenues for disseminating and discussing important ideas in American public life. TCH may need to return to some of the very early premises of the program—that it has a special obligation to foster dialogue on contemporary issues and that such dialogue is enriched through the humanities.

Third, the TCH may need to re-vision that part of its mission having to do with relating the humanities to "the current conditions of national life." Throughout its twenty-five year history, this phrase has been primarily interpreted by the TCH to mean that state councils should sponsor some programs that use the humanities to clarify particular public issues. But dialogue on public issues is not in itself sufficient. We must include action as well as talk. An opportunity now exists to put the humanities to work more directly, more practically, on behalf of the American people, especially in regard to our poverty crisis. While it may be a truism that only education can truly help the poor, there is growing evidence, anecdotal as well as substantive, that education must be grounded in the liberal arts, in the humanities. Such is the claim of Earl Shorris in *New American Blues: A Journey through Poverty to Democracy*. This book documents the worst of American poverty, but it also makes the bold claim that an education in the humanities may be the only real solution to multigenerational poverty. The humanities provide indispensable resources for understanding human behavior and the nature of our society and culture, and such understanding is necessary if one is to participate effectively in our society and its economy. The humanities also provide resources for fostering responsibility, compassion, and hope. Thus the humanities have much to contribute to the solving of some of our most intractable societal problems, and the TCH is in a strong position to encourage, sponsor, and support programs that bring the humanities to those hardest to reach, those who are falling through the cracks of the welfare system, those who have dropped out of school, those who live in public housing, on the street, or in shacks in small villages and rural areas—those whose lives may be forever lost unless opportunities for renewal through education are given to them. TCH would need to work with an entirely new group of potential collaborators, those non-profit organizations whose tasks include feeding the hungry, assisting the illiterate, finding homes for the homeless, helping the addicted, and comforting the afflicted.

TCH will need more money to accomplish this broadened agenda. Renewed bipartisan recognition of the federal government's responsibility to further the arts and humanities would help all the councils in their quest for expanded state funding and for private sector support. A renewed commitment on the part of the federal government, restoring funds that were lost in recent years, would help potential funders see the importance of this work. The worth of these federally-funded programs has been demonstrated through the tough political dialogue that has marked the recent past. For TCH, this federal commitment should mean renewed quests for state funding and for greatly expanded private sector support from Texas foundations, corporations, and philanthropic individuals. Donors need to be informed about the vital role that the humanities can play in helping address some of this nation's most serious challenges. Indeed, the re-visioning of mission to focus more directly on the poverty crisis and on children and youth might assist in greatly expanding nonfederal support.

Money aside, the TCH is well prepared to meet these new challenges. It can draw strength from three important realties that have enveloped the TCH for twenty-five years.

First, through the commitment of its board and staff, TCH has been able to avoid the politicization of its program and the imposition of particular ideologies, giving it the freedom to move ahead in constructive ways. TCH has always taken an expansive view of the humanities. It has stood for the classics and for the value of the study of Western civilization. But it also has stood for the value of new disciplines, new discoveries, new histories, new cultures. It has promoted social history as well as political history. It has not sought to destroy the scholarship of "dead white European males;" indeed, it has treasured the intellectual and spiritual heritages of Western culture. But it has sought to embrace important new scholars, female as well as male, minority as well as majority, who are making tremendous contributions to our ways of understanding the world. TCH has been an important voice for those without a widely-known history; it should embrace and celebrate this history. It has been an important source for new scholarship as well as an important source for the dissemination of previous scholarship. It has tried to transcend rather than join the culture wars, but it has not shied away from stating its position when called upon to do so. The late Konstantin Kolenda, professor of philosophy at Rice University and a remarkable public humanist, maintained that the humanities look forward as well as back. The humanities are about the stories we would like future generations to tell as well as stories about the past. Thus it is free to move in new directions, to find new ways to respond to contemporary circumstances.

Second, the TCH has an intellectual heritage that explores the connections between the humanities and public life and that offers guidance in thinking about future endeavors. This heritage can be found in many places: in the work of grantees, in the programs of the Resource Center, in the issues of *Texas Journal*, perhaps even in a few of the essays in this collection. Three of the most important texts that express what the TCH has been about are: *The Humane Imagination*, the 1983 Texas Lecture in the Humanities presented by poet and legal scholar Charles L. Black, Jr., published as a small booklet by the TCH; *The Humanities and the American Promise*, the report written by Jefferson scholar Merrill D. Peterson for the Colloquium on the Humanities and the American

People, published by the TCH in 1987 (unfortunately, now out of print); and *Building Community in Texas*, by Catherine Williams, published as Vol. 1 in the *Preparing for Texas in the 21st Century* series, 1990. These three texts continue to inspire. Black tells us why the humanities are indispensable to the cultivation of our humanity. Peterson shows us why the humanities are vital to American democracy. Williams tells us how the humanities illuminate the creative visions of humanity, inspire new forms of civic engagement, and lead to enlarged understandings of community.

Third, from almost the very beginning, the TCH made sure that the board and staff would be representative of the state. Over the years, the percentages of blacks, Latinos, and whites on the board have patterned the state's population, and much consideration has always been given to ensuring as well that all geographical areas of the state receive representation. And the staff has been remarkably representative of the state's population as well—and TCH has been much better for it. Out of this shared commitment to diversity, to our recognition that we had a moral and political obligation to ensure a program for all the people of Texas, have come programs of high quality to which Texans of diverse ethnicity and cultural background have been drawn. At the end of my last board meeting, after a presentation was made to me, I responded with this statement, which speaks to this point:

> What I am most proud of, in terms of these years, is that this group was able to do what is so desperately needed in today's world—and that is to come together, to find common ground. If you look at this board right now and you look at the board in the past, it is East Texas, it is West Texas, it's black, it's brown, it's white, it's left, it's right; it's everything you can think of, and yet we are able to talk together and come together and to have a common vision. And that gives us hope. We have tried from the very beginning to make sure that the record of this Council is one in which we see that the story of this state and the story of this nation is richer and fuller than it has been in the past. I think the accomplishment along those lines, of seeing that our history is now much more textured, much more full, much more rich than it was twenty-five years ago, because of all of you, is an incredible achievement, and this should give everyone a lot of hope for the future.

So where does all this leave the TCH as it contemplates its role in a new century? Perhaps with the recognition that TCH has not been about "institution building," about constructing monuments to the public humanities. We have not perceived that to be our role. Rather, TCH has been a program about people, about the insights and opportunities that come to individuals, to communities, to a state, to a nation, when shared learning takes place. I hope that it has contributed to a national movement composed of those Americans who recognize that, as the Congress stated in NEH's authorizing legislation, "The world leadership which has come to the United States cannot rest solely upon superior power, wealth, and technology, but must be solidly founded upon worldwide respect and admiration for the nation's high qualities as a leader in the realm of ideas and of the spirit." This is a movement of people willing to give wings to ideas, knowing full well that the humanities originate in the community as well as in the academy.

So what has the TCH been about? I tried to answer that question in a funding proposal to the NEH in February 1980. Perhaps the answer given then still holds some relevance for today.

> TCH, drawing upon humanistic resources across the state, offers educational opportunities whereby citizens can gain knowledge, perspective, and orientation that will help them function as interpreters of their lives and of their society. The state humanities program encourages citizens to get in touch with their history, with various expressions of culture, with old and new values and ideas. Whether a grant project involves reflection upon the Cowboy ethic, the nearly lost Indian culture of West Texas, the fundamental issue of punishment versus rehabilitation in our criminal justice system, or the way a city's architecture seeks to ensure harmony between the environment and man-made structures, the implications are the same: citizens are encouraged to understand the past, to interpret the present, and to participate in planning the future.
>
> One cannot overstress the importance of this humanistic process to the future of our society and government. Democratic government depends on the ability of the average citizen to understand the world about him [her], to effectively assess challenges confronting this world, and to be in a position to responsibly affect

that world. American society is threatened by the potential inability of our citizens to think for themselves, not in bits and pieces, not hastily and imprecisely, not from worn out or hastily construed ideologies, but humanistically, drawing from the resources that come from a knowledge of history, an understanding of divergent cultures and values, an acknowledgment of the power of an idea, and an empathy for our fellow human beings which can only be gained through communication.

What is this program about? It is about Czechs in Texas, tortilla curtains on the border, Texas ranchers, East Texas Black music, Jewish immigration through Galveston, consumer rights in South Texas, depression history, alcoholism, and Nacogdoches, Victoria, Alpine, and the 5th Ward of Houston. But it is about much more. It is about having resources, knowledge, and intellectual skills needed to participate actively and creatively in our democratic society. The state humanities program involves a humanistic process in a public context, a process through which the American Self is able to reflect upon the American Self. As such, the state humanities program is deeply rooted in the democratic ideals which form the basis of American society and government. It rests on the conviction that the future of our country depends not on the few, but on the many, not on knowledge and skills belonging to a minority, but on the wisdom, decency, and understanding of a majority, not on a vote cast from ignorance and prejudice, but on a vote cast from a sense of history and a vision of the future.

Works Cited

American Identity: Questions and Readings for Community Conversations. Austin: Texas Council for the Humanities, 1996.

Black, Charles L., Jr. *The Humane Imagination in the Great Society.* Austin: Texas Council for the Humanities, 1984.

Buenger, Walter L. and Robert A. Calvert, eds. *Texas Through Time: Evolving Interpretations.* College Station: Texas A&M University Press, 1991.

Building the New Texas. Austin: Texas Council for the Humanities, 1993.

A Call to Civil Society: Why Democracy Needs Moral Truths. New York: Institute for American Values, 1998.

Carter, Stephen. *Civility: Manners, Morals and the Etiquette of Democracy.* New York: Basic Books, 1998.

Cisneros, Henry G. *Understanding the Global Community in the 21st Century.* Austin: Texas Council for the Humanities, 1991.

Cultural Pluralism: Readings in the American Experience. Austin: Texas Council for the Humanities, 1996.

Education for the Future. Austin: Texas Council for the Humanities, 1989.

Fresh Approaches to Public Programs and Special Events. Austin: Texas Humanities Resource Center, 1996.

A Guide to Understanding Texas Myths. Austin: Texas Council for the Humanities, 1984.

Kliever, Lonnie D., ed. *Dax's Case: Essays in Medical Ethics and Human Meaning.* Dallas: Southern Methodist University Press, 1989.

McDonald, Archie P. *The Texas Experience.* College Station: Texas A&M University Press, 1986.

National Foundation on the Arts and the Humanities Act of 1965. Public Law 209. 89th Congress.

O'Connor, Robert F., ed. *Texas Myths.* College Station: Texas A&M University Press, 1986.

Peck, M. Scott. *A World Waiting to be Born: Civility Rediscovered.* New York: Bantam Books, 1993.

Peterson, Merrill D. *The Humanities and the American Promise.* Austin: Texas Council for the Humanities, 1987.

Poyo, Gerald E. and Gilberto M. Hinojosa, eds., *Tejano Origins in Eighteenth-Century San Antonio.* Austin: The University of Texas Press, 1991.

Preparing for Texas in the 21st Century: Summary of a Three-Year Research and Discussion Project. Austin: Texas Council for the Humanities, 1991.

Program Announcement. Austin: Texas Council for the Humanities, 1996.

Shorris, Earl. *New American Blues: A Journey through Poverty to Democracy.* W. W. Norton & Company, 1997.

Texas in the 21st Century: The International Agenda. Austin: Texas Council for the Humanities, 1991.

Toward Thoughtful, Active Citizens: Improving the Public School Curriculum. Austin: Texas Council for the Humanities, 1982.

Veninga, James F. *The Biographer's Gift: Life Histories and Humanism*. College Station: Texas A&M University Press, 1983

_____ and Catherine Williams, eds. *Preparing for Texas in the 21st Century: Building a Future for the Children of Texas*. 5 Vols. Austin: Texas Council for the Humanities, 1990.

Wallis, Jim. "Repairer of the Breach: Reflections on Restoring Our Civil Society." *Texas Journal of Ideas, History and Culture* 20 (Spring/Summer 1998).

Williams, Catherine and Frances Leonard. *Planning Humanities Programs: A Guide for Project Directors*. Austin: Texas Humanities Resource Center, 1976 and 1996.

Woodruff, Paul and Harry A. Wilmer, eds. *Facing Evil: Light at the Core of Darkness*. LaSalle, Ill: Open Court, 1988.

[1] The concluding essay, "The Humanities and the Civic Imagination," documents the contribution TCH has made to academic and public understanding of Mexican American history and culture.

Part One

State Councils, NEH, and the Political Arena

Humanities Programs, Accountability and State Government

State humanities councils were founded in the early 1970s in response to Congressional insistence that the NEH expand its public programming. Senator Claiborne Pell of Rhode Island, one of the Congressional founders of the NEA and NEH, pushed hard for a program that would replicate NEA's state arts agencies.

The NEH experimented with different structures at the state level. For example, in 1970 NEH awarded grants of $100,000 to state arts councils in Oklahoma and Maine, establishing humanities components in these state agencies. These and several other efforts were abandoned when it became clear that the humanities would be diminished if not lost altogether if they were incorporated into existing entities, especially if those entities were state agencies. What emerged was a new and untested structure. Over a period of six years, the NEH invited six consultants from each state, drawn from lists of prominent scholars, cultural leaders, and university administrators, to Washington D.C. to lay the groundwork for establishing independent, volunteer organizations. Thus the NEH decided to use newly-created non-profit organizations rather than agencies of state government, as NEA had done, to meet the Congressional mandate.

Senator Pell expressed his displeasure over this decision during the 1975 confirmation of Joseph Duffey, President Carter's appointee to head the NEH, and again during 1976 reauthorization hearings. Pell believed *that for state humanities councils to attain visibility, to bring the humanities to grass roots America, they should be part of the "warp and woof" of state government. He also felt that state humanities councils, lacking accountability to state governments, might be unduly influenced and managed by the federal government. State councils and the NEH countered by talking about the benefits of independence, the value of volunteer boards, the wisdom of avoiding expensive bureaucratic operations, and the need for autonomy when dealing with perennial questions of the humanities.*

A compromise was reached in the 1976 legislation. The independent status of the state humanities councils was preserved but the legislation required the councils to follow certain procedures regarding recruitment of board directors "to assure broad public representation" and to limit their service to established terms. The legislation also allowed the governor of each state two appointments to the council board, a figure that was increased to twenty-five percent of the board in 1980 legislation. The 1980 reauthorization bill also permitted a governor to convert the state humanities council to a state agency if the state appropriated either fifty percent of the council's basic operating grant from the NEH ($200,000) or twenty-five percent of the total funding received from the NEH, whichever was greater.

These issues provided challenges to the newly-minted state humanities councils through the 1970s, forcing the councils to think hard about matters of accountability, about how to represent the public as well as the academy, about how to be a part of the fabric of state life without being inside the political arena, and about how to be partners with the NEH while retaining program autonomy.

One further dimension to this controversy should be noted. In the expectation that NEH would ultimately allocate humanities funds to state arts agencies, as it had in 1970 in Oklahoma and Maine, a number of arts agencies had incorporated the word "humanities" into their names. The Texas humanities program suffered in its early years from public confusion with the Texas Commission on the Arts and Humanities. That problem was addressed by State Rep. Wilhelmina Delco, an early director of the TCH, who sponsored legislation mandating a change in the name of the arts agency, dropping the word "humanities" from its title.

These issues subsided dramatically after passage of the 1980 NEA and NEH reauthorization bill. The compromise took, and both the arts agencies and the humanities councils moved forward with recognition of their very different mandates, organizational structures, and ways of ensuring accountability in the expenditure of public funds. With the

*election of President Reagan in 1980, new and more urgent issues re-
garding federal funding of the arts and the humanities soon emerged.*

*The following speech was presented at the conference "In the Public
Interest: New Accords Between the Humanities and the Arts," held at the
Spring Hill Center, Wayzata, Minnesota, July 21–22, 1978, sponsored
by the Federation of State Humanities Councils. The Federation was
created by NEH and the state councils in 1978 to advance the work of
the councils. The address was published by the Federation in 1980 in*
Citizens, Scholars, and the Humanities, *edited by Steven Weiland.*

*One of the concerns registered here, that the opportunity to seek state
funding might jeopardize the independent, non-profit status of state
humanities councils, proved to be groundless. Twenty years later, more
than two-thirds of the state councils were receiving state appropriations,
some in amounts that matched or exceeded their federal allocation, and
none had been incorporated into state government. Thus state humanities councils can be seen as early experiments in the privatization of
government services.*

There have been, from time to time, numerous misconceptions and
misunderstandings concerning the nature, function, and purpose of arts
and humanities programs in the various states. Undoubtedly, one explanation for the problem has to do with the relationship between the
arts and the humanities, the similarities and differences, the problem of
definition, and the varying ways in which these activities contribute to
the substance of American cultural life. Another explanation, however,
lies in the different state groups and agencies that have been established to further arts and humanities interests, and the differing organizational structures and programming missions adopted.

I will confine my remarks to, first, a brief outline of the essential
characteristics of our humanities program in Texas, and, secondly, to
an analysis of the organization's structure, with particular reference to
its volunteer, private nature, characteristics which are true of all state
humanities councils.

There are a number of essential organizational characteristics of the
TCH. First, it is a volunteer, private organization, yet functions very
much like a quasi-governmental unit. It is composed of twenty-five
members, with membership drawn from academic and public sectors.

Second, the TCH is an organization whose members and staff are
dedicated to the humanities. This dedication is essential to service on

the Council. Every board director serves by virtue of a desire to further the development of the humanities in Texas. The same is true with the staff of the Council. This commitment has given a unique sense of mission.

Third, the program capitalizes on and expresses the essence of certain aspects of American political thought and experience: the proper and limited role of the federal government, volunteerism, the encouragement of responsibility and dedication in furthering program goals, controlling bureaucracy and limiting, as much as possible, the infamous red tape that Americans are increasingly rejecting.

Fourth, the program has been free from undue political pressure. There is no need to allocate funds according to legislative district, population or any other extraneous factor. The TCH has an obligation to ensure equal access to its funds by qualifying organizations, thereby ensuring that each application is evaluated on the basis of merit.

Fifth, as previously mentioned, the state humanities council is in a unique position to encourage the involvement of the private sector and to form new alliances and partnerships. It can work constructively with public and private universities and schools, with state agencies, with corporations, and with foundations.

In spite of these strengths, it is clear that the state humanities program is still greeted with skepticism in some circles. All serious questions about organizational structure seem to revolve around the issue of accountability, and this issue needs closer analysis.

The strengths of the state program are derived, I believe, from the sense of mission and purpose which has been a part of the program from the beginning. Should this sense of mission and purpose wane, should there be floundering, should a particular state program seem ineffective, where are the controls, one might ask, to ensure integrity and responsibility?

The primary external control lies at the federal level, for the NEH reviews grant proposals from the various states and analyzes state programs to determine compliance with federal legislation. What if a state is in compliance with the law, but is not doing a very good job? Will it continue to receive the minimum level of funding as provided by the legislation? Who would receive these funds if the NEH rules the council to be incompetent or inadequately organized?

At the state level, state government has no control over the program, outside of the appointments made by the governor. Undoubtedly, governors as well as congresspersons and members of state legislatures can express either their pleasure or displeasure over the state humanities council, but state government does not have the authority to exercise control over the program.

Should state councils be more accountable to state governments? The national legislation of 1976 sought to address this question and granted an increasing role to state governments. The governor of each state could, in fact, appoint one-half the membership of the council if the state matched federal funds with state funds. The legislation also provided for additional measures, such as the submittal of an annual report to the chief executive officer and other persons that he might designate.

How can state councils be accountable to the state without losing their private, volunteer nature? Are the minimum requirements of the legislation of 1976 enough? I believe that these requirements should be seen as basic legal requirements and that efforts should be taken to go beyond them in the furtherance of programming objectives, to not just report to the governor, but to seek his advice and suggestions, to work cooperatively with various state agencies, and with state representatives and senators.

Given this challenge, one can identify the key issues confronting state humanities councils as non-profit, independent, volunteer organizations.

First, how can each state council best serve the interests of its state? This question has been raised extensively by the legislation of 1976 which afforded each council new freedom in determining program design. Most states have dealt with the issue of whether to retain their current program or to adopt a broader program. A formal response to this issue is the first step in determining future program directions. Until now, responses to this issue have been based primarily on the use of federal dollars for traditional kinds of projects. For example, state councils have not, by and large, explored the role of the council and all resources that might be open to it, in regard to the development of humanities curricula in secondary and primary schools of the state; the development of local urban humanities councils; means whereby young writers, poets and novelists can be encouraged and the talented can find a market for their work; ways of overcoming the devastating consequences of the underemployment of people trained in the humanities; and cooperative, formal arrangements that can be made with business and the various professions in regard to use of humanistic resources. How far should state councils go in assuming positions of leadership within the states? Where will state councils find the resources to accomplish this? More federal money? Private money? State money?

Is the lure of possible state dollars going to ultimately sacrifice the merits of the volunteer, private structure that has been successful?

Secondly, how can state councils retain the volunteer, private nature of their organizations, which has worked well for this national humanities effort, while being accountable to state government? I am convinced that state humanities councils do not have to be state agencies to be accountable to the state. Perhaps public agencies may have a difficult time accepting this fact. If so, in spite of the evidence that exists regarding present accountability, one can ask the question: Would an organization be more responsive to the needs of citizens and more responsible in terms of handling tax-payers dollars by virtue of being a public agency? The history of state agencies within many states, including Texas, provides an answer with which, I think, most of us would agree.

Should state councils function more and more as public agencies, seeking, for instance, gubernatorial appointments equal to one-half the membership and state funds matching federal funds, tensions might arise as arts commissions and historical commissions and other agencies seek their fair share of limited state resources.

Aside from the fact that the uniqueness of the state humanities program, as seen in the volunteer structure and the sense of mission and dedication, could be threatened, such efforts might, indeed, undermine the unique position that a state council currently holds in furthering the cultural life of its state. State humanities councils can assist arts commissions in their struggle for adequate funding and historical commissions in their need for further state support. The extent to which humanities entities in the various states could function to further new alliances and partnerships, as mentioned earlier, might be in doubt.

What unites those disciplines and activities that we call the humanities is a concern for public and private values. It is appropriate, I think, that given this basis, the NEH and Congress have implemented a public humanities program utilizing private, volunteer citizens councils. There is compatibility between the nature of humanistic inquiry and the private organizational structure of the state humanities program.

Councils as independent non-profit organizations have served well the interests of the public and the interests of the humanities community. There is need, of course, for continual improvement in terms of both quality programming and organizational structure. Likewise, as the history of politics and governmental programs indicate, the evolution of programs and structures designed to meet the purposes of government is a given fact.

State humanities councils, as with state arts commissions, are experiencing considerable change. We are called upon to reflect objectively on where we have been, on the principles and values underlying our present structures and efforts, on opportunities that are before us, and on the best means available to fulfill those opportunities.

It is important to acknowledge the unique and successful experiment of the NEH and Congress in utilizing volunteer citizen councils in the implementation of this public humanities program. At the same time, we must also acknowledge the potential challenges to this effort, particularly in regard to the issue of accountability to state government, as we build upon accomplishments to date. We must be open to new program opportunities, and what is fundamentally important is the fulfillment of those opportunities, rather than the preservation of particular organizational structures. Structures must serve programs. If that point can continually be kept in mind, then this conference will indeed serve the public, for whose benefit both arts commissions and humanities councils were created.

Three New Threats to the State Humanities Program

The following speech was given at an orientation conference for new board directors of state humanities councils, held in San Antonio, Texas, June 30, 1981. The conference was sponsored by the NEH to introduce these directors to their new responsibilities and to demonstrate the multiple ways in which they were now involved in a national effort.

It probably was not a coincidence that these orientation meetings began as the state councils were claiming autonomy. While the 1976 and 1980 reauthorization bills strengthened procedures ensuring accountability to the public, they also underscored Congressional intent that the state councils would be independent of the federal agency. While state councils accepted, sometimes with reservations, the necessity of providing detailed and substantive reports and plans (called by the NEH "funding proposals," language that irritated some since the Congress had already appropriated the funds for the councils) as a primary means of ensuring accountability, some councils were concerned that the NEH was seeking too much control over the councils. This tension between a federal agency desirous of control and many state councils desirous of independence, grounding their accountability more in their responsibility to the citizens of their respective states than to the federal government—a matter that Senator Pell had sought to encourage in the 1970s—festered throughout the 1980s and into the early 1990s, height-

ened, undoubtedly, by state council responses to some of the policies and emphases of Bill Bennett and Lynne Cheney, appointees of Presidents Reagan and Bush to the NEH. This tension remained until Sheldon Hackney, appointed by President Bill Clinton, eliminated the Division of State Programs in 1995, creating instead an Office of Federal-State Partnership, and, out of recognition of the maturity and success of the state councils, acted to greatly reduce reporting requirements.

While these changes were very much needed, NEH staff charged with working with the state councils were genuinely concerned about the vulnerability of federal funding for state councils and thus sought to use the leverage of the federal agency to help strengthen the councils and to demonstrate to real as well as potential critics that these were well-managed councils engaged in programs of excellence and sustained by diversified funding. Orientation conferences for new board directors demonstrated NEH's commitment to the state councils and sustained the perception that this was a "national" program, not just a mechanism for releasing federal dollars to humanities councils in fifty states, the District of Columbia, and the U. S. territories.

It should also be noted that in establishing the state councils in the early 1970s, NEH decreed that the programs funded by the councils should all have a public policy focus. This requirement, which was a useful way for the NEH to separate the work of the councils from the work of the NEH (promoting scholarship, improving the teaching of the humanities, reaching large audiences through national television programs and nationally-significant blockbuster exhibitions, etc.), was designed in part to give uniqueness to the work of the councils, to address national needs, and to involve—it was hoped—large numbers of the public. The 1976 reauthorizing legislation removed this requirement, allowing the state councils the freedom to explore all kinds of humanities projects and initiatives, to become, if they so desired, mini-versions of the NEH. While most state council representatives—board and staff alike—welcomed this change, the state councils by and large have retained some measure of interest in relating the humanities to public issues—a lasting legacy of those NEH officials and state council representatives who helped create the councils.

This short address, however, picks up on what I saw as matters far more important than the relationship of state councils to the NEH, some new "threats" that had the potential to end all federal support for NEH and the state councils. Regrettably, at least two of these threats—briefly outlined in this talk—became increasingly powerful forces in the 1980s and early 1990s.

There are, in every social or political movement of some note, certain public addresses that magically capture the essence of that movement. Indeed, these addresses—powerful, special words spoken on what become special days—last far beyond the movement.

While the public humanities program may or may not be a movement with staying power, state councils have one public address in their ten-year history that seems to have captured the imagination of people involved in this effort. We frequently hear references to it. I am referring to an address by John Barcroft, the former director of the Division of Public Programs, and a key figure in the founding of the state humanities program, at the 1973 national conference of state councils. The address was entitled "The Three Threats to State Programs."

After outlining his hopes for the state program—and they are very interesting ones—Barcroft summarizes three possible threats that could undermine the stated hopes:[1]

1) that the state program will lose its present spirit of adventure, and become just another federal program;

2) that the program will fail to strike a deep enough cord of response in a large enough part of the public;

3) that the program will lose its objectivity, and that advocacy of particular public issues might occur.

I would like to suggest that, if one reflects on the program nationally, these three threats no longer exist, or, more cautiously, they appear as nagging problems, but not dire threats. The spirit of adventure seems alive and well, and we continually remind ourselves, in many ways, of the experimental nature of the program. We have gained the interest and involvement of the public, especially through the important legislative changes in 1976 which opened up new programming opportunities. Undoubtedly, our constituency has expanded greatly over the past number of years, especially among those institutions and organizations that must be our allies: museums, libraries, historical organizations. We have been faithful to our democratic instincts: Program development efforts have resulted in projects in the smallest villages and in the largest cities. Finally, with the shift from public policy questions to broader public issues and to themes and subjects drawn directly from the humanities, the question of objectivity has becomes less important.

It is inevitable that with every new federal program, however meritorious, the social and political circumstances leading to the establishment of that program, as well as the program itself, undergo change. The NEH was conceived in the 1960s quest for The Great Society. The NEH and state humanities councils have grown greatly since their founding. However, barely out of the adolescent stage, we now find ourselves in a world where we no longer are sure of our place—1981 is remarkably different from 1965 when NEH was founded and 1971 when the state councils were launched. Yet our uncertainty is occurring at a time when the spirit of adventure remains high, when we have been able to obtain the interest and participation of the public, and when we have been true to our position of non-advocacy.

Recently, new threats have emerged, replacing those that Barcroft spoke of in 1973. The three new threats are: 1) growing antagonism to humanistic thought from religious and political groups to the far right; 2) the potential disengagement of the scholarly community from public programming in the humanities, and 3) the possible loss of bipartisan support for the Endowment.

Growing Antagonism to Humanistic Thought

There are an increasing number of stories covered by the media that involve verbal attacks upon the humanities and on humanities scholars, attacks that stem from opposition to a perceived outburst of secular humanism. Public libraries are increasingly under pressure to remove certain books. Organized groups of parents are seeking to control the curriculum in the public schools and the selection of textbooks, barring anything that seems anti-God, anti-American, and anti-family. The NEH itself has been under journalistic attack; for example, a June 1981 article in the *Reader's Digest* portrays the scholarship supported by the NEH as silly and trite. This troubling situation reflects a disturbing social and cultural development—a rebirth of anti-intellectualism— and poses a threat to the future of state humanities councils.

Potential Disengagement of the Scholarly Community

In difficult and uncertain times, we are tempted to withdraw, to protect our own, to take few risks. With declining student enrollments in the humanities, with university administrators seeking to make ends meet, with inadequate pay and public support and appreciation, scholars may turn inward, to attend to their classes and college chores, including scholarship. While I obviously support teaching and scholarship, we find little encouragement of and few rewards for public service.

More than ever, state councils need the involvement of the scholarly community, especially serious, provocative, critical, and reflective scholars. Such individuals bring the respect and participation of their colleagues, the interest of professional societies, and—most importantly—substance, drawn from the humanities, to matters of council policy and individual projects. The social, cultural, and political issues that the American people now face provide the context in which state councils function. We must, therefore, involve the best thinkers in every state in our programs.

Possible Loss of Bipartisan Support

The decline in bipartisan support is a sensitive matter and, on this point, I speak only from my own vantage point. Since the Reagan administration came into office, 1) the FY 1982 federal appropriations request for the NEH has been reduced by fifty percent; 2) the president has established a Task Force on the Arts and Humanities which, among other things, will explore the possibility of restructuring the two endowments and possibly creating a new entity altogether; 3) a request to the Congress has been submitted to rescind—at this late date—a portion of the fiscal year 1981 appropriation.

One may or may not question the need to reduce federal expenditures for all federal programs. One may or may not agree with the idea that both endowments should receive a reasonable cut in appropriations. But the issue before the Congress is difficult to resolve since the fifty percent slash is the largest proposed cut for any federal agency, aside from the few that are to be abolished altogether, such as the Institute for Museum Services. Equally important, it is clear that the administration and the Congress are designing current fiscal policy so as to effect social and political change as well as economic change. To what extent, therefore, is the fifty percent proposed cut based on an ideology in which the NEH is viewed negatively, and to what extent on the need to balance the federal budget? The impact of saving approximately $170 million from the two endowments will have a minuscule, hardly detectable effect on the quest for a balanced budget.

Summary

These are three threats with which we currently live. You have become a part of a national effort at a time in our history when that effort is of genuine, however intangible, importance to the nation.

As we confront the current conditions of national life, there must be centers and pockets for, and expressions of, the interrelationship between thought and civic responsibility. In this sense, a state humanities council must serve as a major resource for preserving and deepening our collective memory, thereby avoiding collective amnesia; for under-standing and interpreting those forces, ideas, events, and fears that shape our lives on a daily basis, thereby avoiding the situation wherein we are simply dependent participants in our society; and for unabash-edly claiming the importance of the aesthetic, moral, and spiritual di-mensions of life, thereby avoiding a society where the bottom line is marked with the dollar sign. The business of America must be more than business.

This is the effort that is before us. The state humanities council is more than a regranting agency, more than a non-profit humanities or-ganization, more than an accountable delivery system for federal dol-lars. It is a symbol of a civilized nation, a center for thought, a place for understanding and interpreting, and a source for dreaming, imagining, and hoping.

As with all human endeavors, we will fall short. But the times call for us to give this program our very best effort.

Works Cited

Bancroft, John. "The Three Threats to State Programs," in *Citizens, Scholars and the Humanities: An Introduction to State Humanities Councils*. Steven Weiland, ed. Minneapolis: Federation of Public Programs in the Humanities, 1980.

[1] Barcroft's four hopes: By 1976 (when NEH will be before the Congress for reauthorization), 1) the structure of the program will be solid and able to withstand bad weather in each state, 2) the public policy focus of the program will be fully understood, fully tested, and proved of value to a broad public in each state, 3) the public in significant numbers and significant variety will have participated in the program and found it both of value and worth their confidence, and 4) the humani-ties will have so fully infused the program that everyone in the United States will see this program as manifestly a program in the humanities.

The Humanities and Public Life

I was invited to provide a keynote address at an orientation conference for new board directors of state councils, held in St. Louis, October 15, 1982. I sought to respond to the new environment brought about by the election of President Reagan and the appointment of Bill Bennett to chair the NEH. Although the Congress decided to reduce NEH's budget by $21 million rather than the $55 million requested by the Reagan administration, a new and very challenging era had arrived. The environment had changed dramatically. State councils, if they were to survive, had to turn seemingly negative realities into positive forces. It seemed likely that NEH's budget, and the funds appropriated for state councils, would be further reduced. While the impact of these cuts would not be felt by the state councils until the mid-1980s, due to creative budgeting by NEH's Division of State Programs, it was clear in the fall of 1982 that the best defense had to be a solid offense.

This address offered a redefinition of the work of state councils. It gave in—too readily so, I should add—to the then-current critique that saw political constituencies as clients of the federal government, arguing that we had come to base the value of our work on the numbers reached and that no amount of federal funds would ever be enough to bring the humanities to all the American people. I emphasized another part of our Congressionally mandated mission, that of relating the humanities to the current conditions of national life, in order to preserve the program after funding was slashed. I was concerned that reduced appropriations would provide a near-fatal blow to the councils unless missions were redefined.

The address expressed a growing conviction on the part of many of my colleagues that it was time to balance a responsive but nevertheless passive grant-making role with sponsored projects that the councils thought were timely, important, and consequential. While the Texas Council for the Humanities was not alone in arriving at this conclusion, it was one of the leaders in the early 1980s in developing entirely new arenas for council work—seminars, media projects, publications, task forces on education—that the TCH sponsored itself, with non-federal as well as federal funds. For a few years, creativity at the TCH was unbounded, reinforced by ample funding, with one council-sponsored project after another, until federal reductions finally impacted the TCH in 1985—the same year that the Texas economy took a terrible dive and private funding all but evaporated. By the fall of 1986 we were forced to reduce staff and to jettison some of the initiatives begun a few years earlier. By the end of the decade, the TCH program had recovered, and more council-sponsored projects were again underway, but the era of an expanding program infused with expanding revenues had passed.

The theoretical framework provided in this redefinition of the mission of state councils still tantalizes. Unfortunately, it didn't adequately take into account the independence of the councils, the drive of each council to ensure programs that responded to the interests of the citizens in the various states. For better or for worse, there seems to be more interest in local and state history and culture, in political and social history, in biography and autobiography, in folklore and folk culture, than in public issues confronting the nation. But it is not, of course, an "either/or" situation. Creative programming often brings these diverse interests together, utilizing traditional humanities fields to clarify public issues.

On a lighter note, the reader will find my not-so-hidden concern that the orientation conferences were a form of federal control over the state councils. Why else would one want to talk about the "disorienting" function of the humanities at a conference devoted to orientation?

This address was published in the January/February 1983 issue of Federation Reports: The Journal of the State Humanities Councils.

Even a casual reading of the notebook prepared by the NEH for this orientation conference points to a carefully managed program of the federal government. As new members of state humanities councils, you are learning a seventeen-year history of federal support for the humanities, and a twelve-year history of support for the state councils. You are getting acquainted with program divisions, legislative mandates, compliance plans, application review processes, conflict of interest policies, reporting requirements, and board/staff relationships. You are, in short, being oriented.

The word "orientation" invokes our desire for knowledge and comfort. Surely some of you must have said to yourselves as you boarded planes for this conference: "Finally, someone will tell me what this program is about." That of course is the function of orientation. In *The American Heritage Dictionary* we find this function to be definition seven of the word *orientation*: introductory instruction concerning a new situation. The comfort of orientation comes from its conservative, even nurturing, characteristic. To orient, says the dictionary, is "to align or position with respect to a reference system" and "to cause to become familiar with or adjusted to facts, principles, or a situation." Hence, in this act of orientation, you are gaining knowledge of this situation in which you now find yourself—a member of a state humanities council—while being aligned or positioned within a system, the state humanities program.

Despite the rewards of orientation—knowledge and comfort—there is something disquieting about the process. If someone offers you the opportunity to be aligned or positioned, you want to think twice. Our society is full of people and programs eager to offer orientation, eager to align and position our hearts and minds.

If you are like me, there is within you a bit of the rebel, resisting alignment and positioning unless you are certain that where you end up is where you want to be. Of course, one important function of humanities education is orientation. Humanities disciplines—at their base—deal with alignment and positioning. The humanities in the public schools serve as the primary vehicle whereby the individual is oriented into a society and culture. A language—the basis of communication—is learned, a sense of history is gained, the founding ideas of a civilization are explored. Those who argue that the humanities in the schools are in a state of crisis bemoan the fact that our orientation of the young into a culture and a society is grossly inadequate. Students are not "familiar with or adjusted to" the facts, principles, and situation of our society and culture.

But humanities education at a deeper level is as much about disorientation as it is about orientation. To disorient, says the dictionary, is "to cause to lose one's sense of direction or location, as by removing from a familiar environment." A good example of this is the liberal arts major. Under the best of circumstances, one's son or daughter—freshly oriented in society and culture through twelve years of public education—leaves for college. Humanities education takes on a new twist; now it is Nietzsche as well as Thomas Jefferson who is studied, and when he or she returns home one Christmas it is Zarathustra who speaks. A good liberal arts education takes one away from a "familiar environment." A second language, a second culture, is learned. Different political ideas are encountered and perhaps some even embraced. Sensibilities are heightened, critical faculties sharpened. In this process, disorientation is inescapable. Indeed, it is desirable; psychoanalytic thought tells us that there can be no growth without disorientation. Doubts, confusions, crises that arise through the discovery of environments other than the familiar are the basis of all human growth.

Several weeks ago, I asked Robert Bly, the poet, to consent to an interview that would be published in our bimonthly magazine, *The Texas Humanist*. Mr. Bly's one sentence written response was: "I am tired of interviews and of literary magazines supported by government money." I felt confused and disoriented, for I believe in interviews with poets and public persons and I believe in the appropriateness of federal support for certain "literary" magazines, especially ours. But then I saw the meaning and beauty of his letter. The poet—who sees what we do not see and says what we cannot say—spoke his truth and in so doing, made me question my truth. Why is he "tired," I asked, of interviews and government-supported magazines? Do interviews exploit the individual in order to satisfy the interests of the reading public? Are magazines supported by taxpayer dollars self-serving, inappropriate, and ultimately doomed to financial, if not literary, failure? The purpose of disorientation is ultimately orientation into a larger, deeper, and more meaningful world.

Constituency-based Program

With these preliminary thoughts on orientation, disorientation, and the humanities out in the open, let me try to elucidate the subject that has been given to me, "The Humanities and Public Life." I wish to talk about the humanities and public life within the context of the state humanities program.

The early literature of this program displays a strong conviction that the state humanities program could strengthen the soul of America. Indeed, this sense of mission was undoubtedly derived in part from the inspiring rhetoric used nearly a decade earlier when Congressional leaders urged the adoption of legislation establishing the NEA and the NEH.

Here, for instance, is what Senator Claiborne Pell said during initial hearings on the bill.

> I am convinced that the arts and humanities are central not only to our national welfare today, but to the goals we seek for years ahead. And that is what this legislation, which is now before us, is all about—those cultural areas which widen the understanding of man in relation to his environment as well as to other men; man's ability to appreciate the past, to comprehend the present, to project soaring new thoughts and images, ideas and ideals into the future; man's ability to analyze wisely, to perceive and appreciate, to be fully aware of his particular moment in history in relation to other moments and eons of the past; and, ultimately, man's ability to understand more completely his potentials so that they may be realized. . . . I feel that this legislation can have a most profound beneficial effect on the very core of our country. (Larson 1983)

The legislation passed, and the NEH went quietly about its business in the areas of education, research, and scholarly fellowships. There were, of course, some early critics, such as Representative H. R. Gross of Iowa, who confessed before the Congress that he wouldn't know a humanist from a bale of hay, and who sent President Johnson a telegram requesting a veto of the legislation, arguing that the budget should be balanced "before subsidizing the longhairs and the little twinkletoes" (Larson).

Fears were abated and the few critics were silenced. While the NEH moved forward in administering its scholarly grant programs, the Congress began to take an interest in more visible, public programs that would help create a wise and visionary citizenry. With Congressional encouragement, the Endowment expanded its public programs in the humanities. The state humanities program, born in the early 1970s, inherited the stimulating rhetoric noted above. The intent was to develop a program that would infuse the humanities into public life. The two goals for the state humanities program that existed then and continue to this day are: 1) to foster public understanding and appreciation of the humanities, and 2) to relate the humanities to the current conditions of national life. These goals are distinct and not necessarily compatible, although both are found in the authorizing legislation. The first goal refers to the notion that a large percentage of adult society in this country has little access to and understanding of the humanities; the second, that resources in the humanities should be applied to the human environment, that the humanities can elucidate the character of our national life.

The most important characteristic of the program that emerged was that it was constituency-based. Even in that early period, from 1971 to 1976, when the Endowment defined for state councils the subject matter—that all projects must focus on public policy issues (a too narrow and misguided interpretation of the second goal)—the primary objective was to foster public understanding and appreciation of the humanities. The constituency-based factor was more important than the subject factor, and this characteristic became the primary feature of the state humanities program. The other divisions of the NEH deal with scholarship; we deal with dissemination of scholarship. An important distinction had been made. Here is how John Barcroft, NEH's director of the Division of Public Programs, expressed this in 1972:

> We are creating structures which provide continuity and focus for local adult programs in the humanities, and which can serve as a programmatically important way of increasing the commitment to adult programs in the humanities nationally.

And again in 1976:

> . . . state humanities committees ought to be encouraged to concentrate their planning and their grant-making programs on activities that reach the citizens of the state broadly—that is, the adult, out of school public, and that they ought to be discouraged from support of scholarly research in general.

This objective—to reach the adult public broadly—remains the primary objective of the state program. Indeed, if you will check with the staff of your state council, you will find the most ingenious methods and plans developed over the last decade to reach citizens "broadly." Some of these endeavors came in response to NEH grant award conditions; in the case of Texas, for instance, the need to reach rural towns and villages. Other endeavors flowed from the council's conviction that more had to be done in a particular geographical area, or with a certain constituency, or with certain organizations.

I am amazed at the success that state councils have had in reaching out, in finding ways of soliciting the interest of local, grass-roots organizations to sponsor public humanities programs. If numbers and diversity were the only criteria employed, this program has been an overwhelming success.

Still, there are some troubling aspects to this constituency-based program, and for the sake of *dis*orientation, I would like to offer some thoughts on what they might be. It is best to frame these thoughts in terms of questions, for the state program has been an experiment and conclusive judgments still seem premature. For those who wish to continue to pursue a constituency-based program, however, I think these questions are worth considering.

First, in pursuit of the principle of equal access to state council funds by potential sponsors of public projects, is there a tendency to move away from the scholarly base of the program?

The concept of public accountability in recent years seemed to imply that an organization or agency using tax-payer dollars must ensure equal access by the designated constituency—in our case the public at large—rather than vested or narrow interests. For the state humanities councils, this emphasis can lead to less than high quality programs. If a particular community in your state has not benefited from humanities funds, and a grant application finally arrives, there is an innate tendency to fund the project, even if it might suffer from content weaknesses, for it is assumed that all citizens in the state—in all locations—should be given the opportunity to benefit from the program.

Let me offer a more specific example. In Texas we have sought to ensure that the bulk of our funds would go to public, non-academic agencies and institutions. If the percentage of grants to universities, and the dollar amount awarded, crept beyond twenty-five percent, we expressed alarm. Now, however, I wonder, why the alarm? Are not the primary resources of the humanities normally found in colleges and universities? Perhaps our program development efforts should have been directed toward, rather than away, from the academy. The danger of this principle of equal access—which in our case was not equal access since universities were sometimes discouraged from applying—is that it can lead to inadequate humanistic depth. If this principle were interpreted differently, I wonder if there would be more first-rate scholars sponsoring and participating in our public programs.

Second, in pursuit of the goal to reach citizens broadly, are we tempted to demonstrate worth through numbers?

Peter Drucker points out that there is an innate tendency in public service organizations to demonstrate the worth of given programs by documenting consumer demand, a tendency which gives rise to obsessive concern for numbers of all types. The number of communities reached, new constituencies served, themes and topics covered, scholars who participated, become the benchmarks for determining success. Such a concern leads to heightened interest in computers, but it can also lead to a program without a soul. Subject matter is diluted, and there is a loss of connection between the humanities and public life. The greatest temptation is to fund projects that are primarily arts appreciation programs; you can be sure that more people will attend a dazzling performance of *Waiting for Godot* than a discussion of anti-intellectualism in nineteenth-century America.

Third, in pursuit of the principle that program funds must be restricted to the use of other agencies and organizations, have we encouraged a passive grant-making role for state councils that has diminished the potential for leadership within the states?

If the only activity of a council, in this constituency-based program, is to provide funds for local projects at the grass-roots level, it may overlook critical ways whereby it can exercise leadership and serve as a catalyst in focusing resources on important areas of the humanities and public life. Passivity might very well be a natural tendency in a constituency-based program.

Many states have found creative ways to overcome this apparent dilemma, such as council-initiated conferences, requests for proposals on identified topics, and subtle or not so subtle hints that the Council would like to see this or that topic addressed. Most state councils recognize the importance of this brokering role. Still, passivity remains, and a good deal of pressure for excellence and impact can go unheeded if a passive grant-making role is the only model to be followed. State councils do have the capacity to ascertain critical needs, interests, resources, and to implement successful projects.

Fourth, in pursuit of a constituency-based program, have we overlooked the possibility that reduced appropriations could provide a near-fatal blow to the kind of program that has been established?

This constituency-based program took root during a period of extraordinary budget expansion. For instance, appropriations for the state program increased from $14.1 million in FY 1976 to $23 million in FY 1981. If you inquire as to why we have a constituency-based program, the answer, in part, can be found in an apparently ever-expanding budget. To help ensure the use of funds, an immediate goal was available—to fund more and more programs in more and more cities involving more and more people with more and more scholars. As long as Congress kept appropriating the funds, the goal seemed reasonable.

But how many dollars would it take for the adult out-of-school public to gain an understanding and appreciation of the humanities? If the billions of dollars appropriated by state and local governments every year for public education fail to lead to increased public understanding and appreciation of the humanities, what would it take for the federal government through the state humanities councils to accomplish this goal among the adult public?

It seems as though we failed to foresee the possibility—if not the inevitability—of budgets retracting rather than expanding. If the administration's current budget proposal is approved by the Congress, many state councils will experience thirty to seventy percent reductions in financial resources by the fall of 1983. If and when this happens, a constituency-based program is basically dead. If all we have as the primary means to increase public understanding of the humanities is equal access, strength through numbers, and grant-making activity, we will be in rather desperate shape. State humanities councils are in a state of financial crisis not so much because funds are being reduced, but because of the kind of program that has been created.

A Subject-based Program

What then are we to do? One option is to hope for the best, to work toward higher appropriations that will sustain a constituency-based program while avoiding the negative consequences of the apparent dilemmas I have noted. Our past success demonstrates that these consequences can be avoided. But there is a second option, one that some of us find more attractive, especially in light of status quo or reduced funding: to redefine the phrase "a public humanities program" and to concentrate more on the second of our two missions, that of relating the humanities to the current conditions of national life. The option leads to a subject-based rather than constituency-based program. We must retain our freedom to craft a state humanities program that is substantively involved in approaching the current conditions of national life through the humanities. We have been granted an extraordinary amount of freedom by the Congress, and the best solution to the financial crises we now face may be a redefinition of the program, a re-examination of what it is we can contribute to the relationship between humanistic study and public life.

How do we relate the humanities to the current conditions of national life? We would be focusing on an interpretation—an analysis—of the life of the American people. We are a community held together by common ideas, customs, allegiances, a language, a political structure, and by many other factors. We are also diverse, and there is constant tension between that which unites us and that which separates us. Yet, we remain a community. In looking at this community and its life, four questions can help clarify our task.

First, what are the conditions of our national life?

The word "condition" refers to one's status, situation, fitness, and health; in short, one's state of being. Applied to a community, a nation, we sense the potential richness of this kind of inquiry. Programs and projects that focus on the moral, political, social, spiritual, cultural, and economic well-being of this community form our primary task. At the same time, we cannot understand these conditions without a wider reference; hence, projects and programs involving comparative studies—activities that reflect on our nation from the standpoint of other cultures and nations—are also required.

Second, what forces, events, ideas, and processes have contributed to these conditions?

Answering this primarily historical question can lead to new efforts to document our evolution as a people, to offer explanation and interpretation about how we have arrived at this moment in time with this set of characteristics and conditions. One cannot assess one's own character, or the character of another, without understanding the formative influences; the same principle applies to this endeavor to understand the character of our national life. Every discipline of the humanities includes an historical dimension: the political theorist, the philosopher, the cultural anthropologist, the scholar of literature—as well as the historian—can tell us much about those factors that have led to the current conditions of national life.

Third, what are the positive and negative aspects of the current conditions of national life?

The humanities involve certain methods of analysis that include reason and critical assessment of information. These methods include techniques for identifying evidence and for judging it from context, for discriminating between questions of value and questions of fact, and for determining what conclusions can and cannot be drawn from what we know. Hence, the humanities can help us determine the significance and meaning of the conditions of national life that have been identified. The humanities help us understand where we might be going as a people—in light of these conditions—as well as where we have been.

Fourth, how are these current conditions, with their positive and negative aspects, related to fundamental national myths, ideals, and goals? This question, it seems, is the most important one. What is it that holds us together as a people, as a nation? For what do we aim, and what is the meaning of our national experience? How is this aim and this meaning expressed through myths that we have held about ourselves as a people and about our role in the world?

To identify and interpret these myths is not easy, but it can be done. Obviously, it is easier to identify controlling myths that have influenced the public in the past, such as the Puritan myth of America as the New Israel, a myth that influenced nearly every aspect of life, including the conduct of commerce and foreign affairs, the development of political structures and community institutions, and the formation of personal values and life-styles. It is more difficult to identify the myths by which we now live, and there are those who argue that modern American consciousness is formed more by the process of demythologizing than by the process of mythologizing, that the consequences of industrialization, the uncertainty and pessimism caused by two world wars, the shock of a major depression, the fear of nuclear annihilation, and the loss of confidence in government at all levels, are such that most of us live with only the residue of previous myths and without the benefit of new myths. Yet it is unlikely that the energy of a people can be marshaled, that the common good can prevail over vested interests, that civility can reign over barbarism, without some myths that tell us who we are as a people and for what we strive.

Leon Edel, the noted biographer and literary critic, argues that in every life there is a manifest myth and a secret, inner myth. It is the task of the biographer to move behind the manifest myth—the facade—to bring forth the inner myth, the inner life. The same point can be made about our collective biography. It is the task of scholars who deal with the humanities and public life to tell us about the manifest myth, the way we project ourselves in the world, the way we would like to be, the way we want others to see us, and our inner myth, the myth that tells us that we as a nation have some being, some selfhood, some goal, something to strive for beyond the success of a bubbling economy, low interest rates, full employment, and a computer in every home.

If, indeed, these four questions formed the core of the state humanities program—identifying the current conditions of national life; exploring those forces, events, ideas, and processes that have contributed to these conditions, identifying and analyzing the positive and negative aspects of these conditions, and determining how these conditions relate to fundamental myths and ideals—we would be operating squarely within the humanities and in accordance with the legislation establishing the NEH and the state humanities program. A symposium on the Federalist Papers, a conference on the philosophical thought of John Dewey, a workshop on Herman Melville's *Bartleby the Scrivener*, a discussion program on Alice James' *Diary*, and a public seminar on the televised production of Americo Paredes' *The Ballad of Gregorio Cortez*, are as much in order in this kind of program as a symposium on technology and the evolution of human consciousness, a conference on the inner and manifest myths of the American people, a workshop on perceptions of the United States held by countries of the Third World, a seminar on the promise and practice of equal justice under the law, or a public program focusing on the social expression of male/female archetypes operative in American culture.

To be sure, state humanities councils are doing much of this very thing right now. The difference, however, is that the incorporation of the above points in our program would help provide a sound theoretical framework for unifying the important work being done, for rejecting marginal programs and inappropriate or secondary subject matter, and for allowing us to focus our energies and limited resources on that which is of fundamental importance.

Such an effort would also help us respond to serious criticism that has been leveled against the state humanities program. Here is what social philosopher Robert A. Nisbet says about us in his book *Prejudices: A Philosophical Dictionary:*

> Another contribution of the Endowment was to subject the humanities to the values of populism and egalitarianism. Those in Congress who were so eloquent in behalf of the humanities . . . encouraged these values. . . . Every worthy grant to a scholar in the true sense must be balanced . . . by a proper number of grants to those in America's towns and villages eager to putter

with local history, to revive old and forgotten town festivals, to rummage and to dredge up the sayings of a department store founder half a century earlier. It may be said that all of this is justified by the fact that genuine scholars receive grants too, but this misses the crucial point, which is that bad money drives out good, and that only a few years of such handouts to putterers will be enough to convince the American people that Everyman is a humanist as well as a speaker of prose. It is necessary only to look at the reports of disbursements of funds, especially from the state councils of humanities. There is nothing too trivial, hackneyed, irrelevant, even obscene to get its funding.

While I do not have much sympathy for many of Nisbet's prejudices—especially those concerning the humanities—I do believe that we left ourselves open to such criticism by having an inadequate theoretical base for our work, by thinking of this effort as a continuing education program for all Americans, by sometimes giving in to a remedial role for the humanities, by not stressing original scholarship, and by not seeking to enrich the program through a collective understanding of its purpose and through stimulating and socially useful documentation of its results.

The state humanities program exists in order to relate the humanities to public life. Ideas matter, and good ideas influence the public. The public will respond to our programs, as it has in the past. What ultimately counts is not how many people we reach, but what is written and said. If what is written and said is good, the public will benefit.

The Program and the Idea

If we are successful in relating the humanities to public life, the idea behind the program will flourish. But if we are not successful, if we give into what Nisbet accuses us of—funding trivial, hackneyed, and irrelevant programs in order to reach as many people as possible—then we risk something far more important than a government program; we risk the idea that the humanities are indispensable in helping us understand who we are as a people, where we have been, and where we are going.

In light of the criticism that has been raised, and in view of impending reductions in federal support for our work, the most important thing that we can do is to ensure that the many parts of this program relate to the whole, and that our work at its center exhibits a sound theoretical base, solid scholarship, and a direct relationship to the task of clarifying the current conditions of national life.

You enter this program at a special time in its history. It is possible that you will be helping to oversee your council in a period of declining resources. The only good thing about reduced funding is that such a circumstance requires careful analysis of priorities. Let me offer an improbable example. What if your council had only $20,000 to work with next year? What would you do? I would hope that your council would not divide the money twenty ways, giving various constituencies—from museums to libraries to historical societies to colleges and universities—$1,000 each to provide a public humanities program on whatever subject they chose. Rather, I would hope that your council would address in your state an important condition of national life—a condition that may very well influence our destiny as a people—and that the $20,000 would be expended through whatever means is most appropriate (one or more grants; contracts for services, Council-sponsored activities and publications) to provide a fresh understanding of the nature of that condition, its origins and development within American society and culture, and its implications for our self-understanding as a people.

If we faced such a dire circumstance, perhaps the state council would agree on a single subject worth pursuing. Imagine what could be done with $1 million if fifty state councils committed $20,000 each to creating new knowledge concerning a single condition of our national life. At the end of the year, a committee, perhaps formed by the Federation of State Humanities Councils, could review a gold mine of material—the best papers, presentations, and essays, and produce a coherent, substantive book for commercial release that would shed new light on this condition and that would serve as a lasting symbol and statement of what this program is about. A major media program for national distribution could be a corollary effort. If such a contribution to public life and the humanities could be made with one million, think what might be possible with $13 or $21 million. The state humanities program should be producing the best scholarship and the best ideas in this country on the humanities and public life.

This program serves an idea: that the humanities provide the means whereby we can understand, confront, and influence our destiny. Compliance plans, reporting requirements, grant review processes, are merely secondary factors which, however important and necessary, must be subsequent to the idea. Whether the humanities program has $13 million or $21 million, whether it exists or not, *the idea remains*. Over the next number of years, the greatest contribution that you can make to this program is to concentrate your energy and time on the idea.

I close by reading a paragraph from Czeslaw Milowz's *The Issa Valley*. The setting for the story is Poland, the author's native land. We are told that the Issa River runs deep and dark.

> One winter—there was always that first morning when you went tracking through the snow that had fallen the night before—Thomas spotted an ermine on the Issa. Frost and sunlight made the twigs of the bushes on the steep shore of the opposite bank stand out like bouquets of gold, lightly tinged with gray and bluish purple. It was then that a ballet dancer of remarkable grace and agility made her appearance, a white sickle, arching and straightening. With a gaping mouth, Thomas stared in awe and ached with desire. To have. If he'd had a rifle with him he would have shot it, because one could not simply stand idle when one's wonder demanded that the thing arousing it be preserved forever. But what good would that have done? Then there would have been neither ermine nor any sense of wonder, just dead matter lying on the ground; no, it was better to feast one's eyes and to let it go at that.

We must, once again, imagine that first morning. In the brilliance of that morning, we perceived something far more than an effort of the federal government, more than a state humanities program. We glimpsed, in awe, the possibility that research, writing, and learning in the humanities could, in a new and deepened way, clarify the current conditions of national life, sustain the American spirit, and help shape the American character.

The instinct to preserve must be resisted; it can only lead to dead matter lying on the ground. With Thomas, we must feast our eyes on that which brings us wonder, and let it go at that.

Works Cited

The American Heritage Dictionary of the English Language. William Morris, ed. New York: American Heritage, 1973.

Larson, Gary O. *The Reluctant Patron: The United States Government and the Arts, 1943–1965.* Philadelphia: University of Pensylvania Press, 1983.

Milowz, Czeslaw. *The Issa Valley.* New York: Farrar Straus & Giroux, 1982.

NEH Memorandum. John H. Barcroft, Director, Division of Public Programs, to Robert Kingston, Deputy Chairman. December 14, 1976.

NEH Memorandum. John H. Barcroft, Director, Division of Public Programs, to Ronald S. Berman, Chairman. January 26, 1972.

Nisbet, Robert. *Prejudices: A Philosophical Dictionary.* Cambridge: Harvard University Press, 1982.

Cultural Pluralism: National Interests and Local Needs

Meridian House International, Washington, D.C., in cooperation with the government of Norway, sponsored a colloquium April 11–12, 1983, on "National Cultural Policy: The Norwegian and American Experiences." High-ranking State Department officials from both nations as well as leaders of diverse arts and humanities organizations in the U.S. participated. The colloquium reflected emerging world-wide interest in the relationship of governments to culture. A year earlier, for example, UNESCO sponsored in Mexico a World Conference on Cultural Policies.

Chairman William Bennett spoke on behalf of the NEH. He followed Lars Roar Langslet, minister of Cultural and Scientific Affairs for Norway. Bennett began by letting the audience know that he was not a minister of culture and that the question of U.S. cultural policy "is in a most important sense a non-question" in that the United States does not have a cultural policy. But, he added, the federal government does encourage cultural expression through tax policy and the existence of agencies like NEA and NEH. And that, Bennett added, was consistent with America's founding principles and, he said, "will be true in the future."

I was recruited to address the relationship of the federal government to local needs and interests, especially in the context of cultural pluralism. By the spring of 1983, it was clear that Bennett was working hard to counter the perceived "populism" of his NEH predecessor, Joe Duffey. A blueprint for what he was to do at the NEH could be found in Mandate for Leadership: Policy Management in a Conservative Administration, *published by the conservative Heritage Foundation at the advent of the Reagan administration in 1980. Bennett offered renewed interest in the Western tradition, in the "great books" of Western Culture, in the perceived primary themes and subjects of the humanities. Emerging fields such as social history, women's studies, and ethnic studies were now suspect. Especially troublesome to Bennett were projects and programs that sought to relate the humanities to contemporary public issues, one of the primary interests of the councils in the 1970s.*

This was a time of uncertainty for state humanities councils. I sought to use the occasion of this colloquium to make a fundamental point: local cultural interests and needs, which are often expressed in the context of a pluralistic society, must remain as matters of concern to the federal government.

I wish to explore a particular aspect of federal activity in support of the cultural life of this country. I am interested in the relationship between national interests and local needs in the context of our complex cultural and social pluralism. Although much of what follows may apply to all areas of federal involvement in culture, including the arts and historic preservation, I will concentrate on that area with which I am most familiar, the humanities. I begin, however, with two important assumptions.

First, the well-being of our democratic society depends in part on the health of our cultural life. The federal government has recognized the importance of this relationship most notably in the passage of the National Foundation on the Arts and Humanities Act of 1965.

Second, although I have no doubt but that this nation's cultural life would continue without extensive federal involvement—that we would continue to have symphonic orchestras and ballet companies, public libraries and museums, scholarship and books—programs and policies implemented by the federal government have enhanced our cultural life, resulting in significant achievements, tangible activities and products of which all Americans can be proud. But the federal effort carries the most weight because of its symbolic power. It serves as a visible sign that this nation cares about the human spirit, about ideas, about freedom of expression, about the imagination. It is, therefore, entirely appropriate, indeed necessary, that the federal government remain involved in the cultural life of this country.

A Point of Tension

In the authorizing legislation for the NEH, one finds a bewitching tension between mandated activities that meet definite national interests and mandated activities designed to meet local needs. Put briefly, the primary national interest is the advancement of research and scholarship in the humanities. Primary local needs, which the legislation also addresses, center not so much in the advancement of scholarship in the humanities but in increasing the public's understanding and appreciation of the humanities and using the humanities to interpret local culture and history. Both emphases, of course, are designed to strengthen our nation's intellectual capacities; the first by enhancing scholarship and the second by instilling public appreciation and understanding of the work of scholars and the importance of humanistic study.

These goals—fulfilling national interests and meeting local needs—are shaped, reshaped, and acted upon within a continually shifting social, political, economic, and cultural context. Central to this context, and that which gives this point of tension special meaning, is our collective experience in cultural pluralism.

At first glance, it would seem that achievement of the first goal—the advancement of scholarship in the humanities—would have little if anything to do with cultural pluralism. The Endowment's mission in part is to support the best scholarship meeting the highest possible standards. Here we find the ongoing interpretation of classical texts in the humanistic tradition and the occasional discovery of neglected fields, subjects, events, and people.

Also at first glance, it would seem that meeting local needs would have everything to do with cultural pluralism. While local needs reflect a thirst for traditional subjects and texts, those, for instance, representing the best in North American and European literature, one finds a particularly strong interest in community and regional history and culture and in ethnic history and culture. The pervasive presence of cultural pluralism, therefore, can readily be seen in the kinds of humanities projects and activities that local organizations—libraries, museums, historical societies, and others—wish to sponsor.

I offer examples of these goals. In regard to advancing scholarship in the humanities—a primary national interest—Jean Strouse's recent book, *Alice James*, the result of an NEH fellowship, provides a classic example. The biography instills in the reader a deeper understanding of a wide range of subjects and topics—the history of medicine, the history of women, New England culture, class structure in nineteenth-century America—and invaluable information on and interpretation of William and Henry James and of an entire family that so deeply influenced American culture and society.

In regard to meeting local needs, the second goal, I offer as an example the recent work of the Houston Center for the Humanities, a small non-profit organization composed of scholars and citizens who recently sponsored, through an NEH grant, numerous public programs and produced a series of booklets on various ethnic groups in Houston—blacks, Mexicans, French, Greeks, Scandinavians, Indo-Chinese, Jews, Germans, Japanese, and Chinese. The Center's work, including these publications, reflects the indisputable fact that the public is interested in and concerned about cultural pluralism.

As we deal with this inevitable tension between those policies and programs directed toward the advancement of research and scholarship and those directed toward meeting local needs, two obvious pitfalls must be avoided. First, it is possible that national interests can be so predominate that local needs are not met. Worse, they might be scoffed at for, in comparison to the Alice James project—and the hundreds of other projects designed to advance scholarship in the humanities—they may seem to be inferior in quality, falling short of defined or undefined standards. Second, it is possible that local needs can so flood the federal agenda that the advancement of research and scholarship in the humanities at the highest level possibly becomes a secondary concern.

It is important to make a distinction between national and political interests. National interests have to do with this nation sustaining a position of leadership in the production of humanistic scholarship; political interests, on the other hand, have to do with that which is perceived to be politically valuable. In this regard, it should be noted that when taxpayer dollars are used, political pressure ultimately tends to gravitate not toward that which I have defined as in the national interest but that which supports local needs. Every member of Congress is interested in how federal dollars are being used in his or her district. Support of local projects fosters a political base that permits the government to support other projects less identified with particular constituencies and more clearly in the national interest.

Handling the Tension

The tension that exists between national interests and local needs is not something to be avoided, for it is intrinsic to the nature of democratic society and to the authorizing legislation establishing the arts and humanities endowments. All of us involved in this effort must acknowledge this tension and find ways to use the energy of that tension in positive ways. The federal government has an obligation, I believe, to encourage and initiate efforts that will increase the compatability of the two goals as it seeks to enhance the cultural life of the United States. Three particular efforts might assist in this attempt.

First, the government should recognize that national interests include the production of the best scholarship possible in the interpretation and reinterpretation of our national experience, in the nature of our national character, and in the formative influences on our national spirit. This means, of course, examining our shadows as well as our public profile. This means studies of John Brown as well as of James Madison; of the Kickapoo Indians as well as of the New England Puritans; of internment camps for Japanese Americans as well as of the military triumphs of General Eisenhower.

Second, the government should stimulate additional scholarship—in pursuit of our national interest—on the interpretation and meaning of our unique experience in cultural and social pluralism. Much work has been done, but more remains in regard to understanding the nature, power, and meaning of American pluralism. The better we understand our differences, the better we will be able to understand that which brings us together, that which transcends our differences, that which allows us to see ourselves as a people united.

Third, the government should provide additional encouragement to local, regional, and state organizations and agencies—those who respond most directly to local needs—to carry their concerns one step further and to explore how community history and culture and ethnic history and culture are related to our national experience and history. More effort is needed to show how the many parts form the whole. Missing from the Houston project, I think, is a final booklet, potentially the most important one of all, a booklet that would tie the previous work together, that would relate ethnic history to the comprehensive history of the city and to the character and spirit of that city, and that would place the history and culture of Houston in the broader context of American urban history and, indeed, of American social and economic history. What is needed is a new emphasis that will encourage scholarly work relating local projects to national interests.

Example: A Border Ballad

Community and ethnic history and culture—the understanding of which I have described as being a local need—can be a matter of national interest. Let me illustrate this point by referring to a Mexican/Texas border ballad.

Last year, American viewers were able to see on PBS—thanks to NEH support—a film adaptation of the "Ballad of Gregorio Cortez." Before I mention the nature of the ballad and its meaning, some information on its history—and how it made its way into our national consciousness—might prove helpful.

In the midst of the Depression, a young, shy man from a tiny, poverty-stricken community in East Texas, a young writer with a passion for folk tradition and culture, made his way through Texas, recording ethnic songs. William Owens, who became one of Texas' great teachers and writers, went to the border town of Brownsville and met another young man, Américo Paredes, a singer and guitarist who was working at a newspaper and taking courses at a junior college. Paredes, born in Mexico, became one of Texas' great folklorists. Together, this strange pair made their way through the cantinas of Matamoras "hunting wandering minstrels and listening to their songs." William Owens, in his third autobiographical volume, *Tell me a story, sing me a song*, describes what happened:

> In a cantina in a poorer section of town we found an older man playing a concertina and singing corridos and love songs. The loungers called him "Pepe" and listened respectfully through his long ballads. Finally he sang one called "El Corrido de Gregorio Cortez." I had not heard it before. Neither had Americo. The first time through I got enough of words and tune to know that I wanted to record it. For the others he had sung for cerveza (beer). From me, a gringo, he wanted cerveza and a daime (dime) for each song. For Gregorio Cortez, I was willing to pay. As I had not been permitted to take my recording machine into Mexico, I had to pay singers to cross the Rio Grande and record for me. Pepe would not go. He had too much fear of the Border Patrol and he was not a *mojado*. I offered money. Still he would not go. At last we reached a compromise. He would sing the song over and over, for a daime each time, and Américo would memorize it. He sang it until

Américo had the words and could imitate his voice and manner of singing. When I asked Pepe one more time to go with us he answered cynically, "Los americanos."

Here is the English version of the ballad heard that day by William Owens and Américo Paredes:

In Karnes County
Such a misfortune happened;
The chief sheriff died—
They don't know who killed him.

It must have been two in the afternoon,
About half an hour afterward,
They found that the wrongdoer
Was Gregorio Cortez.

They put out the hound dogs
To follow his trail,
But to catch up with Cortez
Was to follow a star.

But the rangers of the county
Went almost flying
Because they wanted to get
The three thousand pesos they were giving.

In the county of Kenedy
They caught up with him.
A little more than three hundred,
And there he jumped their corral.

Gregorio Cortez said
With his pistol in his hand,
"Don't run, cowardly rangers,
From just one Mexican."

Now with this I take my leave
Underneath this cypress,
Gentlemen, this is the ballad
of Don Gregorio Cortez.

As Owens and Paredes were leaving the cantina, "a little brown man with white hair and white handlebar mustache elbowed his way through the crowd" and approached Owens. "Muy estimado señor," he said, "I have the honor of being the uncle of Gregorio Cortez."

The most popular version of the ballad is brief and sketchy but, as Owens notes, "the image of one lone Mexican 'with his pistol in his hand' standing off more than three hundred Texas Rangers is enough to stir the imagination." Owens writes: "It is not Jesse James in a sombrero but the theme of a man wronged that permeates one ballad and then the other. Gregorio Cortez was not a bad man but a poor Mexican-Texan caught in a set of misunderstandings because of language."

It is in the nature of those misunderstandings that we find something of national interest. Owens tells the history behind the ballad:

> On June 12, 1901, Sheriff W. T. Morris of Karnes County went to the farm home of Gregorio Cortez in search of a stolen horse. Through an interpreter he questioned Cortez about an animal he had acquired. The interpreter used the word *caballo*, horse; Cortez used the exact word, *yegua*, mare. The second misunderstanding came over the interpreter's confusion of *nada*, nothing, and *nadie*, no one, so that Cortez' statement that he had done nothing came out that he would be arrested by no one. According to testimony, the sheriff pulled his pistol and shot. Gregorio Cortez shot and killed the sheriff. The subsequent chase, capture, and trials exposed the Anglo-Mexican conflict and gave rise to many versions of the ballad.

The ballad, of course, is about the application of legal justice in a bicultural setting, an issue that goes to the core of our national experience, to the problem of maintaining a just and fair legal system in the midst of a pluralistic culture and society. But the history of this ballad, and how the ballad made its way into this country and ultimately into our national experience and memory, is about much more. It is about two young writers and scholars—untested, uncredentialed, unworthy at the time of an NEH fellowship, if such a program had existed—an Anglo man from the stubborn soil of Northeast Texas and a Mexican man from a Texas border town, who made an invaluable contribution to humanistic scholarship. Paredes, through the late 1930s, through his military service in World War II, through his years of training at the

University of Texas, never forgot that day in a Mexican cantina; he kept working on the ballad and the history behind it. Eventually he published his work in a biography titled *With His Pistol in His Hand*, a work that has become a significant text in the humanities. As Owens says, "the book is a model of scholarship in folk tradition, but [Paredes] goes beyond the narrative and presents as thorough an analysis of border tensions as may be found."

Conclusion

Here then is the point: As the federal government seeks to meet its primary obligation to advance research and scholarship in the humanities at the highest level possible, it must also respond to local cultural needs. Our government's record is a good one, I think, but additional encouragement can and should be given to meeting these needs and to scholarship that interprets the significance and meaning of community and ethnic history and culture projects, that places these activities and what is learned in a broader and deeper context, so that these local activities are more directly related to primary national interests—the advancement of humanistic learning and scholarship.

I recall a recent conversation with a young professor who had received a grant from the NEH for the translation of an obscure Sanskrit text. I asked him a personal question: What did it mean to him to receive taxpayer money to pursue his study? He told me that he had a tremendous, almost embarrassing—and I am using his words—sense of pride in the United States. He asked himself: What kind of nation would use tax dollars to support this type of work? He concluded, he told me, that it must be a very great nation. Then, he noted that he felt extremely accountable for how he spent his time and for the quality of his work.

That same sense of pride, that same sense of accountability, will be felt by future young scholars poking around in sleepy border towns in search of ballads that speak of a people, a history, a culture, a way of life, if such efforts receive the unequivocal endorsement of the federal government.

That endorsement is crucial to the well-being of our society. Through the work completed we will gain a better understanding of the significance and meaning of our experiment in cultural pluralism, and we will gain a better understanding of the character of our nation, of the soul of the American people, and of the pains and pleasures, the nightmares and the dreams, the shadows and the triumphs, that have formed the American psyche. This understanding of cultural pluralism, therefore, is not only a matter reflecting local needs, but a matter of genuine federal interest as well.

The United States will be a stronger nation if the citizens of Karnes County, Texas, know of the accomplishments of Henry, William, and, yes, Alice James, but it will also be a stronger nation if the citizens of Boston know of the terribly unfortunate but admirably brave life of Gregorio Cortez.

Works Cited

Paredes, Américo. *With His Pistol in His Hand: A Border Ballad.* Austin: The University of Texas Press, 1958.

Owens, William. *Tell me a story, sing me a song.* Austin: The University of Texas Press, 1983.

1984

Congressional Testimony

The Federation of State Humanities Councils asked me to testify on April 14, 1984, on behalf of FY 1985 appropriations for NEH and the state humanities councils before Congressman Sidney Yates's Appropriations Subcommittee on the Interior and Related Agencies. Through most of the 1980s, the councils were put in the disadvantageous position of having to counter funding proposals from the Reagan administration that sought substantial cuts. Perhaps it was good practice for what would come after the 1994 elections as the Congress, under new leadership, sought to defund the NEA and the NEH.

While making as strong a case as I could for the councils, I wanted to speak honestly about the dramatic shift in NEH priorities and funding patterns that was taking place under Chairman William Bennett. To do so, I returned to the statement Bennett made at the colloquium sponsored by the Meridian House in 1983, that the U.S. does not have a cultural policy. I argued that every administration, through its appointed chairs, had expressed policies, based on political ideologies, that inevitably reflected defacto cultural policies. I went on to suggest that the humanities community and the nation as a whole would benefit from the development of a long-range plan for the NEH that would be drafted with the input of organizations and agencies representing the humanities community, and that would be submitted to the Congress as a mat-

ter of record. While I had little expectation that this idea would find fertile soil—and it did not—I thought it helpful and necessary to make the point that Bennett's statement needed clarifying, and that long-range planning would prove helpful.

This spring, while on leave from my position as executive director of the Texas Council for the Humanities, I have served as visiting professor of American studies and history at The University of Texas at Austin. In my graduate seminar on government and culture, I have had an opportunity to examine the history of federal support for the arts and humanities. My comments, therefore, reflect recent observations on the nature of this support, as well as my nine years of experience in the state humanities program.

Through my research and teaching, I have been able to see the state humanities program from the broader perspective of a remarkable national effort—going back to the federal arts projects of the 1930s—marked by intense debate, political ideology of the left and right, priorities and policies sometimes clear and sometimes fuzzy, programs and projects clearly in the national interest and others that one would just as soon forget. But on one point there can be little challenge. Alongside the Declaration of Independence, the Bill of Rights, and major legislation dealing with a vast array of domestic issues, including civil rights, education, and equal opportunity, the National Foundation on the Arts and Humanities Act of 1965 stands as a key document that evidences the aims and purposes of American civilization. The nurturing of the human spirit, the flowering of the arts and letters, the development of a wise and visionary citizenry, the formulation of public policy on the basis of a sense of history and shared values, the balancing of science and technology with humane learning, comprise a language of aims and public purpose.

The state humanities program of the NEH stands as an essential and enduring vehicle through which the federal government contributes to these specific national goals. From its beginning twelve years ago, the objectives for the state program have been to increase public understanding of the humanities and to relate the humanities to contemporary concerns and issues.

An objective review of the history of the state program documents the boldness, imagination, and dedication by which state humanities councils have sought to carry out their mandate. Through the awarding of more than 3,000 grants a year in support of projects that reach millions of citizens, through hundreds of council-conducted projects, and through a variety of publications and media programs, the state humanities councils provide the most visible and continuous program whereby the Congressional statement of aims and purposes is met.

To demonstrate the connection between the objectives of the state humanities program and the aims of American civilization as found in the legislation, I refer to one specific activity of the Texas Council for the Humanities.

The Texas Council selects an annual topic for special emphasis and programming. This year, we are working in the area of Texas myths. The selection of this topic reflects the Council's desire to advance scholarship in, and to increase public understanding of, an extraordinarily important subject, one that is both known and unknown, titled and untitled, comforting and discomforting. During the past ten years, the Council has funded hundreds of projects, small and large, local and statewide, that have sought to interpret Texas history, culture and literature for public audiences. We have funded projects ranging from the history of blacks in the fourth ward of Houston to the history of the Panhandle cowboy, from the border culture of El Paso to the Southern culture of deep East Texas, from the history and future of the small Texas farm to the history and future of Texas' largest cities, from the history of frontier women to the history of twentieth-century oil entrepreneurs.

Our Texas myths project is designed to elucidate the mythological underpinnings of the Texas experience and character, to unravel the powerful and frequently conflicting symbols and images of that experience and character, to clarify the unconscious memory—whether black, Anglo, Mexican, or American Indian—of all time and all place but tempered and shaped in a particular time and a particular place. This elucidating, this unraveling, this clarifying, will provide invaluable perspective on Texas history and culture, for myth refers to stories and legends that display the character of a people, that evidence cultural values, that point to deep-seated failures, aspirations and victories.

As one part of this effort, the Texas Council recently reviewed grant proposals for a variety of projects related to the theme of Texas myths. Of twenty-three applications originally submitted, the Council reviewed sixteen, with applicants requesting $250,000 in definite funds and $94,775 in Treasury funds to match an equal amount in third-party support. Nine applications were approved, with $81,170 awarded in definite funds and $66,000 in Treasury matching funds. Among the projects approved is a film series, symposium and publication on myths related to Spanish exploration in the Southwest, sponsored by the Panhandle Plains Historical Museum. The Southwest Alternate Media Project in Houston will present a series of twelve public discussion programs in which myths of Texas as portrayed in feature films will be analyzed, with scholarly essays to be published in *Southwest Media Review*. The Institute for the Humanities at Salado will host a three-day symposium relating specific Texas myths to larger myths in Western consciousness. KERA-TV, Dallas, will develop a one-hour color video documentary for television focusing on themes of land and environment in the myths of Texas blacks, Hispanics, Anglos, and American Indians.

In addition to awarding grant funds in support of these projects, the Texas Council itself has sponsored a number of important endeavors. A symposium was held on March 3 in conjunction with the annual meeting of the Texas State Historical Association, in which four scholars examined the formative myths behind the nineteenth century clash of cultures in Texas: Anglo, Mexican, Indian, and black. On March 30–31, the Council sponsored its annual lecture and symposium on the humanities, this year focusing on Texas Myths and Texas Writing. The Council's 1984 lecturer, noted Texas writer John Graves, author of *Goodbye to a River* and other works, addressed the topic from the perspective of the Anglo tradition. In a symposium the following day, other scholars examined the role of myth in women's writing, black writing, Mexican American writing, and political writing. Although over four hundred people attended this program, thousands more will benefit through secondary activities, including the publishing of the lecture and symposium papers. The scholars participating in these projects represent the core disciplines of the humanities, especially history, literature and philosophy.

I have discussed our Texas myths emphasis at some length to underscore one important point: Some of the most intriguing and vital work taking place in this country on the relationship between the humanities and public life is sponsored by state humanities councils. This particular emphasis on myth, although only a small part of a program that includes more than eighty grants a year, the sponsorship of other Council-administered conferences, media projects, and publications, including the Council's bimonthly magazine, *The Texas Humanist*, demonstrates our willingness to tackle subjects and issues of importance to the public. Myth lies at the basis of human society, and through the study of Texas myths, citizens will gain a much deeper understanding of their historical and cultural roots.

The state humanities program must be seen as an important means for achieving the aims of American civilization as found in the authorizing legislation, especially that of the development of a wise and visionary citizenry in touch with society's histories and values. But the state humanities program, although strong and vibrant, is still young, and there are some ways that the program could be enhanced.

First, given the critical role assigned to the state humanities program in achieving the purposes of the authorizing legislation, it is clear that an appropriation of $16 million for FY 1985, as proposed by the Reagan administration, is simply inadequate. Since 1980, the Texas Council, along with other state councils, has received basically stable funding, despite deepened recognition of the critical role played by the councils in achieving legislative goals. If the administration's request is approved at the level sought, the state humanities program would receive a twenty percent cut. Since the current leadership at NEH has sought to make that provision of the legislation that requires that twenty percent of definite funds be allocated to state programs a ceiling rather than a floor, even an appropriation of $150 million to the agency could result in a reduction for the state program.

When it comes to federal appropriations, I do not believe that good ideas should chase money, but that money should chase good ideas. The state program, over the years, has represented the most substantial and important work done in relating the humanities to current conditions of state and national life. We have the structure, a proven track record, and plenty of good ideas. Those ideas need to be recognized and appropriate funding made available.

Aside from an adequate level of definite funds appropriated to the state humanities program, I would urge this committee to look closely at the level of appropriations for Treasury funds and the amount that is allocated to the state humanities program. In recent years, we have made significant progress in stimulating support from foundations, corporations, and in some cases, state government. Yet the Treasury funds program has not kept pace with this development. As private, nonprofit organizations, state councils are uniquely positioned to serve as catalysts in increasing private support for public humanities endeavors. Treasury funds provide a key element in achieving this goal, and if the Reagan administration and the Congress wish to see the state humanities program strengthened, the amount of Treasury funds available to the agency should be increased, with a corresponding increase in the amount of such funds available to the state program.

Secondly, efforts must be made to de-politicize the agency. The debate between so-called "populism" and so-called "elitism," which first emerged in 1976, is not a superficial debate. It captures the fact that the NEH, at various times, has fallen victim to ideology of the left and the right. On the one side, we find an appreciation for cultural diversity, for increased federal support, for values of differing groups, for projects that reach the grass roots of American society, for new research and scholarship, especially in regard to minority interests, women's history, and public policy issues, and to the interconnection between the humanities and contemporary public life. On the other side, we find an appreciation for "high culture," for "classical texts," for the important role of the private sector, for traditional values, for unity over diversity, for traditional research in the core disciplines.

These ideologies have deeply influenced internal NEH policy and program direction, including the kind of research and scholarship undertaken, film projects supported, books published, symposia and conferences held, museum exhibitions endorsed, and audiences reached. In my nine years in the state humanities program, I have seen some dramatic shifts in NEH policy, in programming emphasis, in how proposals—and what proposals—are encouraged and then evaluated, in subjects deemed important and in the national interest. Fortunately, state humanities councils, by virtue of their legislatively-granted autonomy from the NEH, have had a degree of protection against the imposition of ideology by the agency. Still, for those of us in the field—for museums, libraries, historical societies, and colleges and universities—long range planning that includes projects possibly supported by NEH funds, becomes very difficult. For what is acceptable and encouraged in one administration is rejected in another. In short, the priorities established for the use of federal funds for the humanities tend to shift dramatically every four years.

The reason for this, of course, is that the United States lacks a formal public cultural policy. To my knowledge, every chairman of the NEH has argued that we do not have such a policy and that the American people do not want such a policy. Most recently, William Bennett, current chairman, noted at a public conference the vast array of art and thought in America, a point that substantiates, he said, Tocqueville's observation that "no sooner do you set foot on American soil than you are surrounded by a tumult of opinions ranging on everything on all subjects and every individual is his own authority." "What kind of country," asked Bennett, "what kind of cultural policy, provides such an array? The answer is, and I think we should be grateful for it, no cultural policy whatsoever. The question of United States cultural policy is in a most important sense a non-question. We do not have a cultural policy and that is, I think, the best that can be said, the fairest that can be said, and a fine thing to be said."

While that may sound admirable, anyone familiar with the NEH knows that everyday decisions are made to support this or that kind of project, to emphasize this or that discipline of the humanities, to reach this or that constituency, to encourage work in the great canon of European and American thought and literature, or to encourage work in books outside this canon, including, for instance, work in American Indian, black, Hispanic, and women's thought and literature. Such decisions inevitably reflect defacto cultural policies. The public proclamation denying the existence of a cultural policy provides extraordinary freedom to NEH chairs to allow particular ideologies—whether from the left or the right—to influence particular policies and programs. Thus the denial of a national policy creates the circumstance that permits the emergence of defacto policies based on ideology. The chairmanship of NEH becomes a prized possession, as evidenced by the intense public controversy over the appointment of the last two chairs. Conservatives, neo-conservatives, liberals, neo-liberals, all want their representative at the NEH. It is in this context that one understands the 1980 request of the Heritage Foundation that, in the coming years, the task of the NEH should be to "teach the nation the limits of egalitarian impulse."

It is neither fair, appropriate, nor in the national interest for the Fort Worth Museum of Science and History, the Texas Historical Commission, Stephen F. Austin State University, or the Lubbock Public Library, to plan special projects, programs and initiatives for which they intend to seek federal funding around program emphases that come and go every four years. These institutions, and similar institutions across the country, need to have access to a well-conceived, long-range, publicly known, humanities policy that governs the work of the NEH.

Looking toward the 1985 reauthorization of the NEH, some thought should be given to this problem. I offer one suggestion. Would it not be possible to assign to the NEH chairman the responsibility for drafting a five year plan—to coincide with the period of authorization—that expresses a national policy, and that this plan be submitted to national organizations representing constituencies involved in and concerned about the humanities for analysis and comment? Organizations such as the American Council of Learned Societies, the National Humanities Alliance, the American Association of Museums, the American Association of State and Local History, the National Black Studies Association, the National Association of Women's Studies, the American Library Association, the National Federation of State Humanities Councils, and others that represent the rich diversity of American intellectual activity, should be solicited to give a response to such a policy statement. Through this involvement, the document could be redrafted by the NEH and then submitted to the Congress as a matter of record, thereby becoming a public document that evidences the policies and programs to be pursued and that relates these policies and programs to a more democratically conceived sense of the relationship between humanistic research and learning and the cultural life of our country.

I cannot speak about other divisions of the NEH, although I am confident that good work is being done. I can, however, assure the members of this committee that the state humanities program is in sound shape, that good ideas far exceed the financial resources currently available, that public humanities programming provides a key means whereby the goals of the authorizing legislation—and the aims of American civilization as found in that document—are being met. The state humanities program would be further strengthened, as I have argued, through a higher level of definite funds appropriated to the Division of State Programs, through increased use of Treasury matching funds, and through a more consistent, long-term, non-ideological, policy governing the NEH that is determined in a more democratic fashion.

Across the country, state humanities councils are at work nourishing the roots of American culture. The public is with us. The academic community is with us. Public libraries, museums, and historical societies are with us. Corporations and foundations are with us. Yet we know that our work has just begun, and that the encouragement of this legislative body means everything to us. It is time for us to dream again of a wise and visionary citizenry in touch with the realm of ideas and of the human spirit. We are doing that, and we thank you for your commitment and support.

Works Cited

Bennett, William J. "View from the United States," in *National Cultural Policy: Norwegian and American Experiences*. Washington, D. C.: Meridian House International, 1983.

Heatherly, Charles, ed. *Mandate for Leadership: Policy Management in a Conservative Administration*. Washington, D. C.: The Heritage Foundation, 1980.

Congressional Testimony

At the invitation of the Federation of State Humanities Councils, I returned to Congressman Yates's subcommittee in the spring of 1987 to make once again the case for adequate appropriations for state humanities councils. I began my testimony by referring to a report, The Humanities and the American Promise, drafted by noted Jefferson scholar Merrill D. Peterson and released by the Colloquium on the Humanities and the American People. The Colloquium was sponsored by the University of Virginia at the invitation of NEH and funded by the Endowment. I served as an advisor to this group of distinguished scholars drawn from across the nation, and I was concerned when the NEH, now chaired by Lynne V. Cheney, withdrew funds from the grant for the publication of the report as an NEH-funded document. The Colloquium had been funded in the waning days of the Bennett chairmanship, through the encouragement of several supportive senior officials at the NEH, and was designed to strengthen state council work by adding to its theoretical base while making a strong case for the importance of the humanities to American democracy. The report was subsequently published by the Texas Council for the Humanities through a grant provided by the Joyce Foundation of Illinois. But without adequate funding for promotion, and without the advantage of its original sponsor, the report did not have as much public impact as we had hoped, although state coun-

cil board directors and staff found it to be immensely useful. The Congressional testimony provided an opportunity to share with members of the Congress and the humanities community the important work of these outstanding scholars, including Edmund Pincoffs, professor of philosophy at the University of Texas at Austin and a former TCH chair.

The reader will find in my remarks several examples of the work sponsored by state councils in the late 1980s. I began with examples from the Texas Council but move on to highlight the work of other councils as well. One project from the Texas program found a very receptive audience in Congressman Yates, the "Understanding Evil" symposium sponsored by the Institute for the Humanities at Salado. Congressman Yates asked me for detailed information from our files on this project as well as the book and the ninety-minute Bill Moyers documentary, Facing Evil, *both based on the symposium. On more than one occasion during hearings in subsequent years, Congressman Yates referred to this project as an example of the creative work being done by the state humanities councils.*

Mr. Chairman, distinguished Members of the Subcommittee:

I am very pleased to appear before you to discuss the vitally important work of the state humanities councils.

I have served as executive director of the Texas Council for the Humanities since 1975. I have had the good fortune of observing and participating in the growth and development of the state humanities program. What began as an experiment in public humanities has become an institutional reality. This remarkable program is serving the humanities well. More importantly, it is serving American democracy very well. I am pleased to offer thoughts as to why this is so.

A very useful report was published this past November by a group of nationally-recognized scholars, writers, and educational administrators, titled *The Humanities and the American Promise*. Over the course of eighteen months, the Colloquium on the Humanities and the American People met at the University of Virginia on four different occasions to "discuss the relationship—as it has been and as it should be—between adult Americans and those areas of intellectual activity known as the humanities."

The report underscores the progress that has been made in our country in providing learning opportunities in the humanities for adult Americans. While the Colloquium did not set out to examine or evaluate any particular institution or program, it did devote considerable space in its report to state humanities councils. The report notes how the state councils have "given shape to a curriculum in the humanities [that] appears to satisfy a real social need, even a hunger, felt by many adults." Every year, according to the Federation of State Humanities Councils, upwards of twenty-five million Americans take part or benefit from approximately four thousand humanities programs—conferences, symposia, library reading programs, lectures, exhibits, film, and special radio and television programs.

But what, one must ask, is the shape and content of this curriculum, and in what ways does this curriculum and the programs that flow from it serve the humanities and American democracy?

The shape is wide and deep. The curriculum encompasses all the traditional disciplines of the humanities as well as newer interdisciplinary studies, including women's studies, black studies, Mexican American studies, Native-American studies, medical and environmental ethics, film studies, and folklore and folk culture. The curriculum includes concern for traditional subjects—the history of ideas in Western culture, major themes in American and European literature, the history of American politics, and so forth. But it also includes concern for newer subjects and interests, including, for example, the impact of television on American society, ethical issues arising from advances in medical technology, land use and other environmental concerns, civil rights, and the issue of punishment versus rehabilitation in recent American penal theory and practice.

As with the case of curricula in schools or universities, this curriculum for public humanities in America can best be described by application—particular projects that provide learning opportunities for Americans. I begin with a few examples of projects funded by the Texas Council for the Humanities.

Last October, twenty-five hundred citizens from San Antonio and surrounding cities attended the third annual Inter-American Bookfair, established by the Guadalupe Cultural Arts Center to highlight contemporary literature south and north of the United States-Mexico border. In conjunction with the Fair, in which seventy presses displayed one thousand new book titles, there were lectures, readings, and discussion programs. Writer and actress Maya Angelou gave a dazzling presentation to an audience of six hundred. Her theme was the power of poetry, the ability of words to lift the human spirit and to understand the human legacy. Chilean novelist Isabel Allende, who has lived in Venezuela since the Pinochet coup in 1973, read passages from her latest novel and discussed its social, political and cultural background.

Literature was also the focus for a project in Dallas, but this time the focus was on classical works. The Dallas Institute of Humanities and Culture, a remarkable community-based organization founded a decade ago, sponsored, with support from the Texas Council, the NEH, and local donors, an intensive four-week summer institute for secondary school teachers in the North Texas area. Fifty-two teachers of English participated in a rigorous course of study in tragedy and comedy, focusing on great works of literature in the Western tradition. Evaluation reports received by the Texas Council for the Humanities from the participants are moving and give hope for the further renewal of the humanities in our schools. "I discovered anew the love of teaching that drew me into the profession in the first place," wrote one teacher. Another: "I think that I can say, without a doubt, that every one of us has been transformed in a profound way by our experience here at the Institute." And another: "The reinforcement received sent us back to our jobs with a renewed sense of excitement and commitment."

Part of the strength of the curriculum that underlies the state humanities program has been a deep concern for the relationship between the humanities and issues of contemporary public life. Last fall, the Institute for the Humanities at Salado, with major funding from the Texas Council, sponsored a three-day conference entitled "Understanding Evil." The Salado Institute, located in a small village fifty miles north of Austin, has emerged as a symbol of the growth of public humanities in the state and nation. The conference, attended by two-hundred citizens—the maximum number that local facilities could handle—brought together an extraordinary group of scholars, writers, and thinkers—psychoanalyst Rollo May, former Member of Congress Barbara Jordan, author and professor of history Jeffrey Russell, author and Rockefeller Foundation president Richard Lyman, professor and minister Samuel Proctor, holocaust scholar Raul Hilberg, to name a few—to cast light on this darkest of subjects, what Sir Laurens Van der Post, speaking to the audience on film from his home in London, described as "the greatest problem of our time."

What an extraordinary event—two hundred Texans, from all walks of life, willing to give up a weekend to learn what some of the world's greatest thinkers have to say about the nature of evil. This conference was covered by most of the major daily newspapers in the state and by the *Boston Globe* and the *Chicago Tribune*. And on the 28th of this month, a ninety-minute documentary film of this event, narrated by Bill Moyers, will be broadcast nationally on PBS.

I believe these Texas programs are representative of the state program nationally and representative of the components of a very rich national curriculum for adult Americans.

For example, the Maine Humanities Council is devoting considerable resources to a multi-faceted project focusing on the history of exploration and settlement in the Northeast region from 1498 to 1700. This project is drawing on the insights of scholars from multiple disciplines in developing a traveling exhibition of maps, a symposium, an international conference, and other public programs.

In the Midwest, the Great Plains Chautauqua, sponsored by humanities councils in North and South Dakota, Nebraska, and Kansas, is in its tenth year. The heart of the Chautauqua program is the nightly open-air tent performance in which an historical character—Thomas Jefferson, Abigail Adams, Henry Adams, Elizabeth Cady Stanton, among others—delivers a thirty-five minute monologue followed by fifty minutes of dialogue with the audience. This program continues to expand, to generate spin-off programs, and to gather such a following that families plan vacations around the programs and communities compete vigorously for the privilege of hosting the scholars who play these historical figures.

The Illinois Humanities Council, with funding from the NEH and the MacArthur Foundation, continues its remarkable six-year emphasis on "Inventing Illinois." The Council is supporting projects throughout the state that explore each year a range of topics: the settlement of the state, working in Illinois, and the nature of leadership.

These and thousands of other efforts sponsored each year demonstrate the extent to which this curriculum and program are *of*, *by*, and *for* the people. The program is *of* the people in that state councils respond to worthy project ideas of local, community-based organizations and institutions. The program is *by* the people in that all councils are governed by volunteer citizens and all councils call upon interested citizens in developing program plans. And the program is *for* the people in that the mission of all the councils is to enhance public understanding and appreciation of the humanities.

Yet it is true that from time to time the state humanities program has had its critics. There have been those who believe that the humanities belong inside the academy, and that endeavors in the humanities outside the academy are somehow inferior. And there have been those who tend to believe that the work of councils, like the work of scholars in the academy, should shy away from controversial issues of contemporary life, that scholars in the humanities have little to contribute to analysis of policy concerns. Fortunately, the work of state councils proves these critics to be wrong.

Indeed, it can be demonstrated that this national curriculum in public humanities has enriched immeasurably scholars in the humanities and the academy itself. I think particularly of the work of state councils on state and regional studies, on women's history, on minority history and culture, on folk culture, and on other subjects that have called for interdisciplinary work. These efforts have had a most positive impact on our schools and colleges and universities.

One of the great challenges facing the next generation of scholars will be that of integration and synthesis. In the development of public school and university curricula, in the writing of history books and in the editing of readers and anthologies, much work needs to be done to incorporate scholarship in the newer disciplines into traditional studies, courses, and programs. In meeting this challenge, these scholars will do well to look to the state humanities program where integration and synthesis form the heart of what we do, melding the old and the new, relating the past to the present, the traditional with the nontraditional, the known with the unknown, the comfortable with the uncomfortable.

The charter for the NEH includes the mandate to help create and sustain a climate that encourages freedom of thought, imagination, and inquiry. It gives me great pleasure to report that the state councils are hard at work meeting this mandate.

Although much has been accomplished, we know that our work to advance public understanding of and appreciation for the humanities has only begun. We also know that recent accomplishments would not have happened without the strong support of this subcommittee.

During the past seven years, state councils have labored in an environment that threatened greatly reduced federal support. Indeed, despite the diligent efforts of many, the amount appropriated in outright funds for state councils for FY 1988, $21.3 million, is $500,000 less than the amount appropriated for FY 1984 and $2.6 million less than the amount appropriated for FY 1981.

State councils continue to make dramatic progress in securing corporate, foundation, and individual contributions—as well as state appropriations—to support their programs, although Treasury matching funds, our best stimulus to private giving, have not kept pace with the expanded opportunities that have come with a maturing program; indeed, there have been reductions in these funds.

Councils in a number of states that have not benefited from generally good economic times have been particularly hard hit. Texas, for instance, remains in a deep recession, and the total revenues of the Texas Council for the Humanities, compared to 1984, are down by approximately thirty percent—a percentage that reflects declines in both federal and private funding.

To ensure a strong and vibrant state humanities program and to move the program forward, I endorse completely the proposal of the Federation of State Humanities Councils that the state program be funded at $25 million in fiscal year 1989.

I also believe that steps should be taken this year to ensure that the National Endowment for the Humanities, by fiscal year 1991, achieve funding parity with the National Endowment for the Arts. I know of no sound argument that can be put forward as to why the present imbalance in funding for the arts and the humanities should continue.

One finds in the authorizing legislation for the NEH a vision of America as a learning society. One finds a vision of citizens in touch with history and culture, a vision of citizens understanding the world about them, and a vision of citizens translating this understanding into civic action. This vision is as important today as it was in 1965. Perhaps it is more important, for the world continues to grow in complexity. The well-being of the nation and of our democratic institutions depends on a thoughtful, reflective citizenry.

The curriculum that I have been describing and the projects that flow from it undergird and carry out this vision. This curriculum, unique in the history of the nation, is, as I have noted, of, by and for the people. It draws its strength from the imagination and creativity of the American people.

Our goal is to help weave the humanities into the social fabric of America. State councils are planning now the programs, emphases and projects that will take them into the 1990s, efforts that involve nothing less in intent than the opening of the American mind. The humanities, like life itself, are inherently forward-looking. We must continue to dream of a wise and visionary citizenry in touch with the realm of ideas and of the human spirit. We are doing that, and I thank you, Mr. Chairman, and the distinguished members of this subcommittee, for your continued commitment and support.

Works Cited

Peterson, Merrill D. *The Humanities and the American Promise*. Austin: Texas Council for the Humanities, 1987.

Woodruff, Paul and Harry A. Wilmer, *Facing Evil: Light at the Core of Darkness*. LaSalle: Open Court Press, 1988.

National Public Radio Commentary

President Reagan's appointment of Lynne V. Cheney to head the NEH, after William Bennett left to become Secretary of Education, en-sured the continuation of a "neo-conservative" stance for the agency. Indeed, soon after her arrival, Cheney made news when she demanded that NEH credit be removed from a soon-to-be broadcast PBS documen-tary, The Africans, *claiming that the program suffered from a Marxist slant and demeaned the United States and Western culture in general. She caught the media's attention. Cheney brought to the NEH remark-able political and public relations skills and, while jumping into the by now hot "culture wars," protected the agency against unwarranted at-tacks from the political and religious right. In the latter years of the Reagan administration, and on into the Bush administration, the agency's relationship with the Congress improved, as did appropriations, resulting in a period of stability for the agency and the state councils.*

Cheney used her position to draw attention to perceived weaknesses in elementary, secondary, and post-secondary education, issuing occa-sional reports during her tenure from 1986 to 1992 that received exten-sive coverage in the nation's media—work that proved to be a prelude to the publication of Telling the Truth: Why Our Culture And Our Country Has Stopped Making Sense And What We Can Do About It *(1996). While I shared many of her concerns, for example, the priority given to research over teaching in higher education, her advocacy of neo-conservative causes was troubling. Many in the state humanities councils were concerned that, despite legislatively-granted autonomy, they too might be criticized, especially through the proposal review process, for supporting projects that often drew on newer scholarship, especially minority and women's studies.*

But Cheney was often a champion of the state humanities councils, as evidenced by her second report, Humanities in America: A Report to the President, the Congress, and the American People *(1988), in which she documented the extraordinary growth and vibrancy of the public humanities while criticizing the status of the humanities in the nation's colleges and universities. Shortly after this report's release, I was asked by National Public Radio for a five-minute commentary, broadcast on September 14, 1988, as was scholar Charles Blitzer. I welcomed the opportunity to offer a different perspective on why the humanities were alive and well in the public arena, and discussed the implications of this success for the future of the humanities in higher education.*

While this commentary points to philosophical differences that often existed between state council personnel and this NEH chair, much cooperative work was accomplished during Cheney's tenure. In Texas, for example, I worked closely and productively with Cheney's senior staff to find ways of promoting the idea of a core curriculum for all undergraduates, even though I knew that our ideas about the content of such a curriculum would inevitably vary. Thus we jointly sponsored a series of workshops across the state on the undergraduate curriculum.

NEH chair Lynne Cheney has published a courageous report on the state of the humanities. *Humanities in America* breaks new ground. Dr. Cheney argues, as no previous official of the U.S. government has argued, that an extraordinary development has occurred in American society—a "remarkable blossoming of the humanities in the public sphere." As the report indicates, we are experiencing nothing less than the opening of the American mind.

Yet not all is well with the humanities in American life. Dr. Cheney argues that, while the humanities blossom in the public arena, the vine of learning withers in our universities. The report strikes hard at humanities scholars who prefer specialized research over generalized teaching. Too many are focusing on the errors of Western culture. Too many are turning their backs on the Western tradition.

The report leads me to believe that the way to revitalize the humanities in the university is to incorporate the virtues of the humanities in the public arena. But to discover these virtues, we must dig much deeper than Lynn Cheney does in her report.

The report inadequately grasps the seriousness, indeed, the revolutionary nature, of this public inquiry. Yes, the public is interested in Plato, Shakespeare, Locke, Madison, and the Western tradition. But the public knows that as we approach the twenty-first century, we must broaden our horizons. We want to know about the cultures of the East. We want to know what Nicaraguans really think. We want to learn more about the experiences of women of all ages and all cultures. And we want to know more about the ethical issues raised by modern science.

An important purpose of education in the humanities is that of understanding the dominant culture. But we cannot stop there. The thirst of the public is to know the rich diversity of American cultures and cultures outside the United States, to ask difficult questions about ourselves and others, to connect our inquiry to the deepest concerns of public and private life. The humanities, while supporting the sacred canopy of established culture, invite us to undertake new and risky journeys.

In the public arena, we are seeing what happens when humanistic inquiry breaks through traditional boundaries. This is the reason for the flowering of the humanities in the public arena. But this can happen in our universities as well.

At the University of California–Santa Barbara, Walter Capps's course on the Vietnam War draws over one thousand students. At the University of Texas at Austin, students literally beg to enroll in Ricardo Romo's class on the history of American civil rights. At hundreds of universities across America, programs in women's studies have been established. Students may be flocking to business and engineering, but they are deeply interested in humanities courses that explore important subjects. More often than not, these courses, like many public humanities projects, are interdisciplinary and involve new methods such as social history and feminist criticism.

When Congress reauthorized the NEH in 1985, it warned against imposing "a limited and restrictive definition of the humanities" grounded in a "mainstream" concept of the western tradition. Indeed, NEH's legislation was amended to encourage interdisciplinary and culturally diverse programs, efforts that would "push the boundaries and question the comfortable assumptions" of the traditional humanities.

The humanities are flowering in the public arena because hundreds of institutions are following this broader concept. New subjects can only enrich the study of old subjects. Revitalization of the humanities in the academy will occur when scholars reclaim faith in the humanities as disciplines that not only preserve our memory but help chart our future.

Works Cited

Cheney, Lynne. *Humanities in America: A Report to the President, the Congress, and the American People.* Washington, D. C.: National Endowment for the Humanities, 1988.

National Foundation on the Arts and the Humanities Act of 1965 (Public Law 209–89th Congress) as Amended through December 10, 1985. Public Law 99-194, with House and Senate Reports.

The Civic Function
of the Humanities

Reflections on the 25th Anniversary of the NEH

On April 20, 1989, I spoke to the Houston Philosophical Society at the invitation of the late Rice University philosopher and former TCH board director, Konstantin Kolenda. The speech was an abbreviated version of a paper I was then working on, but never published, reflecting on the status of the NEH and federal support for the humanities upon the forthcoming twenty-fifth anniversary of the passage of the National Foundation on the Arts and Humanities Act of 1965.

My goal was to provide some historical perspective to the debate about the humanities in America's schools, colleges and universities, and cultural institutions which William Bennett, Lynne Cheney, and various conservative writers had done so much to foster. The neo-conservatives had the upper hand in the debate given access to the media by Reagan appointees to the NEH and the Department of Education. Those who expressed concern over positions taken by the neo-conservatives, especially in regard to issues related to higher education, included most of the academic professional associations and their national organization, the prestigious American Council of Learned Societies.

State humanities council personnel found it necessary to navigate their councils through these turbulent waters. When necessary, the state councils, especially through the Federation of State Humanities Councils, would remind interested parties, including members of the Congress, of the extraordinary vitality of the humanities in the community and of the need to ensure, in a democratic society, an open rather than a rigid understanding of what comprises the humanities. State council personnel—board and staff—worked hard to preserve the autonomy of the councils and to avoid public confrontation.

Most of the humanities councils, however, including the TCH, were concerned that the mission of NEH was shrinking, that a broader notion of its mission was being lost. If so, then it was only a matter of time before the work of state councils would begin to suffer from a restricted view of the humanities. What was being lost, I thought, was a well-rounded perspective of the civic function of the humanities. The following paper sought to provide historical perspective to the origins of NEH, to the early debates regarding the role of the federal government in supporting culture, and to why it was that the Congress in 1965 voted so overwhelmingly in favor of a federal program supporting the arts and humanities.

By 1989, when this paper was written, many members of the Congress who, a few years earlier, had called for a fifty percent cut in NEH funding, had come to admire the way in which the agency was countering the perceived excesses of an earlier, more populist-oriented NEH. The reports published by Lynne Cheney had been well-received by conservative members of the Congress. The NEH budget crisis seemed over. Such was not the case with NEA, which, because of two indirectly funded photographic exhibitions, one by Andres Serrano and the other by Robert Mappelthorpe, came under the gun of Congress when conservative religious and political groups charged that the federal government was funding obscenity. Like a prairie fire, the controversy would come to engulf the NEH as well, not long after Lynne Cheney's departure. Little did we know in 1989 that, six years later, after the stunning 1994 Congressional elections, the Congressional leadership's "Contract with America" would call for ending federal funding for the NEH as well as the NEA, including state humanities councils. Bipartisan support for the humanities had collapsed.

What happened in the culture wars between 1989 and 1995 as they relate to NEA, NEH, and state arts and humanities councils is another story, but the antecedents of these recently fought battles, especially as they were played out on the floor of the House and Senate the last few years, can be found in the debates about cultural funding from the 1930s to the founding of the NEA and NEH in 1965. A look at the historical record is illuminating.

In this paper, I quote extensively from The Reluctant Patron: The

United States Government and the Arts, 1943–1965, *by Gary O. Larson (1983).* Twigs for an Eagle's Nest: Government and the Arts, 1965–1978, *by Michael Straight (1979), also provides useful information. President Nixon's appointee as chairman of the NEH, Ronald Berman, who served from 1965 to 1971, offers a one-sided but still useful history of the early years of the endowment in* Culture & Politics *(1984). Stephen Miller's* Excellence and Equity: The National Endowment for the Humanities *(1984) is also helpful.*

I

Let me begin with the good news. True to the cycles of American history and culture, the humanities are once again experiencing something of a resurgence. The word "humanities" seems far less problematic to the public than it did a decade ago, and in many campuses across the country, enrollments in humanities courses are up for the first time in two decades. One senses growing familiarity with the word. A few weeks ago, when testifying before a committee of the Texas House of Representatives regarding some international initiatives, I received nods of acknowledgement—rather than the blank stares of past years—when I referred to the Texas Council for the Humanities.

What has brought about this change? For one thing, during the past six or seven years, our nation has been about the task of education reform, in part as a result of the April 1983 landmark report of the National Commission on Education, *A Nation at Risk.* The Commission brought chilling news: "We report to the American people that while we can take justifiable pride in what our schools and colleges have historically accomplished and contributed to the United States and the well-being of its people, the educational foundations of our society are presently being eroded by a rising tide of mediocrity that threatens our very future as a Nation and a people." The Commission noted that "Each generation of Americans has outstripped its parents in education, in literacy, and in economic attainment. For the first time in the history of our country, the educational skills of one generation will not surpass, will not equal, will not even approach, those of their parents."

The Commission said that the U.S. was entering into a new era dominated by new technologies and international competition, and that "The people of the United States need to know that individuals in our society who do not possess the levels of skill, literacy, and training essential to this new era will be effectively disenfranchised, not simply from the material rewards that accompany competent performance, but also from the chance to participate fully in our national life."

The record shows that Texas has been a national leader in this effort to improve education in our public schools and colleges and universities. Two years before the National Commission released its report, the Texas Legislature passed House Bill 246, addressing for the first time in a long time, pressing needs in our elementary and secondary schools, and setting the stage for subsequent reforms throughout this decade. Much of the credit for this leadership goes to a small group of enlightened political leaders, including Lt. Governor William Hobby, who had the courage and fortitude to push ahead against formidable opposition and in the midst of difficult economic times.

For those who care about the humanities, about the quality and extent of education in such fields as history, literature, government, and foreign cultures and languages, the educational reform movement provided an extraordinary opportunity. There was now a context for asking: What is it that students should know? What courses and programs should constitute the curricula to be offered our children? What sorts of skills must students have in order to live productive lives and to meet the needs of a changing economy?

Once these questions were asked, the humanities were on the rebound. Best selling books—Alan Bloom's *The Closing of the American Mind* and E. D. Hirsch's *Cultural Literacy*—focused public attention on educational problems. Numerous reports issued by blue-ribbon commissions brought further attention. Press coverage of some of these reports has been extensive.

I think especially of three reports issued by the chairs of the National Endowment for the Humanities over the past six years: Bill Bennett's *To Reclaim a Legacy*, dealing with higher education; Lynne Cheney's *American Memory*, dealing with secondary education; and her sequel, *The Humanities in America*, dealing with higher education and the wider culture.

These reports seek to answer these important questions from a perspective which, for the better part of a decade, has been called "neo-conservatism," that school of thought that fueled much of the intellectual foundation of the Reagan administration. It is the same perspective that supports positions taken by Bloom and Hirsh in their best-selling books. I have referred to these individuals as the "preservationists." Here is what they argue:

The preservationists are concerned about the loss of the preeminence of the Western tradition in our schools and colleges and universities. The legacy that Bill Bennett wants us to reclaim is the legacy of the Western intellectual tradition. These writers are concerned with the loss of cultural memory; that is, the cultural memory drawn from the Western tradition and experience. They believe in a canon of great works that should form the backbone of any curriculum. They are critical of American education over the past several decades because they see an erosion in instruction in traditional history and literature. They want to see a restoration of history taught in linear fashion—one that involves a dramatic story focusing on great moments, great laws, great leaders. They want to see a restoration of literature taught with less regard for issues of class, race, and gender. Neo-conservative thought has dominated much of the public discussion of what it is that our children should be taught and what it is that our college youth should be learning.

In the last several years, however, those representing other viewpoints have responded. Frequent stories in *The Chronicle of Higher Education* document efforts underway to preserve and strengthen a broader approach to the humanities. This alternative perspective, from those I have called the "expansionists," is represented in two reports, *The Humanities and the American Promise*, from the Colloquium on the Humanities and the American People, chaired by noted historian Merrill Peterson of the University of Virginia, and *Speaking for the Humanities*, published by the American Council of Learned Societies.

The expansionists have not shared in political power in the 1980s. They have not held important positions at the NEH or in the Department of Education. Rather, they have been teachers, scholars, and independent grass-roots writers who have argued over the course of the past several decades that we need secondary and post-secondary curricula that are responsive to the realities of American and world demographics. They have sought to expand the canon of "great" literature through the inclusion of black, Hispanic, and women authors. Their intellectual roots reach back to the American civil rights movement, to the women's movement, and to the progressive tradition in American politics. The expansionists believe that, to understand a nation's history, it is important to know about average people, including the poor and the disen-franchised. Expansionists have promoted social history, ethnic history, and family history. When it comes to teaching literature, they argue that it is impossible to understand a text and its author without addressing issues of class, race, and gender. For the expansionists, the turmoil that confronts the humanities community in deciding what and how to teach is a sign of life and not death.

We could dismiss this division in the humanities community as an intramural conflict if it were not for one important fact—there is a deep and abiding connection between the humanities in our public schools and colleges and universities and wider, public culture. This debate, which has moved from a small circle of educators to the wider public and now to the political arena, is about much more than what we teach our students. It is about the shape of American intellectual life, about the breadth and depth of our culture, about shared history and values, and about the ideas that sustain American politics and society.

The enhanced public profile that has come to the NEH in recent years is, in large measure, due to the fact that the recent chairs of that agency, Bill Bennett and Lynne Cheney, saw the educational reform movement that was sweeping the country as an ideal opportunity to make the case for the humanities, to help restore the humanities to a central place in American education. We should be very glad they did. At the same time, however, the fact that Bennett and Cheney belong so squarely in the camp of the preservationists, that they represent so faithfully the neo-conservative philosophy, means that the federal government, using taxpayer dollars, has become centrally involved in answering as well as asking the question: "What is it that students should know?" and in promoting particular approaches to curricular questions. In so doing, they are shaping the wider public culture. My reflections, therefore, have to do with the proper role of the federal government in regard to support of the humanities.

II

Twenty-five years ago this spring, as Lyndon Johnson shaped his vision of The Great Society, a small group of influential members of the Congress made plans to submit legislation that ultimately would lead to the establishment of the National Endowment for the Arts and the National Endowment for the Humanities.

These members of the Congress knew that opposition to such support was formidable. Central to the concerns of most members was the fear of state control over the cultural life of the country and fear of the imposition of political ideology in federal programs in support of the arts.

From the late 1940s to the early 1960s, various members of the Congress had proposed legislation, always in support of the arts, never in support of the humanities, but such legislation was continually defeated. Some initial efforts even had presidential backing. Dwight

Eisenhower, in his State of the Union address in 1955, made the first significant presidential plea for the arts since the New Deal. "In the advancement of the various activities which will make our civilization endure and flourish," he said, "the Federal government should do more to give official recognition to the importance of the arts and other cultural activities." The president proposed a Federal Advisory Commission on the Arts within the Department of Health, Education, and Welfare.

According to historian Gary Larson, later that spring, Oveta Culp Hobby, secretary of HEW, sent a draft of a bill establishing such a Commission to House Speaker Sam Rayburn. The bill, written in large measure by Undersecretary Nelson Rockefeller, argued that the encouragement and creativity of the arts, and widespread participation in the arts, while primarily a matter of individual initiative, promotes the general welfare and is therefore in the national interest.

In her letter accompanying the draft legislation, Secretary Hobby made some telling points. "Throughout the great epochs of history," she declared, "civilization has been importantly exemplified by masterworks of art and architecture, music and the dance, drama, and literature. Achievements in these fields represent . . . one of the enduring criteria by which history appraises every nation." She argued that although the United States is a young nation, it has made substantial contributions in these fields. Yet, despite our various cultural triumphs, much remains to be accomplished, especially in bringing the arts into the mainstream of American life. "There are many respects," she noted "in which we lag behind other nations in the general position we accord the arts in our society." She argued that "new ways should be sought to bring the enjoyment of and participation in the arts to more of our people."

While Secretary Hobby offered some of the best reasons for government support of the arts, other bills submitted in the 1950s rested on the premise that culture was one of the weapons of the Cold War, and that the United States was falling behind the Soviet Union, which was pumping substantial funds into its state-operated arts establishment and was conducting a vigorous campaign of international cultural exchange. In supporting an arts bill in 1954, Senator Herbert Lehman of New York argued that "We in the United States have fallen into the habit of letting the rest of the world believe in the myth that there is no real cultural base in the United States—that the creative artists of the United States have little to contribute to the cultural growth of our civilization." According to Lehman, "The Communists have exploited this myth by propagandizing the peoples of the world with the story that we in the United States are materialistic barbarians."

120

Arguments in favor of some kind of federally-subsidized arts program coalesced around this need to counter the perceived Soviet advance worldwide through cultural initiatives. A Congressional hearing in 1955 revealed, probably erroneously, that the Soviet Union was spending $2 billion a year on cultural exchange, far in excess of the $2.5 million spent by the U.S. government. Two separate hearings were conducted in 1956 to discuss how the United States could best respond to this Soviet threat.

This apparent need formed the rationale for a sweeping bill proposed that year by Representative Frank Thompson, the "American National Arts, Sports and Recreation Act." The premise of the bill was that the program of the U.S. to build armed strength against the Communists should be broadened to include cultural advances in this country and the exportation of American culture, through exchange programs, to other parts of the world. According to Thompson, "it is through cultural interchange and development, more than superhighways, science, and statistics, that the real answer to communism must be sought."

These bills went down to defeat. In analyzing the response of the Congress in the 1950s to these legislative initiatives, it is important to remember the intense dislike, if not disgust, that some members of the Congress in the 1950s had to U.S. involvement in the arts in the late 1930s. The Works Progress Administration, established in 1935, included the Federal Arts Project, Federal Theater Project, Federal Music Project, and Federal Writers Project. These projects, launched originally as a way of providing useful employment for artists and writers in the midst of the Great Depression, became an extraordinary experiment in the democratization of culture. Countless paintings, photographs, theatrical productions, musical performances, tape recordings, and writings, gave expression to the way Americans really are—in the coal fields of West Virginia, in the wheat fields of Kansas, in the ghettos of our urban centers, and in the coffee shops and cafes of our small towns. Never before in the history of Western civilization were so many human and financial resources spent documenting and expressing the lives of ordinary citizens. Many of these artists and writers had extensive impact at the time, and fifty years after the WPA, books are still being published, and video documentaries being made, on their important work.

But not everyone liked this work. By the late 1930s, these projects were distrusted by some members of the Congress who felt that the projects seemed to heighten the possibility of class warfare. For others, these projects were nesting grounds for communist conspirators, especially the Federal Theater and Writers Projects. In 1938, the House

Committee on Un-American Activities, chaired by Texas Congressman Martin Dies, conducted hearings on the projects. He argued that the projects were "doing more to spread communist propaganda than the Communist Party itself." The administrators were "purveyors of class hatred," and he doubted that federal guidelines regarding objectivity could be maintained for the Writers' Project.

While it was impossible for the Committee to find enough evidence to pull the plug on the program in 1938, the hearings fueled the Congressional revolt from New Deal art programs. From that point on, the program was in demise. What was left of it, especially the Writers' Project, ultimately was swallowed up in the war effort, with remaining writers assigned through the War Services Subdivision of the Works Progress Administration to writing everything from air raid manuals to books on home gardening to a guide to the U.S. Naval Academy.

Thus when some members of the Congress began making plans in 1964 for a new program of federal support of American culture, the federal projects of the 1930s projected a long and troubling shadow, one that provoked the fear of radicalism and the possible imposition of leftist ideology on cultural activities supported by the federal government.

Even some very modest adventures into the arts in the years between Roosevelt and Johnson brought forth the wrath of the most conservative members of the Congress. In 1946, the State Department, to demonstrate, according to Assistant Secretary of State William Benton, "to all those abroad who thought of the United States as a nation of materialists, that the same country which produces brilliant scientists and engineers also produces creative artists," put together through $50,000 in federal money a collection of contemporary American art for touring in Europe and South America. Shortly after opening at the Metropolitan Museum of Art, the collection and the State Department program came under bitter public and political attack. Many found the modernist art represented in the collection to represent European radicalism, art not indigenous to American soil. Conservative newspapers, eager then as now to identify federal boondoggles, charged that the federal government was creating a monopoly for abstract art. It did not take long for the Congress to conduct hearings. Representative Fred Busbey of Illinois called the exhibit a "disgrace to the United States," but typical, he said, of an administration "infected by Communists." For many Congressmen, this program was the last straw, further evidence of how radicals could use government support of the arts for their own sinister purposes. Using material furnished by the House Un-American Activities Committee, Busbey charged that "the records of more than 20 of the 45 artists are definite New Deal in various shades of Communism."

Even after the State Department canceled the tour of the collection and unloaded the paintings for less than one-tenth their appraised value, Congressional criticism continued. Congressmen like George Dondero of Michigan saw federal support for the arts as nothing short of a communist conspiracy. In 1949, when the Library of Congress awarded its top literary prize to Ezra Pound, then under indictment for treason and recently committed to an institution for the insane, the Congress reacted quickly, canceling this prize and similar prizes for music and art. Government-funded exhibits in the late 1950s, such as the art exhibit that appeared at the Brussels World Fair in 1958 and the American National Exhibit in Moscow in 1959, faired better, but the suspicions remained.

Thus proponents of federal support for culture in the early 1960s had their work cut out for them. However, there had been, beginning in the late 1950s, growing public recognition that in order for the United States to compete successfully on the world stage, it needed to do more to foster the arts. In 1960, President Eisenhower's Commission on National Goals captured this sentiment when it devoted an entire essay to American culture. The Commission argued that American art had not kept pace with developments in science and technology. "In the eyes of posterity," the Commission argued, "the success of the United States as a civilized society will be largely judged by the creative activities of its citizens in art, architecture, literature, music, and the sciences."

That spirit was advanced by the Kennedy administration, thereby broadening support for a new federal arts initiative. But Congressional proponents still met stiff resistance, and that resistance was not broken until the focus of cultural support shifted from the arts to the humanities.

In April 1964, twenty-five years ago, almost to the day, the Commission on the Humanities, sponsored by the American Council of Learned Societies, issued a report on the state of the humanities in America. This carefully-crafted document made the case for public support of those fields of inquiry known as the humanities.

"We propose," the Commission said, "a program for all our people, a program to meet a need no less serious than that for national defense. We speak, in truth, for what is being defended—our beliefs, our ideas, our highest achievements." The Commission "conceives of the humanities, not merely as academic disciplines confined to schools and colleges, but as functioning components of society which affect the lives and well-being of all the population."

"Over the centuries," the Commission noted, "the humanities have sustained mankind at the deepest level of being. They prospered in Greece and Rome, in the Middle Ages, in the Renaissance, and in the Enlightenment." The Commission observed, importantly so, that "in the formative years of our own country it was a group of statesmen steeped in the humanities who fused their own experience with that of the past to create the enduring Constitution of the Republic."

The Commission observed that during the early history of the Republic, Americans were occupied in mastering the physical environment. "No sooner was this mastery within sight than advancing technology opened up a new range of possibilities, putting a new claim on energies which might otherwise have gone into humane and artistic endeavors." According to the Commission, the result was that "our social, moral and aesthetic development lagged behind our material advances. . . . Now more than ever, with the rapid growth of knowledge and its transformation of society's material base, the humanities must command men of talent, intellect, and spirit."

The Commission argued that the state of the humanities today "creates a crisis for national leadership." The Commission called for a new commitment to ensure that the United States would be a leader in the realm of ideas and of the human spirit. "World leadership of the kind which has come upon the United States cannot rest solely upon superior force, vast wealth, or preponderant technology. . . . If we appear to discourage creativity, to demean the fanciful and the beautiful, to have no concern for man's ultimate destiny—if, in short, we ignore the humanities—both our goals and our efforts to attain them will be measured with suspicion."

The Commission warned of a growing imbalance between the sciences and technology, on the one hand, and the arts and humanities on the other. Academic institutions in particular experience this imbalance, given dramatically increasing federal funds for research in the sciences. As a result, the arts and humanities are demeaned and trivialized. It is time, the Commission argued, for a National Foundation on the Humanities.

The Commission's report was read and enthusiastically accepted by many members of the Congress. Later that spring, various members of the Congress took the first steps in drafting new legislation. In January 1965, on the first day that the new Congress met, fifty-seven representatives introduced arts and humanities legislation. Ultimately over one hundred bills were introduced. The movement received a boost from President Johnson's 1965 State of the Union Address when he called for a new federal initiative. On March 10, 1965, President Johnson submitted to the Congress a bill calling for a National Foundation on the Arts and Humanities with two independent endowments, one administering arts programs, the other humanities programs.

In his analysis of the founding of NEH, Stephen Miller notes that much of the language of the Commission on the Humanities was incorporated into the bill that was passed later in 1965. Ironically, after years of seeking support for the arts, it was the language of the humanities that made this new venture into federal support of American culture possible.

The legislation was crafted to take into account the twenty-five-year debate on the role of the federal government in cultural affairs and to answer the charges of critics who feared political meddling and ideological imposition. "Under no conditions," argued the Commission on the Humanities, "should [the Foundation] attempt to direct or control the scholarship, teaching, or artistic endeavors which it supports." That recommendation was incorporated into the legislation. More important, however, was the eloquent language of the preamble—drawing from the report—that laid out the civic function of the humanities.

One finds in the report a vision of an educated society. According to the report, "Democracy demands wisdom of the average man." Through the humanities, we grasp the significance of the past. Through the humanities, we are able to wrestle with such enduring values as justice, freedom, virtue, beauty and truth. Without the exercise of wisdom by the average person, "free institutions and personal liberty are inevitably imperiled." Further, "to know the best that has been thought and said in former times can make us wiser than we otherwise might be." Without the humanities, we cannot begin to judge the effects of particular technologies. The humanities can nourish the creative and imaginative abilities of the American people. To defend the humanities, to provide much needed financial support for the humanities, is indeed in the national interest. "Upon the humanities depend the national ethic and morality, the national aesthetic and beauty or the lack of it, the national use of our environment and our material accomplishments," the report stated. Through the humanities we, as citizens, might make better judgments about our lives, about our relationship to nature and to each other, about our very destiny. It is in the national interest that these judgments about contemporary life be strong and good.

III

There are those who would argue that this uplifting language about the civic function of the humanities and what the humanities can do for America, was really a ploy for support for humanities research. These skeptics point to the fact that it was the American Council of Learned Societies, representing the academic community, that sponsored the Commission that lobbied the Congress for passage of the National Arts and Humanities Act of 1965. They would argue that humanities scholars, envious of the dollars flowing to their colleagues in the sciences from the National Science Foundation, simply wanted a slice of the federal pie. These skeptics buttress their argument by pointing to the record of the Endowment during its very early years—nearly all sums appropriated by the Congress went for fellowships and other scholarly endeavors rather than for public programs.

To a limited extent, these skeptics have a valid point. The record shows that it was the Congress, during these early years, that reminded the agency of its public function, of the need to establish programs that would reach out to citizens at large, if the original mandate were to be realized. By the early 1970s, the agency had learned that, if it wanted its appropriations to be increased in the years ahead, it had to move aggressively in sponsoring programs for the benefit of all Americans. Since that time, funding for the agency has been more evenly balanced between public and scholarly activities, although the debate over funding balance took a heavy toll when Nixon appointee Ronald Berman resisted pressures in 1975 from Senator Claiborne Pell to further expand public activities, especially through proposed collaboration between state governments and state humanities councils, with Pell blocking the re-appointment of Berman to a second four-year term of office. President Jimmy Carter instructed his appointee to the NEH, Joseph Duffey, to shed the elitist image of the agency.

While these skeptics may be partially correct in their assessment, it is important to recognize that it took time and great effort to determine what kinds of structures and what kinds of programs could best fulfill that part of the agency's mandate having to do with the public. Because of the deliberation that went into these decisions, the programs that have evolved have had a level of accountability of which the administrators of the federal projects of the 1930s would surely be in awe. The most important means whereby the agency would strive to meet the mandate to relate the humanities to the current conditions of national life was through the state humanities program, created in the early 1970s. Without much enthusiasm from the agency, the Congress amended the authorizing legislation in the mid-1970s to ensure that at least twenty percent of program funding received by the agency would be allocated to the newly established humanities councils operating in all fifty states. These councils, with the mandate to provide public programs, were authorized to make funding decisions based on local needs and interests, thereby assuring that at least a portion of federal funds would be outside direct federal control—an early form of privatization of government services.

Over the past twenty-five years, the NEH has spent upwards of $1.8 billion dollars to further the humanities in American life. During this period of time, there have been, in comparison with the cultural programs of the 1930s, surprisingly few political attacks. But those that have come have been sharp, consequential, and worthy of some reflection.

The most serious challenge came at the dawn of the Reagan administration eight years ago. Much of the intellectual foundation of the Reagan administration was contained in the document, *Mandate for Leadership: Policy management in a Conservative Administration*, which provided blueprints for the administration. In its report, the not-for-profit, tax-exempt Heritage Foundation included a chapter on the NEH and the NEA. The report argued that federal support had grown excessive and that the federal government had usurped the private sector in providing support for the arts and humanities. More importantly, it argued that the Endowments, especially the NEH, had become politicized under the Carter administration.

The Heritage Foundation report charged that the NEH, in pursuit of the civic function of the humanities, had given in to the excesses of populism. In pursuit of new constituencies, it had left behind high culture for popular culture. It had emphasized "politically inspired social policies at the expense of the independence" of the humanities. To the detriment of "excellence," NEH administrators had shown "a slavish devotion to innovation and a fascination with public media and public programs." The report decried the "unfortunate employment of humanists in settings where they are asked to speak of things about which they know nothing," especially in regard to public policy questions in programs sponsored by the state humanities councils. In short, the report charged that the Endowment had become the tool of the liberal left.

To set things right, President Reagan brought in Bill Bennett, the former head of the National Humanities Center in North Carolina. One of the first things that Bennett did was to make the front page of *The New York Times* with a strident condemnation of a documentary film produced by a grant from the Wisconsin Council for the Humanities, "From the Ashes . . . Nicaragua." According to Bennett, the documentary was "unabashed socialist-realism propaganda" and not an appropriate object for federal funding (Friedman 1984).

Bill Bennett went to work righting the perceived wrongs of the agency, carrying out the mandate for leadership given by the Heritage Foundation. In pursuit of the neo-conservative cause, he and many colleagues, inside and outside of government, who were willing to do what the Heritage Foundation asked: "to teach the nation the limits of the egalitarian impulse." Many of these spirited colleagues, over the next six or seven years, wrote books—some of them best sellers—decrying what they saw as the sorry state of the humanities in America.

Some very conservative members of the Congress, while applauding the new direction, kept their eye on possible offenses that would indicate the survival of past errors. In October 1983, Senator Steve Symms and Congressman Denny Smith asked the General Accounting Office to conduct an audit of the state councils in Idaho and Oregon, as well as other state humanities councils, "to determine whether or not [federal] dollars are being misused in the cause of political advocacy." It had come to their attention, they said, after reviewing grant awards by the Idaho and Oregon councils, that some programs might involve political partisanship. They pointed to two grants in particular, a grant of $11,000 from the Idaho council for a program entitled "Russian Awareness Week," and a $5,056 grant from the Oregon council for a seminar entitled "What about the Russians?" Another grant from the Oregon council for a project entitled "Understanding the Soviets—a Path to Peace," was also cited (Molotsky 1983).

The Senator and Congressman acknowledged in their request that the NEH was now trying to ensure that projects funded by federal grants would avoid contemporary and controversial topics. But these and other projects that they had seen—such as a grant from the Oregon Council to the Salem Committee on Latin America for a project entitled "Violence in Central America: Causes and Responses"—"do not fit the definition of humanities," said these members of Congress, "since the sponsored events revolve around current political subjects, rather than educational, cultural opportunities."

By and large, such attacks by the political right on federally-funded humanities programs have stopped. And the reason is clear: the NEH, after eight years of neo-conservative leadership, has achieved much of what the Heritage Foundation wanted. In the war of ideas in American culture, the Endowment has succeeded in pushing the neo-conservative cause. At the heart of that cause, one finds the disengagement of the humanities from questions of public policy, the restoration of traditional humanities disciplines as opposed to newer disciplines such as social history and women's studies, and so-called "high culture" over "popular" culture.

By refocusing the work of the NEH, by using the NEH as a bully pulpit, the recent chairs of the NEH, Bill Bennett and then Lynne Cheney, have succeeded in drawing public attention to the state of the humanities. Their positive contributions in this regard should not be underestimated. Lynne Cheney's 1987 report, *American Memory*, which focused on the plight of the humanities in our nation's elementary and secondary schools, has helped to galvanize public support for new and expanded efforts to improve instruction in history, English, and other humanities subjects. Likewise, Bill Bennett's earlier report, *To Reclaim a Legacy*, and Lynne Cheney's most recent report, *The Humanities in America*, have focused needed attention on the status of the humanities in institutions of higher education.

While promoting the advancement of the humanities, while trying to restore the humanities to a prominent position in American life, these reports offer stinging criticism of the academy and of many aspects of the contemporary humanistic enterprise. Of particular concern to Bennett and Cheney is the apparent loss of the pre-eminence of the Western tradition in the curriculum and the alleged tendency, in studying texts, to focus more on political questions than questions of truth, beauty, and excellence. Bennett and Cheney see the humanities in our institutions of higher education controlled by individuals with leftist political ideology.

Ironically, argues Cheney, the humanities in the academy remain in decline at the very time when the humanities in the public arena are alive and well. "Public programming in the humanities is now so substantial and extensive," says Cheney, that it has become a kind of parallel school, one that has grown up outside established institutions of education." Citing programs offered by museums, libraries, study groups, public television stations, and many others, and frequently funded by the state humanities councils, Cheney argues that the public humanities have evolved into an intellectually rigorous pursuit. No previous chairs of the NEH championed public programs and the state councils like Lynne Cheney. Given the high marks granted to public programs, one can assume that, in her view, they must be essentially free of the kind of politicization that apparently plagues the humanities in academic settings. It was Cheney, after all, who, borrowing a page from Bennett, withdrew NEH sponsorship of the PBS series, *The Africans*, when she concluded that portions of that series were unfair to the U.S. and suffered from a Marxist slant.

Although this extolling of the humanities in the public arena while criticizing the humanities in the academy has won the praise of political conservatives and many journalists, it has generated criticism from the scholarly community, even though it is a difficult thing to bite the hand that feeds one. On the twenty-fifth anniversary of its sponsorship of the report that led to the establishment of the NEH, the American Council of Learned Societies published another report, *Speaking for the Humanities*. This report, written by six distinguished professors of the humanities, tackles head-on the criticism of the humanities in America raised by Bennett, Bloom, Cheney and other neo-conservatives. The report argues that "We are, in fact, living through a revival of the humanities on campuses where, until recently, the focus of students was overwhelmingly on business and technological studies." Exciting things are taking place in the humanities, and many of those things identified as failings in the humanities by the neo-conservatives are, in reality, "enlivening transformations." The broadening out of the canon to include works by minorities and women, the willingness to see great texts in their historical and political contexts, the eagerness to study the literature and political works of other cultures, the willingness to use the humanities to clarify important issues of public life—all these endeavors which bother the neo-conservatives, the report maintains, are renewing the humanities.

This report argues that NEH leadership, and allied writers outside the endowment, while accusing the professoriate of ideological bias, fail to see their own ideology. While hiding under the banner of objectivity, of an apolitical approach to federal support for the humanities, they fall victim to that which they criticize—the politicization of federal funding and, indeed, of education itself.

Make no mistake about it, the report implies, this truncated view of the humanities, this desire to tame the humanities, this penchant for seeing the humanities as the intellectual stuff which preserves order, instills traditional values, teaches transcendent truths, and preserves the predominantly white, privileged, and male Western intellectual tradition, is heavily politicized.

Ironically, this neo-conservative, political approach to the humanities, in an era of great fiscal constraints, has helped to ensure the continued appropriation of federal dollars for the humanities. But one must raise the question: What might we be losing? It is much easier to see what we have gained. We have gained some very articulate spokespeople who have worked very hard raising the banner of the humanities. Lynne Cheney's report, *The Humanities in America*, was covered by most major newspapers in the country. Ironically, Bennett and Cheney have helped preserve federal support for the humanities, even though they officially blessed administration-proposed cuts in NEH's funding. But what have we lost?

My fear is that we may be in danger of losing a larger notion of the civic function of the humanities as promised in the original legislation of 1965. That notion, as articulated by the Commission on the Humanities in 1964, by the Congress in 1965, and most certainly by thousands of scholars, institutions, and public agencies since that time, recognizes, first of all, that the humanities belong to the people—all the people. As such, in this democratic society, the humanities must represent the traditions and values of all our citizens, including those whose historic and ethnic roots lie outside the Western tradition.

In this broader understanding of the civic function of the humanities, one finds a recognition that, while the humanities do play a conserving role, reminding us of the traditions, beliefs, and experiences of the dominant culture that have molded society, they may be and often are disturbers of the peace. In the words of another recent report, *The Humanities and the American Promise*, which sets forth a more expansive view of the humanities in America, the humanities "ask troubling questions, heighten consciousness, start revolutions in the mind, challenge the status quo, and raise expectations for ourselves and society. The humanities should be cultivated, not for intellectual adornment, even less to legitimate existing social and political institutions, but as instruments of self-discovery, of critical understanding, and creative social imagination."

This broader interpretation of the civic function of the humanities, while recognizing the importance of the conserving role advocated by the neo-conservatives, invites Americans to reflect deeply on their society, to see our failings as well as our accomplishments, to see ourselves as a people in relationship to other peoples, and to hear new voices while remembering old and familiar voices.

As we move into the last decade of this century and millennium, as we face the challenges of the twenty-first century, it is my belief that we must reclaim this broader understanding of the civic function of the humanities. Our government justifies its authority on the claim that it embodies "the will of the people." In that regard, *The Humanities and the American Promise* says:

The mobilization of consent in a highly differentiated electorate, to say nothing of the implementation of the popular will once registered, is a difficult and uncertain process. But the degree to which it is achieved depends fundamentally on the quality of public debate and discussion. The giant liberties of the First Amendment—of thought, speech, press, and assembly—are not only guarantees of individual rights against government; they are also the positive means for carrying forward the civic discourse that is the lifeblood of democratic government. Political liberty is but one necessary condition, however. Another is the education of citizens in ways that strengthen responsible participation.

I would argue that such education for citizenship should be grounded in this broader understanding of the humanities. I offer three reasons.

First, we can no longer hide from the realities of American cultural pluralism. We must come to grips with what it means to be a nation composed of citizens drawn from all corners of the world. We must ensure as much universal understanding of our multiple traditions, faiths, and values as is possible. We must recognize that we still have a long way to go in creating an environment, in education as well as in work, that ensures equality of opportunity. We must find new ways to combat racism and prejudice, to rectify our past mistakes, and to foster cross-cultural understanding and goodwill.

Second, we can no longer hide under the protective intellectual blanket of the Western tradition. We are living through a time of unprecedented national and international restructuring of political and economic power. To our west, we see the rapid emergence of nations with enormous economic power. To our east, we see an old foe, once thought of as an "evil empire," a nation which forced us to adopt policies and to structure our society in ways that have literally shaped our way of being, undergo such profound change that some of the most important assumptions held by our nation undoubtedly will have to be re-visited. To our south, we see nations in great pain and turmoil. If we are to succeed in the next century as a nation, it is imperative that we grasp these dramatically changing world conditions, and to do that we must incorporate in far more extensive ways the study of other nations and cultures in our public school and college and university curricula.

Third, we can no longer ignore the tremendous challenges involved in helping citizens understand and discuss complex contemporary public issues. Issues related to the environment, to the application of new technologies, to national and international debt, to food production and distribution, to the horrible plague of drugs, to crime and ever-expanding prisons, to rampant illiteracy, to chronic poverty, to the proliferation of nuclear weapons—all these issues and many more—beg for public understanding. If such understanding is absent, we lose our ability to govern ourselves. It is time to reconnect the humanities to these issues of national life, to encourage citizen understanding of these difficult issues through perspectives that the humanities bring. The media can help, and public humanities programs can help, but our schools and colleges and universities bear special responsibility in helping young citizens understand the historical, social, and moral dimensions of these issues.

This commitment to civic conversation, the application of this broader understanding of the civic function of the humanities, may be slipping from our grasp. Perhaps it is inappropriate to ask the federal government to assist in this effort. Perhaps, despite the legislative mandate given to it in 1965, it is inevitable that the NEH would offer a tamer, more restricted, and less self-critical understanding of the civic function of the humanities. Would not the alternative result in only more GAO audits, more House Committee investigations, more denunciations of offending programs, and finally, the withdrawal of the humanities as a matter of national concern and general welfare?

Perhaps, but I don't think so. In this exciting arena of government and ideas, we must press ahead. "For the government to invest in the humanistic learning and action of its citizens," says *The Humanities and the American Promise*, "is an act of national faith and national courage. . . . It may not guarantee anything, but it declares the willingness to take seriously the moral and intellectual requirements for the good health of a nation conceived in liberty." We must test that faith by reclaiming the full dimensions of the civic function of the humanities.

From where will encouragement for this testing come? Not, I suspect, from federal office holders, from Congressional committees, or blue-ribbon commissions. If it comes, it will come from the people, from concerned citizens from all walks of life who recognize that something must be done to enhance our civic conversation, to expand and improve educational opportunities so that citizens have the opportunity to deepen their knowledge and understanding of the contemporary world. We need citizens who will take an active role in shaping public school curricula, citizens who will actively serve on the boards of museums and libraries and other cultural institutions in order to encourage and plan programs that meet pressing public needs and interests, citizens who will encourage their local newspapers and television stations to provide deeper and more meaningful coverage of difficult public issues, citizens who will establish new organizations to bring the humanities to their communities, citizens who will ask administrators and faculty members difficult questions about the missions, programs, and courses of study of their local colleges and universities, citizens who will tell their elected public officials, "We need help in finding new ways of ensuring public conversation of the complex and difficult issues that you deal with."

If we can re-incorporate this broader vision of the civic function of the humanities into our lives at the local and state level, we will have a much better chance of ensuring that the federal government fulfills its promise, as stated in NEH's founding legislation, to help all Americans "achieve a better understanding of the past, a better analysis of the present, and a better view of the future . . . so that the world leadership that has come to the United States will rest not solely upon our superior power, wealth, and technology, but upon worldwide respect and admiration for the Nation's high qualities as a leader in the realm of ideas and of the [human] spirit."

Works Cited

Bennett, William J. *To Reclaim a Legacy: A Report on the Humanities in Higher Education*. National Endowment for the Humanities, 1983.

Berman, Ronald. *Culture & Politics*. Lanham, MD: University Press of America, 1984.

Bloom, Alan. *The Closing of the American Mind*. New York: Simon & Schuster, 1987.

Cheney, Lynne V. *American Memory: A Report on the Humanities in the Nation's Public Schools*. National Endowment for the Humanities, 1987.

_____. *The Humanities in America: A Report to the President, the Congress, and the American People*. National Endowment for the Humanities, 1988.

Friedman, John S. and Eric Nadler. "Hard Right Rudder at the NEH." *The Nation* (April 14, 1984.)

Goldstein, Richard. "The War for America's Mind." *The Village Voice* (June 8, 1982).

Heatherly, Charles L., ed. *Mandate for Leadership: Policy Management in a Conservative Administration*. Washington, D. C.: The Heritage Foundation, 1981.

Hirsch, E. D. Jr. *Cultural Literacy: What Every American Needs to Know*, 1987. Reprint: New York: Vintage Books, 1988.

Larson, Gary O. *The Reluctant Patron: The United States Government and the Arts, 1943–1965*. Philadelphia: University of Pennsylvania Press, 1983.

Levine, George. *Peter Brooks, Jonathan Culler, Marjorie Garber, E. Ann Kaplan, Catharine R. Stimpson, Speaking for the Humanities*. New York: American Council of Learned Societies, 1989.

McCombs, Phil. "NEH Backs The Basics." *The Washington Post* (November 22, 1982).

Miller, Stephen. *Excellence and Equity: The National Endowment for the Humanities*. Lexington: University Press of Kentucky, 1984.

Molotsky, Irvin. "Congressmen Say Three States Misused Federal Humanities Funds." *The New York Times* (November 6, 1983).

A Nation at Risk: The Imperatives for Education Reform. National Commission on Excellence in Education, 1983.

Peterson, Merrill D. *The Humanities and the American Promise*. Austin: Texas Council for the Humanities, 1987.

Report of the Commission on the Humanities. New York: American Council of Learned Societies, 1964.

Scully, Malcolm G. "Audit Asked of How States Use NEH Funds." *The Chronicle of Higher Education* (January 4, 1984).

Straight, Michael. *Twigs for an Eagle's Nest: Government and the Arts, 1965–1978*. New York: Devon Press, 1979.

Engaging the Public: New Roles for Scholars

A preview of the post-1994 Congressional attacks on the NEH can be found in two events that show the extent to which the Endowment had been pulled into the culture wars.

In 1991, when President Bush, with Lynne Cheney's backing, nominated Carol Iannone to the National Council on the Humanities, several professional organizations in the humanities sought to block the nomination, arguing that she was insufficiently qualified to serve on the panel. Conservative scholars charged that this resistance was politically motivated, that Iannone was opposed not because of her qualifications but because she failed to conform to the political views of the academic establishment. Press coverage of the ill-fated nomination was extensive, and for the first time the charge of "political correctness" entered into the popular press. Conservative members of the Congress, responding to the charges leveled by Lynne Cheney and others, began to take keen interest in the NEH.

The second incident was the nomination of Sheldon Hackney by newly-elected President Clinton to head the NEH. Several campus incidents at the University of Pennsylvania, where he was president, were blown out of proportion by the opposition and then the press as examples of the perceived problem of "political correctness" in higher education. Hackney was finally confirmed by the Senate, but not without much controversy and with deepening interest in the NEH, for the wrong reasons, on the part of some members of the Congress. For the most conservative members, those already predisposed to the idea that federal funds were being used to further an agenda of multiculturalism and political correctness, the change in administrations and the appointment of Sheldon Hackney signaled that it was time to keep close watch over the NEH. They found support among a small group of conservative scholars headed by former colleagues of Lynne Cheney, now organized as the National Association of Scholars. After the 1994 mid-term elections, these forces, including Lynne Cheney, coalesced to try and convince the Congress that it should stop funding the NEH altogether.

Shortly after taking office, Sheldon Hackney announced that his top priority would be to broaden the work of the NEH to reach more of the American public. The centerpiece of this emphasis was an Endowment-led "National Conversation on American Pluralism and Identity," a warm-up, as it turned out to be, for President Clinton's less-than-successful 1997–1998 initiative calling for a national conversation on race relations. Ultimately, the Hackney administration had to tend to a massive restructuring of the NEH in light of draconian budget cuts and to a reprioritizing of the agency's work, both of which deflected staff energy and financial resources from the national conversation initiative.

I found the initiative to be a positive response to two obvious needs: first, to find a way to recapture for the public and the Congress the essential mission of the agency as contained in the original 1965 legislation; and, secondly, to find a new program that had the potential of bringing together the academic left and right on a matter of growing public concern—the challenges of a remarkably pluralistic society beset by ethnic and racial conflict.

Hackney's project furthered my own interest in finding fresh ways to use the humanities in dealing constructively with many problems of contemporary society. A burst of new scholarship emerged in the 1980s and early 1990s on the problems of civil society, building on the work of German philosopher Jurgan Habermas and his important book, The Structural Transformation of the Public Sphere *(1962). An opportunity emerged, I thought, to reconnect the humanities to, as the founding legislation said, "the current conditions of national life." In the fall of 1994, I took a one-year leave of absence from the TCH to direct The Humanities and Public Engagement Project, a collaborative effort of the NEH, the Kettering Foundation, and the Federation of State Humanities Councils. Our goal was to rethink the ways whereby state councils could enliven the civic sphere with projects that brought Americans together to talk about important public issues, and to experiment with a few innovative projects in a number of states. Unfortunately, the work was cut short when the state councils were forced into a survival mode by the growing movement in Congress, after the 1994 elections, to defund the NEH and the councils. One product of our work, however, is a collections of essays that Noëlle McAfee and I edited and published in 1997,* Standing with the Public: The Humanities and Democratic Practice.

The following article, published in the Spring/Summer 1995 issue of Texas Journal of Ideas, History and Culture, *addressed one of my fundamental concerns: Was the academic community sufficiently prepared for and interested in a new model for the public humanities, a model implicit in Hackney's national conversation project and in the joint project that I was directing? After nearly twenty-five years of state council programming, it was clear that thousands of scholars across the nation were interested in and committed to public activities. A study conducted by the Modern Language Association in 1990, surveying the Association's members, discovered that one-third of its members had participated as scholars in public programs. But what was not known, and what remains unknown, is how many of America's humanities scholars are interested in the kinds of projects that seek to relate the humanities to the problems of civil society and to contemporary public issues. Unfortunately, the answer, undoubtedly, is not enough.*

Sheldon Hackney's call for a "national conversation" on pluralism and American identity poses challenges as well as opportunities for scholars in the humanities. It is, after all, the National Endowment for the *Humanities* that is sponsoring this effort, and somewhere, somehow, scholars of history, literature, philosophy, religion, political theory, and other disciplines are expected to make substantial contributions to this conversation.

The thesis of this article is that the promise of this initiative may not be realized unless the humanities community itself enthusiastically backs this effort and develops models of engagement that will successfully integrate the humanities into the proposed conversation.

What will scholars of the humanities contribute? Few would doubt the appropriateness of pluralism and American identity as a subject for humanistic scholarship. Issues of diversity and unity have been at the core of the American experience, and these issues have occupied the minds of many brilliant scholars over the years. It's not difficult to put together a bookshelf—perhaps even a bookcase—of important works on American pluralism and identity. And few would doubt the importance of making this scholarship available to the public through conferences, lectures, exhibits, and television documentaries.

But that's not what this invitation is about. Although I'm confident that the NEH would welcome proposals for new scholarship on American identity, and although I'm equally confident that state humanities councils across the country would be pleased to support first-rate public programs that would make old and new scholarship available to the public, such activities appear secondary to the national project as proposed.

Yet it would be a mistake to dismiss the contribution of scholarship to American self-understanding. There has been an ongoing conversation among Americans for well over two-hundred years on issues of pluralism and national identity, and this conversation has benefited immensely from humanistic scholarship. Although only small numbers of Americans may have had the opportunity to explore these issues at some depth in advanced college and university studies, many more have made their acquaintance in American history and literature survey courses in secondary and post-secondary education. The history of the United States cannot be adequately taught or discussed without the benefit of scholarship that informs our understanding of the dynamics of pluralism and unity in American life.

But Hackney's proposal for a national conversation extends beyond the bounds of promoting and disseminating scholarship on American identity. He has invited Americans of all backgrounds, all ages, and all locations, to study, learn, and speak face-to-face about our differences of race, ethnicity, and culture, as well as about those values that we might share. Yes, he says, the conversation should take place in schools and colleges, but also in public libraries, in museums, in church basements, and at PTA and Chamber of Commerce meetings and gatherings of civic organizations.

A sense of urgency underlies this call. Ethnic and cultural strife is on the rise world wide, and we know that the United States is not immune to the kind of social fragmentation that tears nations apart. Tension, conflict, sporadic violence, and urban terrorism already mar the American landscape, leaving legacies of failure and fear. All too often we would rather shout than talk, convince than share, demand than compromise. Even debates over school and university curricula get caught up in ideology and politics.

One of the organizations working with the NEH in promoting this national conversation is the National Issues Forums of the Kettering Foundation. In an open letter to convenors of these forums and to chairs of the state humanities councils, David Mathews, Kettering President, and Sheldon Hackney offered these questions for the national conversation: What is our image of America of the twenty-first century? Is America to become a collection of groups, whose members think of themselves first as members of an ethnic community, race, or culture and only second as Americans? Can our ideal be an America of shared values and commitment that nonetheless retains cultural differences? Can we identify those values and commitments that we need to share if we are to be a successful society? What picture of an ideal America will inform our struggles with current problems?

And, in another piece, Hackney noted:

> All of our people—left, right, and center—have a responsibility to examine and discuss what unites us as a country, what we share as common American values in a nation comprised of so many divergent groups and beliefs. For too long, we have let what divides us capture the headlines and sound bites, polarizing us rather than bringing us together. The NEH is proposing a national conversation open to all Americans, a conversation in which all voices are heard and in which we grapple seriously with the meaning of American pluralism.

In launching this conversation, something new is being asked of the humanities community. If the promotion and dissemination of scholarship has a secondary role, what is it that scholars are being asked to do? We know that they are being asked to join in the conversation, to sit at the conversation table with their fellow Americans. Yet stripped of the lectern and the overhead projector, what exactly will scholars do? How will they interact? And what unique contribution might they make to the discussion?

One would hope that each citizen who participates in this conversation would bring to the discussion his or her unique resources—personal experiences, ideas, impressions, values, knowledge. For the humanities scholar, such resources include, as historian Merrill Peterson points out, "certain ways of thinking—of inquiring, evaluating, judging, funding, and articulating meaning." The value of a reflective approach to life, says Peterson, can be best appreciated by considering the alternative: a life unilluminated by imagination, uninformed by history, unguided by reasoning. Undoubtedly, each scholar's contribution to the discussion will be unique. The historian will bring resources different from that of the philosopher or the literary critic. But if Peterson is right, that "certain ways of thinking" unite the disciplines of the humanities in common pursuit, we can be sure that the discussion will be enriched through the involvement of scholars. Framing issues, defining terms, clarifying assumptions, discovering ambiguities, exploring ethical dimensions, outlining options—such ought to form the primary contribution of those scholars who choose to participate. Through such participation, the quality of the conversation will be enhanced, and participants will be more capable of confronting diversity, overcoming prejudice and self-interest, enlarging sympathies, and finding common ground.

One would hope as well that some scholars would take the lead in organizing and moderating such discussions. Where this happens, the scholars' contribution might be more extensive; for example, as in the development of multiple discussion programs that extend over a period of time and that draw more extensively on texts, films, and other humanities resources—products of past scholarship.

There is something fresh in this invitation to scholars to participate in a national conversation on American identity. It is an invitation that asks scholars to sit with their fellow citizens, to listen, to share, to bring to the discussion their own special gifts, as is asked of all who participate. There is nothing in the scholar's academic background that has especially encouraged or prepared him or her for this role. Yet what one finds here is an image of how scholars might interact with the public on issues of importance to American society.

Hackney is not alone in wanting to discover new public roles for humanities scholars. For over a year, beginning in December 1993, a group of state humanities council representatives and scholars in the humanities met on three separate occasions at the Kettering Foundation in Dayton, Ohio to discuss ways of enhancing the role of the humanities in American public life. Recent polls documenting growing citizen cynicism and estrangement from traditional institutions of American society reinforced the belief that American civic life was in trouble, and that the state humanities councils, with more than twenty years of experience in developing and funding programs for the public, were well positioned to identify and promote models of engagement that might work to connect citizens with key public issues and to help restore commitment to those structures and institutions of democratic culture that have helped sustain American society. The humanities community bears particular responsibility, it was argued, to ensure the continuation of democratic culture and the capacity for self-government. We have seen in recent years the tremendous growth of self-help and support groups that focus on problems of the individual. What is needed now is similar growth in community groups and associations willing to work through common problems and issues, an expansion of what Robert Putnam and other scholars are calling "social capital."

The group that met at the Kettering Foundation agreed that the model to be pursued should be one that would reconceptualize the role of scholars as humanists engaged in building long-term relationships with local communities. Such a model would depart from the predominant model of public humanities programming, that of state councils providing financial support and human resources for placing scholars before public audiences at essentially one-time events—a conference, a lecture, a symposium. The dissemination of the humanities as taught and experienced in schools, colleges, and universities has been a driving force behind many public humanities activities. While this model has many strengths—it represents the extension of teaching—there are also limitations. The episodic nature of such programming lessens opportunity for forming long-term relationships between humanities scholars and local communities.

In reconceptualizing the role of the scholar, the group realized that it might be possible to draw upon a different kind of model that has been present but not always visible in programs of state councils. This model involves projects initiated and developed by communities seeking to use the resources of the humanities; for example, in community histories. This alternative model would help to ensure that programs launched would deal with issues, concerns, and interests generated from within those local communities, whether those issues, concerns, and interests be local, regional, national, or global in character.

Out of these discussions the Humanities and Public Engagement project, a collaborative endeavor of the Kettering Foundation, NEH, and the Federation of State Humanities Councils, was born. It is hoped that by September 1995 a dozen or so state humanities councils will be launching experimental projects of not less than three years duration that focus on specific communities and seek to establish ongoing relationships between scholars and those communities. After an initial period of listening closely to the community, key scholars would work cooperatively with local leadership in developing programs that respond to identified needs and interests.

Thus in regard to the interaction of scholars with the public, what Hackney anticipates happening through NEH's national conversation initiative might find further fulfillment in the Humanities and Public Engagement project. Both efforts seek to establish a sense of equality between the scholar and the public. Both emphasize the need for good listening. Both seek to reconnect the humanities with important issues of public life. And both offer models of involvement that depart from the dissemination model that has tended to dominate public activities in the humanities. But the Humanities and Public Engagement Project goes a few steps further by emphasizing the need for more sustained relationships between scholars and communities, partnerships that will help address needs and interests as identified by those communities.

These are initiatives that seek to align the work of scholars with public needs and interests. The implications of such alignment for those colleges and universities eager to provide more helpful services to the wider community should not be dismissed. In response to growing public concern over higher education, colleges and universities are now seeking new ways of demonstrating their contributions to public life and to the civic structure of American society beyond those contributions focused on economic development and the preparation of individuals for the work force. Of all the disciplines represented in American higher education, the humanities have the most to contribute to the urgent task we now face of rebuilding the nation's civic infrastructure. We should not be surprised if college and university administrators increasingly call upon humanities faculty to engage the public on critical issues facing local communities as well as the state and nation.

Community institutions and organizations that might assist with this engagement abound. In addition to more formal institutions with well-developed missions and constituencies, there are countless informal and ad hoc groups in every community that have been formed to deal with particular problems or to represent the needs of particular segments of the population. And there are various alliances that have formed with the expressed purpose of promoting public dialogue. Since 1981, the Kettering Foundation and the Public Agenda have linked up to prepare discussion booklets on policy issues for National Issues Forums. More than five thousand organizations across the country—leagues and leadership programs, churches and synagogues, high schools and colleges, libraries and adult literacy programs—hold NIF deliberations annually as part of their own local programs. NIF is a voluntary network of civic and educational organizations to promote public dialogue. The forums of this network are modern versions of America's oldest political institution, the town meeting. This year's forums have focused on immigration, values in the school curriculum, and juvenile justice. NIF provides an ideal mechanism for building relationships between institutions of higher education and communities by involving faculty in these programs.

Recognition of a heightened public role for scholars does not imply denigration of more traditional roles operative inside and outside the university. We need excellent researchers and teachers. We need to be concerned about the production of new knowledge and the dissemination of that knowledge. These traditional humanistic activities will continue. Rather, what is needed is increased recognition of the important public service that scholars in the humanities are uniquely qualified to provide and more disciplined efforts to find the most promising models of engagement with the public. Such models, when proven effective, should be fully capable of replication elsewhere. Any college or university that wishes to roll up its institutional sleeves to strengthen neighborhood schools or address local environmental problems or help communities deal constructively with the arrival of new immigrants, should be able to draw upon models that have worked well elsewhere.

A good starting point, of course, is to take seriously the invitation of Sheldon Hackney to promote and participate in the national conversation on pluralism and American identity. College and university faculty, with the enthusiastic encouragement of institutional administrators, should identify key community organizations that might sponsor these conversations and they should provide assistance to them to help ensure program success. Without this leadership from the humanities community, we may be left with a national conversation sponsored by the NEH which ironically is devoid of the humanities. And that would be a tragic loss to the humanities as well as to the nation. With this leadership, scholars will connect with the public in new and informative ways, and the public, at this critical moment in the life of the nation, might gain fresh understanding of those values and commitments that bind Americans in common pursuit.

Works Cited

Coleman, James S. "Social Capital in the Creation of Human Capital." *American Journal of Sociology* (supplement) 94 (1998).

Habermas, Jurgen. *Structural Transformation of the Public Sphere: An Inquiry into a Category of Bourgeois Society*, 1962. Reprint: Cambridge, MA: MIT Press, 1991.

Hackney, Sheldon. "Out of Many, One: Renewing the American Promise." *Texas Journal of Ideas, History and Culture* (Spring/Summer, 1995).

Mathews, David and Sheldon Hackney. "An Open Letter to the Chairs of State Humanities Councils and the Conveners of National Issues Forums." Kettering Foundation, 1994.

Peterson, Merrill D. *The Humanities and the American Promise.* Austin: Texas Council for the Humanities, 1987.

Putnam, Robert D. "Bowling Alone." *Journal of Democracy* (January 1995).

Veninga, James F. and Noëlle McAfee. *Standing with the Public: The Humanities and Democratic Practice.* Dayton: Kettering Foundation Press, 1997.

Humanities Councils and the Current Crisis of Democracy

The following remarks were given at a session on "The Common Good" at the September 1995 National Humanities Conference sponsored by the Federation of State Humanities Councils. Reflecting on what had been learned through The Humanities and Public Engagement project, I suggested that we now had a "special obligation and a special opportunity" to bring vitally important resources to American public life.

The TCH, with its long-standing interest in contemporary public issues, had approved in late 1995 several new initiatives that would seek to further civic conversation through small-scale projects in Texas communities. Among five new "packaged programs," the TCH included three that focused on pressing concerns and that included materials for reading and discussion programs, one on "American Identity," the second on "American Pluralism," and the third on topics covered by the National Issues Forums of the Kettering Foundation. These programs would be incorporated into the TCH program in 1997, although on a smaller scale than originally envisioned. These programs should be seen from the larger perspective of state council work: weaving the humanities into the civic life of the nation. There is room for traditional activities, such as TCH's Speakers Bureau, in which scholars share topics of interest

*with public audiences, as well as those that seek to further public delib-
eration on specific contemporary public issues.*

*The 1995 national conference, like the 1994 conference held in San
Antonio immediately following the mid-term elections, was preoccupied
with survival, with finding the most constructive ways to respond to the
proposals from the Republican leadership in Congress to eliminate all
funding for NEH and NEA. While working hard to make the case for
continued support, it was important that the TCH move forward in carrying out its mission, building on a remarkable record that now spanned
twenty-five years. And that it did.*

To even raise the question "What happened to the common good?"
is to align one's self with a growing number of observers of contemporary American society who believe that American democracy is in trouble.
We are unable, so it seems, to unite in common cause to address issues
and to solve problems both local and national in scope.

Common good talk is, of course, academic talk. For most Americans, the questions are even more direct and perhaps even more challenging than "What happened to the common good? Why are we failing
our children? Why are we working more and earning less? Why can't
we feel safe in our own homes? Why are we killing each other? Why
does racism still abound? Where's our moral compass? Why is there so
much greed in high places? Why are doors of opportunity closing to so
many of us?"

My task is to offer some thoughts on what connections—if any—
there might be between the work of state humanities councils—and the
current crisis in American democracy. My thoughts are sketchy; what
follows should be thought of as a preliminary treatment of an important
matter that deserves much fuller analysis, for the state humanities councils, like NEH itself, were created by the Congress to strengthen democracy. How well we have measured up to this expectation, how well we
have succeeded in shoring up the practice of democracy in the midst of
powerful forces that undermine it, and how and where we may have
fallen short, are matters that demand our attention.

The Absence of the Common Good

A recent book by historian Robert Wiebe, *Self-Rule: A Cultural History of American Democracy,* provides us with a point of embarkation.

Wiebe sees democracy in decline, and he groups the growing number of serious issues facing democracy as identified by many other writers around three broad topics: issues having to do with (a) polarization, (b) citizen participation, and (c) individualism—issues that emerged with particular force beginning in the 1960s.

Scholars and other writers interested in these topics have offered much evidence to support the idea that our society is increasingly polarized along racial, ethnic, economic, ideological, and cultural lines; that too many citizens are disengaged from public life, indifferent to politics, and ill-equipped to participate in democratic governance; and that individualism, that bedrock of American democratic life, has turned against itself, as we fail to recognize that individual rights must be linked to community processes and to the common good. Scholars and others who have identified and explored these issues have also proposed many solutions. How to bring Americans together again, how to increase citizen participation, and how to strengthen community, have been important themes in some recent American philosophical and political writing, and have also been the focus of some specific political and social initiatives, many of which hold promise.

But Wiebe believes that however impressive this work has been and however important proposed solutions might be, the analyses and the solutions suffer from a lack of historical perspective, for these contemporary challenges to democracy are deeply imbedded in major social transformations that occurred between the 1890s and the 1920s and that generated "the two great constraints on modern democracy—centralization and hierarchy." The lack of this historical perspective has kept us from seeing how these two major constraints have gradually eroded our capacity to ensure what he calls "the twin mandates for democratic participation—popular access to the governing process and a responsive governing system." The first step toward a revitalized democracy, Wiebe maintains, "is a relentless attack on those primary constraints."

Thus Wiebe joins those who argue that the time has come for a radical decentralization of power. He suggests that a metaphor and a model of such decentralization can be found in the "devolution of mainframe computing centers into networks of small, adjustable work stations." The true democrat "pulls down the large structures so that ordinary citizens can move in and participate," not in traditional hierarchies but in truly interactive structures. Citizens have a chance of achieving, he says, Benjamin Barber's definition of democracy, "a form of government in which all of the people govern themselves in at least some public matters at least some of the time.'" This is no small undertaking, for "major changes in democracy rise only out of systemic breakdowns." Small adjustments, tinkering with the prevailing systems here and there, won't cut it.

In a revitalized democracy, politics will reflect "what happens to people day by day," and such a politics will "expand the number of citizens who initiate and monitor, who raise the new issues and keep the old ones from getting lost. As it joins citizens in common causes, this kind of politics even makes human connections among people who have never seen or spoken with one another."

The key to revitalizing democracy is the dramatic expansion of public space and public dialogue. In the public sphere, as citizen concerns, issues, and interests are dealt with, the two great constraints placed on democracy, centralization and hierarchy, are consciously countered. The values, policies, and practices of public and private sectors are open for scrutiny. Established political parties, which all too often reflect the values of hierarchy and centralization, are countered. "What the democrat seeks," he says, "is a reaffirmation of the American heritage that draws people with all kinds of identities and loyalties into a collective self-governing process." Countless publics are created, and, taken as a whole, "a national gathering of these participating publics creates an exhilarating prospect: citizens divided by race and nationality, sex and sexual preference, social class and physical condition, sundry goods and many lifestyles, contributing equally to decisions that some win, others lose, but all accept as a fact of life. It is a civic affair."

State Councils and the Crisis of Democracy

For some, Wiebe's position might seem too extreme. But consider the alternative, the divorce of more and more citizens from politics, angry citizens at that; the dilemma of a society increasingly polarized; a society where individualism has degenerated into crude self-interest; and the continued presence of powerful centralized bureaucracies and impenetrable and far-reaching hierarchies, both taking power away from the people.

Perhaps we can agree on this basic point: The future of American democracy, of our ability to find and nurture those avenues that lead to the common good, will depend upon the dramatic expansion of public space at the grass roots, on a new form of citizen involvement in the affairs of their communities and of the nation, and in the claiming of values that counter the deadly weight of centralized power and the exercise of that power through hierarchical, non-democratic structures.

If there is agreement on this point, we can then ask the question: Where do state humanities councils stand in regard to the present unraveling of American democracy and to those efforts now underway to revitalize citizenship and the practice of democracy? What have we done to deal with the challenges of polarization, citizen alienation, and unrestrained individualism? And to what extent does our work counter those powerful constraints on modern democracy that sap the public of its strength and rob it of its potential?

These are powerful questions. And to these there are more. To what extent have we avoided the problems of contemporary democracy? To what extent have we unknowingly contributed to those problems? To what extent and in what ways have we sought to counter those problems?

The starting point in answering these questions must surely lie in the special relationship that state humanities councils have to the federal government. The insistence by the Congress that there be a significant measure of decentralization in the NEH, that a portion of program support be given directly to not-for-profit citizen councils in each of the states, provides a powerful incentive to think creatively about how scarce resources can best be used on behalf of local communities, free from the usual strings tied to federal agencies and federal funding.

But we can begin to answer these questions as well by studying the relationship of state councils to the public sphere, to all those public places in which the humanities councils have a presence. If there has been a decline in such space in the past several decades, as Robert Putnam and other scholars maintain, with the consequence that opportunities for serious public conversation have dwindled, one can only conclude that without state councils, the amount of such space and the quality of dialogue that occurs therein, would be all the more limited. If there is one contribution that state councils have made to American democracy during the past twenty-five years, surely it is this—the expansion of public opportunities whereby citizens have an opportunity to meet and learn. We have worked closely with cultural and educational institutions to help them expand programs for the public, and we have often, on our own and with others, created entirely new spaces for public programs.

Yet we must ask: Who, representing what interests, creates these public spaces? Who occupies them once created? And what happens in them? More importantly, what do we want to happen in them? To what extent might these programs perpetuate rather than counter the two great constraints on modern democracy noted by Wiebe? To what extent are we encouraging programs that take on the critical issues of our time, including issues related to the polarization of our society, to the rule of self-interest, and to the disengagement of citizens from politics? Are we institutions that preserve the status quo or institutions that seek fundamental change? If we seek change, what kind of change are we promoting? Are we effective subverters of centralization and hierarchy on behalf of a revitalized American democracy, or are we extensions of existing centers of power and their hierarchies?

We can find answers to some of these questions by looking at the projects supported by state councils. If one thinks of reading and discussion programs in local public libraries, of community-based projects that collect oral histories to weave new community histories, of public issues programs sponsored by civic organizations, of projects where scholars spend time in housing projects, of efforts to document and discuss untold ethnic histories and cultures, the answer seems quite clear—we are undergirders of the public sphere and we are expanding public spaces for public dialogue, bringing citizens together to talk about their lives and those issues that matter to them. But other projects and programs may be less clear, and there are reasons why this is so.

We have often tied our existence to that provocative preamble to the founding legislation for NEA and NEH, that democracy demands wisdom and vision in its citizens. Perhaps too often, we have allowed the authority of the humanities to define what this statement means. In our quest for leadership roles, especially during the 1980s, there was a tendency to see ourselves as important institutions of what Lynne Cheney called "the parallel school," as a continuing education program in the humanities for adult citizens, offering to citizens in innovative and highly visible ways the very best in the humanistic tradition. A top-down model emerged, a model that seems to be based on the premise that there is a body of knowledge that citizens need to know, and that state councils are well-positioned to deliver in exciting ways that knowledge. Of course this model, which does have a legitimate place in our work, often seemed to exist in uneasy relationship with the kind of grass roots, activist, citizen and civic-centered model noted above, and although we kept this latter kind of public programming alive, incentives encouraged extensive focus on the top-down, dissemination model.

We should not be surprised by the pull of this model, for many humanists, like their colleagues in the sciences, have become increasingly professionalized, persons of expertise, persons whose specialized bodies of knowledge often seem separated from the knowledge, concerns, and interests of average people, especially if efforts are not made to bridge these arenas. Thus we in the public humanities often have focused our attention on the transmission of knowledge, on what various disciplines might contribute to public life, rather than on what we might learn from the public, and, more importantly, on what we might learn together. The central question is this: Are we creating public spaces to impart bodies of knowledge or are we creating public spaces to do something very different?

Civic Engagement

These concerns lie behind the formation of The Humanities and Public Engagement project in which I have been involved this past year. This initiative, which has sought to encourage opportunities for more citizen-based and citizen-planned programming, developed out of a series of meetings of scholars and state council and NEH representatives at the Kettering Foundation. This group concluded that, while councils have experimented with much success with very diverse forms of engaging citizens, the predominant model has been that of providing financial support and human resources for placing scholars before public audiences. The dissemination of the humanities as taught and experienced in more formal educational settings has been, as noted above, a driving force behind many council projects and activities. While recognizing the strengths of this model, the group recognized its limitations; for example:

• Programs sponsored by traditional and well-established institutions may not always focus on what the broad public is hungry to understand.

• The emphasis of such programs may lead us to missed opportunities to deal with pressing issues that ordinary Americans are talking about.

• Such programs tend to neglect the intellectual resources and indigenous insights communities provide into both the myriad problems and the myriad solutions.

• Sometimes the episodic nature of the programming provided by the model—a one-time lecture, a one-day conference, a two-day symposium—lessens the prospect for forming long term relationships between the humanities community and grass-roots community organizations.

• Such a model may further rather than counter the fragmentation of the scholarly community into self-contained disciplines and specialties, thus preventing public programming from helping to renew the humanities themselves.

A different kind of model, present but less common, can be found in those projects which have used the assistance provided by state councils to address local interests and needs and in reaching those citizens most cut off or alienated from traditional educational, cultural and other centers of power. Building on this past experience, this engagement model, if fully developed, would seek to:

• Re-conceptualize the role of humanities scholars as humanists engaged in building long-term relationships with local communities, with scholars experiencing a relationship of equality with participating citizens;

• Help ensure that programs undertaken would deal with issues, concerns, and interests generated from within those local communities, whether those issues, concerns, and interests be local, regional, national, or global in character;

• Help connect these communities with other kinds of resources that might be helpful, such as resources provided by the media and local philanthropic interests; and

• Provide the capacity to help with the renewal of the humanities in post-secondary settings.

This model seeks to take seriously the challenges confronting American democracy, and it seeks to use the public spaces created to give expression to the deepest concerns of the American public. As such, it proposes a realignment of the public humanities scholar with the public, offering new forms of collaboration. It puts emphasis on the listening and collaborating roles of the scholar. It recognizes that the polarization that exists in America and that threatens democracy can include, and now often does, a division between scholars and the public. Recent national controversies involving the humanities, especially the unfortunate episodes surrounding the National History Standards project and the Enola Gay exhibition, have resulted in further divisions between the scholarly community and various segments of the public. Scholars are portrayed as wild-eyed revisionists; public critics are seen as promoters of patriotically-correct history and culture.

The philosophical premise behind this engagement model is that the ways of knowing common to the enterprise of the humanities and the ways of knowing common to the public in its quest for insight and understanding, are not all that different and, in fact, may be the same. Historian Merrill Peterson reminds us that "Wherever human beings remember, think, interpret, analyze; wherever they deal seriously with each other's conduct; wherever they try to understand life's meaning, giving to life that examining without which it was long ago said to be not worth living—there we see the fundamentally human impulse from which the humanities spring." To be sure, scholar and layperson alike bring to the public square his or her own unique voice, the fruits of each person's own journey. What the scholar brings to the public dialogue—the historical antecedent, the powerful literary reference, the penetrating question, the forgotten citizen, the moral dilemma, the wisdom of a folktale—provide content, in the same way that personal experience, personal knowledge, and personal judgments provide content for civic conversation. The creation of a public voice, the formation of public sentiments and public wisdom, thus emerges out of a form of reflection that is known by citizens and scholars alike.

Laboratories for a Revitalized Democracy

In proposing that more attention be given to this model of engagement, I am not suggesting that we abandon more traditional formats that have worked so well in infusing the humanities into American public life, formats that enhance the public sphere even if they don't engage citizens in discussions of issues with which they may wrestle day in and day out. This form of public programming, like classes in the humanities in educational institutions, is worthy in and of itself and critically important to the development of educated citizens, to the preservation of collective memory, to the expansion of imagination, and to the furtherance of democratic life. It's not an either/or situation. The philosopher Charles Frankel once wrote that "What keeps the humanities going is that people really want to know, does man have free will; that people really respond to Hamlet's predicament and to his eloquence; that people really would like to get some sense of how the past held together and why it fell apart. All of these are permanent . . . impulses in any civilized society." Given this thirst for knowledge, and given the importance of humanistic study to the development of thoughtful citizens, perhaps one of our greatest tasks in the coming years will be to see how these two models of public programming might be pulled together in some sort of new and exciting synthesis.

What I do want to propose, however, is that in response to the growing crisis of contemporary democracy, we have an obligation and an opportunity to use more of our resources to bring something very special and very needed to the public spaces that we are helping to create and sustain, to use the humanities as sources for public knowing, for finding solutions to the pressing problems of a polarized and divided society, a society in which many people find themselves alienated, losing confidence in the institutions that have shaped our social, political, and cultural landscape, a society in which the potential for finding the common good lessens as self-interest mushrooms.

Perhaps we need to ask the question, over and over, "How might this project, this program, this initiative contribute to a revitalized democracy?" Building upon our past successes in promoting and sponsoring civic engagement projects, in programs that bring citizens together to talk about their issues, concerns, and interests, perhaps we can expand our efforts to promote public spaces where the public can do its work. Wiebe calls this a form of "guerrilla politics," and local groups, with agendas set by them, can spread outward to encompass wider and wider networks through the connectedness that dialogue and political involvement encourages. If scholars are important participants in this dialogue, we might be setting the stage for the infusion of the humanities in an energized, vibrant democracy.

The risks of this enterprise are innumerable. If we take seriously the two great constraints on modern democracy noted by Wiebe—centralized power and hierarchies that freeze people out—we may encounter forces hostile to us. We may find that our fund-raising plans need rethinking, for money all too often sets agendas for discussions, and in this model of civic engagement, no one sets the public agendas but the various publics themselves. We may find ourselves at odds with the political parties, for those parties often forget that popular government "works up from [the] publics, not down to them." We may find ourselves criticized by those scholars who believe that the humanities have no business helping to form publics, helping to give expression to many voices, scholars who see citizens as students in need of instruction, those who would see state councils as institutions of the parallel school rather than as unique laboratories for democratic renewal. As Wiebe points out, guerrilla politics means, among other things, pulling away from centers of power, whether they be in legislative bodies, large bureaucracies, or universities, and pulling down hierarchies, so that the people can speak.

But if the risks are innumerable, so are the potential benefits. American democracy is being tested in new and unprecedented ways, and if state councils can play a vital role in democratic renewal, the confidence placed in us by the Congress and the American people will have been well rewarded. And in the meantime, we may be doing something that holds special relevance to the survival and future development of the humanities themselves.

Recent developments at the NEH seem to provide support for taking this engagement model more seriously than we have. Chairman

Hackney's decision to abolish the Division of State Programs in order to make room for an Office of Federal-State Partnership, recognizes the value of decentralization, and affords an opportunity to develop a new kind of relationship between the federal government and state humanities councils, a relationship that further legitimates our own efforts to promote collaborations among equal partners. And the National Conversation initiative, which encourages citizen-based and citizen-controlled public dialogue in public spaces across the nation, parallels what this civic engagement model is after.

The pursuit of the common good does not begin in the Congress, in corporate board rooms, in government agencies, or in any other powerful, centralized base. Rather, it begins in our neighborhoods, villages, towns, and cities and in public places not defined by geography, ethnicity, religion or any other barrier. It begins where people gather, and where people gather to pursue the public's business, that's where the humanities are and that's where we need to be.

Works Cited

Cheney, Lynne V. *The Humanities in America: A Report to the President, the Congress, and the American People*. National Endowment for the Humanities, 1988.

Frankel, Charles. "Why the Humanities?" in *The Humanist as Citizen*, John Agressto and Peter Riesenberg, eds. Chapel Hill: National Humanities Center, 1981.

Peterson, Merrill. *The Humanities and the American Promise*. Austin: Texas Council for the Humanities, 1987.

Putnam, Robert D. "Bowling Alone: America's Declining Social Capital." *Journal of Democracy* (January 1995).

Wiebe, Robert. *Self Rule: A Cultural History of American Democracy*. Chicago: The University of Chicago Press, 1995.

Part Two

Education

1983

Improving our Public Schools: The Role of the University

The TCH board of directors recognized in the early 1980s that, although the council's primary responsibility was to the general public, supporting programs for adult learners and enriching the civic life of the state, it could provide an important voice for improving elementary and secondary education. No other statewide organization had as its primary purpose the promotion of the humanities, and if the Council's goal was to foster citizen appreciation for the humanities, it made sense to pay more attention to the status of the study of history, literature, foreign languages, government, and other humanities-related courses in the public schools of Texas. Today's students would be tomorrow's adult learners.

TCH established in 1981 a Task Force on the Humanities in the Public Schools of Texas, comprised of several board directors, several school teachers and administrators, several university faculty members involved in elementary and secondary education, a state representative, a member of the Texas Association of School Boards, and a representative of the corporate community. It was chaired by civic leader Betty Anderson of Lubbock. The task force was assigned the responsibility of reviewing the existing curriculum and making recommendations on the future public school curriculum. Detailed analysis was made of the existing curricula in six school districts: Austin, Athens, Junction, Midland, Rio Grande City, and Houston.

The task force's goal was to build on important changes taking place in public education. The Texas Legislature, in the Spring of 1981, passed House Bill 246, amending the Texas Education Code's section on curriculum, requiring every school district to offer a well-balanced curriculum, with the State Board of Education designating the essential elements of each subject and developing optional subjects as appropriate for the various districts.

The report that I drafted for the task force, Toward Thoughtful, Active Citizens: Improving the Public School Curriculum, *provided eleven specific recommendations for improving public education and the teaching of humanities subjects. One recommendation called upon colleges and universities in Texas to strengthen entrance requirements, since those requirements weighed heavily on the curriculum taught in our public schools. We recommended that colleges and universities move toward requiring more substantial work in academic fields for entrance into post-secondary institutions.*

The following article, published in the Spring 1983 issue of Texas Academe, *the journal of the Texas Conference of the American Association of University Professors, addressed the matter of what universities might do to improve public education and to enhance the public school curriculum.*

Professor Alan Bloom of the University of Chicago says in a recent essay that a young person of today "does not generally go off to the university with the expectation of having an intellectual adventure, of discovering strange new worlds, of finding out what the comprehensive truth about man is." In analyzing this predicament, Bloom places primary blame on "listless" universities. A more common view, however, is that the source of the problem lies in inferior public schooling. It is argued that, despite twelve years of public education, many students arrive on the university campus with inadequate language skills, scant knowledge of our culture and history, blunted analytic capacities, and underdeveloped imaginations. Indeed, many university administrators and teachers have concluded that the public schools are failing in their task to prepare students adequately for either productive vocations or further study at the university level.

Unfortunately, most analyses of the problem focus on either the state of the university or that of the public school; we frequently fail to see the educational enterprise in its totality, ignoring the symbiotic relationship between public and higher education. It is no wonder, then, that efforts to improve university and public school curricula are frequently carried out without the benefit of collaboration. In Texas, this collaboration is long overdue. A report to be released soon by the Carnegie Foundation for the Advancement of Teaching, *School and College: Partnerships in Education*, offers recommendations for collaboration.

As we seek to foster a new partnership between higher education and public education, between the local university and the local school district, we must recognize special as well as common problems. Above all, however, we must recognize the impact of one system on the other, of one curriculum on the other.

The Public School

The public seems to support the view of many university teachers that far too many students receive inadequate schooling. A 1981 Gallup Poll of the public's attitudes toward our schools documents concern. People interviewed were asked the question:

Students are often given the grades of A, B, C, D, or Fail to denote the quality of their work. Suppose the public schools themselves, in this community, were graded in the same way. What grade would you give the public schools here—A, B, C, D, or Fail?

The findings are not surprising: A rating, 9%; B, 27%; C, 34%; D, 13%; Fail, 7%; Don't know, 10%. Although it can be argued that two-thirds of those polled give their public schools a C or higher rating, a figure which indicates a continuing reservoir of support, the public schools are under pressure today to encourage discipline, to increase educational standards, to improve the curriculum. Only through such efforts, it is argued, can we reverse a seventeen-year decline in national results on the Scholastic Aptitude Test, taken annually by more than one million college-bound seniors.

An analysis of the public school curriculum lends support to those university teachers who contend that their freshmen students are inadequately prepared for college studies. The Texas Council for the Humanities appointed in 1981 a task force to review the public school curriculum in Texas. The task force's report, *Toward Thoughtful, Active Citizens: Improving the Public School Curriculum* (1982), offered specific recommendations to strengthen the curriculum.

The report maintains that curriculum reform must be based on a deeper understanding of the purposes of public education and the role of the curriculum. The task force endorsed the notion,. as found in the Texas Legislature's Curriculum Act of 1981, that the purpose of the curriculum is to "prepare thoughtful, active citizens," but offers an interpretation of what this mission means. The curriculum should lead to the education of citizens who 1) understand the relationship between the individual, government, and society; 2) contribute to our society and culture; 3) understand and appreciate democratic values, including concepts such as freedom and civic responsibility; 4) understand and appreciate our state and national heritage; and 5) have a grasp of world affairs and those conditions and issues that will confront citizens of the twenty-first century.

Pursuant to the 1981 legislation, a revised state curriculum is now being formed by the State Board of Education. With that in mind, the task force offers specific suggestions for improving the curriculum, emphasizing 1) an earlier attainment of basic communication skills; 2) an increase in the number of units required for graduation from high school; 3) an increase in the number of units required in humanities subjects; 4) the availability of advanced courses in English and Social Studies; 5) the availability of at least three years of study in a second language; and 6) the opportunity to study the fine arts. By increasing the number of units required for graduation, by increasing the basic requirements in the liberal arts, and by ensuring that every school district make available a minimum number of electives in the humanities and social studies as well as the sciences and mathematics, the task force believes that there can be marked improvement in the education of our students.

These recommendations are designed, in part, to better prepare students for university studies. Especially, we need to ensure solid courses in the senior year for the university-bound student. By increasing the number of units required for graduation, the public schools would have additional reasons to encourage high school seniors to take advanced courses in English, history, cultural studies, science, mathematics—studies that will increase knowledge, foster reading and writing skills, stimulate imagination, and enhance analytic abilities.

For those who wish to improve the public school curriculum, now is the time to act. The Curriculum Act of 1981 provides the broad framework for the future curriculum by listing twelve general subjects that must be included in the instruction of all school districts offering kindergarten through grade twelve. The State Board of Education is obligated to identify the "essential" elements of these subjects and must make available instructional plans and program standards. The legislation helps overcome a fragmented and diluted curriculum within the public schools of Texas, but the critical matter—that of identifying the content of the curriculum—is now before the State Board of Education. Hearings have been and will continue to be conducted throughout the state in order to assist the Board in its decisions. The new law will be on its way to full implementation by 1984. All citizens, but especially university administrators and faculty members, have an opportunity to strengthen the curriculum. What should the university expect a freshman to understand about United States history? How many United States history courses should be required in high school, and at what levels should they be taught? What elective courses in United States history should be available in the senior year? Similar questions can be asked about other fields, including world history, mathematics, the sciences, the arts, and English. These questions should be discussed by university faculty members at departmental meetings. Members of the State Board of Education and officials of the Texas Education Agency should be informed of positions held.

What if these efforts proved to be successful? Contemplate, if you will, this fanciful possibility. A few years from now, a university history teacher hands out a syllabus on the first day of class of his Western Civilization course for freshmen. Immediately he is under good-natured attack from his students for leaving out this or that person, movement, or book. Why Plato but not Thucydides? Why the Protestant Reformation but not the Counter Reformation? Full of curiosity, skilled in analysis, comfortable in discussion, these freshmen are prepared for college studies.

The university community, overwhelmed by the turn of events, overhauls the curriculum. The remedial reading program is downgraded from a full-fledged component of the English Department to an evening course for a handful of students (a few teachers are retrained to teach literature); the freshman composition program is reworked to include more difficult assignments; senior faculty members beg for the opportunity to teach United States and Western Civilization survey courses; the remedial mathematics program is dropped from the curriculum; more courses are offered in second-year than first-year French, German, and Spanish; sophomore literature courses are redesigned so that more time is spent on Shelley and less time on Woody Allen.

The University

Before we get carried away with this dream, before we offer advice on the improvement of the public school curriculum, we would do well to take a more comprehensive look at the educational enterprise, at the health of the university teaching profession, and, indeed, at the impact of the current university curriculum on the public school curriculum.

Alan Booth contends that "the university (of today) has no vision, no view of what a human being must know in order to be considered educated." As we seek to improve the public school curriculum, we must recognize and understand those challenges now facing the university and how these challenges relate to the status of public school education.

(1) University Entrance and Exit Requirements

Universities need to reevaluate both entrance and exit requirements. Entrance requirements bear directly on the public school curriculum. If administrators and teachers in institutions of higher education wish to see improvements in the public school curriculum, they would do well to review their own entrance requirements and to raise standards as much as possible. For example, if study in a foreign language is not required for entrance into the university, school districts will probably place low priority on such instruction. The same holds true with other fields, including history and English. The more that is required in terms of substantial work completed in academic fields for entrance into the university, the greater the probability of school districts increasing their high school graduation requirements.

In addition, periodic review of what should be required for graduation from the university—beyond credits and courses—is necessary. Faculty members and administrators need to move toward common agreement on what should be expected of the student in terms of knowledge gained and analytic abilities acquired. What should be expected of a person receiving a bachelor's degree? We need the vision of an educated person that Alan Booth says is now missing from the university. Through this vision, universities can better define entrance and exit requirements on the basis of a sound philosophy of education, and this philosophy, in turn, can influence greatly the quality of secondary-education.

(2) The University Curriculum

Many universities are now engaged in serious efforts to reassess educational goals and to strengthen their curriculum. Numerous challenges will have to be met; four problems are especially perplexing and worthy of ongoing consideration.

First, as Robert Nisbett and other writers have pointed out, the curriculum has been marked by the expansion of secondary and even trivial courses, especially in the humanities and the social sciences, and interdisciplinary studies that too frequently lack a foundation in the disciplines.

Second, universities have given in to, rather than resisted, the "two cultures" phenomenon, with the result that there has been a further decline in the unity of knowledge and the further separation of science and the humanities, especially in our ability to see science *as* culture.

Third, the curriculum has suffered from the increasing specialization of our teachers, by the loss of interest in teaching freshman and sophomore survey courses, by single-minded interest in teaching narrow subjects and topics, by scholarly activities that too often are directed only toward a small group of peers with similar interests.

Fourth, the curriculum has suffered from our inability to understand the relationship between career education and the liberal arts. Edwin J. Delattie, President of St. Johns College, wrote recently that "it is through the liberal arts that a person gains the chance to learn what a career is," and without the liberal arts, students are taught that a career is nothing more than "a succession of jobs" in which success is determined "by rate of promotion and rate of income." Career education and the liberal arts have gone separate ways with the consequence that the liberal arts appear to be less useful in the preparation of a career than specific professionally-oriented university programs.

(3) The Professionalization of the Teaching Profession

In pursuit of the goal to improve public education, we must ask the fundamental question: Who teaches the teachers? The teaching profession became increasingly professionalized as schools of education assumed primary responsibility for the preparation of future public school instructors. While educational theory, history, practice, and technique must be known, future teachers should be required to focus their studies in their academic disciplines. They need to be trained as biologists, as historians, as students of literature, as mathematicians. Academic departments in our universities need to claim these students, to resist the trend toward seeing public school teachers as being primarily the products of schools of education. School teachers must be well prepared and competent in their respective academic fields, and that competence should be recognized and affirmed.

(4) A Fragmented Profession

Too often future public school teachers are not only "unclaimed" by academic departments, but once they leave the university campus, they frequently find themselves cut off from their counterparts in the disciplines within the university. The professional societies—American Historical Association, Modern Language Association, American Studies Association, American Academy of Religion, and others—have made only modest progress in recent years in soliciting the interest and involvement of public school teachers. Worse, there is little contact at the local level between the university and the public school.

There are numerous possibilities for cooperation. University departments can maintain contact with their graduates who become teachers. Departments can encourage local teachers to undertake study at the master's degree level. Departments can implement occasional workshops and seminars that bring together the university and public school teachers. University faculty members can participate in co-curricular activities of high schools, including history, philosophy, literature, and language clubs, as well as writing contests and other programs launched to improve the role of the liberal arts in the secondary school. Occasional workshops could be conducted on new books and teaching resources. Efforts such as these might contribute substantially to furthering mutual interests, thereby reducing discriminatory attitudes that often exist between the two groups.

Collaboration

To improve the public school curriculum and further the education of our children, the entire educational system must face some critical challenges. We need a substantive, comprehensive policy toward education. We need to review our educational goals from kindergarten to the bachelor's degree (and beyond), establishing benchmarks all along the way so that students progress, within a consistent framework, in fundamental skills and knowledge. That total curriculum should reflect a deeper understanding of what makes a person educated. It falls upon the university to set the ultimate standards.

We must overcome any artificial and self-protective barriers that may have contributed to our present educational challenges. Faculty members in the sciences and liberal arts and those in schools of education need to form a new partnership. University teachers and their associates in the public schools need to form a new spirit of collegiality and cooperation. Public schools need to solicit the involvement and interest of universities, especially individual departments, in co-curricular activities and special programs that can enhance the teaching profession at all levels. University faculty members need to reach out to their colleagues in the public schools. The more we recognize that we are all engaged in a common pursuit—the cultivation of the human mind and spirit—the better chance we have that these barriers will fall and that one day, perhaps, our "fanciful possibility" might be reality.

Works Cited

Bloom, Alan. "Our Listless Universities," *National Review,* December 10, 1982.

Deleattie, Edwin J. "Real Career Education Comes from the Liberal Arts," *The Chronicle of Higher Education,* January 5, 1983.

Maeroff, Gene I. *School and College: Partnership in Education.* Princeton: Carnegie Foundation for the Advancement of Teaching, 1983.

Nisbet, Robert. *Prejudices: A Philosophical Dictionary.* Cambridge: Harvard University Press, 1982.

Toward Thoughtful, Active Citizens: Improving the Public School Curriculum. Austin: Texas Council for the Humanities, 1982.

Texas: The End of Laissez Faire Education

The following essay focuses on Texas at a unique moment in its history. The old Texas, with a rural, frontier orientation and a cattle and oil-based economy, was finally giving way to the new Texas, an urban state with a diversified economy that emphasized high technology. Political, corporate, and civic leaders realized that to complete this change, vast improvements were needed in the state's educational system. The essay chronicled the change underway and offered thoughts on the potential benefits and risks.

The essay was published in the September-October 1984 issue of The Texas Humanist, *TCH's public humanities magazine. The magazine was renamed* Texas Journal of Ideas, History and Culture *in 1986, and published biannually.*

◆ ◆ ◆

In a recent essay on the history of education in Texas, historian James Smallwood claims that "from the early Spanish era down to the 1980s, the story of education, allowing for occasional setbacks, has been one of great strides forward . . ." He ends his article, published in the collection of essays *Texas: A Sesquicentennial Celebration,* by saying that "The Spaniards would have marveled to see one of the best educational networks—from primary grades to graduate schools—in the United States."

Compare Smallwood's optimistic analysis with an announcement made by the Texas Education Agency on July 13, 1984, concerning the results of the first pre-professional skills test given primarily to sophomore college students who wish to be enrolled in schools of education to become future teachers of the children of Texas. The students had to earn passing scores in math, reading, and writing. Of the 2,738 students who took the test at fifty-one of the sixty-five teacher training institutions in the state, forty-six percent failed. Worse, only ten percent of the blacks and nineteen percent of the Hispanics who took the test passed, compared to sixty-two percent of the Anglos.

Education officials with the TEA called the results "depressing." Disastrous might be a better word. The results of this test, like many other achievement tests given to students and teachers alike, point to a fundamentally troubled public education system. "I don't blame the students per se," said Education Commissioner Raymond Bynum. "After all, they graduated from a high school and passed some college English and math courses. I don't know who's to blame."

A look at the history of education in Texas substantiates Bynum's reluctance to blame any single interest: educators, students, local government, colleges and universities, or state government. Texas's educational crisis is the product of one hundred and fifty years of laissez faire public education. Texas education has been, until now, a matter of low priority; most Texans have been indifferent to the quality of instruction in their schools.

That is not to say that there have been no high moments, times when a few leaders pushed for educational improvement. Take, for instance, the educational reforms under Governor E. J. Davis and the Radical Republicans in the era of Reconstruction. A strong, centralized public school system directed by a state superintendent of public instruction and adequately financed through taxation, was central to the Radical Constitution of 1869. In documenting this development, Smallwood notes: "In September 1871 public free schools opened at a time when Texas had 229,568 youngsters in its scholastic population. By the end of the year, 1,324 schools had opened, and 63,504 students had enrolled. The next academic term (1872–1873) saw enrollment explode, with 129,542 children attending."

But the reforms of the Radical Republicans did not last long. Texans were hostile to the progress that had been made in developing schools for black children, to the centralized nature of the system, to the power of the state superintendent, and perhaps most telling of all, to the taxes that were imposed to support the system. White Texans claimed that it was "an injustice to use forced taxation to compel one person to educate the children of someone else," Smallwood writes. Once the Democrats overthrew the Radical Republicans in 1873, the educational reforms went out the window. The Constitution of 1875 established the basic characteristics of public education that lasted until the 1980s, including primary control granted to local governmental bodies, inequity in the financing of education, and a loss of coordination between schools of higher education and the public schools.

Yet there has been some progress in the past one-hundred years. The progressive movement in the early part of this century had its benefits in Texas: the consolidation of school districts, the passing of compulsory education laws, some equalizing of educational opportunities in rural and urban areas, free textbooks, and modest taxation programs. And in 1949 Representative Claude Gilmer and State Senator A. M. Aiken combined their educational interests to pass a series of bills in the Texas legislature that resulted in needed improvements—an elective state board of education that would appoint a commissioner of education, a state agency (Texas Education Agency) that would head the public school system, and "minimum foundations" in instruction to help ensure basic literacy and citizenship. For over three decades, the legislation of 1949 remained virtually intact, with little further progress made to enhance public education in Texas.

By 1980, the results of laissez faire were known. Despite the high moments in the history of education in Texas, our public school system was a failure. Many students were still graduating from high school as functional illiterates. Many teachers could not pass basic skills tests. Affluent urban school districts offered courses and programs unimaginable to the administrators of rural schools and impoverished communities. Student achievement scores lagged behind national averages. Per capita expenditure for education was a disgrace. Foreign languages had been dropped from many school curricula. United States history was taught by football coaches who had the first and second periods free. And the world was changing.

✦

It is impossible to understand the desperate plight of public education in Texas without a deeper look at the history, culture, and politics of the state. Until the last decade or so, Texas had been dominated by rural values and a frontier ethic. The Texas frontier fostered a form of rugged individualism that blessed entrepreneurs and oppressed minorities and the impoverished. In this land of untold dreams and opportunities, proof of worth rested in tangible, economic accomplishments: in acquisition, in ownership, in conquest of land and people.

Every society has its institutions that reinforce morality, prevailing ideas and beliefs, and the existing economic structure. Educational systems are, by and large, institutions that maintain a culture. As such, they play an indisputably important role in holding together a society. Although Texans are at times proud of their diversity, pressure is needed to ensure a common thread that holds the diverse parts together. The fear of unraveling is so great that pressure is exerted through society's institutions—church, family, school, government—to maintain the status quo, to ensure that divergent, threatening ideas, values, and lifestyles do not undermine the dominant society and culture. In Texas, that dominant society and culture is primarily the product of Protestant Anglos who migrated to Texas from the East and South in search of freedom, land, and wealth.

Sociologist Will Herberg, in his book *Protestant, Catholic and Jew,* identified the predominant secular religion that held things together nationally as "The American Way of Life." This religion, functioning very much like any other religion, has its own set of values, symbols, and practices. There is also a "Texan Way of Life," and the educational system has worked over the years to ensure the preservation of that myth. Individualism, limited government, low taxation, free enterprise, support of traditional Protestantism (and to a much lesser extent, Catholicism and Judaism), opportunism, non-interference by government or institutions in personal and family life, unlimited use of natural resources—all these serve as primary characteristics of the Texan Way of Life.

Given the rural, frontier orientation of Texas—which television and film producers still seek to convey despite fundamental societal and cultural changes—and the predominance of the Texan Way of Life, it is not surprising that public education in Texas has suffered. A comprehensive public education system held little priority in the beliefs and values supporting the Texan Way of Life. Citizens have to be able to read and write a little, and be able to do simple arithmetic. They should know something about the history of Texas (hence the required course for all public school students) and something about a democratic form of government, free enterprise, and citizenship. But as long as the state's economy was based on agriculture, oil, and some heavy manufacturing, there was little need to have a populace and a work force with higher, more advanced skills and knowledge. One didn't need to know calculus or even United States history to be an effective roughneck in the oil fields of West Texas.

The worst aspects of the Texan Way of Life and its educational system can be found in the practices and policies that were inherently discriminatory toward blacks and Hispanics. One sees racial discrimination in the legislature's dismantling of the educational reforms of the 1870s, in the way public schools were financed, in the inability to deal constructively with students who possess a native language other than English, and in the intolerably slow response to the Supreme Court's decision in *Brown v. Topeka*. Racism was a part of the Texan Way of Life, and that racism was reflected in the educational system.

While primary and secondary education suffered through laissez faire, higher education in Texas blossomed. Public higher education began in 1876 with the founding of the Agricultural and Mechanical College of Texas (Texas A&M University) through resources provided by the 180,000 acres of land granted under the federal Morrill Act of 1862. The University of Texas at Austin opened its doors in 1883. Over the years, many new four-year colleges and universities were established, including teachers' colleges in different regions of the state. For the state's colleges and universities, ever-increasing federal involvement in higher education over the past four decades has resulted in extensive growth. The GI Bill of Rights, the National Defense Education Act of 1958, and the various educational bills passed under Presidents Kennedy, Nixon, Ford and Carter expanded student enrollment. The population explosion in Texas, coupled with local and regional pride, added to the demand for new institutions of public learning. Smallwood reports that between 1960 and 1980, thirty new public senior colleges, systems, or branch campuses were created. To this expansion of public higher education institutions, one must also add the explosive growth of private colleges and universities, beginning with the founding of Baylor University in 1845.

The state's remarkable commitment to higher education ensured that a select group of the best and the brightest—the future leaders in religion, government, commerce, and the professions—would have ample opportunity to gain knowledge and professional skills. But Texas was, until recently, a segregated society; the select group included few Hispanics and even fewer blacks. The University of Texas at Austin enrolled its first black student in 1950. And at Texas A&M, the first written policy of non-discrimination wasn't instituted until 1965. The ongoing financial plight of Prairie View A&M University and Texas Southern University—public institutions established for the education of blacks—substantiates continued discrimination in the Texan Way of Life. The number of blacks attending private and public universities remains disturbingly low, far below the percentage of black population in the state.

Although official segregation ended in our state universities in the 1950s and 1960s, education policies prevented the development of a public school system that would ensure equal opportunity for a solid secondary education for all children, an education that would prepare able students for college and university studies. The children of rural white parents, of Mexican American parents living in the small communities of the Valley, the children of blacks in poverty-ridden urban areas, had far less chance of a decent, challenging public school education than their peers who were the sons and daughters of predominantly middle-class whites living in far more affluent cities and suburbs. Inequity in the financing of public education, as well as broader educational policies, resulted in unequal educational opportunity.

As long as the state's economy could thrive without a first rate educational system that provided equal opportunity for all the children of Texas, no one seemed to worry too much about the status of the schools. Few worried about a continually fragmented and eroding curriculum, about poverty-line salaries for public school teachers, about the quality of instruction in colleges and universities for future teachers, about incompetent school administrators, about an ineffective state Board of Education.

At a national meeting of state school systems' directors in Los Angeles this past May, a meeting devoted to finding ways of strengthening the humanities disciplines in the public school curriculum, the superintendent of schools in another state commented to me: "I don't understand it. The Texas economy is still booming. Texas is a leader in so many areas. But your public schools are in disastrous shape, and your educational leadership fails to do anything about it. Can you tell me why?"

The answer to this question lies in the history of the state, in its culture, economy and way of life. There simply has been little pressure—until now—to do better. The economy did not need large numbers of well-educated people. An innate anti-intellectualism scorned education for the sake of education. The Texan Way of Life could be preserved if large numbers of blacks and Hispanics were kept out of institutions of higher education, or at least the best institutions.

From this perspective, Smallwood's optimistic interpretation of the status of public education in Texas is more understandable. Given the dominance of frontier culture for most of the state's history, it is surprising that the educational system is as far along as it is. The future historian might smile at our consternation that forty-six percent of would-be teachers in our colleges and universities failed their basic skills exam; the figure could be worse. The historian of one hundred years from now will have a better grasp of our transition from a predominantly rural state to an unmistakably urban state, of our slow but growing recognition that the educational system must change if Texas is to achieve its true potential, and of our growing awareness that the withholding of quality education from certain segments of society is a moral injustice and an act of social and economic suicide.

✦

Although education issues have made page one headlines only in the past year, an intense drive to improve the quality of public education has been underway since 1979. This modest revolt, ultimately swelling to a public outcry, corresponds to developments at the national level, with the release in recent years of important reports from various private and public blue-ribbon panels and commissions. But there has been something indigenous about the Texas movement, and a brief look at the past five years is useful.

Republican Governor William Clements created in June 1979 an Advisory Committee on Education to provide a "meaningful mechanism" of communication between the educational community and the governor to address the quality of basic education in the primary and secondary schools of Texas. While the recommendations made by the committee in June 1980 addressed various aspects of public education, the status of the curriculum received special consideration. The report made a strong plea to return to a more essential or basic curriculum. Too many subjects and courses had been added to the curriculum in an attempt to address perceived social ills or single-interest purposes, and the total curriculum had become fragmented and diluted, with many students not mastering basic skills.

Also in the spring of 1979, House Concurrent Resolution 90 of the 66th Texas Legislature created the Curriculum Study Panel to undertake a state-wide review of the curriculum, a study administered by the State Board of Education in cooperation with appropriate Senate and House subcommittees. In its September 1980 report, the panel focused on the need for legislative change, repealing laws mandating specific courses and subjects so that curriculum decisions could be made in a pedagogically sound manner. The panel recommended that new legislation require school districts to offer a well-balanced curriculum that includes English language arts, mathematics, science, health, physical education, fine arts, social studies, economics, business education, foreign languages, and vocational education. The State Board of Education should be directed to designate the most essential part of each of the subjects that all students should be expected to master.

In response to these reports and to lobbying efforts of various educational groups, the Texas Legislature passed in the spring of 1981 House Bill 246, which amended the Texas Education Code's basic section on curriculum. The legislature overhauled the curriculum, identified the subjects of a well-balanced curriculum and authorized the State Board of Education to designate the essential elements of each subject that all school districts must teach. It should be noted that the act provides a concise statement of the purpose of public education, a statement that indicates some understanding of and appreciation for the importance of instruction in the social sciences, English, and other humanities subjects—that of preparing "thoughtful, active" citizens who have an "appreciation for the basic democratic values of our state and national heritage." Since 1981 the State Board of Education and the Texas Education Agency have been defining and implementing the curriculum act, with sweeping changes to go into effect this fall.

But improving the curriculum was only half of the battle. Governor Mark White, making true on his campaign pledge to improve public education, appointed in 1983 a Select Committee on Public Education chaired by corporate leader H. Ross Perot. Using Madison Avenue techniques, the Perot Commission tackled in the winter and spring of 1984 important issues, including merit pay for teachers, standardized achievement tests, the role of sports, and inequities in public school financing. Texans know the results. The 1984 special session of the Texas Legislature completely revamped the educational system and, miracle of miracles, voted a tax increase to make it all happen.

By any standard, the sweeping changes of the last few years mark a bright spot in Texas history. That is not to say that there are no difficulties with the new curriculum requirements or with specific policies adopted by the Texas legislature this summer. But, on balance, the changes represent one of the most extensive educational reforms ever to occur in the United States. The most intriguing aspect of this development is that while the educational establishment was behind the curriculum changes in 1981, the more fundamental changes dealing with structure, policy formulation, administration, teaching, and taxation, completely bypassed the educational establishment. For the first time in Texas history, outsiders to the educational system said that something had to be done, and in Perot these outsiders found a spokesman that challenged the educational establishment, top to bottom. The corporate community, brought directly into the discussion, forced the Legislature to deal constructively with far-reaching educational issues. When H. Ross Perot speaks, the Legislature listens.

The entrance of the corporate community into the public school debate signified the extent to which the existing educational system was tied to an agricultural and manufacturing economy that had gradually eroded. No longer could Texas afford an educational system that produced a large number of functional illiterates and citizens with limited scientific knowledge, technological know-how, and language skills. An agricultural/blue collar economy was slowly disappearing from Texas, and in its place, a high-tech economy was fast emerging, an economy in need of highly skilled workers trained in languages, mathematics, and the natural and computer sciences.

As the Perot Commission started rolling, so too did Microelectronics and Computer Corporation (MCC) headed by former CIA Deputy Director Bobby Inman, an advanced research company supported by seventeen leading high-tech firms as well as by financial commitments totaling in the millions of dollars from the University of Texas, Texas A&M University, and the State of Texas. The corporate community saw that the emerging economy of Texas demanded radical changes in the quality of public education. Lockheed, 3-M Company, Motorola, Electronic Data Systems Corporation, Texas Instruments, Tandy Corporation, and a score of other major high-tech firms, as well as many more smaller firms, will need a work force different from that which met the previously dominant needs of the oil, gas, and agricultural-based economy.

The entrance of the corporate community into issues of public education represents the end of laissez faire education in Texas. Now that quality education is perceived to be intimately tied to the economic well-being of Texas, the chances are good that laissez faire will never again appear. But a most important question remains: Who and what will feed the curious minds of our children?

Although the Perot Commission deserves the deepest gratitude from all Texans who care about their public schools, there is danger in a vision of public education that comes so forcefully and so singularly from the corporate community. The extent to which the corporate community has already deeply influenced the direction of higher education in the state can be seen in the one hundred plus new chairs created in the last few years by the University of Texas at Austin in the natural and computer sciences, with only a small number established in the humanities and the social sciences. Will the corporate community exert direct pressure on the State Board of Education and the Texas Education Agency regarding how the curriculum is ultimately defined and shaped? Will mathematics and the natural and computer sciences so dominate the curriculum that secondary education will produce a work force highly skilled in the application of high-technology but terribly deficient in civic and moral responsibility? Will graduating seniors be able to exercise personal judgment and freedom of choice? Will students know much about computers and little about American and world history? What opportunity will exist to study the fine arts and to improve aesthetic sensitivity and matters of taste? Will students know as much about Martin Luther, Copernicus, Rembrandt, Karl Marx, Sigmund Freud, John Dewey, Virginia Woolf, and Pablo Picasso, as they will know about computer software?

Given the fact that the new economy has brought educational reform, it is possible that the sciences will be perceived as continually expanding fields worthy of more and more courses taught at deeper and deeper levels, while the humanities—history, literature, government, languages—will be perceived as frozen subjects, with dissected parts of those subjects learned at minimal levels.

Even the National Endowment for the Humanities has recently circulated a letter among a diverse group of educators and cultural leaders, to obtain suggestions for a list of ten books in the humanities that every high school student in the United States should be expected to have read and mastered before graduation. In such matters, floors tend to become ceilings if the overall momentum is in a different direction, and ideology has a way of becoming policy.

Who then will provide the leadership and vision for a truly well-balanced public school education as our high-tech society marches on? Will the moral and aesthetic dimensions of education be forgotten? Will students be exposed to great ideas and to the drama of human history? Will students gain knowledge of the diverse American cultures through study of many recently published texts and primary literature that disclose previously hidden black, Mexican American, and Native American experiences and culture? Will our children's knowledge of current international issues, including, for instance, the relationship between developed and developing countries, and issues related to poverty, hunger, racism, and runaway nuclear armament, be enriched through the study of world cultures? Will the recently published diaries, novels, poetry, and essays that illuminate and clarify women's history and experiences be incorporated into the curriculum? Will schools of education be significantly upgraded to provide substantial instruction and solid training for tomorrow's teachers?

✦

The old Texan Way of Life is disappearing. In its place, a new Texan Way of Life is emerging. The new Texan Way of Life shares the characteristics of what some sociologists have called post-modern society. The recent history of Texas has been marked by the gradual deterioration of a nineteenth-century frontier world view, with certain fundamental beliefs and myths no longer internalized by the citizenry. In its place, we have brought forth a new knowledge system with new images and values. The chief quality of this system is its scientific and technological nature. A special kind of relationship has developed between our economic system and our faith in applied knowledge. The new knowledge system that has emerged in post-modern Texas involves knowledge production, organization, storage, retrieval, distribution, and application. While modern Texas was born of economic development stimulated by new technologies—those in the oil and gas industries, for instance—the post-modern society is based on widespread and comprehensively organized applied knowledge made applicable to virtually all areas of our social life.

Daniel Bell points out in *The Coming of Post-Industrial Society* that the chief resource of this new society is the well-educated, specialized person, whose technical and scientific skills can be applied to numerous aspects of current life. Not only does the Texas economy need such people for its work force, it also needs consumers who will buy the products of the new technology. The producers, distributors, and consumers of the new forms of knowledge are the people valued in post-modern society. Professional textbooks, manuals, and monographs become the new literary trademarks of this society, along with the now-familiar computer.

Will only the world of high-technology feed the minds and souls of our children? For the first time, Texans may get an educational system that provides a genuine measure of educational opportunity for all children, a system remarkably free of overt discrimination, a system with a much stronger and equitable financial base. But here's the bottom line: Will our state's resources be as devoted to stimulating the moral, civic, and aesthetic imaginations of our children as it will be devoted to enhancing our children's scientific knowledge and technological job skills?

Moral, civic, and aesthetic education comes primarily by way of the humanities and the arts. It is through the poem, the novel, the essay, the interpretive book of an historical event or person, that the imaginative life grows. We become familiar with other places, times, people, and thoughts, and through this exercise of the imagination, we learn more deeply what it means to be human. And when we truly reach out to read the literature of cultures and societies other than our own, our notion of the unity of humankind is greatly enhanced.

A new Texan Way of Life is taking shape, complete with new experiences, images, symbols, values and beliefs. But at its core is a support system for an economy increasingly based on high-tech culture. The opportunities are immense, and I for one am optimistic about the potential results. But the dangers are also enormous, and the greater the rush to high technology and a public education system in tune with that technology, the greater the need for Texans to ensure that education in the humanities forms the heart of the curriculum. The new Texan Way of Life can include respect for the life of the imagination, and our public schools can be the place where the imagination is loved and nourished.

Works Cited

Bell, Daniel. *The Coming of Post-Industrial Society*. New York: Basic Books, 1973.

Governor's Advisory Committee on Education: *Report and Recommendations*. Office of the Governor, 1980.

Herberg, Will. *Protestant, Catholic and Jew: An Essay in American Religious Sociology*. Reprint. Chicago: University of Chicago Press, 1983.

Select Committee on Public Education: *Recommendations of the Select Committee on Public Education*. State of Texas, 1984.

Smallwood, James. *Texas: A Sesquicentennial Celebration*, Donald W. Whisenhunt, ed. Austin: Eakin Publications, 1984.

Education for Tomorrow: What do Citizens Need to Know?

I spoke before the El Paso Rotary Club on November 14, 1985. Remarks given on the importance of the humanities to the development of well-educated citizens solidified into a short, all-purpose speech on education which I used on a number of occasions in the 1980s.

I have been invited to talk about the role of the humanities in education, about what the humanities might do for today's youth who will be dealing with the challenges of the twenty-first century.

The emerging field of future studies brings us diverse scenarios of life in the next century, many of which focus on continued breakthroughs in technology. We hear of being able to jet from Los Angeles to Hong Kong in a few hours. We are told of the possibility of increased longevity through new drugs and genetic engineering. There are predictions for new breakthroughs in telecommunications, bringing people closer together, and the continued development of an information society as computer technology grows in sophistication. Future studies scholars tell us that more and more people will be able to work at home, freeing many to live where they want to.

But there is, of course, a dark side in these studies. We are told that the world of tomorrow will be far more complex than that of today. The application of many of these technologies generate serious value questions which as yet have received little public scrutiny. We also know that citizens of the twenty-first century may have to deal with catastrophic environmental problems. They may be forced to wrestle with an increasingly divided world between the "haves" and the "have nots." Overpopulation may pose another serious threat, with the world's sustainable resources disappearing. We are told that defined borders, geographic and cultural, will break down, as the global village becomes a reality. And the continued development of biological and chemical weapons, as well as the continued deployment of nuclear weapons, will undoubtedly pose serious threats to people everywhere.

What is it that citizens of tomorrow may need to know in order to cope with a world of increasing promise and peril? And how might our children and youth be prepared to do more than "cope," to interact with the world of tomorrow, to be able to define this world, to understand it, to make it work for them rather than against them?

These questions are of critical importance for us in part because we live in a democracy where ultimate authority for dealing with these challenges rests with the citizenry. However much we may depend upon "experts" for guidance, democratic society rests or falls on the knowledge and involvement of its citizens. To capitulate in favor of the experts is to rid us of political and moral responsibility, opening the gates to non-democratic forms of governance. We are called, therefore, to think deeply about what it is that our children and youth ought to know, what it is that they ought to value, and what we might do now to help prepare them for active, responsible citizenship in the century ahead.

Some Trends in Education

There are several positive developments concerning education that give us hope. Among these are two that I consider to be especially important.

First, there is growing concern about the quality of education in America, a concern that leads me to believe that we may finally be prepared to address in serious ways current deficiencies. There is more discussion in Washington, in state capitols, and in local communities. Numerous agencies have issued reports on education, among them the Rockefeller Foundation, the Carnegie Foundation, the National Endowment for the Humanities and, here in Texas, the Perot Commission. These and many other reports respond to heighten public awareness that our educational system does not measure up to what it ought to be. A 1981 Gallop Poll documents the dramatic loss of public confidence in our schools. For the past seventeen years, average scores on the Scholastic Aptitude Test, taken by one million college-bound seniors, have declined. All these reports speak to particular problems and offer ideas that are now gaining public circulation.

Second, we are breathing new life into Robert Hutchins's idea of America as a Learning Society.[1] The quest for life-long education is growing, and educational institutions are responding to the adult public's interest in continued learning. We see industry providing more educational programs for their employees. Colleges and universities are expanding continuing education programs, developing innovative programs and structures that appeal to busy adults. More established programs are reaching out to adult learners in new ways, as evidenced, for example, by the number of middle-aged homemakers who are now entering professional schools. Cultural institutions—libraries, museums, historical societies—are developing extended opportunities for learning for citizens of all ages, becoming educational institutions in their own right.

Unfortunately, there are negative trends as well, and these trends tend to lower optimism over the long-range consequences of such positive developments.

First, vocational and professional careerism dominate this learning society, with scant recognition given to the liberal arts, especially the humanities. Students are taught that a career is nothing more than a succession of jobs in which success is determined by the rate of promotion and the rate of income. Career education and the liberal arts have gone separate ways.

Second, the "two cultures" phenomenon as described by C. P. Snow, the separation of sciences and technology from the arts and the humanities, dominates secondary and post-secondary learning. We have done little to bring these fields together. Indeed, these "cultures" seem to have gone their own way, with the result that our society finds itself increasingly split by these differing pursuits.

Third, the increasing professionalization of modern society brings with it a narrowness that threatens ideals associated with the well-rounded and well-educated person. Specialization runs rampant, first in scientific, technological, and professional pursuits, but now in the humanities as well. Our ability to pull diverse experiences together, to approach the problems of our society in multidisciplinary ways, to communicate easily across fields and professions, has eroded.

Finally, let me note that we may not be making enough progress in ensuring equal educational opportunity, with the result that we run the risk that successful entrance into tomorrow's information society may be restricted to those of privilege, those who can afford private schooling, have computers in the home, and have access to advanced educational opportunities. At times it almost seems as though we are regressing, especially in regard to public schooling, as we abandon hope for our inner city schools and, in many places, for poor rural schools as well.

New Directions

These trends—positive and negative—require a strong, substantive, and far-reaching response from those who care deeply about the humanities. Obviously, we must raise questions about the aims and purposes of our society, and we must take the lead in talking about the importance of providing equality of educational opportunity and about the necessary role of the arts and humanities in a culture dominated by scientific and technological pursuits.

Most importantly, however, we must say, over and over, wherever and whenever we can, that there is more to education than mastery of skills that will lead to successful vocations and professions. No one can disagree with the notion that public schooling should help educate students for future jobs, providing them with the technical skills needed for a constantly changing economy. But if this is our only goal, at secondary and post-secondary levels, we are in deep trouble, leaving our children and youth poorly prepared for the challenges of tomorrow.

There is a new buzzword in educational circles that provides focus for what we ought to be talking about: cultural literacy. Properly defined, this term provides a framework for thinking about elementary, secondary, and post-secondary schooling in a rapidly changing world. It implies literacy itself, the ability to read, to think, to communicate, but, more importantly, it also points to the kind of curriculum that will help prepare citizens for the challenges of the twenty-first century. It leads to the question: What must students understand about their world that will allow them to live out their citizenship in productive ways? That is the question we—the public—now need to ask.

We cannot adequately answer that question without talking about the importance of the study of history, literature, politics—all those fields that encompass the humanities. Citizens of the next century will not be able to wrestle satisfactorily with the profound challenges facing our nation and the world community without these disciplines. Will they be prepared to confront these challenges without the benefit of knowing the history and culture of this nation, knowing something of the history and cultures of other nations, without exposure to the fundamental questions of value that emerge through the study of history and literature?

It can be argued that the two major foreign policy failures of our lifetime, Vietnam and Iran, were made in the context of nearly total lack of knowledge of the cultures and societies of those nations. We can never underestimate the high price we pay for ignorance, and when we think of the issues that may well dominate the next century—profound ethical issues in medicine and the application of new technologies, the growing environmental crisis, the widening gap between "developed" and "developing" nations, ongoing and perhaps heightened ethnic and racial conflicts—we gain new insight into what ought to comprise our notion of "cultural literacy."

Age-old questions of the humanities, questions about the nature of truth, beauty, honesty, and justice, come alive when we think about these challenges. We need an educational system, from primary to secondary to post-secondary to adult education, wherein these humanistic questions are front and center. Perhaps the most important question of all is this: For what do we hope? This question concerns human ends, what life is all about, and if we keep this question before us, we will be in a better position to talk about means, about what is necessary to help us achieve the most fundamental aims of civilization.

Thus we end up with a focus that is so very basic, so very human, one that has the potential of uniting rather than dividing, of inspiring rather than deadening. The challenges of the next century require a return to the humanities as the means to ensure citizens who have the background, temperament, and ability to live full, productive, and happy lives. Education in the humanities doesn't guarantee survivability and success, but without the humanities, the odds against us become overwhelming. With the humanities, we increase the odds that tomorrow's citizens will have the capacity to be constructively engaged with the challenges that await them.

Our task, then, and our opportunity, is to counter the negative trends in education and to build on positive developments, by returning to the importance of the humanities to education at all levels and for all ages. The humanities ought to be at the very center of a learning society. The challenges of tomorrow require nothing less.

Works Cited

Hirsh, E. D. *Cultural Literacy: What Every American Needs to Know*. New York: Vintage Books, 1988.

Hutchins, Robert. *A Learning Society*. Chicago: University of Chicago Press, 1968.

Snow, C. P. *The Two Cultures*. Reprint. Cambridge: Cambridge University Press, 1993.

[1] Hutchins, one of this century's great American educators, argued persuasively that American democracy will not be realized until its citizens are liberally educated. Co-editor with Mortimer J. Adler of the fifty-four volume set of classics, *Great Books of the Western World*, Hutchins promoted "shared inquiry," a method of learning through the structured group discussion of great literature. The Great Books Foundation continues to promote Hutchins's goals. There are some important parallels between these goals and those of the state humanities councils.

Liberal Arts Education and the Challenges of the 21st Century

I was invited by Jessie Fletcher, president of Hardin-Simmons University, to deliver the school's fall 1989 convocation address. By the late 1980s, TCH's interest in education had expanded to include higher education as it became increasingly clear that the humanities were being squeezed out of the undergraduate curriculum in Texas and throughout the country. This expanding interest did not lead to new grant programs or large scale projects—curriculum reform projects, for example—because of a lack of financial resources. But we could help bring attention to this matter, and thus TCH allocated some modest resources for several initiatives as noted in the introductions to several essays in this collection. This TCH interest also provided me an opportunity to explore in speeches and writings some of the pressing concerns in undergraduate humanities education. I was pleased to talk about the importance of the humanities to quality undergraduate education.

How very pleased I am to be with you to share in this happy occasion. Convocation captures what a university is all about. Here we are—administrators, faculty, staff, students, and friends—celebrating together the beginning of a new academic year, giving thanks for the opportunities that are before us. May that spirit of togetherness, that spirit of sharing a common pursuit, stay with you throughout the year.

I want to talk this morning about the relationship between the liberal arts and the challenges of the twenty-first century. Each of you has associated with this fine university for your own reasons. But among those reasons, I am sure that one would find the shared belief that HSU, beyond preparing students for chosen careers, will enrich your lives. If I were to press you about that belief, I think you would talk about the distinctive character of this university, about its mission, values, and tradition. Central to this character is the value placed by this university on the liberal arts, on a well-rounded education that unites in a meaningful way what is in too many universities separate and disconnected areas of study—the sciences, the arts, the humanities, and the various professions. I too believe in that value, and I want to offer some thoughts on how a sound education in the liberal arts is indeed the best education that one can get in order to deal thoughtfully, constructively, and successfully with the challenges of the future. A new century and a new millennium are around the corner. Those of you who are students today will be the leaders of the next century. You will have the extraordinary opportunity of shaping the twenty-first century, for the first decades of every new century exert powerful influences on the decades that follow.

The challenges that citizens of the twenty-first century will face will be extraordinary ones, and most of them, in one way or another, involve the phenomenon and consequences of change. But before we take a look at the future, I want to look back. The American philosopher and journalist Walter Lippmann once wrote that it is very difficult for Americans to see themselves in the present from the perspectives offered by the past and by the future. We inadequately grasp our relationship to those who went before, just as we inadequately grasp the connection between our lives and the decisions that we make and those who will come after us. Yet we are all connected.

To look back, to see the extent to which the twentieth century itself has been marked by change, I refer to a 1928 graduate of this university, Hendley Varner Williams, Jr. Sixty-two years ago, this young man from Snyder was preparing for his senior year, undoubtedly attending a convocation such as this, although I suspect that the speaker that day was probably better than the one today.

Hendley was from a family of modest means. His father, who came to Texas as a young man in the 1880s when economic conditions in his native Georgia failed to recover from the devastation of the Civil War and Reconstruction, was a photographer, recording for posterity the pioneer lives of the Snyder settlers. Hendley had some older sisters, school teachers, who assisted him financially as he enrolled in a two-year program in a teachers' college. He received a certificate and taught for several years in one-room schools in West Texas. As a young teacher, Hendley read widely, attracted to the poets and essayists of nineteenth century romanticism. He yearned for new experiences, for foreign encounters, for the testing of young adulthood. He went to New Orleans one summer and before long set sail on a nineteenth century schooner, delivering cargo throughout the Caribbean, docking at Central American ports. Many years later, these experiences were still fresh in his mind, and he would tell those who listened his stories of the sea. Although the captain of the ship, a man named Eden, selected Hendley for his first mate and begged him to stay, Hendley left the crew to teach for a year in a small school in a village in Puerto Rico.

Despite the pleasure of this adventure, Hendley longed for more education, and decided to return home to West Texas. He enrolled in Hardin-Simmons, graduating in 1928. He then taught and served as principal in a number of country schools in West Texas and in several small towns, including one, Clara, where he fell in love with, and married, a fellow school teacher. Summers found Hendley studying at Southern Methodist University, working on a Masters degree. A decade or so later, summers took him to Colorado State University in Boulder where he ultimately received a doctorate in education. Better, he said, to spend summers in the mountains than on the Texas plains. Too young for World War I, too old for World War II, he escaped much of the carnage of the twentieth century. In the late 1940s, he served as principal of Bowie High School in El Paso, a border school in a border city. A doctoral degree led to university appointments, first at Sul Ross State University and then Baylor University. In his fifties, his idealism found fulfillment in new opportunities with the U.S. State Department and the United Nations, working to build elementary schools in Guatemala and Costa Rica. He returned to Baylor and taught until his retirement, at age seventy, in 1974. This lover of Kipling, however, could not stay still. Retirement brought several trips to Central America as well as a short-term teaching post at Hong Kong Baptist College. He died in Waco in 1982 at the age of seventy-nine.

I cite this biography of one Hardin-Simmons graduate for a reason. During his life—one person's life—here are a few things that happened, events and developments and challenges which shaped his life and to which he, as an American, as a Texan, had to respond.

the closing of the American frontier
mustard gas and World War I
Spindletop
prohibition
end of Western colonialism
the vote for women
Dr. Pepper
population explosion
stock market crash and the Great Depression
the ball point pen
the Dust Bowl
the Russian Revolution
the Mexican Revolution
small pox and polio vaccines
Babe Ruth
Novocaine and the high speed drill
Carter's Little Liver Pills
statehood for New Mexico
the radio, the phonograph, and television
Suez Canal
Ann Landers
Will Rogers
Chairman Mao
refrigerators
rebirth of Israel
Mary Pickford, Marilyn Monroe and Meryl Streep
Live from the Met
Pearl Harbor and World War II
Fidel Castro and the missile crisis of 1962
Somoza Brothers
Tele-evangelism
bikinis
marijuana and LSD
Ford Model T, Chevy Impala, and Mazda RX7
the airplane
Sputnik, Apollo, and men on the moon
indoor plumbing
heart transplants
Birth control pills
Gandhi and Martin Luther King
test tube babies

theory of relativity
Auschwitz and the murder of 7 million Jews
Hiroshima
Korea, South Vietnam, and Cambodia
acid rain and Love Canal
Tea Pot Dome and Watergate
November 22, 1963
interstate highways
urban sprawl
the Black Panthers
Hoover Dam
Hippies
Social Security
electric can openers
mini-skirts and designer jeans
War of the Worlds
microwave oven
satellites and telecommunication
nuclear-powered submarines
shopping malls
toothpaste
Big Macs
Teddy Roosevelt and Ronald Reagan
Panama Canal
central air conditioning
gas-powered lawnmowers
contact lenses
disposable diapers
Walter Cronkite and the Evening News
the KKK
The Spirit of St. Louis
W. C. Fields and Charlie Chaplin
Sigmund Freud and Dr. Spock
asbestos
Dale Carnegie and how to win friends and influence people
Ma Ferguson
John Deere Tractors and International Harvesters
Billy Sunday and Billy Graham
VCRs
Robert Byrd and the north pole
D. H. Lawrence, Ernest Hemingway, and J. D. Salinger

the Titanic
bomb shelters
drive-in movies
John Dewey
AFL-CIO
Leave it to Beaver

The question, of course, that one must ask is: How well did Hendley Williams's undergraduate education prepare him to deal with the momentous cultural, social, economic, and political changes that occurred during his lifetime?

This question is quite different from the kinds of questions that students and parents tend to ask today about university education. Traditional liberal arts education has received a beating during the past several decades. Increasing emphasis has been placed on the short-term, economic utility of a university education. Priority has been placed on professional programs that can guarantee upon graduation employability at high introductory salaries. As a result, students and parents have shied away from traditional liberal arts programs, favoring instead programs in business, engineering, and other professions. This trend has led many educators to wonder what the long-term consequences to the nation will be of a citizenry increasingly ignorant of history, literature, philosophy, and other fields of learning associated with the liberal arts.

Numerous reports issued by blue-ribbon commissions have sought to underscore the importance of the liberal arts education and the humanities. That is, there is growing recognition that we must counter the specialization and vocationalism that has crept into the undergraduate curriculum in recent decades. This trend has been most visible in our state universities. Interestingly, it has been the smaller private colleges and universities, such as Hardin-Simmons, that have resisted this trend and that provide curriculum models to which state schools may now be turning. Here in Texas, the Legislature has mandated the establishment of expanded core curriculum programs in all public universities, undergraduate requirements that must include fairly extensive course work in traditional liberal arts fields.

Hendley Williams lived most of his life during a period of *rapid* change that began in the early 1800s with industrialization and ended in the mid-twentieth century as we entered an era more accurately described as one of *radical* change. Yet some scholars now talk about a new era, beginning in the later decades of the twentieth century and continuing through the twenty-first century, marked by *convulsive* change. As a society, as individuals, we must ask the question: How can we educate citizens for the challenges of the twenty-first century? Given the profound changes that are now taking place and will take place, undergraduate education must be for a much broader purpose than just getting a job or, from the perspective of the state and nation, achieving economic competitiveness.

The issues that citizens of the twenty-first century will face will be grave ones indeed. It is impossible to provide definitive illustrations of the changes that citizens of the twenty-first century will experience, but it is possible to group some of the more important possibilities around major public issues. Let me mention five:

The Environment

It is likely that the most pressing public issue of the first half of the twenty-first century will be that of preserving the environment. The rise and fall of the Mayan civilization in Guatemala provides a chilling account of what can happen when the environment deteriorates. For nearly seventeen centuries, from 800 B. C. until A. D. 900, Mayan civilization prospered, with a total population of about 5 million by A. D. 900. Mayan civilization was remarkably advanced in agriculture, architecture, and culture. Yet, around A. D. 900, the civilization collapsed. Researchers from the University of Chicago concluded in the 1970s that within a matter of decades, the Mayan population fell to less than one-tenth of what it had been. The civilization collapsed because of severe environmental stresses brought on by excessive population. In order to grow more and more crops, the land had been deforested. Soil erosion occurred, draining the cropland of its productivity. There simply was not enough food for the population.

What separates us from the Mayans, of course, is our understanding of our environment and our current predicament. In the last several decades, many policy makers have concluded that we are on an unsustainable path. Grave environmental crises now span the globe and threaten all societies. Deforestation, soil erosion, depletion of fertile croplands, pollution of our waters, lands, and air, have threatened all biological systems.

Growing public recognition of the seriousness of the problem is leading to significant national and international initiatives to preserve the environment. It is likely that over the course of the next fifty years such efforts will intensify. The pessimists, however, think that corrective action will be too little and too late. They predict water shortages, continual smog alerts in our major cities, power blackouts, more oil spills, the death of oceans, rivers, and lakes, the continued warming of the planet, nuclear waste dumped indiscriminately, the death of species of animals at a staggering rate, and the collapse of entire civilizations, much like the Mayan situation. Others believe that, because we are aware of the challenge, we can act to prevent this catastrophe. If so, the cost will be high, not only in dollars but also in terms of personal and national sacrifice. We will have to accept controls over the world's resources in ways that we cannot now imagine, including water and energy fuels. It may affect what we eat, how we live, the amount of days a year that we will be allowed to use remaining recreational land, how we move from one city to another, from home to work, the materials with which we build our homes and office buildings, how we stay warm in the winter and cool in the summer.

Environmental issues will dominate life in the twenty-first century. We will be forced to respond to these issues, and to do that, we will need to fully understand them. Ultimately, these issues will be dealt with both privately, in how we live, and publicly, in the policies that we as a people encourage or discourage, pay for or don't pay for.

International Issues

The late twentieth century has been a time of increased recognition of the extent to which all nations are interrelated. Think, for instance, about the impact of environmental problems on international relations. The developed countries are the chief polluters of the environment, a process that is intimately tied to industrialization since the 1800s. Developed nations, with strong economies, are now taking the lead in encouraging international action. Such action, however, could have a dramatic impact on underdeveloped nations who only now are prepared to industrialize their economies. International restrictions on the use of remaining forests, on the burning of fossil fuels, on fishing restrictions, on cropland usage, may very well be perceived as efforts to curtail economic development among these poorer nations. One can predict, therefore, open hostility toward the developed nations.

We have gained new appreciation for the roots of political instability which can lead to international conflict. Chronic poverty, starvation, the loss of hope for economic improvement, provide the context for revolution and for international conflict.

A major new challenge to education has thus emerged—that of increasing citizen understanding of other nations and cultures. Indeed, the incorporation of global concerns and issues may be the most important educational challenge of the next decade. Education can no longer be shaped by parochial and insular perspectives. The world has grown smaller; the fruits of modern technology break down insularity. How can we forget the dramatic television images that flooded into our homes the first weekend of June. In China, live television coverage brought us the ghastly sight of slaughter as government troops and tanks suppressed student demands for simple democratic reforms. In Iran, television brought us the inexplicable sight of thousands of Iranians living out their frenzied passion for religious and political zealotry as they mourned the death of their leader Khomeni. Meanwhile, in Poland, we witnessed through television the triumph of Solidarity and the rebirth of democracy in Eastern Europe as Poles participated in free elections for the first time in decades.

We are, of course, citizens of the world as well as of the United States, and thus we must, if we are to be effective, responsible citizens, gain global perspective. Economic self-interest alone dictates this perspective. The jobs that university graduates will seek in the 1990s and into the twenty-first century will be increasingly tied to the development of a single world economy with closely linked worldwide economic institutions. Famine in Africa, the closing of borders in China, the opening of borders in the Soviet Union and Eastern Europe, the level of production of remaining oil in the Middle East, third-world default of loans from developed nations, free trade among nations of the European Economic Community—these and many other developments have grave consequences for our economy here in Texas and on your prospects for future employment. To gain global perspective, more time must be spent studying the histories and cultures of those nations whose futures bear so much on our own. We must hear their interpretations, not just ours, of their histories, cultures, religions, and interactions with the world community. Survivability in the twenty-first century means broad public understanding of global problems that demand global solutions. We must think internationally.

Multiculturalism

Issues related to the multicultural makeup of Texas and the United States will also dominate personal and public agendas in the twenty-first century. Texas's population will increase from 16.8 million to at least 29.6 million by the year 2025, and the Texas Department of Commerce estimates that fifty percent of the population will be minority by that date.

Coming to terms with our multiculturalism is one of the unfinished public agenda items of the twentieth century. Segregation may be gone, but all to often prejudice remains. Even where prejudice does not exist, we struggle with the challenge of developing a shared culture. Public school curricula, as well as many college and university curricula, inadequately incorporate the histories and literatures of our nation's major minority groups. Serious efforts to open up the curriculum, to incorporate into the study of history, literature, and culture the true demographic, social, and cultural realities of American and Texan life, must continue. Much progress has been made; but more needs to be done.

Multicultural understanding and appreciation is the foundation for ensuring equal opportunity. And without equal opportunity, we are in danger of becoming a society of two classes—those of privilege and wealth and those of limited opportunity and poverty. A recent report, *One-Third of a Nation*, issued by the American Council on Education, argues that after years of impressive gains, the United States is now moving backward in providing equal opportunity for blacks, Hispanics, and American Indians. The report, issued by a panel of forty civic leaders, including former presidents Carter and Ford, calls for immediate, widespread reforms to open doors to minorities in education, business, and government. In education, income, health, longevity, and other basic measures of individual and social well-being, there are widening gaps between members of minority groups and the majority population. The report points to "a dangerous split between haves and have-nots" and states that "If we allow these disparities to continue, the United States inevitably will suffer compromised quality of life and a lower standard of living." For states like Texas, with a heavy minority population, the issue is particularly acute.

We have little hope of addressing this issue without efforts made by the majority to gain new understanding of the histories and cultures of the minority. One of the great challenges of the twenty-first century, then, is an old one—how to develop a shared culture out of our multiple and at times conflicting histories and cultures.

Technology

One of the seeds of the convulsive change now taking place and that will continue into the twenty-first century flows from technological development. Many scholars argue that modern technology is literally shaping our lives and culture. Or, to put it more bluntly, technology is controlling us rather than we controlling technology.

To argue that technology is driving culture is to acknowledge two basic facts. First, we often simply do not know the long term consequences of a particular technology that has been developed, and second, we deal with the ethical implications after the fact. Take, for instance, what is now a rather old technology. Edward Cornish of the World Future Society asks a troubling question in *The Study of the Future*: Suppose the American people were asked to vote on whether to accept a new technology that would have the following costs:

- 50,000 people killed each year (through the years, more killed than in all the wars the U.S. has ever fought)
- 2,000,000 disabled each year, including perhaps 100,000 maimed for life
- $20 billion in property damage
- urban sprawl, leading to the decay of downtown areas
- a deterioration in public transportation
- sexual promiscuity and weakening of parental control
- pollution resulting in unknown thousands of deaths from lung cancer, heart disease and other ailments
- U.S. subservience to Middle Eastern nations
- billboards that obscure natural scenery
- conversion of thousands of acres of rich farm land and scenic countryside into asphalt
- the placing of a large burden of debt on individual citizens
- unsightly graveyards for rusting vehicles.

How would the American people vote?

The automobile shows how we can end up paying a terrible price for something that most people would say is beneficial. The point is, we often don't know the results, the price we may have to pay, or the full dimensions of ethical issues raised, until the technology is in place for many years.

We now can begin to assess some of the impact of newer technologies, including nuclear power and computers. We are less clear about extraordinary technological developments in other fields, especially biology and medicine. Extensive media coverage is being given these days to the surprising and difficult ethical questions that baffle experts and courts of law as new technologies are perfected. Implanted organs give life to many, but the practice leads to shortages and the prospects of black markets for donor organs. Personality control drugs may counter depression and other forms of mental stress and illness, but could lead to the development of drugged super-soldiers and terrorists. Drugs that expand the life span might provide years of happy retirement living, but raise serious questions about how society will pay for this increased longevity. Genetic engineering might lead to the prevention of mental retardation, but could result in nations creating entire classes of people, from menials who do the dirty work of civilization to superhumans who have power, privilege, and wealth. The availability of mass-administered contraceptive agents might lead to controlling the world's population explosion so that life on this planet can continue, but whole nations, cultures, and civilizations could die in the process.

It will take a wise citizenry if technology is to be controlled. Not only must we understand the issues, we must bring to those issues highly developed thinking skills and sound ethical values. We must weigh costs and benefits. We must weigh values associated with the market place with values associated with long-range, carefully-developed national policy. These issues must not be left exclusively in the hands of the experts. Citizens must understand them in order to ensure productive policies that make technology the servant of the human spirit.

Democracy and Representative Government

A fifth challenge that I mention is that of ensuring the well-being of our democracy and representative government. We have no guarantee that this nation will survive forever. We have no guarantee that our representative form of government will survive forever.

Indeed, there are forces at work that, unless controlled, give us a bleak picture of our nation fifty years from now. We have witnessed in the last half of the twentieth century the growth of huge bureaucracies, private as well as public, that, while exercising enormous power over our lives, are far removed from us. These seem impenetrable, and often are. Bureaucrats may know a lot about us—our bank accounts, our debts, the square feet of our home, our work, our families, our personal and family histories, the status of our health—but we know little if anything about them. They make decisions that affect our lives, thousands of miles from where we live—in the Congress, in the offices of massive government buildings, in corporate offices in New Jersey, Michigan or Minnesota. Without knowing us, without talking, without the human touch, decisions are made.

Parallel to this trend, one finds another development—the loss of a sense of community, of seeing our inter-connectedness, of knowing that we are related to each other, of having some sense of the common good. Some interpreters of the American scene tell us that rampant individualism, the pursuit of individual material gain without concern for the common good, is undermining the very fabric of American society.

One of the great challenges of the twenty-first century then is that of ensuring the well-being of the nation and of representative government through cultivation of community. Community begins at home—in our churches, schools, towns and cities. But it must also extend to the state and to the nation. Sound public policy—the ability of our political leaders to make the right choices—will depend upon this sense of community. As the twenty-first century approaches, we must ask what it is that you and I and all Americans can do to instill a rebirth of community in our nation. Without that sense of community, bureaucracies can run wild, trampling on individual rights, ignoring individual realities and needs; and governments, out of touch with citizens, can make the wrong choices.

✦

If these are the primary issues, what kind of university education can best prepare an individual for life in the next century? The answer, I believe, is an undergraduate experience that is grounded in the liberal arts. I recognize the need for students to gain particular skills in particular fields—whether that be business, engineering, medical technology, or any other field. But at the minimum, the first two years of undergraduate education should be devoted to general education—to the study of science, the arts, literature, history, philosophy and religion. Every university needs a strong core curriculum that all students participate in and that all faculty teach.

Interestingly, some important studies show that, while university graduates who have pursued narrow professional studies may secure higher paid positions in the private sector upon graduation, over the long haul traditional liberal arts graduates ultimately overtake these specialists because they have the general knowledge and more advanced skills in writing, reading, and thinking that are required for senior leadership positions.

But that is an inadequate reason for defending traditional liberal arts programs. A more profound reason is that our society cannot deal adequately with the challenges of the twenty-first century without citizens who understand the world about them. Are we not already paying the price of the gradual loss of traditional liberal arts study in this country? Surely there is a connection between the erosion of study of the arts, social sciences, and humanities in our public schools and universities and the scandals of recent years—in banking, government, real estate, and on Wall Street. Surely there is a connection between runaway technology, where little thought is given to long-range consequences and to ensuing ethical dilemmas, and the quality and kind of education offered our citizens. Surely there is a connection between the educational trends and practices of the past twenty years or so and the disturbing fact that citizens feel alienated from their government, with fewer than fifty percent bothering to vote in presidential elections.

Undergraduate education should prepare individuals for active, thoughtful citizenship. Being a responsible, knowledgeable citizen of Texas and the United States in the twenty-first century will be a challenge. Indeed, the challenges that will face us as a republic—challenges of the environment, of technology, of international relations, of unity in the midst of diversity, of faceless bureaucracies—place new burdens on citizens. These burdens cannot be adequately understood without the insight that is gained through the study of history, literature, society, and culture.

But there is another dimension to this as well, the personal one. It is difficult to deal with the issues of society and culture without a strong sense of self—knowing who you are, where you come from, what you hope for, what you fear, what you love, what you value. This search is what gives the liberal arts, and especially the humanities, their relevance. I began this presentation by talking about Hendley Williams and the dramatic changes that he experienced over the course of his life. Dr. Williams was my father-in-law, and I knew him well. I'm convinced that Hendley Williams was a better citizen by virtue of his liberal arts education at HSU, but I am also convinced that he was a better person—better able to shape his life, to give meaning to his life, to discover and appreciate his values—because of his liberal arts education.

For those of you who are students, I offer these observations. This is the time to wrestle with great thoughts and great minds. This is the time to study the literature of one's own tradition as well as the literature of other traditions. This is the time to familiarize oneself with the uniqueness of world cultures and the flow of history, with the dramatic story of Western civilization, with the wonders of the human personality, with the captivating history of science, with the stunning truths of the physical universe. This is the time to explore complex moral and ethical issues. This is the time to learn to read, write, and think well.

Whether or not your university experience prepares you for living and for citizenship, as well as for a career, will depend upon you. Ultimately, it is about what you do with your books and how you relate to your teachers and your classmates. It is about how you bring together faith and knowledge, personal goals and public duties, freedom and responsibility. What a great opportunity it is to study in a university that supports this quest, a university that values the liberal arts. If this is the path you take, I am confident that you will enter through the doors of the twenty-first century well prepared. You will meet successfully the challenges that await you. Like Hendley Williams, that young man from Snyder, you will have a spiritual and intellectual foundation that will last a lifetime.

Works Cited

Cornish, Edward. *The Study of the Future: An Introduction to the Art and Science of Understanding and Shaping Tomorrow's World*. World Future Society, 1977.
American Council on Education. *One Third of a Nation: A Report*, 1988.

Core Curriculum:
Making the
Connections

College and university administrators and faculty met in Houston July 20–21, 1990 for a conference on undergraduate core curriculum, sponsored by the Texas Higher Education Coordinating Board. I was asked to provide the keynote speech.

The Coordinating Board had established a panel more than a year before to offer recommendations concerning legislation passed in 1987, H.B. 2183. This bill sought to respond to the report of the Select Committee on Higher Education which had been established by the Legislature to address particular needs in higher education, a development that brought the 1980s higher education reform movement to Texas. The TCH had been strongly supportive of H.B. 2183 and the proposed requirement that all public colleges and universities have a core curriculum. Indeed, the need for undergraduate curricular reform had been prominently featured in TCH's Texas in the 21st Century project and the publications released earlier in 1990 as part of that project.

In collaboration with the NEH, TCH sought to provide ideas and assistance as colleges and universities began to consider the new mandate. We sponsored with NEH's Division of Education a series of five workshops in different regions of Texas. A team from the NEH was able to share information on developments nationally and to encourage grant requests. It was one of the most concentrated program development ef-

forts of the division as it promoted funding opportunities for colleges and universities to refashion the undergraduate curriculum.

I was supportive of Lynne Cheney's campaign to strengthen under-graduate education, even though I differed with her, as many in Texas did, regarding the makeup of the curriculum. I was confident that the colleges and universities of Texas, as they moved forward in thinking about a core curriculum in this pluralistic state with its emerging inter-national orientation, would recognize the necessity of having a cur-riculum that included but went beyond the Western Tradition/Great Books curriculum that most neo-conservative writers were promoting. While it was vitally important to ensure student learning in the Western tradition, a point that I continually made, much more was now re-quired. New ways had to be found to give fuller expression to the civic function of higher education.

Proceedings of the 1990 conference were published by the Texas Higher Education Coordinating Board. The address included in that publication, with minimal changes, was given again January 26, 1991 at a program for academic vice presidents sponsored by the Coordinat-ing Board. This latter version is printed here.

I have been asked to share with you an address that I originally gave last July at a conference sponsored by the Texas Higher Education Coordinating Board. I do so with several reservations, for I am well aware of the fact that higher education—like American society itself—is experiencing rapid change, and one's perspective on the status of undergraduate education, because of this change, is bound to shift.

Our concern today is with the core curriculum. H.B. 2183, which requires all colleges and universities to establish a core curriculum, evidences the leadership role of key legislators concerned about our colleges and universities. That bill, passed in 1987 in response to a recommendation of the Select Committee on Higher Education, pro-vides a state mandate to move forward with ideas generated by the national reform movement of the 1980s. As such, it stands as a unique effort of a legislative body to deal with important challenges confront-ing undergraduate education in the United States.

Some observers of higher education mark the beginning of this latest reform movement with the core curriculum put in place at Harvard University in 1979. That curriculum, nearly six years in the making, was the first major attempt to overhaul the undergraduate curriculum at

Harvard since 1945, when a general education program was introduced following the release of the Harvard Report, the so-called "Red Book." That report provided a philosophical groundwork for an approach to general education that by and large has dominated higher education in America for the last four decades.

The report was deeply concerned with the problem of how to provide a general education to the postwar generations. It noted that American democracy was threatened by a dramatic shift in political power from an educated elite to the unenlightened many. A democracy of equal citizens was replacing a small privileged class of well-trained leaders. Thus Harvard proposed to democratize what had once been the education of a gentleman.

Unfortunately, practice did not live up to rhetoric. What developed was quite different from what the original committee anticipated, and what happened at Harvard was repeated in the vast majority of colleges and universities across the country. In place of tightly focused core curriculum courses that required a high degree of faculty cooperativeness, availability, and willingness to move beyond specialized fields, the University, responding to departmental and faculty pressures, went for breadth, with the consequence that the contemporary cafeteria-like approach to general education evolved, in which a system of distribution requirements and electives have center stage. In 1975, David Riesman described Harvard's general education requirements as "minimal, not much more than a mild expectation that a student will take several courses outside his own area of specialization." By the late 1970s, to meet general education requirements at Harvard, students were free to choose from over one-hundred courses listed in the catalogue.

Thus from the end of World War II through the 1970s, general education in the United States became increasingly, as Ernest Boyer points out, "the neglected stepchild of undergraduate education." The concept of a core curriculum all but disappeared in the majority of institutions of higher education. The reinstitution of a core curriculum at Harvard in 1979 signaled a swing of the curriculum pendulum once again, moving back toward prescription and away from permissiveness. The Harvard committee proposed that students take eight courses from five core areas: literature and the arts; history; social and philosophical analysis; science and mathematics; and foreign languages and cultures. While this may seem like a dramatic change in requirements, the level of prescription in this core curriculum is quite modest. Indeed, it is highly questionable whether what existed at Harvard in the 1980s can genuinely be called a "core" curriculum. At best, it may be what former Secretary of Education William Bennett called "core light," a description that did not sit well with the Harvard faculty.

But I cite the Harvard effort because it seems to mark—despite its weakness—the beginning of renewed interest to fashion general education programs that meet new needs. Throughout the 1980s, report after report of various blue-ribbon commissions have sought to restore general education to its rightful place in American higher education.

Critics have recognized growing public disenchantment with higher education. Public concerns have centered on the apparent cheapening of college and university degrees; on the inability of large numbers of graduates to have the writing, reading and analytical skills needed in today's economic marketplace; on the abundance of narrow and sometimes esoteric scholarship; and on the growing isolation of the university from community needs and public issues.

Building on these public concerns, the critics have argued that higher education is beset with major problems. For too long we have witnessed the decline of the liberal arts and the ascendancy of professional and vocational programs. The undergraduate curriculum appears fragmented, lacking an overriding coherence based on a vision of what a college-educated person should know. Introductory classes in our larger universities, frequently enrolling hundreds of students, are most often taught by graduate students, part-time lecturers, and young assistant professors rather than by experienced faculty members.

Despite the growing public recognition of the need for curricular reform, despite the numerous reports issued, and despite new experimental programs at a number of institutions, a 1989 survey commissioned by the NEH of five hundred and four colleges and universities found little change in undergraduate general education requirements. For example, at four-year colleges, requirements in the humanities were increased an average of only 1.5 hours in the preceding five years. While approximately ninety-five percent of all baccalaureate-granting institutions have general education requirements for all undergraduate students, most of these institutions do not have genuine core curricula. Thus even though general education requirements may be high, it was possible in 1988, as Lynne Cheney points out, to graduate from almost eighty percent of the nation's colleges and universities without taking a course in Western civilization, from more than eighty percent without taking a course in American history, from forty-five percent without taking a course in English or American literature, and from seventy-seven percent without studying a foreign language.

Here in Texas, undergraduate education faces the same challenges that confront colleges and universities across the country. Of course some institutions have given much thought to general education in recent years, with very positive results, and the report released last year by the Coordinating Board's Subcommittee on Core Curriculum has proved most helpful. In spite of these and other efforts, however, much work remains.

Many factors have contributed to the current status of general education and to the difficulty institutions have in establishing coherent and integrated core curricula, including, most certainly, factors that seem to reinforce one another: the career-orientation of students; a society that tends to place more value on the practical than the theoretical; the supremacy of departments within the university structure; the over-specialization of faculty; the nature of graduate education; the priority placed on research at the expense of teaching; and so forth.

But I would like to propose to you that as important as these factors are, there is another reason—one more sweeping and one more disturbing. I am referring to the gradual erosion of a sense of the civic function of our institutions of higher education, a sense of how our colleges and universities are related to a society of self-governing people, how these institutions might be able to contribute in new and deeper ways to the development of community through which challenging social, cultural, and political problems can be addressed. It is my belief that this loss has contributed to the increasing marginalization of our colleges and universities.

This difficulty can be seen in the February 1987 report of the Select Committee on Higher Education. That report identified three goals for higher education in Texas: 1) strengthening the traditional role of higher education; 2) firmly establishing the critical role of higher education as a powerful instrument for economic development and an indispensable factor in producing a brighter economic future, especially through research, and 3) managing and controlling higher education for better results.

I do not want to dismiss the contribution made by the Select Committee in recommending ways of strengthening accountability and management, and the progress made by our colleges and universities since 1987. Nor do I want to minimize the importance of higher education to economic development. But the Committee's description of the "traditional role" of higher education is troubling. The introduction to that section of the report dealing with the "traditional role" states:

> Higher education traditionally has been valued as an end in itself for personal enrichment. Its role has been to transmit culture through general education, to impart and extend knowledge, and to teach and train students for vocations and professions. At the turn of the next century, our intensely competitive society will require a highly capable work force prepared to cope with change. Education, more than ever before in Texas, will be the road to individual success and achievement.

We are left with the argument that higher education is important for a) individual enrichment and advancement, and b) economic development, primarily through research. The connections between higher education and the body politic, between college and university education and the well-being of democracy and free institutions, between university education and civic responsibility, and between our universities and pressing social and cultural issues tend to be missing.

The missing links may reflect the peculiar historical and cultural background of the state, including our penchant for individualism and our passion for economic achievement. Missing is the recognition of Texas as a community, with our institutions of higher education playing a central role in supporting that community. The relationships between our colleges and universities and broad-based goals—the extension of freedom and opportunity, the development of healthy environments, the elimination of racial, ethnic and gender discrimination, the quest for good and honest government, the application of sound values in public and private spheres—are not articulated.

The report of the Select Committee was used in developing a series of bills passed in 1987 by the Texas Legislature. Some of those bills were designed to dramatically increase scientific and technological research, as an important dimension to the state's economic recovery. Others were designed to improve the quality of undergraduate education in the state, including H.B. 2183, dealing with the core curriculum. But these latter bills and the initiatives that have ensued from them, do little to reestablish the civic function of our colleges and universities beyond that of ensuring a literate and skilled work force for a post-industrial, service-oriented economy. As a result, insufficient incentive has been given to think about general education and the core curriculum in ways that will make the kinds of connections that are needed if the broader civic function of higher education is to be achieved. Without this incentive, intellectual frameworks for thinking about the core curriculum are limited, focusing primarily on skills and competencies to be gained, on the one hand, and the transmission of culture through the study of traditional disciplines, on the other hand. In the end, we are shortchanging society, for the enormous resources of our colleges and universities and the multiple talents of the faculty are insufficiently brought to bear on fundamentally important issues of democratic culture.

In pushing for reform, it has become fashionable to cite statistics. Report after report issued in the past decade provided us with dismal statistics regarding what it is that college graduates know about history and culture. For example, in one recent poll, two-thirds of graduating seniors could not identify the authors of the *Divine Comedy* and *Paradise Lost,* and fully one-quarter of graduating seniors thought that Karl Marx's phrase "from each according to his ability, to each according to his need," is part of the U.S. Constitution.

But there is a problem more serious than literary and historical gaps in the knowledge of our college seniors, and that has to do with the troubling health of our democratic society and culture as revealed through statistics that hold relevance to the design of general education and a core curriculum.

Take, for example, statistics about the status of children in our society. Twenty-five percent of pre-schoolers live in poverty. One out of three girls and one out of every five boys born in the U.S. will experience sexual abuse by the time she or he is eighteen. Nearly ten thousand children in the U.S. die annually from poverty. Eighty percent of the children eligible for Head Start never get a chance to participate.

How about statistics on poverty? There are an estimated thirty-three million Americans who live in poverty. Approximately three million Americans are homeless, including 500,000 children.

Regarding violence: The United States leads all industrialized nations in homicides. In the United States, a woman is beaten every eighteen seconds and raped every six minutes.

Regarding education and literacy: Nearly thirty percent of our students nationally do not finish high school. There are now over four million young Americans, age eighteen to thirty, who are dropouts. Here in Texas, eighty thousand kids drop out each year—that's more than four hundred every school day. One out of three Texans is functionally illiterate. Approximately thirty million American adults cannot read well enough to function effectively at work.

Regarding greed: The Savings & Loan scandal ultimately will cost $2,000 per U.S. citizen—perhaps much more.

Regarding productivity: American productivity has dropped so significantly since 1973—the growth rate has been cut in half—that many observers believe the United States is about to slip into the second rank of nations in terms of wealth and income, with the consequence that, as we move toward the twenty-first century, the high standard of living that we have known is in jeopardy.

Regarding the environment: Acid rain damage, normally associated with industrialized nations and regions, now can be seen in the virgin forests of Central America. We are told that the average temperature may increase as much as seven degrees Fahrenheit over the next century, promising dramatic climatic changes, unless major new environmental policies are put in place worldwide.

Regarding growing American cynicism: A recent survey found that forty-three percent of Americans—and more than half of those under age twenty-four—believe selfishness and fakery are at the core of human nature, and that most Americans will lie and cheat if they can gain from it.

Regarding civic involvement: Fewer and few Americans bother to vote. Young adults, aged eighteen to thirty, in recent years have come to know and care less about public affairs than any other generation in the past half-century, according to a recent poll. Young Americans are less likely to read newspapers, less likely to watch news on television, less able to identify newsmakers, and consistently register less interest in public events, than the preceding generation. In the last twenty-five years, the percentage of young adults who read newspapers has dropped from sixty-seven to twenty-four percent.

These statistics point to a democratic society that faces major challenges that confront us at the very time when democratic values are taking hold around the world and in the most unlikely of places. To be sure, all students who come through our general education programs should have some knowledge of Dante and Milton—courses in Western culture and literature, including American history and literature, should be central to the core curriculum. But they also should know the problems that our society faces and the basic threats to American democracy as we move toward the twenty-first century, and what options might be available to us as a people in addressing these problems and threats.

But even if one takes the longer look, if one identifies certain trends that will extend well into the twenty-first century, it is impossible to escape the conclusion that the future of our democratic society should be a fundamental concern of the core curriculum. All students—no matter what their professional pursuits might be—need a prescribed curriculum in their general education program that familiarizes them with the most important issues facing our state, nation, and world.

For example, what is the connection between literacy and the well-being of democratic institutions and values? And what do we mean by literacy, and who should define what we mean?

What about multiculturalism, the extraordinary shift in demographics now occurring? How does a democratic culture deal with the questions of pluralism? What risks do we run if they are not dealt with successfully? Why do we have such a difficult time incorporating into our ideals of a common and shared culture the experiences, realities, and traditions of our multiple cultures?

What about internationalism, the maturing of the global village? We know that there are global problems demanding global solutions—environmental problems, international debt, third-world political instability, drug trafficking, hunger and poverty, and terrorism and aggression—and we know that the world's economies are increasingly interrelated. But what do these realities mean for citizens of a democracy? For ranchers and electricians and computer programmers and corporate executives and homemakers and engineers and doctors and bankers and teachers? Why must we know of these things? What is the danger to society if we don't?

What about technology? How is technology affecting our collective and individual lives, and how can American society deal with the moral and ethical dilemmas posed by modern technology?

What about equal opportunity? How important is equal opportunity to a maturing democratic society, and how does a society keep a commitment to equal opportunity alive?

And what about ethics and citizenship? A poll undertaken last year by the *Los Angeles Times* indicated that as we moved into the 1990s, issues of morality and ethics dominated the concerns of our fellow Americans.

If we wish to improve undergraduate education to meet in new ways the ends of a democratic culture, we must ask the right kinds of questions. I'm sure it is highly appropriate to ask, as did the Select Committee on Higher Education, whether or not our college and university students are graduating with the skills needed in a dramatically changing economy. And it is also appropriate to ask, as so many blue-ribbon commissions have asked in the past decade, whether or not our colleges and universities are successful in transmitting to this generation of youth the cultural wisdom of the past—whether that wisdom is conceived narrowly in the sense of the Western tradition or more broadly in the sense of minority and non-Western traditions as well. And it is appropriate to ask, as so many faculty committees engaged in curricular reform have asked in recent years, whether students are gaining sufficient familiarity with the methods of inquiry of the various disciplines.

Those are important questions, but they are not the only ones that we must ask. Indeed, they may not even be the most important ones. If we stop with these questions, we will fall short in developing core curricula that might help us to reclaim in far-reaching ways the civic function of higher education. Thus to these questions we must add others:

As we move closer to the next century, what problems and issues of our society will need to be addressed by our college-educated citizens?

And what kinds of knowledge, what forms of inquiry, and what methods of teaching might work to further democratic institutions and values, to develop a sense of community, and to extend to an ever-increasing number of our citizens the fruits of democracy and the joys of participating in this community?

To ask these questions is to ask whether or not it is possible for us to further develop a vision of higher education in which our colleges and universities are at the very center of democratic life. In such a vision, general education programs would take on new priority, for through such programs graduates of our colleges and universities would be prepared for creative and responsible membership in the self-governing body politic, graduates who would possess an understanding of the most important public issues that need to be addressed by our society if democratic culture is to flourish.

The development of such a vision is the challenge now facing our colleges and universities. A remarkable opportunity has come your way. You have an open invitation from the State of Texas to develop general education programs that will meet the needs of students and society well into the twenty-first century. The mandate given to the higher education community by the state to develop core curricula should not be perceived as a burden, but as a chance to move our colleges and universities into the very center of society, a chance to reclaim in new ways the civic function of higher learning, to demonstrate that colleges and universities are important to the state not just because they feed the engines of economic growth, not just because they provide opportunity for individual advancement, and not just because they transmit the cultural wisdom of the past, but because they are absolutely essential to the well-being of democracy, to the preservation of free institutions, to the development of community, and to the quest for a more just, peaceful, and happier world.

But what will it take to reclaim the civic function of higher learning through general education programs that meet in new and far deeper ways the needs of democratic culture?

It will take college and university administrators who are willing to place the advancement of general education at the top of their institutions' agendas.

It will take senior faculty members who are willing to allocate considerable time to the difficult process of undergraduate curriculum reform.

It will take faculty who are willing to reclaim the importance of teaching and to work toward a tenure system in our research universities in which devotion to and excellence in teaching are given new and expanded priority.

It will take faculty members who are willing to move beyond the boundaries of their disciplines in order to develop new interdisciplinary and multidisciplinary programs and courses, and a willingness to engage in team teaching in introductory courses.

It will take departments that are willing to give up useless turf battles.

It will take a remarkable level of collegiality as the intellectual frameworks for new core curricula are developed.

It will take new mechanisms for sharing information among colleges and universities, so that schools can learn from each other.

It will take a new appreciation for synthesis and coherence, and a willingness to make connections between the sciences and the humanities, between technology and human values, between history and literature, between general education and professional programs, and between general education and departmental majors.

It will take a new brand of public service scholarship that focuses on timely public questions and problems, on critical issues facing our society, with this scholarship enriching general education programs.

It will take new efforts to inform the public about what is going on, to solicit input from the community, and to demonstrate that our colleges and universities are repositioning themselves in society.

And it will take money, significant sums of money.

We cannot expect the reform of general education, we cannot expect the emplacement of substantial new core curricula, without significant new funding. If the public is serious about this business of reform, if the political leadership of the state wants to see our institutions of higher education functioning creatively in society, institutions that develop outstanding general education programs that meet the future needs of society and that relate directly to the challenges facing the state and the nation, then they should take the lead in pressing for new financial resources.

No institution can reform undergraduate education on a shoestring budget. In the process of funding higher education, new priority must be given to general education programs. Funding must take into account the critical need to reduce class size, to employ more faculty, to assign larger numbers of senior faculty to general education courses, and to improve curricula.

Faculty need time off from teaching and research in order to develop new core curriculum courses. Colleges and universities need special funding to organize workshops and summer institutes whereby faculty can be introduced to all components of the core curriculum so that coherence and integration can be assured, and whereby new faculty can be introduced to the program. And we need a Public Service Scholarship fund, modeled after the $60 million programs established to encourage university research in science and technology, with this fund earmarked for research in the humanities and social sciences, with the bulk of funds reserved for projects that deal with issues and topics of grave importance to the state and nation, projects that also would help support core curricula programs. A fund that is even one-tenth the amount appropriated for science and technology would be welcomed and would make a major difference.

To those who believe that the state already is appropriating enough money for new initiatives in undergraduate education, I would suggest they take a close look at these recent NEH grants to Texas institutions for curricular development:

- Amarillo College, $95,000 to develop a new Western Civilization course;
- Galveston College, $25,967 to plan a core humanities course;
- Tarrant County Junior College, $92,000 for faculty development in support of a core curriculum;
- University of Texas at San Antonio, $100,000 to develop core courses for a new interdisciplinary degree for elementary school teachers.

These figures demonstrate the kind of money that is needed when colleges and universities take on the task of curricular reform. It is difficult to see how major progress in achieving the reform of under-graduate education can take place without significant new funding from the state. These grants from the federal government are extraordinarily important, and I am most grateful—and I know you are most grateful—for the Endowment's ability to support worthwhile projects in Texas, but it is not the responsibility of the federal government to do for Texas what Texas ought to be able to do for itself. Nor is there enough federal money—even if every college and university in the state could submit competitive proposals to NEH—to make a sustained and major differ-ence in undergraduate education in Texas, given the number of institu-tions in the state. In short, the state must accept its responsibility to provide enough funds to ensure that colleges and universities can pro-ceed with the improvement of general education and can achieve the broad objectives established in the last several years.

Of course we must not let the lack of significant new funding keep us from moving ahead in the best possible ways; the risk to society of doing nothing is unacceptably high. But if adequate financial resources are made available, I am confident that the 1990s can be a decade marked by the further advancement of undergraduate education in Texas and the repositioning of our colleges and universities for leadership in the twenty-first century.

Establishing in every college and university a first-rate core curricu-lum will be critical to achieving these goals. The dictionary tells us that the word "core" refers to "the innermost or most important part of anything," to the heart, center, essence. A core curriculum is the heart of undergraduate education—the heart of the college and university—and it should include those courses that *all* students must take, and it should be based on what it is that society needs these students to know and understand in order to function effectively in democratic society.

I recognize the need for institutional autonomy, and the desire of each institution to determine what this center, this heart, ought to be. The core will undoubtedly be thought of differently across the state, in part because of the varying missions, resources, and constituencies of our institutions.

But this autonomy and variance should not foreclose discussion on an important question: Should there not be some common elements in the core curriculum of all colleges and universities in Texas?

Can we not take it for granted that there are certain issues of society and democratic culture that we want all college and university students in Texas to understand, and that there are certain traditions and subjects and modes of inquiry in the liberal arts that all students need to master in order to understand these issues?

I am of course suggesting that there is a core within a core—an inner core that ought to be fully transferable and that ought to be fairly uniform in all our institutions, from Amarillo to McAllen, El Paso to Beaumont. This inner core would include those introductory courses frequently associated with liberal education, for example, the history and literature of Western civilization. But it would also include multidisciplinary courses that seek to achieve with great clarity the civic function of general education; for example, courses in modern technology and human values, global issues of the twenty-first century, and contemporary democracy and its crises and opportunities.

It might be time for institutions to give up just a little bit of autonomy when it comes to the curriculum in order to help achieve the statewide reform of general education that all of us desire.

H.B. 2183 does provide a mandate to think about undergraduate education in new ways. It's time for all of us to dream about what undergraduate education in Texas could be, about how it might respond to social and political and spiritual needs as well as economic needs.

We should not underestimate the ultimate damage done when economic needs are excessively used to justify increased state appropriations for higher education. In the area of cultural policy, we have a similar problem. I cannot tell you how many times I have heard the argument that Texas should fund the arts because the arts are important to economic development by creating jobs, encouraging the relocation of businesses, and stimulating tourism. I cringe every time I hear those arguments. I don't believe we fund the arts in this country because the arts are good for economic development. We fund the arts because the arts are central to civilization, because the arts provide meaning and joy and perspective, and because the arts help all of us to be more human.

The taxpayers of Texas provide funds for undergraduate education not just because undergraduate education is important to the economy, not just because we need skilled workers, not just because undergraduate education provides opportunities for individual advancement, indeed, not just because it is a wise and noble and good thing to transmit culture from one generation to another, but because Texas needs citizens who understand the world about them, citizens who will vote and vote thoughtfully, citizens who are fully engaged in the issues of their time, citizens who can provide models of civility and decency and honesty and compassion, citizens who can dream of a better world and citizens who are not afraid to work hard to achieve that dream.

I believe that's why the State of Texas funds undergraduate education. That's why we who are outside the academy are going to press hard for increased appropriations for undergraduate education. And that's why I hope all of you who hold senior administrative positions in our colleges and universities will continue to move forward in building the very best general education programs possible. It's clear that our institutions are off to a great start—a start that promises only good things for undergraduate education in Texas in the 1990s.

Works Cited

"Americans Satisfied, According to Survey: Moral Values Reported to Cause Concern." *Austin American-Statesman*, January 2, 1990.

Boyer, Ernest L. *College: The Undergraduate Experience in America*. New York: Harper & Row/The Carnegie Foundation for the Advancement of Teaching, 1987.

Cheney, Lynne V. *50 Hours: A Core Curriculum for College Students*. Washington, D. C. : National Endowment for the Humanities, 1989.

General Education in a Free Society: Report of the Harvard Committee. Cambridge, Mass: Harvard University Press, 1945.

One-third of a Nation: A Report. American Council on Education, 1988.

Report of the Select Committee on Higher Education. State of Texas, 1987.

Report: Subcommittee on Core Curriculum. Texas Higher Education Coordinating Board, 1988.

A Survey of College Seniors: Knowledge of History and Literature, Conducted for the National Endowment for the Humanities. Princeton, N. J.: The Gallup Organization, 1989.

Texas in a Changing World

In the late 1980s, TCH launched a number of efforts to expand the study of languages and cultures in secondary and post-secondary education and to increase Texans' understanding of global issues. We were responding with enthusiasm to House Concurrent Resolution 236, adopted by the Texas Legislature in 1989, requesting TCH to initiate and sponsor programs in international studies and cultural exchange with the state's leading trade partners and to provide the Governor and the Legislature with a long-range plan for a sustained effort in this area.

In response to the first part of this request, TCH devoted, over the course of two years, considerable resources to cultural exchange opportunities. Here are a few examples:

• The Canadian government donated a series of photographic exhibitions to the Texas Humanities Resource Center and awarded $12,000 for their circulation.

• TCH assisted the Japanese Consulate in Houston with promoting programs funded by Japan for Texas teachers of Japanese history, culture, and language, and provided support for summer institutes for teachers at Southwest Texas State University and the University of Houston.

• The photographic exhibition, "Texas Visions," funded by TCH and sponsored by the Texas Photographic Society, was shown in Mexico City,

Guadalajara, and Saltillo, accompanied by a bilingual catalogue and a one-day symposium.

• Grants funds were provided to the University of Texas at Austin for a conference focusing on a major translation project for twentieth-century Mexican literature, with scholars from Mexico and Texas participating.

• Meetings to explore cultural exchange opportunities were held with consular officials of Canada, Mexico, Japan, and the People's Republic of China.

• TCH revised its grant guidelines, to include public projects focused on other nations and cultures, with the result that many local projects were funded in subsequent years.

While this work was going on, TCH developed the long-range report as requested. Texas in the 21st Century: The International Agenda, *was submitted to the Governor and the Legislature in January 1991. The report resulted in a legislative package, with sponsorship by Rep. Henry Cuellar and Senator Judith Zaffirini, of five bills filed for the 1991 session. These bills focused on the expansion of international studies and foreign languages in school and university curricula, the expansion of regional studies programs in research universities, the establishment of a division of International Affairs in the Office of the Governor, the creation of an International Education Fund, and the authorization for a Texas Academy of Foreign Languages and Cultures, with programs to be administered by the TCH.*

Unfortunately, a deficit in excess of $4 billion prevented the Legislature from enacting virtually any new program proposed in the session, including those noted above, with one exception: authorization for a program of research abroad to be administered by the Texas Higher Education Coordinating Board, when funded. Although much momentum was lost, some of the proposals resurfaced in subsequent legislative sessions, and an authorizing bill establishing the Texas Academy of Foreign Languages and Cultures was finally passed in 1993. Much to the disappointment of TCH and modern language teachers across the state, it has yet to be funded.

TCH's work in this area has continued to the extent that financial resources have permitted. In 1993 it collaborated with the Association of Texas Colleges and Universities, a statewide organization of college and university presidents, to fund and sponsor a fifteen-city program in which nine presidents made presentations before key civic organizations on the need to expand international education. A five-minute video introduction, taken from the previously-funded thirty-minute television program, Achieving Global Awareness, *a video produced for PBS stations in collaboration with the Association and TCH by KERA-TV, Dallas, was used in each program. TCH continues to encourage local projects focused on international issues and the history and culture of other nations.*

The report for the Governor and Legislature that I wrote included a short introduction, "Texas in a Changing World," reprinted here.

During the past several years, numerous blue-ribbon national commissions have argued eloquently that we as a nation must make a major new commitment to international education if the United States is to remain a global power in the twenty-first century.

Many of the reports, while recognizing that the federal government has an appropriate role to play in advancing international education, contend that state and local leadership are essential in creating a citizenry knowledgeable about key international issues and the histories and cultures of other nations. In a 1989 report, the National Governors' Association maintained that "international education must be an integral part of the education of every student" and called upon state government to expand and improve international education programs at all levels.

Across the country, various states are moving aggressively to establish overseas offices, to expand and improve foreign language study in elementary and secondary education, to strengthen university courses and programs in foreign languages and cultures, and to expand research in international issues.

In Texas, the severe economic downturn of the mid-1980s provided the impetus to move in this direction. As the state sought to diversify its economy, it paid increasing attention to the infrastructure needed to support a service-oriented, high-technology-based economy fostering international trade. An economy that solicits foreign investment, while emphasizing the exportation of knowledge, skills, and services, ultimately depends upon an education system radically different from one that is handcuffed to an insular economy dependent upon natural resources and heavy manufacturing.

In regard to state policy, initial efforts were devoted almost exclusively to primary economic considerations—for example, the establishment of the Texas Department of Commerce and the creation by the

Texas Legislature in 1987 of new scientific and technological research programs with $60 million in new funds invested. More recently, other aspects of this infrastructure have received modest attention. For example, in 1989 the Texas Legislature authorized the Department of Commerce to open overseas offices in Mexico, Europe, and the Asia Pacific region and to make these offices available to the state's colleges and universities and cultural organizations; adopted a series of resolutions calling for increased cultural and educational exchange with the state's major trade partners; adopted a resolution calling upon the State Board of Education to develop a program that will include international studies and a foreign language curriculum for Texas public schools; and asked the Texas Council for the Humanities to "initiate and sponsor . . . programs in international studies and to foster cultural and educational exchange programs, especially with the state's leading trade partners."

The primary motive behind this concern with the infrastructure supporting global awareness and international studies is the quest for a vibrant, expanding economy that will help ensure the future of Texas well into the twenty-first century. There is growing recognition that the future of the state is intimately tied to our ability to compete internationally as well as nationally. The Council on International Educational Exchange reports that thirty-three percent of U.S. corporate profits are generated by international trade, and four of every five new jobs in the United States are generated as a direct result of foreign trade.

But while the economic dimension must remain paramount, we cannot overlook other dimensions of national and international leadership. Among these dimensions, we find four to be of extraordinary importance:

• The ability of Texans to be strong and articulate advocates for democracy and free market economies throughout the world, and to lend knowledge and expertise to the many democracies and market economies now emerging;

• The ability of Texans to offer knowledge and expertise toward the resolution of major international problems that threaten peace and prosperity, including the environmental crisis, the pervasive challenges of poverty and hunger, and the economic, cultural, and political development of Third-World nations;

• The ability of Texans to promote the free exchange of ideas across borders and to further human rights worldwide; and

• The ability of Texans to understand and respect the diverse perspectives of other nations as the basis for international dialogue in meeting mutual challenges.

From this perspective, global leadership in the twenty-first century will depend upon far more than economic acumen and abundant scientific knowledge and technological skills. The new global leadership will require deep pockets of knowledge and expertise for which Texas heretofore has not generally been known. Such leadership demands a higher education system in which international studies hold a place of priority. Such leadership will require new avenues for educational and cultural exchange. And such leadership will depend upon a citizenry in touch with global issues and with knowledge of other nations and cultures, especially those that will weigh heavily on Texas and the United States in the next century.

Although policy makers have made considerable progress in the last few years in positioning the state for such leadership, it is clear that we have a long way to go. We began the process with some terrible deficiencies: rampant illiteracy; the under-education of thousands of Texas children and youth through a public school system that was failing; the continued erosion of the liberal arts in our colleges and universities; and a pervasive insularity that stultified citizen curiosity in the history and cultures of other nations and in global developments in general.

But this is changing. The deficiencies are being addressed, and gradually, persistently, we are recognizing that our own fate is increasingly tied to the fate of the world. We recognize in new and far more profound ways that, just as Texas can be a constructive economic force in the global community of the twenty-first century, so it can be a leader in building international understanding, good will, and cooperation, and in helping to resolve some of the most important social, cultural, and political challenges that confront the global community.

In the long run, these international and very human challenges pose the most serious threat to sustained economic development worldwide and to the global economic leadership of Texas. Political instability, racism, sex discrimination, religious bigotry, terrorism, debilitating debt, persistent and widespread poverty and hunger, and oppression and displacement are powerful forces that can quickly and devastatingly undermine the very best plans for commercial partnerships, international trade, and economic growth. Thus we are called upon to exercise leadership abroad in new and sometimes unfamiliar territory. The development of such leadership may very well be the principal challenge of Texas as it prepares for the twenty-first century.

The University and Society

The following address was given April 16, 1991, at the Janet and Chester H. Roth Public Affairs Symposium sponsored by Texas Woman's University and the University of North Texas. TCH's multi-year project, Texas in the 21st Century, provided the context for this address, for the relationship of the university to the public was one of the major concerns of this project.

Begun in 1988, the project was supported by a $75,000 Exemplary Project grant from the NEH and other revenues allocated by the board of directors. The economic collapse of Texas in the mid-1980s created an element of "public space" for self scrutiny as Texans pondered their past and future.

TCH pursued four important questions: 1) What are the major cultural and historical forces shaping individual and collective life as Texans approach the twenty-first century? 2) What are the primary public issues confronting Texans preparing for life in the next century, and how can the humanities be used to identify, clarify, and interpret these issues? 3) How is Texas increasingly tied to the global community, and what is the impact of these ties? 4) How can education in the humanities—in our schools, colleges and universities, and community organizations—be strenghthened and expanded?

These questions were pursued in a variety of ways. TCH sponsored

*seven university-based study groups involving over one hundred schol-
ars to provide a scholarly base for the project. TCH sponsored November
14, 1988, a major statewide public symposium involving key state officials and over four hundred attendees. TCH published in 1990 a five-
volume book series, condensing the work of the study groups. Press
conferences announcing the series were held in Austin, San Antonio,
Lubbock, Houston, and Corpus Christi. Through a request for proposals,
TCH funded projects in twelve communities. Over two hundred presentations were given by scholars on various aspects of the twenty-first century theme. Finally, I wrote an eleven-part weekly newspaper series,
summarizing the major points coming out of the project, published by
twenty-five Texas newspapers.*

*In contemplating the future of Texas, the relationship of the univer-
sity to society became for me an important issue. The following address
sought to explore this relationship. In preparing these remarks, I relied
on several previous addresses and one published work: "Great Expectations and the Politics of the Humanities," Houston Community College
Faculty Conference, February 25, 1989;* Education for the Twenty-First
Century, *Vol. 5 in the series* Preparing for Texas in the 21st Century:
Building a Future for the Children of Texas *(Austin: Texas Council for
the Humanities), 1990; and "The Humanities and the Public Interest,"
University of Nebraska Conference, Lincoln, March 11, 1991.*

Catherine Williams, in her opening essay in TCH's five-volume series, *Preparing for Texas in the 21st Century*, begins with a quotation
from Houston author Phillip Lopate: "What will happen in the latter
part of the twenty-first century God only knows. We may be ruled by
penguins or cockroaches of a higher order, but the start of the twenty-
first century is not so far away that we cannot reasonably project from
current patterns. More importantly, what do we *want* to happen?"

That question, it seems to me, should be central to our discussions
about education in the twenty-first century. Yet that is a question that
all too infrequently is asked, especially in a public context.

Education in Texas is at a genuine crossroads. The people of this
state, through their elected officials, are deciding whether or not we
will allocate the financial and human resources needed to ensure an
education system that promises a bright and productive future for Texans of the twenty-first century. At stake is the future of every elementary and secondary public school and every public college and university.

You know the issues. Can the state ensure equal educational opportunity? Can the state provide sufficient financial resources to ensure quality education in our elementary and secondary schools? Can the state find the will and the revenue to develop the kind of higher education system that Texas will need in meeting the challenges of the twenty-first century?

But the public discussion that is occurring in Austin and around the state on these questions by and large fails to address what it is that we *want* to happen. The discussion tends to focus on immediate problems, especially on funding, and not on what it is that we as citizens may want and need from our system of education. Missing is a shared vision of the interrelationship between education and the long-range needs of our society and culture, a vision that surely would help inform our discussion of these particular issues.

The development of such a shared vision is an awesome challenge, one that can be met only through symposia like this one, and through conferences and workshops that bring together professionals in education, policy makers, and the wider public.

Today you had an opportunity to explore issues related to elementary and secondary public education. Building on that inquiry, I would like to focus my remarks on public higher education, on the relationship between society and our tax-supported colleges and universities.

There is an urgent need to reclaim the civic function of our institutions of higher learning, to regain a sense of how our colleges and universities are related to a society of self-governing people, and how these institutions might be able to contribute in new and deeper ways to the satisfactory resolution of challenging social, cultural, and political problems.

This need is evident in the 1987 report of the Select Committee on Higher Education. That Committee undertook its work during another of this state's fiscal crises. The Committee conducted hearings to determine what might be ailing higher education in Texas and to obtain fresh ideas for advancing college and university study. The Committee did heroic work, and many of the sound ideas presented found their way into legislation. But the state's economic difficulty cast a long shadow on the Committee's work, and thus the report focused on the contributions that higher education can make to the diversification of the state's economy and to the education of college graduates who will have the skills needed for the post-industrial, service-oriented economy projected for the twenty-first century.

The report issued by the Select Committee identified broad goals for higher education in Texas. While the goals outlined are laudable, something is missing, for we are left with the argument that higher education is important for a) individual enrichment and advancement, and b) economic development, primarily through research. The connections between higher education and the body politic, between college and university education and the well-being of democracy and free institutions, between university education and civic responsibility, and between our universities and pressing social and cultural issues are absent.

The missing links may reflect the peculiar historical and cultural background of the state, including our penchant for individualism and our passion for economic achievement. Missing is the recognition of Texas as a community, with our institutions of higher education playing a central role in supporting that community. The relationships between our colleges and universities and broad-based goals—the extension of freedom and opportunity, the development of healthy environments, the elimination of racial, ethnic and gender discrimination, the quest for good and honest government, the application of sound values in public and private spheres—tend not to be articulated.

This report reflects a troubling fact—we simply have an inadequate framework for talking about the civic function of higher education, about the relationship between the university and the wider society. Indeed, it seems to me that many of the complaints levelled against the university in the last few years reflect this lost connection. These complaints include the decline of general education, the inability of many graduates to know important historical events and personages, the decline of geographic knowledge, the inability of many graduates to write clearly, and so forth.

The defining element in this relationship between higher education and the public for many Americans, certainly for many public officials, has been science, technology, and professional programs, as evidenced by the growth of federal and state appropriations for these fields, compared to relatively paltry revenue growth in the arts, humanities, and social sciences.

That imbalance was not always the case. This is not the time to explore the ascendancy of science, technology, and professional programs over the humanities, arts, and social sciences in the history of American higher education, but one point needs to be made. At an earlier time in the life of this nation, the defining characteristic in the relationship between the academy and the public could be found in the humanities, in a belief that the very welfare of the Republic rests upon an educated citizenry, and that liberal education grounded in the humanities has a genuine civic purpose.

Of course that belief held sway at a time when only a tiny percentage of the population—composed of men, I should add—was able to pursue college studies. It is most unfortunate that this fundamental connection between the humanities and society, between the university and the public, waned at the very time when the doors of our colleges and universities were opened to more and more citizens, including women and minorities. The defining element in the relationship between the academy and the public—the betterment of society through education in the liberal arts—tended to lose out to vocationalism and technical and professional pursuits just at the time when higher education ceased to be the elitist institution that it had been.

From this perspective, it can be argued that only now are we in a position to explore the full dimension of the civic function of higher education. But this exploration will not be an easy task. The fact that most Americans continue to define the relationship between the academy and the public in terms of individual advancement and economic payoffs, means that in many places the humanities tend to be poorly understood and inadequately funded. And when the humanities are brought into the equation, all too often the discussion seems to focus on the humanities as the handmaiden of economic development, as those disciplines that will help ensure a skilled, literate work force for a post-industrial, high tech economy. All too often one finds scant recognition of the importance of the humanities to the well-being of democracy, to the development of free institutions, to the education of citizens who will claim their civic responsibility and who will have the knowledge and wisdom to tackle the most difficult challenges facing these citizens in the twenty-first century.

So the starting point in developing this broader vision of the civic function of public higher education might be to ascertain what it is that we want from our college and university graduates. Allow me to offer five very basic perspectives that we as a society will need from our college graduates, individuals who will be the leaders of tomorrow.

We will need college-educated citizens who will be fully literate. The educational reform movement of the past decade has placed considerable emphasis on the concept of literacy. To be sure, we need citizens who can read and write and who possess the kinds of skills needed in our post-industrial economy. We should expect such skills of every college graduate. But we cannot stop with literacy at that level. A higher level of literacy is needed. Ernest Boyer of the Carnegie Foundation for the Advancement of Teaching argues that literacy must mean "teaching students to think critically, listen with discernment, and communicate with power and precision. . . . It means teaching students that language is a sacred trust . . . [and] that values are sustained by the honesty of our own words and by the confidence we have in the words of others." In this expanded notion of literacy, increasing emphasis will be placed on questions of ethics and values and on the needs and practice of democracy—that is, on ethical and civic literacy.

We will need college-educated citizens who are informed of the critical issues facing our society and culture. Public policy issues seem to grow increasingly complex, understood by only a handful of technocrats, bureaucrats, and specialized professionals. Issues related to the environment, science and technology, the economy, public finance, medicine, mass media, and so forth, are increasingly difficult to understand, beyond the comprehension of millions of Americans. And yet democracy depends on the ability of citizens to understand the world around them, to comprehend difficult and pressing public issues, to vote with knowledge and care. The future of democracy in the United States may very well depend upon our ability to overcome a growing knowledge deficit on the part of citizens in regard to policy choices.

We will need college-educated citizens who will have a grasp of the history, politics, and culture of other nations. The maturing of the global village, the free flow of ideas across borders, the development of new trade alliances and free market economies, the persistent threat of global environmental disaster, the pervasive demand for economic justice on the part of Third-World nations, all dictate the need for American citizens who speak more than one language, who are sensitive to diverse traditions and cultures, and who can serve internationally as ambassadors of good will, peace, and prosperity.

We need college-educated citizens who can help foster a new birth of community in America. In TCH's three-year project focusing on the future of Texas, the most critical need that emerged in our study was that of fostering community in Texas, and the need for community that exists in this state is surely a need that exists nationally as well. If communities are defined by common moral understandings and the necessity to reach workable compromises when agreement about those understandings fails, as writer Robert Bellah maintains, then surely community in America is threatened. The "acids of modernity," to use a Walter Lipmann phrase, continue to chip away at our sense of community, undermining our sense of connectedness. Our ability to solve difficult public issues, to imagine the lives of others, to foster mutuality and civic responsibility, to overcome the splintering effect of contemporary culture, and to counter the pervasive racism that marrs our society, are all at stake.

We will need college-educated citizens whose private pursuits contribute to public purpose. To be sure, this includes one's professional endeavors, which has public benefits, as the Select Committee on Higher Education noted. But it also includes something more—the personal quest for truth, wisdom, and beauty. That quest was once the hallmark of a liberal education. It is time that it be restored to its rightful place in higher learning. We need citizens who read widely and deeply, who reflect on "the best that has been thought and said," citizens who develop in their college years a hunger for learning, a sense of purpose and meaning that goes far beyond the economic dimension of life, beyond the desire for a decent job and a good paycheck, citizens who have a commitment to counter the shallowness, meanness, and emptiness that all too often surrounds us as we prepare to embark on a new century.

I offer these five perspectives of what we as a society need from our college-educated citizens because of the threats we face—the threat of illiteracy, the threat of public ignorance of policy issues, the threat of isolationism, the threat of unchecked individualism, and the threat of civic purposelessness.

These perspectives, and I know you would have your list as well, might help us rethink the role of higher education in the twenty-first century. Especially, I think they might help us in a number of areas:

First, general education. In many institutions of higher learning, new emphasis is being placed on general education, on programs of instruction that all undergraduates must take—regardless of professional interests—in order to graduate. In *The Meaning of General Education: The Emergence of a Curriculum Paradigm*, Gary Miller offers characteristics that might help define a general education.

General education should promote knowledge not just for the sake of the individual, but for the sake of the wider society as well.

General education should be concerned with the total environment of student and teacher and should give equal weight to the goals, methods, and content of the curriculum.

General education should be concerned with democratic processes, public issues, and the needs of a democratic society.

General education should provide ethical perspective and should help prepare students for responsible membership in society, rather than simply acquainting students with the methods and perspectives of the different disciplines.

General education should be more concerned with themes and issues than skills and competencies. The driving force behind the curriculum should be an intellectual framework rather than a statement of competencies to be gained.

If these are some of the more important characteristics of general education, it can be seen that the enemy of general education so understood is the traditional view that promotes general education as an end in itself. The traditional view supports disciplined-based departments whose tasks are to acquaint students with the work of historians, literary critics, biologists, and so forth. The traditional view sees distribution requirements as the primary structure for organizing the curriculum, with priority given to student attainment of certain skills and competencies, and to mastery of facts.

We need more than that from general education. Here in Texas, a remarkable opportunity has come our way with the state-mandated requirement of a core curriculum. An open invitation has been given to our colleges and universities—an invitation that some have accepted with enthusiasm—to rethink what it is that all students should learn during their fifty-four credit hours of general studies. This mandate should not be perceived as a burden, but as a chance to move our colleges and universities into the very center of society, a chance to reclaim in new ways the civic function of higher learning, to demonstrate that colleges and universities are important to the state not just because they feed the engines of economic growth, not just because they provide opportunity for individual advancement, and not just because they transmit the cultural wisdom of the past, but because they are absolutely essential to the well-being of democracy, to the preservation of free institutions, to the development of community, and to the quest for a more just, peaceful, and happier world.

Second, teaching. Critics of contemporary higher education are at least partially right in their belief that the languishing of general education is attributable in part to higher education values that place more emphasis on scholarship than on teaching. In a system that rewards professors for published books and articles placed in an ever-growing number of little-read academic journals, the importance and art of teaching have been neglected. As NEH Chair Lynne Cheney has noted, one talks about research opportunities and teaching loads, never the reverse. Graduate students learn early on that the ticket to success is good research rather than good teaching.

Since it is the faculty who by and large set the rules for promotion and tenure, it is the faculty who bear special responsibility in restoring teaching to its historic place—creative, imaginative teaching. Graduate programs must provide assistance and training in the art of teaching. New teacher-scholar programs need to be established so that professors are able to concentrate on teaching. Endowed chairs, now restricted to those who are accomplished in research, need to be established for those who are accomplished in teaching. Financial resources need to be secured for smaller classes, and for placing more senior faculty in general education courses.

Third, public service. All of us present here are familiar with the third category that governs promotion within the university—public service. More often than not, this category is inadequately defined and receives only token recognition. Yet public service is absolutely critical to the restoration of the civic function of higher education.

That indeed was the premise behind a report released last year by the National Task Force on Scholarship and the Public Humanities, jointly sponsored by the American Council of Learned Societies and the Federation of State Humanities Councils.

In this report, to which I had the privilege of contributing, an argument is made that we need to think more in terms of *public service scholarship* than simply *public service*. By redefining this activity, the document encourages scholarship that is determined in part by the public, through invitations extended to the scholar.

Just as the needs of our democratic society should inform our discussion of general education, so they should inform our discussion of the nature of public service performed by the scholar. The development of such scholarship on timely public issues could lead to new institutional connections between the academy and society, and would provide a basis for enriching our national cultural conversation. I am referring to public conferences, museum programming, public radio and television productions, public lectures and symposia, print media, and to collaborative endeavors with state and federal agencies and private institutions as well.

We need public service scholarship that focuses on the future of American democracy, on the impact of technology on our collective and individual lives, on how fast-changing world developments—in the Soviet Union, Eastern Europe, the Middle East, Central America, and Africa—might affect the lives and values of Americans, on the continued growth of bureaucracy and the power of institutions over individuals, on the future of freedom, on the future of the family in American society, and on the opportunities and limitations posed by the multicultural, multiracial dimensions of the United States.

Obviously, many scholars are at work on components of these issues. What we need is more public service scholarship focused on subjects of critical importance to the public, and we need new mechanisms for sharing this scholarship with the public.

Such scholarship would also undergird general education programs, since the focus of such programs would in part seek to elucidate the very same issues.

And to this I would also add the critical need to develop new partnerships between universities and public schools. The potential for public service scholarship in this arena is unlimited.

Finally, the university as a community of learners. The perspective offered earlier might help to recast the university as a community of learners in which teachers and students share a common bond, the love of learning.

The university does have a special, unique, privileged place in society. Here, where the pursuit of truth and wisdom are nourished, the imaginative life can grow, setting patterns and values that can last a lifetime. "Enchantment" occurs, the absorption of our minds in other minds, the pure pleasure that comes from the mind at play, whether student or faculty. And thus traditional scholarship, as well as the public service scholarship noted earlier, needs to be acknowledged and supported.

This is an important point, for much of what I have said underscores the social, cultural, and political significance of the humanities. My profession is that of the public humanities, and I believe strongly that new efforts must be found, if public higher education in Texas is to achieve its potential, to undergird the civic function of our colleges and universities. But I'm also a traditionalist, and I think it is important, in this quest to reclaim the social significance of the liberal arts, to remember where it all begins, in the sheer exhilaration of learning, in our individual encounter with great minds and great books, in the overpowering experience of making sense of one's own life. The wellspring of public humanities, after all, is the exercise of individual imagination. Communal vision depends upon private vision, upon the ability of each of us to see ourselves as not alone, not isolated, but as living members of the human community that stretches from the distant past through the present and on into the future, a community of men and women whose collective history is much like our personal history, a moving, dramatic story of failure and achievement, fear and hope, uncertainty and certainty, stupidity and wisdom, hate and love, deceit and honesty, tragedy and triumph, death and birth.

And therein lies the mystery. The magic of words and images. The power to see. The power to understand. The power to feel. The power to empathize. The power to heal. The passion to make whole that which all too often is broken.

So, less you think that I am emphasizing too much the connections between the university and society that ought to be made, I'll confess to you that, to maintain my balance, I not infrequently read a favorite poem, published over a decade ago by *The Chronicle of Higher Education*. Its author is Carol Jin Evans, who at the time was a junior at Metropolitan State College in Denver. The poem, titled "I Tell Them I'm a Liberal-Arts Major," speaks of a time when the humanities were out of fashion. More important, it speaks of a universal time when enchantment means everything.

> And then of course, they say:
> how quaint; and what are you going to *do* with it?
> What am I going to *do* with it?
> As though these four phenomenal years
> were an object I could cart away from college—
> a bachelor's degree across my back like an ermine jacket,
> or my education hung from a ceiling on a string.
> What am I going to *do* with it?
> Well, I thought perhaps I'd put it in a cage
> to see if it multiplies or does tricks or something
> so I could enter it in a circus
> and realize a sound dollar-for-dollar return
> on my investment.
> Then, too, I am exploring the possibility of
> whipping it out like a folding chair
> at V.F.W. parades and Kiwanis picnics.
> I might have it shipped and drive it through Italy.
> Or sand it down and sail it.
> What am I going to *do* with it?
> I'll tell you one thing:
> I'm probably never going to plant sod around it.
> You see, I'm making it a definitive work:
> repapering parts of my soul
> that can never be toured by my friends;
> wine glass balanced in one hand,

warning guests to watch the beam that hits people on the head
when they go downstairs to see the den.
You don't understand—
I'm using every breath to tread water
in all-night swimming competitions
with Hegel, Marx, and Wittegenstein;
I am a reckless diver fondling the bottom of civilization
for ropes of pearls;
I am whispering late into the night on a river bank with Zola;
I am stopping often, soaking wet and exhausted, to weep
at the Bastille.
What am I going to *do* with it?

I'm going to sneak it away from my family
gathered for my commencement
and roam the high desert
making love to it.

What do you think? Will our society be better off because of this
young woman's passion for the humanities? I suspect that it won't be
worse off and I have a hunch that in the end there are far more connections between her enchantment and the problems of our society than
we are willing to recognize. That is, the restoration of the civic function
of our colleges and universities and the continued fulfillment of human
life in the twenty-first century may well depend on the enchantment of
which this young poet speaks.

Works Cited

Boyer, Ernest L. *College: The Undergraduate Experience in America*. New York: Harper
& Row, 1987.
Cheney, Lynne, *Humanities in America: A Report to the President, the Congress, and
the American People*. Washington, D.C.: National Endowment for the Humanities,
1988.
Evans, Carol Jill. *The Chronicle of Higher Education*, Vol. 20, Number 15, June 9,
1980.
Miller, Gary E. *The Meaning of General Education: The Emergence of a Curriculum
Paradigm*. New York: Teachers College Press, 1988.
Report of the Select Committee on Higher Education, State of Texas, 1987.

Veninga, James F. and Catherine Williams, eds. *Preparing for Texas in the 21st Century: Building a Future for the Children of Texas.* Austin: Texas Council for the Humanities, 1990.

On the Future
of Public Education

John D. Moseley, former president of Austin College, took on a major responsibility in the early 1990s, managing a project to improve the public schools of his community, Sherman, Texas. Through his leadership, the Consortium for Community Education Development, Inc. was founded, with the goal of bringing together community leaders, corporate executives, teachers, parents, and concerned citizens to rethink what it is that the community should expect from its schools and what might be done to transform the educational enterprise. The TCH funded several of his community discussion programs. The results of this discussion were published for the community along with much of his personal research.

I was asked to speak at an October 28, 1993, community seminar. I wrestled with the assignment, for I wanted to do something more than simply catalog perceived ills and proposed solutions, most of which seemed to be leading nowhere. So I proposed taking a step back, to think about the primary "stories" that we once told about public schooling in America, and a step forward, to see how we might go about the task of figuring out what story it is that we hope future generations of Americans will be able to tell about public education.

My presentation, published here, offers only a framework, and not a very complete one at that. But the warm reception that I received to these

remarks told me that the exercise proposed might work at the commu-
nity level, if not at the state and national level. It seemed to be a starting
point.

For those interested in the approach suggested, I would recommend
Neil Postman's book, The End of Education: Redefining the Value of
School *(Knopf, 1995). In this provocative book, Postman argues that the*
debate over the purpose of our schools centers too much on "engineer-
ing" concerns, the nuts and bolts of testing, curricula development, teach-
ing methods, and so forth, and not enough about the "metaphysics" of
education, the ultimate purpose or "end" of education. He proceeds to
discuss five stories that might help us develop a sense of such purpose
and thus provide a sustaining rationale for our schools.

I would like for us to step back from the immediate crisis confronting public education in the U.S. in order to take in a longer, deeper
look at the role of education in American society.

We are having a difficult time dealing with serious problems confronting our schools. We seem paralyzed. Bad news is everywhere—in
newspapers, on television, in government reports. And there are a lot
of pundits who seem to be making careers off the public education
crisis. We are inundated with bad news and multiple perspectives on
what is wrong. And we know that there also are many members of
legislative bodies eager to find quick solutions to very complex problems. A little distance to all of this is in order if we are to gain fresh
insight.

I also know that many of you are on the front line dealing with
these problems day in and day out, and understand them far better
than those of us who are a few steps removed. So I'm not going to offer
my thoughts on possible solutions. Instead, I want to offer the perspective of one who is in the humanities—the public humanities. And perspective, I believe, is what the humanities help provide when it comes
to discussions of vital public issues.

So what are we going to do about education in America? In Texas?
It seems as though we really don't know what to do. Why can't we
solve the problems that are now well identified? And given the difficult
nature of these problems, what are the likely *scenarios*? What will happen?

Before we take a plunge into the unknown, into what might happen, let's remind ourselves, as best we can, of the multiple criticisms that we hear every day.

Public Education: A System in Crisis

Here are some commonly-heard complaints:

1. Children are not learning—as demonstrated by declining scores on achievement tests.

2. Far too many youth are dropping out of school.

3. Our schools are drowning in state-imposed regulations.

4. There's just too much bureaucracy in education.

5. There's too much paperwork—teachers don't have time to teach any more.

6. The curriculum is out of date—students won't be prepared for life in the twenty-first century.

7. Public education costs too much, and the way we fund public education is a mess.

8. The community seems to have lost ownership of its schools.

9. Kids are out of control—there is too much violence in our schools.

10. Teacher morale is low—the result of low pay, over-work, and an indifferent public.

11. School boards are often divided and can hardly agree on anything.

The consequence of these complaints, heard month after month, year after year, is the growing loss of public confidence across political and ideological lines.

Can we can find some explanations for this depressing situation? Let me propose a starting point. It is this: *The core myth that has sustained public education through the latter part of the nineteenth century and the first half of the twentieth century has collapsed.* As a result, we don't know how to tackle these problems. We have lost a framework for understanding them, for acting upon them. It seems as though these are problems that can't be solved within the context of the present system *and its collapsed myth*.

What Basic Myth has Sustained Public Education in the Past?

I need to define what I mean by myth. I shall take *The American Heritage Dictionary* (1973) definition: "Any real or fictional story, recurring theme, or character type that appeals to the consciousness of a people by embodying its cultural ideals or by giving expression to deep, commonly felt emotions." These are stories that we tell about ourselves to help us understand human experience. Myths are found in all cultures. For example, here in the United States, the myth of America as the "City on the Hill" has had profound impact, from the early Puritans, who drew on Biblical and Reformation images, to President Reagan, who used the myth so successfully in the 1980s. Another powerful American myth is centered in the notion of "Manifest Destiny," the story that was told in the nineteenth century as the nation conquered an entire continent and cast our eyes covetously on lands far away.

I believe that public schooling through much of our history was grounded in a myth, in a powerful story that we told, in various forms, over and over. It was this: *Our free public education system, the best in the world, prepares students to participate in the American dream.* The emphasis in this myth was placed on what education does to help the individual achieve economic success.

As I see it, here are the elements of this myth:

1. Getting a good public school education is *the* ticket to success.

2. Public schools instill a strong work ethic and provide students with a sense of personal responsibility.

3. Public schools are efficient and spend the funds they receive very well.

4. Public schools provide a well-organized and planned curriculum.

5. Neighborhood schools form the heart of our public education system.

6. Our communities take great pride in their schools.

7. Our schools are known for their order and discipline.

8. The primary emphasis in our schools is on academics.

9. Our teachers are well-educated and are greatly esteemed in their communities.

10. Our students have great respect for authority.

This myth (and its component understandings) functions as a legitimator of society and cultural values. This core myth about public education functioned to support our schools, and in doing so, society as a whole.

As the myth began to collapse, as it unraveled, we had an emerging crisis in education, locally and nationally. And because our schools have been vitally important institutions of American society and carriers of cultural values, this crisis has had a profound impact on society, on our very sense of national identity.

Why Did this Myth Collapse?

The process by which this myth disintegrated is an inadequately known and understood chapter in American history. But let me venture some thoughts on what transpired to undermine the myth.

1. Most states increased attendance requirements in the early decades of this century, making the attainment of a public education more strenuous and difficult for some students.

2. Access to public schooling was broadened to include the poor, the previously disenfranchised, and new immigrants.

3. Desegregation—the end of "separate but equal" schools, while having a profound impact on our notion of neighborhood schools, had an even greater, more lasting impact in that it destroyed (appropriately so) one component of the old myth, that *quality* education was meant for only a privileged (white) few. Henceforth, quality education must be available for everyone.

4. A public education no longer served as the ticket to individual economic success. By the mid-twentieth century, it was clear that most positions promising decent wages required some higher education, or at least specialized trade school education. And if one aimed higher, a baccalaureate degree was mandatory. For increasing numbers of students, secondary education became a stepping stone, not an end unto itself.

5. The over-professionalization of education and the emergence of powerful schools of education, with future teachers studying more and more educational theory and less and less specific subject matter, brought new problems to the educational enterprise. The existence of multiple theories of education tended, over time, to create doubt about the nature and purpose of education.

6. Increasing regulation by state legislators and central education agencies made local communities feel that they were losing control.

7. The "feminization" of the teaching profession, with the decline of male teachers, tended to undermine, in a society that still evidences patriarchal values, the prestige once associated with teaching.

8. Many pressures were brought to bear to expand the curriculum, to include, for example, "values" education and multicultural perspectives. Such expansion tended to undermine the economically driven curriculum of the past with its goal of providing the keys to economic success.

9. The last half of the twentieth century has brought widespread public distrust of leading institutions of society, including public schools.

10. We have seen in recent decades heightened fear of government and distrust of government involvement in education.

11. Violence in society was brought into the school, thus undermining that component of the myth that saw schools as safe havens.

12. We experience skyrocketing costs not related to instructional needs as schools sought to respond to new mandates.

13. Funding crises in many states happened when various methods for financing public schooling proved to be unconstitutional. Such crises left the impression that schools were troubled institutions, like many other institutions in American society.

14. We have seen the development of growing alternatives to public schooling, the emergence of private schools with the consequence that the uniqueness and prestige of public schools have been undermined.

When a myth collapses, public confidence declines, doubt sets in, and chaos reigns. We have moved, so it seems, from one stage to the next, with the crisis deepening.

Toward a New Myth

What sort of myth ought to drive public education ten, twenty years from now? Can we envision a powerful new myth that gives a grounding, a *raison d'etre*, for public education?

I recognize that one can't call a new myth into being, even though we are as human beings always creating new myths. Myths spring from the creative energies of our minds as individuals and cultures experience reality and strive for meaning. They develop over time, and we know that there are bad myths and good myths, myths that destroy and myths that ennoble. But public myths that are good and that serve humanity emerge out of conversation, out of shared experiences and shared stories. Thus it is not inappropriate for us to think about the kind of myth that we wish for public education in the coming century. Indeed, it may be absolutely necessary.

Let me propose the following as a core myth: *Our schools are indispensable institutions of American democracy, preparing our children for full citizenship in the American and global communities.*

Is this the "story" we want to tell? Note that the emphasis in this formulation of a new myth is on society rather than the individual. What might the key elements of the myth be? Here are some possibilities:

1. Our public schools are key protectors of American democratic institutions.

2. Our schools provide all students—to the best of their ability—

with an excellent foundation for participation in the national and international economy.

3. Our schools provide all students with an excellent foundation for participation in American civic life.

4. Our public schools help prepare children and youth for personally meaningful and rewarding lives.

5. Our public schools have established strong collaborations and partnerships with community organizations, agencies, institutions.

6. In our public schools, instruction and learning are geared to the abilities of each individual.

7. Since learning is dependent upon a strong sense of self-worth, our schools pay close attention to personal growth.

8. Our schools have learned to balance teaching appreciation for cultural differences with teaching that emphasizes the commonalty of human experience and values.

9. Extracurricular activities complement rather than interfere with academic programs.

10. In our public schools, all critical decisions are made at the local level, and each school is responsible for its successes and failures.

11. Faculty comprise the heart and soul of the educational enterprise, and these well-educated and highly-motivated persons are greatly esteemed in their communities and compensated accordingly.

12. Our public schools are efficient and indispensable institutions of American society, and because they have the confidence of the public, they are all adequately funded.

13. Parents and guardians are intimately involved in the educational process, provide regular input into school governance and goals, and help foster a sense of individual responsibility.

14. Our schools are helping citizens renew (remythologize) the American Dream.

"Reinventing" Public Education

Now comes the test for such a myth. Can it help us "reinvent" public education? Can it provide the framework we need for constructive action? What does it point to?

First, this myth calls for nothing less than a transformation of public schooling in America. Tinkering will not do. Radical change is needed.

Second, this myth might also help us deal with possible scenarios for public education in Texas and the U.S., to anticipate these scenarios and to determine how to respond to them.

Scenario One: Voucher/Free Market System

This scenario involves the following.

• Parental choice, with a set amount of funds appropriated by the state for each child.

• Responsibility is placed on parents/guardians for selecting specific schools for their children.

• Schools are run by churches, cultural groups, for-profit entities, and local governments.

• There will be increased national and state standards and testing of children to ensure adequacy of very diverse institutions.

• We will see great diversity in curriculum which most likely will reinforce American cultural diversity, given the dramatically different institutions sponsoring schools, thereby further dividing the American public along cultural, racial, ethnic, and political lines.

Clearly, the new core myth that we have outlined does not seem to fit very well with this scenario.

Scenario Two: A Modified Public Education System

This scenario might involve three key elements:

• Governmentally-supported schools through middle school, with a free market system (vouchers) for high schools, allowing for both public and private schools.

• Governmentally-supported schools covering kindergarten through grade twelve, but with state funding (from a more stable source than is now the case) tied to base amounts for all schools with school districts having the option to spend more.

• More autonomy/authority granted to schools at the local level.

Scenario Three: Renewal of Current Public School System

The key elements here include:

• "Reinvention" of the current system.

• Communities reclaiming their schools as vital institutions over which they have responsibility and control.

• Reformulating the funding system to ensure equality of opportunity statewide. This would imply a new and deeper state commitment.

• Developing alternatives for secondary education (magnet schools, public school voucher system allowing students to attend any institution, etc.)

• Developing strong and innovative collaborations with other community entities: businesses, libraries, civic organization, museums, public radio and television, etc.

- A curriculum that truly prepares students for the challenges of the twenty-first century.
- The enhancement of the teaching profession, including adequate pay and professional development opportunities.
- Having as the main goal of education the preparation of students for active and responsible citizenship.

Conclusion

You may of course disagree with my formulation of a new core myth or with the key components of that myth as identified. You may also disagree with the conclusion that this formation points to: the need to renew our commitment to public education, rather than adopting an exclusive free market model with government subsidies to both public and private entities.

What is important is not my particular formulation, or the conclusions drawn, but the process suggested for thinking about the future of education. Telling new stories—mythologizing—helps provide a framework for talking in new ways about what it is we want and need from our schools. It helps us distinguish between a) determining how to be, and b) determining what to do. Given the demise of the old myth supporting public education, we need sustained conversations, locally as well as nationally, about the kind of story we hope the next generation will be able to tell about schooling in America.

While it is possible to find the origins of some cultural myths in heroic acts of individuals thinking and working alone, my hunch is that the true heroes for this new myth will most likely be communities rather than individuals, people talking and working together. Through the sharing of our stories about what we hope American education might become, we might arrive at shared understandings that transcend those differences that tend to divide and immobilize.

1995

Universities and Communities: Keys to Engagement

One of the most hopeful moments in higher education in Texas in the 1990s came when Jerome Supple, president of Southwest Texas State University, raised the question, first with his faculty, then with the public, about the role of the secular university in teaching values. Given the growing public concern about perceived lost values, about moral disarray and relativism, he wanted to explore what sorts of values might be upheld and taught by the publicly-supported university.

On February 4, 1995, Southwest Texas State conducted a public symposium, held not on the university campus but, significantly so, at the local high school, on a related theme: "Civic Responsibility and Higher Education," a topic that would place the discussion of values that might be taught in a wider framework. The auditorium was full with several hundred people in attendance. Questions raised by Jerome Supple had connected with concerns of the public.

My task was to approach the subject by talking about the kind of engagement that might exist between universities and communities.

✦ ✦ ✦

This symposium—exploring the civic responsibility of the public university—is a unique event in the life of Texas. To my knowledge, this public conversation has not happened before.

243

Perhaps you are asking the same questions that I am. Why now? What has happened in our society and culture to make this conversation possible, to bring us together to talk about "the moral role of the public university in a deliberately secular state?" What has happened to make this a question of public importance?

I want to suggest that the answers to these questions can be found in two encouraging developments. The first has to do with *revisioning higher education*; the second has to do with *revisioning citizenship*. These developments are of course related, for there are deep connections between the challenges facing public higher education and challenges we face as a people in ensuring the well-being of our democratic society.

I want to offer some thoughts on how higher education might be more connected to the needs of American society, but before I do, let me speculate on why issues related to the civic responsibility of our universities have emerged at this time in the life of our state and nation, and why this revisioning of higher education and citizenship is now taking place.

Public Higher Education

We are coming to an end of an extraordinary era in higher education, an era that has made American colleges and universities the envy of the world. This era began fifty years ago, immediately following World War II. Three dominant characteristics have marked this era.

1. Expansion and access. The G. I. Bill of Rights, coupled with the desegregation of our colleges and universities, allowed many more Americans to pursue higher education. Increased public awareness of the importance of higher education to individual opportunity and economic growth led to large-scale student loan programs, increased funding, and the expansion of facilities. The percentage of persons with four or more years of college increased from around four percent in 1940 to nearly twenty percent in 1990. And the number of persons with less than four years of college but at least twelve years of school jumped from twenty to fifty-five percent in the same period.

2. Research funding. This era saw a tremendous explosion in research funding. Contracts from the Department of Defense to universities, stimulated by the Cold War, became common place. More funds came available through the National Science Foundation, the Department of Education, NASA, the National Institutes of Health, the National Endowment for the Humanities, and other federal programs. Major corporations and foundations, which looked upon universities as think-tanks for scientific discovery, technological innovation, and social problem-solving, also got on this fast-moving train. This external funding had a tremendous impact on values of the university, as seen in the prominent place that research came to assume in the higher education community.

3. Growth of professional schools and professionalism. This era also brought an explosion of new professional schools. A two-tiered system developed, with medicine, law, and business getting the university penthouse, and public administration, education, social work, public health, and other helping professions getting a lower floor. Unfortunately, the priority placed on professional schools often meant that the arts and humanities got, as Joan Mondale once observed, the university basement. But even in the basement professionalism thrived as departments became small bureaucracies and departmental loyalties shifted away from the university to powerful professional societies.

The extraordinary growth of higher education led Daniel Bell to proclaim a few years ago that the modern university has become *the* central institution of post-industrial society. But it seems clear that this era is coming to a close. We have seen in the last decade or so the emergence of powerful new realities that have placed tremendous pressures on the university, and these realities serve to mark the end of this era. Our current response to these realities—the kind of response we now offer—will help determine the nature and shape of tomorrow's university. Let me mention three such realities.

The first is *diminished public revenues.* It has become increasingly difficult to maintain our higher education system. Clearly, the kind of expansion that occurred in recent decades is over. Static public revenues, in federal research dollars as well as appropriations in many states, have led in the last few years to a greatly broadened search for new revenues, particularly from corporations, foundations, and individuals, a search which often shapes priorities within the university. Educators seeking to preserve access, retain quality, and control expenditures while trying to respond creatively to new needs and opportunities, have an impossible task.

The second new reality is *diminished public confidence* in institutions of higher learning. Citizen alienation from the primary institutions of our society has been well documented. Although polls indicate that colleges and universities, in comparison with other institutions, retain a higher level of confidence among citizens, they hold no immunity from tough public judgments. It doesn't take much these days for the public to lose confidence. Media coverage—fair or unfair—of athletic scandals, canon wars, so-called political correctness, reports of students under-prepared for today's economy, and claims that priority is often placed on research over teaching, tend to erode citizen confidence.

The third new reality focuses on the *diminished expectation that our universities can help solve the problems of society.* The public all too often perceives universities as institutions that are isolated from societal problems—poverty, illiteracy, inferior public schools, family disintegration, crime, greed, and corruption in government and business. Sometimes, even those within the university draw the same conclusion, as Derek Bok did in 1990 in his book, *Universities and the Future of America*, where he states that American universities are failing in at least part of the great challenge facing the nation: "How to build a society that combines a healthy, growing economy with an adequate measure of security, opportunity, and well-being for all its citizens."

And, if we dig a little deeper, should we not ask: Was not the growth of the professional schools within the comprehensive university supposed to solve these problems? There may be a connection between a perception of university remoteness and growing distrust of the professions. As Donald Schon points out in his book, *The Reflective Practitioner,* throughout this century we turned increasingly to professionals to solve the problems of society, only to find that designed solutions sometimes had consequences worse than the problems they were designed to solve.

Those of us involved in higher education have had a difficult time facing the prospect that the preceding era of higher education—an era of extraordinary growth, of ever-expanding research funds, of the invention and inclusion of more and more professions—is coming to an end. Indeed, attention in recent years has been primarily focused on preserving the current structure rather than working for fundamental change. To keep the current system in place, leadership has had to concentrate on expanding revenues, and, for those who must make the case over and over again to increasingly reluctant state legislatures, this tended to translate into singular focus on the importance of the economic dimensions of higher education. There, so it seems, we are walking on solid ground, avoiding the shifting sands of social and cultural problems and the quagmire of moral values.

But this defensive posture seems to be giving way now to a serious reassessment of the mission of higher education, to thinking about accountability in new ways, to reassessing priorities, to reconsidering the importance of liberal learning in an advanced technological society, to preparing students for responsible leadership in the new global community, to forming promising partnerships with community organizations and institutions, to seeing the crisis in secondary education as a matter of great relevance to all dimensions of higher education, to responding to the need for lifelong learning, and, most certainly, to addressing the loss of civility and the erosion of community in American society. New realities have created an opportunity for fresh ideas.

So now we have one answer to the question with which we began, why this inquiry into the moral role of the public university comes at this time. Nothing could be more important to the revisioning of higher education than to take on this inquiry and to have as our reference for it the curriculum and what happens inside the classroom. If the public university has a moral role to play, that role will be felt in all areas of university life, including research and community involvement. But the core of this moral role undoubtedly centers in developing the character of students—their moral capacities—and fostering in them a strong sense of civic responsibility. To engage this inquiry, one is putting one of the most important concerns of the public on the agenda of higher education—how to restore civility, decency, honesty, respect, empathy, and other cardinal virtues to American society, and in so doing one is making a significant contribution to the revisioning of higher education.

Citizenship

There is a second reason why this matter of the civic responsibility of institutions of higher education has emerged as a public concern at this time—the growing recognition that we need to revision and reinvigorate our understanding of citizenship.

We Americans are coming to another kind of ending, what Harry Boyte of the Humphrey Institute of Public Affairs at the University of Minnesota refers to as the relocation in this century of politics to the state. In an article for *Kettering Review,* Boyte argues that the origins of our current civic crisis can be found in the decline of citizen involvement in politics, in the gradual loss through the course of most of this century of a sense of having a stake and ownership in the nation. We came to see government less as an instrument of and by the people and more as a solver of problems and a provider of services. We entrusted our future to government officials and a wide range of professionals assigned the task of administering a vast array of well-intentioned but not always successful public and private programs. As a result, a vacuum was created in the public life of the nation that "had disastrous consequences for both office holders and citizens."

Boyte reminds us, however, that a different kind of politics—a different understanding of citizenship—continued to survive, at times even flourish, through much of the century. This understanding, flowing from the abundance of voluntary, civic, and reform efforts that existed in the nineteenth century, can be seen in various "mediating political institutions," like local political parties, labor unions, ethnic groups, local business organizations, settlement houses, publicly-minded churches and synagogues, and even the local press. It was alive and well in the women's suffrage organizations which taught politics and citizenship while working for enfranchisement of women voters and which inspired organizations such as the League of Women Voters. Boyte argues as well that the civil rights movement was an extension of this tradition of citizen-centered politics, as seen for instance in the Citizenship Schools of the Southern Christian Leadership Conference which provided "teaching skills of public problem solving and politics to black communities across the South."

But Boyte's point is that these developments could not counter the powerful trend of the twentieth century to relocate politics to government and professionals. The nation's civic capital, or what some scholars are calling social capital—a term used to measure the quantity of public life—has substantially eroded. In a recent article, Harvard University's Robert Putnam surveys trends in social capital in contemporary America and concludes that there has been a fundamental erosion of such capital in the last three decades. Such loss has contributed to "democratic disarray," for networks of civic engagement encourage trust, facilitate coordination and communication, promote collaboration, and make possible the discovery of shared values and purposes.

But now we have the opportunity to revision citizenship and to encourage civic engagement for a very different kind of era. The era of hoping that large-scale, publicly-funded, and traditionally-managed programs will expand employment and eliminate poverty, improve our public schools, solve the drug problem, control crime, and improve the environment appears to be over. A very different kind of effort, one combining national leadership with greatly expanded state and local responsibility, will be required. The successful exercise of that responsibility will depend upon an adequate supply of social capital. Without it, we will fail.

I believe the federal government has the capacity to make a positive difference in the quality of life, for surely it has, and I remain optimistic that the important work of professionals can be aligned with the public in healthy and productive ways. But such a belief and such an optimism do not undercut Boyte's central argument that politics needs to be re-centered in the lives of people, that we need to overcome the disconnection that now exists between ordinary people and democracy, and that, as he says, "we need a practical politics in which citizens claim and develop their own self-directed efforts in a world of diverse communities, values, and points of view." This effort calls out for new resources.

Boyte himself has helped launch a new organization, the American Civic Forum, which seeks a new role for government. "Instead of mainly providing services and making top-down decisions," Boyte said, "it should act as a catalyst . . . and provide tools for citizens and communities to solve their own problems." The name is borrowed from Vaclav Havel's grass roots group which overthrew the Communist regime in Czechoslovakia. A similar kind of effort can be found in the New Alliance for National Renewal, a network that links over one hundred organizations in nurturing local leadership.

Columnist William Broder refers to this and other new initiatives to reclaim politics as "The Citizenship Movement." For Broder and other observers, the end of this era of federal government as comprehensive problem solver must be to dramatically increase responsibility at the local level, for the problems won't go away; indeed, they may become worse. And the truth of the matter is that we are probably ill-prepared for this responsibility. Our civic infrastructure is fragile, suffering from lack of attention. Columnist William Raspberry argues that "civic duty" has come to mean only one thing—voting, and that the last period of American history in which millions of Americans saw civic duty as something more was three decades ago, during the Kennedy years, when people believed that change was possible and that they could play a direct role in bringing it about. Yes, he says, those were the days of the Peace Corps and other government-sponsored interventions, "but also the time of massive citizen participation in direct problem solving." A new generation of Americans has come to adulthood without direct experience in—or even memories of—citizen-centered politics that understands civic responsibility as something more than voting.

So now we have a second answer to our initial question, why this inquiry into the moral role of the university has emerged at this time. The second answer is that a citizens movement is underway, and many Americans are working hard to revision the meaning of citizenship as the federal role is redefined and transformed and as local communities face the challenging prospect of increased responsibility in dealing with deep social and cultural issues and problems.

We will need to strengthen our civic life by encouraging all those organizations that make up the so-called third sector of American society, to become political, not in a party or an ideological sense, but in the sense of exercising the responsibilities of citizenship, to revision what it means to be an engaged citizen. And with this task, the university has a vital role to play.

Keys to Engagement

To further this role, we will need to see the university as having certain capacities and resources that have been under-utilized in recent decades. It's ironic that in a fifty-year era of enormous expansion of higher education, our perception of the university as an institution critical to the practice of American democracy has shrunk.

I have noted elsewhere that we saw this shrinkage here in Texas in a disturbing way in the 1987 report of the Select Committee on Higher Education of the Texas Legislature, the recommendations of which helped shape higher education policy in the past seven years. In response to public concern in the 1980s over higher education, the Select Committee identified broad goals for higher education. Higher Education is important to the state, the Select Committee tells us, for two reasons. First, it provides the means for individual advancement and achievement, and secondly, it makes possible economic development. The role that higher education might play in meeting the needs of American democracy beyond these two dimensions is missing. The damage of this shrunken view should not be minimized, for this "grand design" for higher education in Texas included the recommendation, subsequently accepted by the Legislature, to require every public college and university to develop a public statement of mission that, while reflecting the nature and strengths of each institution, would tie back to this overarching understanding of the role of higher education.

When the purposes of higher education are framed in this way, what's missing, of course, is what we are discussing today—the moral role of higher education in a democratic society, a notion of civic responsibility that is broader and deeper than providing opportunities for individual advancement and economic growth. Despite the gains made through the work of the Select Committee, we paid a price for this omission.

I would like to propose that the most fundamental connection between the revisioning of higher education and the revisioning of citizenship can be found in the capacity of the public university to foster civic imagination.

If the imagination serves as a bridge between human beings, then the *civic* imagination allows us to grasp and nurture those social, cultural, and political connections and structures that can invigorate our public life, bringing together citizens to tackle public problems.

All activities of a university, from athletics to performing arts to internship programs to formal course work, can and should contribute to the development of civic imagination. For this to happen in more extensive ways than is usually the case, I would suggest the following three possibilities.

First, we need to claim and promote the public role of the scholar.

The professionalization of the scholar in the twentieth century brought with it the tendency to see the pursuit of academic knowledge as something that takes place outside of or apart from the public arena. Where this occurs, not only is there a tendency to separate scholarship from the public, there is also the propensity to write for and speak with an ever-decreasing audience. We are familiar with the criticisms often raised against some of today's scholars, that their research and writings can be understood by only their peers, that is, persons who are working within their area of specialization.

There has been, however, a powerful countertrend, especially in the humanities. Former National Endowment for the Humanities Chair Lynne Cheney noted in 1988 that "the remarkable blossoming of the humanities in the public sphere is one of the least noted, though most important, cultural developments of the last few decades."

Public programming in the humanities—conferences, seminars, lectures, exhibits, television documentaries—represents one important dimension of this public role, the dissemination and translation of scholarship to the public. Another dimension can be found in the application of scholarship to pressing social problems and issues, such as the impressive work that some humanities scholars have made in the field of biomedical ethics. And a third dimension can be found among those scholars who have chosen to write for general audiences, selecting themes and topics that hold broad public and commercial appeal.

But there is an additional and even more profound dimension to this public role—a relational dimension—that needs cultivation, a dimension that should undergird traditional forms of public programming as well as research and teaching. This relational dimension nourishes equality and mutuality between scholars and the public. It requires an openness to the public, a deep concern for democracy, and a willingness to embrace and participate in public life. As historian Thomas Bender points out, through such participation, the public benefits from "the intellectual power of theoretical abstraction that derives from an academic discipline," while the public "offers to the academic the particularity, the concreteness, of lived experience in time and place." These benefits can only be realized through public conversation.

If we are able to claim and promote the scholar's public role, including its profound relational dimension, we would be recognizing that intellectual work in American universities takes place within a democratic culture, and the heritage, experiences, problems, and promises of that culture should have a powerful influence on all activities of the scholar—research, teaching, and public service scholarship. We would be helping to ensure that the intellectual seeds we sow will be nourished by fertile democratic soil.

Second, we need to work toward a university curriculum that enhances opportunities for the cultivation of the civic imagination.

Unfortunately, students matriculating into colleges and universities in the 1990s have shown little interest in civic life. The twenty-ninth annual survey of freshmen at four hundred and sixty-one colleges and universities undertaken by the Higher Education Research Institute at the University of California and released last September, indicates that students entering college in 1994 "are more disengaged from politics than any previous class." A record low number—less than a third—said that keeping up with political affairs is an important goal in life. And only sixteen percent said they frequently discussed politics. The survey director, reflecting on the poll's results, described this year's freshmen as "people who don't see themselves as being part of the democratic process, who don't even understand how democracy works."

As this poll indicates, the cultivation of civic understanding and imagination must become a priority. The future of our democratic way of life may well depend upon it. Not all courses will contribute to this cultivation in equal ways, but all should in some way, and some should in very special ways.

General education courses—those courses that all undergraduates are required to take—bear special responsibility for the enhancement of civic imagination. "General" and "liberal" education are often used interchangeably to describe that portion of the undergraduate curriculum that all students should study. But there is an important difference. "General" education tends to draw more from the Jeffersonian and pragmatic traditions of American education, while "liberal" education draws more from a classical and "great books" tradition. Gary Miller, in *The Meaning of General Education,* makes the following distinction:

> Liberal education . . . is concerned with ideas in the abstract, with the conservation of universal truths handed down through the years, and with the development of the intellect. General education . . . is concerned with experimentation and problem solving for individual and social action, with the problems of the present and future, and with the development of the individual.

We can say that general education carries out the civic function of higher education by promoting knowledge not for its own sake but for the sake of the wider community. It is concerned with democratic processes, public issues, and the needs of a democratic society. It should provide value-oriented education that prepares individuals for, as Leland Miles says, "critical, creative, and responsible membership in the self-governing body politic," rather than simply offering students "an increasing accumulation of human knowledge," or an equally futile sample of the "perspectives and methods of multiplying disciplines and subdisciplines."

However, I should add that it is possible, indeed necessary, to incorporate traditional liberal learning—the pursuit and love of truth through the study of the greatest philosophical, historical, literary, political, and theological works inside and outside Western culture—into general education, but general education should provide the framework.

In such a curriculum, students will gain certain understandings that can help enhance the civic imagination; for example, an understanding of the most important public issues of our time; an understanding of how democracy works; an understanding of how public policy is made; an understanding of the relationships between public, private, and nonprofit sectors; and an understanding of the diverse literary, cultural, and philosophical heritages that have helped shape American society.

Such education should be participatory, and students should have ample opportunity in their general education to practice public dialogue, to talk and listen with civility, to question assumptions, to explore together possible solutions to pressing public issues, to test the waters in how a public voice might emerge from very diverse voices. In short, general education should provide ample opportunity for students to gain competence in practicing as well as preparing for citizenship.

Third, we need to expand the level of engagement between the university and the community to help rejuvenate democratic culture.

The focal point of this engagement should be with the many civic organizations and institutions that are ideally positioned to enhance the practice of citizenship.

Public libraries, service clubs and organizations, chambers of commerce, museums and historical societies, churches and synagogues, schools and PTAs, and numerous ad hoc groups organized for specific purposes, provide the civic infrastructure that can be tapped to enhance every community's capacity to bring people together to discuss and act upon difficult and pressing public issues.

A 1991 report prepared by The Harwood Group for the Kettering Foundation, *Citizens and Politics: A View from Main Street America*, maintains that in the midst of the current widespread public reaction against the political system—against politicians, lobbyists, special interests, big government, and party politics—there is a deep sense of civic responsibility, a willingness to find fresh ways of restoring integrity and vitality to the political process. Research based on focus group discussions indicates that although citizens are indeed cynical about politics as now practiced, they care deeply about public life and are troubled by their cynicism. "On Main Street America," the report says, "we have discovered a strong . . . foundation for building healthy democratic practices and new traditions of public participation in politics."

The question for today's universities, then, is how to strengthen this foundation and how to build these new traditions. The institutions and organizations that comprise our civic infrastructure need to foster more sustained opportunities whereby citizens can learn about, discuss, and ultimately act upon pressing public issues. This means finding new ways of connecting university resources with these civic groups. And the most important resource that a university has is its faculty. We need to connect faculty members with these community organizations to foster public dialogue, to promote reciprocity between academic and public knowledge, and to expand and enhance the practice of citizenship.

It would be a mistake for us to expect the university to solve major social problems such as crime, poverty, environmental deterioration, racial violence, even inadequate public schooling. But the university can provide certain kinds of resources that will assist citizens in dealing with these problems. In the past, we thought the university could help solve such problems by producing experts—professionals who would possess the knowledge and skills needed to solve these problems. Although such experts still have a role to play, we now know that a different strategy is needed. What the university can do is to enhance the capacity for the exercise of citizenship in our villages, towns, and cities so that we, the American people, are in a position to tackle tough issues and to shape our future. Federal and state governments have an obligation to encourage and financially support this university work.

All academic disciplines and fields have important contributions to make toward the enhancement of this capacity, but especially those disciplines that comprise the humanities, for the humanities provide the historical, cultural, and ethical perspectives that broaden and deepen our understanding of public issues, and provide invaluable assistance in imagining the lives of others, in discovering shared values in the midst of very diverse opinions and beliefs, and in working our way through difficult problems.

Summary

By exploring these three possibilities—claiming and promoting the public role of the scholar, working toward a university curriculum that cultivates the civic imagination in its students, and expanding the level of engagement between universities and communities—we would be making an invaluable contribution to American democracy. We would be recognizing that deep concerns of the public are also concerns of the university, and we would be putting public issues high on the agenda of higher education.

This is a unique moment in the life of the nation. It is not a coincidence that we are revisioning citizenship at the very time when we are revisioning higher education. If we can press forward with these tasks, we will be in a much stronger position to deal with the multitude of challenges that await us.

We are discovering, I think, the important contributions that universities can make to the reinvigoration of citizenship. Those universities that are taking the lead in this effort, like Southwest Texas State University, deserve the public's deepest gratitude and support. Yes, our public universities are vitally important for their contribution to economic development, and yes, they are just as important for the opportunities they offer our young people in preparing them for successful careers. But we must say as well that they are equally important—perhaps more important—for the invaluable contributions that they can make to our democratic way of life by fostering citizenship in their students and in the wider public.

Works Cited

Bender, Thomas. *Intellect and Public Life: Essays on the Social History of Academic Intellectuals in the United States*. Baltimore: The Johns Hopkins University Press, 1993.

Bok, Derek. *Universities and the Future of America*. Durham: Duke University Press, 1990.

Boyte, Harry C. "Reinventing Citizenship," *Kettering Review*, Winter 1994.

Broder, William. "The Citizenship Movement," *The Washington Post*, 27 November 1994.

Citizens and Politics: A View from Main Street America. Dayton: Kettering Foundation, 1991.

Miles, Leland. "Liberal Arts in an Age of Technology," *American Education*, June 1984.

Miller, Gary E. *The Meaning of General Education: The Emergence of a Curriculum Paradigm*. New York: Teachers College Press, 1988.

Putman, Robert. "Bowling Alone," *Journal of Democracy*, January 1995.

Raspberry, William. "Our Declining Civic-Mindedness," *The Washington Post*, November 1994.

Schon, Donald A. *The Reflective Practitioner: How Professionals Think in Action*. New York: Basic Books, 1983.

Veninga, James F. *Education for the Twenty-First Century*. Austin: Texas Council for the Humanities, 1990.

Wallace, Amy. "College Freshmen Tune-Out Politics," *Austin American-Statesman*, January 9, 1995.

What Campus Walls? The Democratization of the Humanities

The reward structure for college and university teachers has been under intense review in recent years. For those whose professional lives are centered in the public humanities, these discussions have been followed with much interest, for without a large pool of outstanding scholars committed to public programming, our work would wither.

Jamil Zainaldin, past president of the Federation of State Humanities Councils, and several of us state council executive directors, sought in the early 1990s to encourage colleges and universities to give satisfactory consideration to professional activities in the public humanities in promotion and tenure decisions. We spoke on a number of occasions before professional organizations to make the case for the value of such work.

The majority of scholars participating in public programs in Texas tend to be drawn from the ranks of senior, tenured faculty. Younger, untenured faculty by and large are too involved in establishing records as excellent teachers and researchers to take on public responsibilities. Or, to put the matter another way, public activities, while occasionally contributing to positive promotion and tenure decisions, tend to be discouraged in research universities until tenure has been achieved.

Thus while TCH has been blessed with an abundance of senior faculty members with top-rate credentials who are eager to participate in its programs, one can't help but be concerned by the lack of participation by younger scholars in public activities and by a reward system that all too often places too little emphasis on public work.

Yet on balance it is clear that after twenty-five years, the TCH, like sister councils across the country, have solicited the interest and involvement of large numbers of humanities scholars. Some serve on state humanities council boards. Others work with councils as consultants. But most are involved as panelists, lecturers, discussion leaders, resource persons, writers, and media advisors. They serve primarily for personal reasons, rather than for reasons having to do with professional advancement within their institution.

The following paper focuses on the great expansion in recent decades of the public activity of scholars. It was given at the American Association of Higher Education 1995 national conference on "The Engaged Campus: Organizing to Serve Society's Needs."

I have been assigned the task at this national conference on "The Engaged Campus" to provide commentary on the role of the public intellectual based on my experience as an executive director of a state humanities council.

I take as my launching point the cover story on "The New Intellectuals" by Robert Boynton in the March 1995 *Atlantic Monthly*. This is an important piece of reporting, not only for what it says but for what it does not say about the public intellectual. My concern is that the model followed by Boynton, however important, not lead us astray as we contemplate how scholars might better respond to the needs of American society and culture.

Boynton begins with a commonplace critique: "One of the few things most intellectuals will agree on in public is that the age of the public intellectual is over. By and large, American intellectuals are private figures, their difficult books written for colleagues only, their critical judgments constrained by the boundaries of well-defined disciplines. Think an intellectual today, and chances are he is a college professor whose 'public' barely extends beyond the campus walls."

This critique was the lament of Russell Jacoby in his 1987 book, *The Last Intellectuals*. Jacoby argued that the grand age of the public intellectual—of those predominantly Jewish writers who gathered around the *Partisan Review* in the 1930s, 1940s, and 1950s—eminent thinkers such as Edmund Wilson, Alfred Kazin, Lionel Trilling, Daniel Bell, and

Irving Howe—came to an end in the 1960s as the second generation of these intellectuals took academic posts and assimilated into American culture. For Jacoby and others writing on these influential thinkers, the public intellectual was, as Boyton says, a writer, usually independent of a university commitment, "informed by a strong moral impulse, who addressed a general, educated audience in accessible language about the most important issues of the day."

Boynton believes that a new group of public intellectuals has emerged. They differ from their predecessors in a number of ways—they are African American and not Jewish, they are inside rather than outside the university, and their primary interest has shifted from a concern with Communism and international issues to a concern with American Democracy and its racial divisions. Yet he sees these writers—Cornel West, Henry Louis Gates, Shelby Steele, Toni Morrison, Stephen Carter, Patricia Williams, among others—"as the legitimate inheritors of the mantle of the New York intellectuals."

Thus Jacoby, Boynton says, got it only "half right." Although it's true that today's scholars no longer know how to communicate with the public, there is good news: We now have a handful of academics who are speaking to a new public, intellectuals who have unprecedented access to the print media, who appear regularly on radio and television talk shows and news programs, and who write for a general audience. Although Boynton wonders whether these writers have been so assimilated by the media and American culture that they will lose their moral stance and become "mere pundits or intellectual celebrities," he expresses cautious optimism about their enduring influence.

Scholars and the Public

My central point is this: We must not let this model of the public intellectual—however important it might be—limit our understanding of how today's scholars are interacting with the American public. Indeed, I want to suggest that in the last three decades, we have seen an extraordinary array of new avenues in which scholars have transcended traditional limits placed by their disciplines and/or their institutions in order to engage the public. I, too, agree that we have had too much specialization and that too many scholars still show little interest in speaking to anyone but their peers. But it's difficult to generalize about the academic profession. For in the midst of this era marked by a propensity in some academic circles to overspecialize and to communicate only with one's fellow academics, one finds deep scholarly interest in other circles in public issues as well as a blossoming of the public humanities—the involvement of thousands of American scholars in public activities. And one finds expressions of this interest and public involvement in arenas entirely missed by Jacoby and Boynton.

One finds evidence of this interest and involvement in how scholars in recent decades have changed the disciplines of the humanities. Peter Stearns notes in his book, *Meaning Over Memory*, that the humanities disciplines, once primarily limited to describing and evaluating the great ideas and value systems embedded in the great thoughts and deeds of Western history, philosophy, and literature, have expanded outward "to considering how diverse cultures themselves are shaped and how they in turn inform institutions, expressions, behaviors, and values." In so doing, today's humanities scholars have become more, not less, responsive to the needs of American society. The growth in international studies and in studies of the history and cultures of other nations, for example, surely respond to new global realities that we can no longer afford to ignore. The same point can be made in regard to the "new social history" which responds not only to the reality of our nation's pluralism but to our need to understand in far more profound ways the historic development of American society and culture. Stearns correctly points out that after several decades of innovation in the humanities—innovation often criticized for its specialization—today's scholars are working more and more on the problem of coherence, offering exciting ways of integrating new knowledge and arriving at the kind of synthesis that contributes much to successful classroom teaching. These and other developments in the disciplines reflect important connections between scholars and the public.

One finds further evidence in the increasing numbers of scholars who write with enthusiasm and without apology for a broad public. Not too many years ago, academics who published trade books ran the risk of ridicule and ostracism. Fortunately, that situation has changed as more and more scholars publish for general audiences.

Think of the recent work of Paul Kennedy, Robert Coles, Mary Ruether, N. Scott Momaday, Robert Reich, Amitai Etzioni, Christopher Lasch, Gertrude Himmelfarb, Robert Bellah, Allan Bloom, David McCollough, and Thomas More, among many others, including those writers identified by Boynton as "the new intellectuals." These scholars, most of whom have or had academic appointments, represent very diverse disciplines, viewpoints, and interests. They are setting new standards, and in an ever-expanding circle of scholars connected with the public, these writers are often admired and envied for their skill in writing outward to an expanding public readership, even when there are fundamental philosophical or political disagreements with them.

Think too of the rich diversity of books written by these writers. Some scholars take on public issues with powerful moral analysis, including, but not limited to, those African American scholars identified by Boynton. Others offer fresh and compelling interpretations of the American experience and reflections on American culture. And still others give us crisp and clean prose that reflects on personal experience and that deepens our understanding of what it means to be human. To underscore this last point, think of the present popularity of biography and the prominent visibility given to biographers when their new books appear.

One also finds expression of this connection with the public in what might be called a public humanities movement. We tend to reserve the word "movement" for broad social and cultural developments that are easily identifiable with the passage of time. Thus some might say that it is too early to use this word in regard to the explosion of public activity in the humanities in the past three decades. But on this matter I would like to err on the side of enthusiasm, for this development in American culture is both broad and deep and provides, I believe, the most significant and promising evidence that scholars and the public are traveling the same roads.

In her 1988 report on the status of the humanities in America, Lynne Cheney noted that "Public programming in the humanities is now so substantial and extensive that it has become a kind of parallel school, one that has grown up outside established institutions of education." The parallel school finds its home among public libraries, museums, historical societies, PBS and NPR stations, independent humanities centers and institutes, and countless civic organizations, for it is these institutions and organizations that sponsor public programs in the humanities: reading and discussion programs, conferences and seminars, chautauquas, interpretive exhibits, public radio and television programs, oral and community history programs, and community forums on public issues. And in each and every one of these endeavors, scholars from colleges and universities are centrally involved.

State humanities councils have been at the center of the public humanities movement. In reflecting on state council work at a 1994 conference of the American Association of Higher Education, my colleague Jamil Zainaldin, President of the Federation of State Humanities Councils, pointed out the ways in which state councils were contributing to important social ends, including the expansion of public space where free inquiry, tolerance, and mutual respect can take place. But above all, Zainaldin said, the state humanities councils offered programs that preserve and assert "the moral worth of seriousness," a quality often in short supply in today's culture.

Dissemination and Engagement

From modest beginnings twenty-five years ago in a handful of public libraries, church basements, and city parks, the public humanities movement can now be seen in cities, towns, and villages across the country. In Texas, projects funded by the humanities council and sponsored by the many institutions and organizations that comprise the parallel school result in well over two hundred and fifty public programs a year. In addition, nearly two hundred community programs are provided by the Texas Humanities Resource Center, a component of the state council, which makes available interpretive exhibits and accompanying resources, including bibliographies, discussion guides, and films and videos. In these programs, more than seven hundred and fifty humanities scholars participate annually as planners, speakers, panelists, moderators, media consultants, and evaluators. While some of these scholars may participate in more than one program each year, the figure still points to extensive public activity on the part of Texas scholars.

Nationally, the Federation of State Humanities Councils reports that in 1993 more than twenty thousand humanities scholars participated in programs for the public, funded or sponsored by the councils. State humanities councils nationwide awarded more than eight thousand grants to local organizations and groups, enabling them to produce many times that number of humanities activities. In addition, most councils, like Texas, offer exhibits and other ready-to-use programs. Based on reports submitted by the councils, the Federation states that the total audience for council programs including lectures, exhibits, book discussions, public forums, and films, was one-hundred twenty-five million. None of these statistics take into account programs funded directly by the National Endowment for the Humanities or programs sponsored by local institutions without NEH or state council support.

Regarding this work, it is important to distinguish two very different kinds of scholarly involvement. One form of involvement centers on the *dissemination of the humanities.* This form is an extension of teaching. One's classroom is extended into the community. The scholar is invited to participate in a public program—to give a talk, to be on a panel, to serve as a consultant to a film project, to write an opening essay for an interpretive exhibit. It is this form of involvement with which most scholars are the most comfortable. Most often, original research is not required, nor is it necessary to make significant commitments to the sponsoring organization or those in attendance. They represent essentially one-time efforts. Yet this work is important, for it involves the diffusion of humanistic knowledge into the wider society.

A second form of involvement, less prominent but perhaps most promising, involves *civic engagement*. Here the scholar is working with rather than speaking to the public. A form of equality and partnership exists between the scholar and the public, and a much deeper level of commitment is required. Sometimes this involvement requires new scholarship on the part of the scholar, as he or she responds to needs and interests identified by the community. In other cases this involvement might lead to a role in which the scholar helps communities frame key public issues, discover options for dealing with those issues, and explore values underlying options identified. Here the scholar makes a direct contribution in helping communities solve public problems.

In the day-to-day work of state humanities councils, one finds many projects that include variations of these two forms of involvement. Some projects that center on a scholar working in partnership with a civic organization might also include programs where dissemination of humanistic knowledge is the goal. And some projects that begin with an event like a public lecture or seminar unexpectedly lead to more sustained efforts in which the scholar works collaboratively with the sponsoring entity on identified public interests and needs.

Such diversity in roles can be found in many projects supported or sponsored by the Texas council. Recently I have been exploring the kind of scholarly involvement that undergirded one of the major thrusts of the council since its beginning, that of discovering, documenting, interpreting, and disseminating the history and culture of the Mexican American community in Texas.

Mexican American studies in Texas, as an emerging interdisciplinary field in the humanities, received its impetus not from the academy, which in many places showed little interest, if not outright resistance, but from the community. In 1973, when the TCH program got started, the Mexican American community was demanding that the history and culture of Mexican Americans be studied, written, taught, and disseminated, for without a public history, it was argued, full participation in society is impossible. For an emerging number of Chicanos who had pursued graduate studies in the humanities, new opportunities arose for documenting Mexican American history and culture, thus providing the scholarly and intellectual foundation for a broadly-based social and cultural movement.

During the past two decades, the Texas council has supported hundreds of programs focusing on Mexican American history and culture. The cumulative impact of these programs has been extraordinary. On the one hand, these programs have contributed to a far more inclusive society in which many more Mexican Americans have assumed a rightful place in Texas and the nation. On the other hand, the academy itself has been transformed, not only in the number of Mexican American scholars who are now teaching but in the development of Mexican American studies as a field of study in the humanities and in the infusion of Mexican American history and culture into the study of American literature and history. The role of the state humanities council was that of a catalyst.

What I discovered in my review of these projects, is the close relationship that existed between the participating scholars and the Mexican American community. They seemed to derive their intellectual interests and energy from the people with whom they had maintained or had established genuine conversation. They saw themselves as inside, not above or outside, this community. Thus public programs—conferences, reading and discussion programs, interpretive exhibits, and public television documentaries—came naturally, the most logical way of bringing together community interests and academic pursuits. Community leaders and scholars worked together to sponsor these projects.

The key factor in these endeavors was not that of bringing scholars before the public, although that was done, but rather in bringing the interests and concerns of the public to the scholars. In the scholars' response, one sees a blending of the public humanities as civic engagement and as dissemination of scholarship. Indeed, the process was circular: civic engagement stimulated research; research stimulated dissemination; dissemination stimulated further civic engagement.

Community Work

This example of the public humanities tells us that if we rely only on the model of the public intellectual as presented by Jacoby and most recently Boynton, we will have a very shrunken understanding of the current interaction of scholars with the public. These writers have missed an extraordinary American phenomenon, the dismantling of traditional "campus walls," the blossoming of public service scholarship. Not only have they missed the increasing numbers of scholars who write highly successful books for general audiences, beyond the handful of stars identified by Boynton as inheritors of the earlier tradition of public intellectuals, they have failed to see the extent to which the public sphere is being enriched by scholars engaged in local community work.

I have no explanation for this limited perspective, except to suggest that perhaps they are far from the trenches where much of the action is taking place. For the work supported by state humanities councils, work that is at the core of the public humanities movement, is local and involves particular communities forming alliances and partnerships with institutions of higher education and scholars.

This kind of public scholar most likely will not appear on *Nightline*, but she may very well appear on a noon news program of the local television station. The *New York Times* probably won't publish her editorial, but the local newspaper will. She won't get paid a large stipend for a lecture on contemporary American race relations before a well-groomed audience of convention-goers, but she will receive a very modest stipend for moderating a community forum on that topic.

By clinging to a romanticized vision of the public intellectual, Jacoby and Boynton have missed the movement. In his book *Intellectuals and the Crisis of Modernity*, Carl Boggs makes the point that "older modes of understanding the role of intellectuals are obsolete, demanding fundamental new theories and concepts." Indeed, the time has come for scholars to study this public humanities movement, to analyze the forms of engagement, to study its consequences on American society and culture. My own hunch is that the public humanities movement of the past three decades has had considerable influence on American society and culture. Its impact on public ideals, beliefs, and values, which are not always, perhaps not even often, consistent with the cultural and political passions of the moment, should not be minimized.

I am now involved in a project strengthening connections between scholars and the public by promoting civic engagement. Perhaps too often in our work the dissemination of the humanities has received priority over civic engagement. The Humanities and Public Engagement project, a collaborative effort of the Kettering Foundation, the National Endowment for the Humanities, and the Federation of State Humanities Councils, seeks to answer this question: How can public programs in the humanities encourage citizenship, enhance the capacity of local communities to deal with tough public issues, and strengthen the practice of democracy? Those involved in this project wish to build upon that aspect of the public humanities movement that has helped to promote civic engagement on the part of scholars. Given the pressures now placed on American civic life, this project is indeed timely.

Importance to Higher Education

The potential impact of the public humanities movement on American higher education should not be minimized. Institutions of higher education are increasingly being called upon to rethink their mission for an era strikingly different from the era that began with the tremendous expansion of higher education immediately following World War II. As part of this rethinking, college and university administrators and faculty are now dealing with tough, knotty questions regarding the moral purposes of their institutions and what obligations their institutions have to society beyond that of providing excellent educational opportunities for their students and supporting research and technological innovations that will help ensure an expanding and robust economy. While it may be possible to argue that institutions of higher education are not in a position to solve major social problems such as crime, poverty, environmental deterioration, racial violence, and inadequate public schooling, it is difficult to conclude that they don't have an obligation to help communities deal with these social problems, to expand America's social capital, to strengthen local civic infrastructures, to encourage more and more Americans to participate in finding solutions to these problems.

If institutions of higher education respond to America's contemporary civic crisis, the public humanities movement will provide far more instructive models for how to engage scholars with the public than the tradition—lost or recently regained—of the public intellectual that has been bandied about the last few years. There are few institutions of higher education that can compete for the services of these few academic stars. Nor should they. For most institutions, the task of connecting with the public can and should be done in other ways. There is here a rich history and a tradition, one that connects with people at the grass roots. It is a practice easily replicated in new settings. There is much experience out there in connecting scholarship to the public and the public with scholarship. There is much upon which every interested institution of higher education can build. In so doing, American higher education will be connecting with an even richer and longer tradition, that of civic humanism.

Works Cited

Boggs, Carol. *Intellectuals and the Crisis of Modernity*. Albany: State University of New York Press, 1993.

Boynton, Robert S. "The New Intellectuals," *The Atlantic Monthly*, March 1995.

Cheney, Lynne V. *Humanities in America: A Report to the President, the Congress, and the American People*. National Endowment for the Humanities, 1988.

Mackintosh, Esther. *Good Cents: A Federal-Private Partnership in the Humanities*. Federation of State Humanities Councils, 1995.

Jacoby, Russell. *The Last Intellectuals*. New York: Simon and Schuster, 1987.

Steans, Peter. *Meaning Over Memory: Recasting the Teaching of Culture and History*. Chapel Hill: The University of North Carolina Press, 1993.

Zainaldin, Jamil. "An Approach to Thinking About the Public Role of the Humanities Scholar," *Standing with the Public: The Humanities and Democratic Practice,* James F. Veninga and Noëlle McAfee, eds. Dayton: Kettering Foundation Press, 1997.

Part Three

The Humanities
and Society

Biography:
The Self and
the Sacred Canopy

TCH sponsored in 1982 the Texas Lecture and Symposium on the Humanities, a program that was repeated, with different subjects, for the next eight years. To launch this series, TCH selected as its lecturer historian, biographer, and university president Frank E. Vandiver. The Institute featured four successful biographers: Robert H. Abzug, Stephen B. Oates, Ronald Steel, and Jean Strouse. These five scholars had written twenty-two books, including full biographies of eight men and women.

An important goal of this program was to bring together not only biographers and persons with professional interest in the writing of biography, but avid and critical readers: schoolteachers, physicians, lawyers, ranchers, business men and women—people who wished to learn more about the nature and meaning of biographical studies. The program was immensely successful.

I edited the presentations of these scholars, along with interviews that had been conducted with four of them and published earlier in The Texas Humanist *(Vol. 4, No. 4, 1982), for* The Biographer's Gift: Life Histories and Humanism, *published by Texas A&M University Press in 1983. I wrote an essay for this collection, reprinted here. My interest was in clarifying the broader meaning of biography for the general public.*

✦ ✦ ✦

"At its best," says Frank Vandiver, "biography brings a touch of humanity from the past and can, if deftly done, offer a glimpse of humanity in microcosm." Unlike its distant cousins—profiles of living politicians, Hollywood stars, and other notables, books that tend to stimulate prurient instincts—a good biography can lead to a more thoughtful understanding of human life. The avid reader of true biography evidences a curiosity about the nature and meaning of human life as well as a special interest in particular lives. What we learn through biography and how we learn needs examining.

In my reading of recounted lives, certain patterns have emerged about the kinds of insight into human life that are gained through biography. I shall discuss three such patterns, though the reader may detect others as well.

I shall deny the temptation to discuss the obvious significance of biography for the scholar: that of a deepened understanding of one's academic field. If one teaches nineteenth-century American social history, Robert Abzug's biography of Theodore Weld surely enhances that person's scholarly pursuits. If one's academic interest is in modern military history, Frank Vandiver's biography of Black Jack Pershing makes an invaluable contribution. Although many interesting questions arise about the relationship between biography and academic fields, I shall confine myself to the implications of biography for more general humanistic inquiry. I have in mind the lay reader, regardless of profession, occupation, or intellectual interests. For the person whose life includes humanistic inquiry, the central question is, What is gained through the reading of biography?

Patterns of Insight

Biography provides us with insight into how other people have given shape to their lives; our knowledge of human personality is deepened. Hagiographic and moralistic biography provides little such insight, for we are given a false portrait of the subject, one that lacks truth and objectivity. The personality is camouflaged by the writer's motives. A biography that is a mere chronicle of a person's life also fails in this regard; we learn many facts about the subject's life—presented in "proper" sequence—but the real person of flesh, bone, and spirit is missing.

Thoughtful, carefully crafted biography seeks, as Jean Strouse says, "to illuminate aspects of a life from inside." The biographer's insight into the psychology of the subject is requisite to providing the reader with an understanding of how that person managed the vicissitudes of life and shaped his or her life amidst the numerous realities that impinged upon that life.

Leon Edel argues that in every life there is a manifest myth and a secret, inner myth. It is the task of the biographer to move behind the manifest myth—the facade—to bring forth the inner myth, the inner life. This is an extraordinarily difficult challenge demanding great insight and skill, especially since biographers are frequently confronted by "the oppressive weight" of archival material and by lives that sought to hide the inner myth and to extol the manifest myth. Faced with these problems the biographer must ask the right questions, and his method, as Edel says, "is related to the methods of Sherlock Holmes and also to those of Sigmund Freud." For Edel,

> Biography stated in these terms begins to become more than a recital of facts, more than a description of an individual's minute doings, more than a study of achievement, when we allow ourselves to glimpse the myths within and behind the individuals the inner myth we all create in order to live, the myth that tells us we have some being, some selfhood, some goal, something to strive for beyond the fulfillments of food or sex or creature comforts.

Justin Kaplan likewise argues for the necessity of discovering the inner life, the "naked self." Kaplan takes his clue from Yeats: "There is some one myth for every man, which, if we but knew it, would make us understand all that he did and thought." To unravel that myth (or myths) is to find the key to the story of a life. The good biographer, argues Kaplan, must go to the "underpinnings of personal mythologies," to the supporting structures of beliefs and values.

Biographies that evoke full lives—inner and outer persons—provide us with knowledge about how other persons have shaped their existence. We see the process by which that shape comes into being. We may like that shape, be disgusted by it, or stand in total awe of it, but, in an immediate sense, our reaction to the shape of the life is of less importance than the fact that we see the shape and the process that led to it. This knowledge is unique and it can be argued that only through biography do we have the opportunity to see a human life in its totality, a human life in its final shape, a life lived on the basis of inner myths. It is impossible to gain such knowledge of oneself and nearly impossible in regard to one's family members, friends, or associates, even if these persons no longer live. We may, in the case of a deceased parent, for instance, have a firm grasp of the course of his or her life and the dynamics of the personality, if our insight and psychological skills of analysis are up to the task. But rarely do we have access to the kind of evidence that skilled writers use in developing a biography, or spend the time and attain the objectivity needed to understand fully how the life of that parent was shaped. It is remarkable that this knowledge of another life may come to us in a weekend of reading. The biographer may spend five, ten, or fifteen years studying analyzing, and writing; the reader devours the results of this scholarly effort over a few days' time. We may spend an adult lifetime thinking now and then about our grandfather's life, piecing together history and personality; we come to know Abraham Lincoln, Walt Whitman, or Theodore Weld in a matter of hours in ways that we can never know our grandfather.

And what are the specifics of this knowledge? To use Edel's distinction, we learn much more than the events and acts that express the outer myth. We learn more than a life history. We glimpse inside the person to see a life unfold. We see the influence of environment on personality and of personality on environment. We discover anew the nature and meaning of the seasons of life. We see the fragility of the human psyche as it braces against the strong winds that would blow it asunder. We see the joy of success and the tribulation of failure. We see the magic of love and the power of hate.

We see individuals in pursuit of wholeness and meaning, and we trace their steps along this journey. We see individuals devoid of purpose and we follow them to their fateful end. If the subject is magnanimous and mature, we learn why. If the subject is cruel and deranged, we learn the reason. If the subject is pursued by demons, we have an explanation if not a reason. If the subject glides through life as easily as one could ever hope, we find a clue, if not a cause.

This knowledge, of course, comes to us by way of art, not science. The reasons, the explanations, the causes are ultimately those of the artist, not the scientist. Insight gained from biography derives from the artist's vision of a life lived on the basis of inner myths. The more we know of the subject's soul, the greater the writer's gift. The more we know of how the subject sought to shape his or her life, the greater the writer's vision.

◆

Good biography provides us with insight of another age. Frank Vandiver notes that biography is "history made personal," and to support his thesis concerning the use of biography in elucidating history he refers to Barbara W. Tuchman's essay "Biography as a Prism of History."

Tuchman's interest in biography lies in its ability to serve as a "vehicle for exhibiting an age." Biography "attracts and holds the reader's interest in the larger subject." Tuchman clarifies this point by referring to her own biographical studies. In *A Distant Mirror*, Enguerland de Coucy VII, the remarkable fourteenth-century French knight, "supplies leads to every subject—marriage and divorce, religion, insurrection, literature, Italy, England, war, politics and a wonderful range of the most interesting people of his time, from pope to peasant." In *The Proud Tower*, House Speaker Thomas B. Reed provides the means to understand fundamental ideas that helped shape America: "Reed led, through the anti-imperialist causes to Samuel Gompers, E. L. Godkin, Charles Eliot Norton, William James, Charles William Eliot, Carl K. Schurz, Andrew Carnegie, Moorfield Storey, and to their attitudes and beliefs about America." Thus biography is a most useful tool in understanding history and clarifying forces, ideas, and values that expressed an age, a country, a civilization.

Unfortunately, Tuchman's thesis that biography serves as a "prism of history" leads her to depreciate biography as psychological study. Tuchman claims that Lytton Strachey's "influence on psychological interpretation . . . has been followed to excess." She argues that "since Strachey, and of course Freud, the hidden secrets, especially if they are shady, are the biographer's goal and the reader's delight." She pokes fun at Erik H. Erikson's biographical work: "A whole book is written to show that Martin Luther was constipated. This may be fascinating to some, but is it, in fact, historically significant?"

Here we find the sharpest contrast between those who argue that the primary knowledge gained through biography is an understanding of how other persons have shaped their lives amidst the realities of human existence and those who argue that biography primarily leads to deepened knowledge and awareness of other times and places. Whereas Erikson's concern is primarily with the inner myth, Tuchman's concern is with the outer myth. Erikson's intent in *Young Man Luther* is to understand how profound psychological crises and processes shaped a life and how that life in turn helped shape a culture. Tuchman's interest, on the other hand, is to understand a culture through the public experience—the outer life—of a primary player. Tuchman provides a rationale for her rejection of the former effort: "Having a strong instinctive sense of privacy myself, I feel no great obligation to pry into a subject's private life."

This conflict, however, should not lead us astray from our immediate goal of determining what and how we learn from biography. Tuchman and Vandiver make the point well: through the study of one life we may learn a great deal about history and culture. Vandiver's biography of Black Jack Pershing is a case in point. Through Pershing's life we learn more about the history and culture of the Great Plains, the western frontier, the Philippines, Mexico, Europe, and South America, as well as a half-century of United States military history. Our knowledge of the history of American foreign policy and the process whereby the United States became a world power is enhanced. We learn about the growth of bureaucracy in a nation come of age, and our knowledge of the changing values and ideals of a culture in transition is deepened.

◆

Through biography we gain knowledge of the universal conditions under which all lives are formed and lived, the conditions of freedom and fate. By fate I mean the limits of circumstance, the conditions of a person's life that can be affirmed or transcended only by choice. One's destiny is forged through the constant interplay between fate and freedom. If freedom is not exercised—choices made—then circumstance becomes the dominant force in a person's life.

It is interesting to speculate on how the kind of biography written in this century—biography that explores the inner myth and its consequence on human behavior—might someday influence our collective understanding and vision of human life. We tend to think that the craft of biography is influenced by seminal thinkers, and it is, but the obverse may be true as well. The use of biographical studies in philosophy, theology, and artistic endeavor remains, by and large, unexplored. In particular, much can be learned about freedom and fate, the two conditions that no life can escape.

Robert Abzug, in his response to Frank Vandiver's paper, provides a preliminary framework for understanding this kind of insight. In reviewing a few successful biographies, Abzug notes that

> . . . in each case the author had made me feel at once
> the presence of the core of his or her subject and the
> illusion that that subject was yet to be created. . . . In a

sense each biographer had created the old Calvinist drama, the struggle between free will and predestination. The universe of the biography became one in which the presupposition of a fate had been reinforced by prefiguring and foreshadowing intrusions, images, and the like; yet the expectation of a life to be relived, with all its turns and accidents, had not been destroyed. Indeed, it had been made more compelling.

Abzug concludes with the provocative statement that "good biography worked for me when it hinted in some quiet way that even as it assayed one life it ritually enacted every life."

All lives evidence the struggle between freedom and fate. Through biography we learn more of the intensity of this struggle; we perceive new dimensions to these most powerful conditions of human existence. In the life of Alice James we see the extent to which a human soul is unable to surmount, despite sometimes heroic efforts, the heavy weight of those forces determining personality. In the life of Abraham Lincoln we see the capacity of a human being to claim the freedom that does exist and to transcend, as much as might be possible, determining influences. Yet for Lincoln as well as James the struggle between freedom and fate was lifelong and peculiarly intense.

Unless the subject is a minor figure about whom we know very little, we begin a biography with a general awareness of a person's life and possibly death. What we do not know, by and large, is the course of the life—the early influences, the psychological dispositions, the weight of a culture, the molding events, and how the individual worked his or her way through, around, and beyond these fateful factors. We learn how the individual succeeded or failed to claim the freedom inherent in human existence, to make fundamental choices affirming or transcending the limits of circumstance.

The struggle between freedom and fate takes place within a context. We are not left to ponder these conditions of human existence without a reference. "Every individual biography," states sociologist Peter Berger, "is an episode within the history of society, which both precedes and survives it." Hence the individual's struggle with freedom and fate takes place within a societal and cultural context. The ideas, values, and institutions of a society influence greatly the individual's self-understanding.

Berger's work in the sociology of knowledge focuses on how we as human beings construct, maintain, change, and discard those fundamental ideas and values that sustain a society. The human community, in its pursuit of order and meaning, creates necessary structures, an objective world of ideas and values that, after a time, comes to confront the individual as a powerful reality separated from its human origins. Order in a society is preserved as long as this objective reality is affirmed by the individual. In periods of great social, cultural, and political turmoil, individuals doubt the truth of this objective reality, and such alienation gives way to new ideas and new values. Creating and sustaining an objective reality is thus an ongoing process.

Berger has an apt metaphor for the objective reality that man creates: the sacred canopy. If this canopy is convincingly in place, the institutions of a society are strong, and fundamental ideas and values are clear. No society, however, can sustain for very long a canopy that does not change. Individuals begin to doubt the prevailing canopy, and new ideas and values are projected onto it.

The fate and freedom that we learn about through biography have as their foundation the sacred canopies of a given time and place. Although one discovers some constants in these canopies, some factors that do not vary from one society to another or one time to another, one is struck by the extent of variance and change. Within our own culture and society one need look only at the biographies of two presidents, Stephen Oates's of Abraham Lincoln and Doris Kearns's of Lyndon Johnson, to see the extent to which the canopy upholding American society and culture changed from the nineteenth to the twentieth century. We see this change through the lives of two American boys who grew up to be president of the United States. The Lincoln and Johnson biographies evidence the subtle changes made in the prevailing American canopy by the communities and families of the subjects. Regional, local, and familial incorporation of certain aspects of the canopy and rejection or disdain of others can be seen. Certain ideas, values, ethics, and institutions are given sacred status in one place but not another, or in one family and not another.

Good biography is dramatic, for we see the struggle between freedom and fate within the context of a sacred canopy. To be born poor and on the frontier in the early years of the Republic is fate; we understand the meaning of this fate—and how Lincoln, in his freedom, responded to it from the perspective of a society that upholds a canopy that includes specific ideas about the common man, about individualism and success, about honesty and simplicity. To be born in 1908 in a farmhouse alongside the Pedernales River in the Hill Country of Texas, the son of a hard-drinking, domino-playing father and a self-denying,

Browning-loving mother, is fate; we understand the power and nature of this fate in the context of Lyndon Johnson's claim on the American dream, on aspirations and ideals rooted in the sacred canopy of twentieth-century America. To be born into the James family of Boston in the mid-nineteenth century is also fate, but the power and dimensions of that fate can be known only by looking at the peculiar Jamesian adaptation of the nineteenth-century American sacred canopy.

Every life story, then, is about an individual's relationship to a sacred canopy. Our journey through life is ultimately a solitary affair, for we are forced to deal with that canopy. We internalize parts of it, making those parts our own, and that contributes to our fate. We reject other parts, and that too is our fate, but, in our human creativity, we exercise our freedom to create our own reality, to change the canopy (with the consequence that our children and grandchildren must struggle with those changes). If the canopy crumbles through our experience, we must endure the confusion of a world that no longer makes sense. Therein lie our freedom and fate as well.

Ronald Steel makes an interesting point about the kind of biography read by this generation: ". . . we seek not reassuring tales of people who conform to society's restrictions but inspiring accounts of those who overcome obstacle and tradition. We are exalted not by lives of the saints but by heroic exploits against great odds and unfeeling bureaucracies." Our penchant for this kind of biography reflects the fact that the sacred canopy of our society is filled with holes. Confused over what is true, right, good, and beautiful, we cast about for stories of people who struggled to find a way—through freedom and fate—to wholeness and purpose. At the same time we are curious about those who fail, those who go mad when "obstacle and tradition" cannot be overcome and "heroic exploits" cannot be undertaken. Here we find the other side of the coin, the path that some follow when the sacred canopy disintegrates. Both types of biography provide lessons, not in morality but in the intense, lonely struggle between freedom and fate.

Two Lives

Biography is a prism of history and also of the human personality, naked and clothed; and of the universal conditions of freedom and fate. Biography is the handmaiden of psychology and philosophy as well as of history.

The kinds of insight gained through biography—knowledge of how people have given shape to their lives, knowledge of other ages and cultures, knowledge of the conditions of freedom and fate—cannot be separated. Good biography and good reading depend upon the imaginative interplay of all three.

This interplay can be seen in the works of the biographers who have contributed to this volume: Robert Abzug, Stephen Oates, Ronald Steel, Jean Strouse, and Frank Vandiver. For the purpose of this essay, however, I would like to concentrate on two biographies, Ronald Steel's *Walter Lippmann* and Jean Strouse's *Alice James*. A brief summary of these helps us understand the importance of biography to humanistic inquiry.

◆

In 1955, when he was sixty-six, Walter Lippmann suffered a nervous breakdown, requiring hospitalization and weeks of recuperation. Lippmann provided an explanation: the collapse had been brought on by "trying to swim so long against the current of public opinion." Lippmann added, "Sometimes I wish I had a profession, like law or medicine or chemistry, which has recognizable subject matter and methods." The fundamental human problem of belonging to a profession that is still ill-defined cannot be minimized. Put simply, from the perspective of our earlier frame of reference, Lippmann, for much of his life, stood alone, a professional man whose profession was inadequately grounded in the sacred canopy of American society. One should not be surprised by Lippmann's breakdown after decades of exhausting work. But the reason for the breakdown, according to Lippmann, was not the work but the circumstance that his profession was insufficiently defined and understood.

Yet this most remarkable journalistic career, spanning decades from 1910 to 1970, helped Americans understand and come to terms with a world that was changing dramatically. Events and processes frequently challenged, undermined, and destroyed various elements of the sacred canopy that held late nineteenth-century America together: World War I, the Depression, World War II, the Cold War and reality of annihilation, civil disorder, the tragedy of Vietnam. Lippmann was a voice of reason for millions of Americans, a man of wisdom seeking to make sense out of events and changes that threatened the well-being of our sacred canopy and the society served by that canopy. But Lippmann provided an interpretation for new ideas, values, and structures that tended to rework and reshape this canopy. With eyes on the future, Lippmann was in the business of refurbishing a sacred canopy.

Lippmann's personal life and ideas shared a common characteristic:

a continuing search for order, structure, and purpose. Lippmann was not comfortable with the irrational. With the exception of a few years of association with anarchists and revolutionists following his Harvard education, Lippmann shunned eccentricity, rejected iconoclasm, and distrusted emotionalism, while embracing objectivity, stoicism, and abstract intellectualism. Growing maturity and World War I transformed the young Lippmann, the author of the progressive *A Preface to Politics* (1913), into the serious, ascetic, and objective journalist and philosopher of *A Preface To Morals* (1929).

Lippmann's work, grounded in a quest for order, helped legitimize the changing nature of the sacred canopy under which Americans lived, worked, played, and died. Steel hints at this when he states that Lippmann "had a remarkable facility for not straying too far from the main thrust of public opinion." Lippmann took that opinion, sometimes rough and embryonic, and made sense out of it: "When the dominant mood was progressivist, he was a progressive; when it was for intervention, he was a Wilsonian idealist; when it was disillusioned, he was the skeptic of *Public Opinion* and *A Preface To Morals*; when it was for social change, he embraced FDR's experiments." He was not, however, a propagandist or an echoer of opinion. When he fought for Roosevelt's program, for instance, it was to give content to nascent ideas and to sharpen proposed solutions to pressing problems.

Occasionally, however, Lippmann challenged the sacred canopy of his time, questioning fundamental assumptions, values, and attitudes. To some extent, his denial of a traditional religious faith and his affirmation of secular humanism involved a rejection of some important elements in the sacred canopy of Western civilization. More important, his intellectual integrity, his willingness to confront the canopy when necessary, can be seen in a number of major issues with which he dealt, especially issues related to the early years of the Cold War. Going against the grain, he argued that the increasing militancy of the United States government should be denounced. Rejecting both the idealists, who believed that world law and international parliaments would preserve the peace, and the interventionists, who preached United States military influence worldwide, Lippmann offered, in two books published in 1943 and in his many newspaper columns, an alternative: a political accord between the Soviet Union and the United States based on mutual recognition of the need for security. Peace lay in great-power cooperation; just as Russia could not deny our sphere of influence in Latin America, so we could not deny Russia's sphere of influence in eastern Europe. As United States foreign policy sought more and more to contain communism through United States military presence worldwide, Lippmann argued against specific policy decisions of the United States, including the crusade in Turkey and Greece to suppress Communist-led rebellions, the division of Germany into two nations and the rearmament of "our" Germany, and military support for Chiang Kai-shek. What Lippmann feared ultimately happened: the dissipation of American strength and morality as the United States bolstered discredited governments in regions around the world where it had no vested interests, including Vietnam. For Lippmann, United States foreign policy had lost sight of rational objectives.

One finds in the biography a tension between Lippmann's legitimating, even with modification, certain political and social facets of the sacred canopy of twentieth-century America and his occasional challenges to such facets. Steel points out that Lippmann "felt an insider's responsibility for making the system work. He was never alienated and was in no sense a radical. He operated entirely within the system." Yet he constantly pressed beyond political platforms, bureaucratic practices, and administrative policies to the real and inherently more important values and ideas that would preserve a democratic society and maintain world order. In this process Lippmann sometimes seemed the troublemaker, the destroyer of images, persons, and policies.

Lippmann's personal life bears a strong resemblance to his intellectual life. A man of great discipline, he followed a schedule that simply could not be broken. He was, says Steel, "a person accustomed to having what he wanted." His personal life-style was so morally correct that he endured a twenty-year emotionally and intellectually barren marriage. Lippmann thought about divorce, but he did not want to be the agent of excessive pain or the recipient of hate and rejection. Instead, he withdrew and concentrated on his work; indeed, his many associations seemed to lack emotional involvement. Operating under a set of given principles and ideas, Lippmann assumed a peculiar stoicism.

All of this changed in 1937, when, at the age of forty-eight, Lippmann fell in love with the wife of one of his few close friends. For the first time in his life Lippmann was able to let go, to break through his loneliness and sense of propriety to embrace the irrationality of passionate love, whatever the costs. He divorced his wife, giving her all his financial assets, and married his lover. A new optimism and confidence emerged. In his newfound passion he could put aside the opinions and ethics of the world, and, though he worked to minimize the pain the divorce and remarriage brought to the other partners and to his colleagues, he gave in to the happiness of love.

✦

As much as Walter Lippmann was a public person, Alice James was a private person. While Lippmann was consumed with the political content of the twentieth-century American canopy, Alice James was preoccupied with the psychological realities of the late-nineteenth-century canopy. Living was extraordinarily difficult for Alice, for she had to deal as a woman not only with the larger cultural canopy but also with the peculiar adjustments the James family made to this objectivated reality.

Jean Strouse writes that "though Alice's life can be seen in several contexts—including the history of nineteenth-century women, the science of nervous disorders and the literature of the private life—it was in the family group that she lived with greatest intensity." The family "constituted a self-consciously special case, self-enclosed and self-referring." Independently wealthy, the James family (Henry, Sr.; Mary; and five children—William; Henry, Jr.; Alice; Garth Wilkinson; and Robertson) lived by virtue of a canopy within a canopy. Henry, Sr., the strong father, never held a conventional job; he spent his life "in pursuit of religious truth" and in support of his family's intellectual and cultural quest. Henry, Sr., while rejecting much of New England Calvinism, nevertheless retained a good deal of the Puritan spirit, and the story of Alice James is a story of one unable to come to terms with that Jamesian interpretation of the meaning and nature of life.

"Most families," writes Strouse, "generate myths about themselves, but few place the kind of premium the Jameses did on simultaneously reinforcing the myths and presenting private perceptions of truth for public consumption." At the heart of the James family myth, as Alice grew up, was a peculiar twist on the old Calvinist notion of the importance of success. Henry, Sr., endorsed a "strenuous individualism that stressed being extraordinary no matter what one chose actually to do" in life. The inner life was far more important than the outer life, says Strouse, and success "had nothing to do with the temporal rewards of laurels, lucre, and fame," but lay in perception and the ability to communicate a sense of self that had to do with a quality of being and the ability to see life steadily (as Matthew Arnold put it) and to see it whole."

This Jamesian understanding of success was achieved by two of the four sons, Henry, Jr., and William. The objectivated reality of nineteenth-century America presented many problems for women—as seen in the growing protest movement toward the end of the century—but the peculiar interpretation and shaping of this reality in the James family made the challenge of living doubly difficult for Alice. Strouse quotes Henry, Jr.: "In our family group girls seem scarcely to have had a chance." Strouse adds that "to be a James and a girl . . . was a contradiction in terms. The story of Alice James is one of intense "struggle to resolve that essential contradiction."

It is difficult to imagine anyone struggling harder and suffering more to resolve the contradiction than did Alice James. While her nervous susceptibility can be seen at an early age—at age fourteen, says Strouse, Alice concluded that life for her meant renunciation—she did not suffer a total collapse until 1868, when she was nineteen. Strouse describes the most fundamental dilemma faced by Alice. She was caught between two impossibilities: identifying with her father and brothers, on the one hand, and with her mother and aunt, on the other. "To use her mind productively would have meant entering the lists in competition with Henry, William, and Henry Sr." To compete with men, despite her abundant intelligence and proclivity, she found inappropriate and impossible. Thus, every time Alice began to do intellectual work, attacks of hysteria followed. But to give in to being the self-sacrificing, self-renouncing woman, as her mother and aunt had, was also impossible, for "turning in that direction would have required Alice to relinquish her sense of superior intelligence and her desire to be something more than her mother and aunt."

Alice's escape was illness. Although there were periods during the next twenty-four years when her health was more normal and she found partial outlets for her intelligence and creativity—such as teaching history with the progressive Society to Encourage Studies at Home—her life was dominated by illness and by her attempt to make sense of that illness. Strouse writes that Alice's illness "provided her with an escape route—a way out of having to choose between a safe boring life of devotion to others and a dangerous assertion of intellectual competence." It also "justified her failure to achieve while allowing her to preserve a sense of potent capacity." As Alice moved into middle age, her career as an invalid took on other meanings as well. Her illness, which increasingly involved somatic symptoms, was a form of self-assertion, with power cast over family and doctors, all of whom were unable to help. It was also a way of ensuring that she would be cared for, that someone would be looking after her, that she would not be alone in the world.

At the age of forty, three years before her death, Alice, as her illness intensified, arrived at a Jamesian solution—partial as it was—to her struggle: the keeping of a diary.

> All of her life Alice had needed an outlet for her energy and ideas. Now, at the age of forty, she found a form that suited her purposes. A diary is private, making no claim as a sort of art or an intellectual argument. She could have it all her own way because "it" was simply experience—her experience—and no objective standard could measure or condemn it. In the privacy of her own journals she could feel safe from the kind of withering judgment George Eliot had made about the "feminine incapacity for literature," as well as from the criticism she might anticipate from her brothers. The anomalous literary realm occupied by the diary lay safely within the feminine province of the personal; Alice took no overt risk of appearing to compete either with men or with successful women like Eliot.

Alice died of cancer in 1892. Strouse notes that Henry's novels, William's psychology, and Alice's invalidism were careers that grew out of "moral concerns and personal conflicts." "All three careers," says Strouse, "expressed private experience, but two addressed themselves to the world and were crowned with public success, whereas Alice's work affected only herself—and by anybody's standards, a life of incapacitating illness denoted failure and waste." Yet here was her genius and here was a way out. Illness and failure became, in the last years of her life, the raw material of life. "Failure was a bedrock human experience she could claim as her own. An expert at suffering, she could convert the waste of her life into something more lasting than private unhappiness." The diary thus became the means for a partial triumph of will over matter, freedom over fate. Born a James, Alice died a James.

Understanding

Our understanding of human life is enriched by knowing Walter Lippmann and Alice James. We see contrasting lives in their totality. We see beginnings, endings, and quests in-between.

We learn much about nineteenth- and twentieth-century history and culture through these two lives. In Lippmann, a public person who gave the world twenty-three books, several hundred articles, and several thousand editorials and newspaper columns, we find a journey though nearly all the major events and developments of this century. We see the behind-the-scenes activity of a single man and his associates, observers, and participants in twentieth-century American history. Lippmann's relationship to Lyndon Johnson, for instance, leads to a deeper perspective on the American political scene of the 1960s. Lippmann's feeling that he had been betrayed by Johnson is symbolic of the American public's feeling of betrayal over broken campaign pledges. In Alice James we find a person who leads us to the remnants of Puritanism in nineteenth-century New England; to the intellectual elite of Boston; to the social, economic, and cultural status of American women in the nineteenth century; to the history of medicine and psychology. At a more particular level, one sees the impact of the Civil War on a family's identity, provoking crises of both masculinity and femininity. William's description of Alice as an "idle and useless young female" describes prevailing male attitudes and the plight of thousands of Alices.

But we learn much more than this, for we gain insight into human psychology by knowing how Alice James and Walter Lippmann gave shape to their lives. We see, as Leon Edel says, the inner myths. The various meanings that Alice gave to her illness provide the key to her perception of herself. Some of these meanings were gleaned from prevailing cultural myths. "Illness," writes Strouse, "made women ethereal and interesting." As understood by Alice, illness was an expression of mid-Victorian ideas of femininity. Women were by nature delicate, and "a graceful languor, pallor, and vulnerability" went with the ideal of beauty. Nervousness, a particular illness, was also seen as characteristic of women with intelligence, sensitivity, and shyness. Finally, one finds the incorporation of the "bank account theory" of health: the James family was entitled to just so much good health, and the intense suffering of one would ensure that sufficient resources were left to others. By exploring these and other perceptions of illness, one begins to understand the inner myth by which Alice James lived, suffered, and died.

It is possible that the sheer weight of Lippmann's intellectual productivity can overshadow the inner myths by which he lived. The strength of Steel's biography rests in part, however, on the extent to which he demonstrates the connection between Lippmann's life and ideas and his perceptions of himself, his inner myths. In spite of his accomplishments, his apparent self-confidence, his associations with the movers and shakers of his age, and his influence on twentieth-century history, Lippmann was insecure and vulnerable. His aloofness, even coldness, and his sense of isolation were clearly recognized by Lippmann; in fact, he seemed to turn these weaknesses into strengths as America's most eminent journalist. Whether it was a contributing cause or an expression of this problem, one finds in the early Lippmann consuming ambivalence over his Jewishness. As anti-Semitism grew in the 1920s, Lippmann was forced, privately and publicly, to come to terms with his identity. In response to the question whether Harvard University should limit the enrollment of Jews, Lippmann provided, says Steel, "a masterpiece of equivocation" based on his own ambivalence. Lippmann was disturbed, he said, by the "distressing personal and social habits of Jews brought on . . . by a bitter history and intensified by a pharisaical theology." Lippmann refused throughout his life to belong to or identify with Jewish organizations. Jews must not be ostentatious or conspicuous; they should identify with the wider culture and society. Assimilation is the goal. Lippmann, while not denying his Jewishness, never spoke about it, and his associates avoided the subject. Steel notes, "In rejecting, or at least circumnavigating, his Jewishness, Lippmann had to deny a part of himself." Lippmann learned to conceal his vulnerability. Through choices affecting his career, subject matter, and associations, Lippmann successfully protected himself during a very long life. The extent to which this quest robbed him of the potential for deep and lasting friendship, derived from sharing one's most vulnerable self with others, can only be surmised.

In addition to these kinds of contributions that the two biographies make to our insight into life, the ultimate contribution comes to us, as Robert Abzug says, through the ritual enactment of every life. Lippmann and James are two very different players in the universal drama of human life. We see the nature of the sacred canopy under which they lived, the power of ideas, attitudes, institutions, and collective self-understanding. We see what they inherited, what they accommodated to, and what they sought to change. We see what was "given" to them, what they did with that which was given, and what they left behind.

Above all, we come to see the meaning of freedom and fate. Being born a Jew in New York City in 1889 or being born a female member of the James family in 1848 is fate; helping to found the New Republic or making sense out of one's invalid life through the keeping of a diary is freedom. All lives are shaped by the creative tension between freedom and fate, and good biography gives us a peculiar and special vision of the nature of this tension and the consequence on individual lives and, for public persons, on society as well.

We gain a sense of lives well lived or not so well lived. We learn a lot about dispositions, influences, values, controlling ideas, prejudices, fears, and the power of institutions. But we also learn a lot about risk, creativity, good luck, brilliance, and fortitude. We learn about suffering, failure, and death, and we learn about happiness, success, and rebirth.

What we see are lives lived under sacred canopies, whether such canopies are complete, powerful, and assuring or disintegrated, impotent, and troubling. Like the chorus of a Sophoclean play, we participate in the unfolding drama, projecting onto the story our understanding of the life being told, our assessment of the life being lived. But when the weekend is over and the biography is read, the tear that we shed is as much over our life as it is over the one whom we have come to know. We suck in our gut and go about our business, but we know more about that mysterious canopy and about the limits of circumstance and the awesomeness of choice. We are not given answers, only insight.

Frank Vandiver makes a telling point: persistence is the essence of humanism. When Alice James, in the last years of her illness-ridden life, takes up the pen and writes the first line on the first page of a small leather-bound volume in order to give meaning to her experience, we learn about persistence. When we see Walter Lippmann, a frail, totally exhausted man of eighty-four, manage to leave his bed in a nursing home to walk, with the aid of only his crutches, down the aisle of a New York Unitarian church for the funeral service of his beloved wife, we learn about human persistence. "Shockingly thin, his fine cheekbones protruding under his flaccid skin, his black suit hanging loosely on his emaciated frame, he seemed terribly alone—a solitary and immensely courageous figure."

Like Lippmann, we meet fate solitarily. With Walter Lippmann, Alice James, Theodore Weld, Abraham Lincoln, John Pershing, Martin Luther King, Jr., and many others, we may be able to meet fate with courage. Therein lies our freedom. Therein lies the gift and beauty of good biography.

Works Cited

Abzug, Robert. "Response," in James F. Veninga, ed., *The Biographer's Gift: Life Histories and Humanism*. College Station: Texas A&M University Press, 1983.

Berger, Peter L. *The Sacred Canopy: Elements of a Sociological Theory of Religion*. Garden City, N. J.: Doubleday, 1967.

_____ and Thomas Luckmann. *The Social Construction of Reality: A Treatise in the Sociology of Knowledge*. Garden City, N.J.: Doubleday, 1966.

Edel, Leon. "The Figure Under the Carpet," in Marc Pachter, ed. *Telling Lives: The Biographer's Art*. Washington, D.C: New Republic Books, 1979; reprint, Philadelphia: University of Pennsylvania Press, 1981.

_____. *Literary Biography*. London: R. Hart-Davis, 1957.

Erickson, Erik H. *Young Man Luther*. New York: Norton, 1958.

Kaplan, Justin. "The Naked Self and Other Problems," in Marc Pachter, ed. *Telling Lives: The Biographer's Art*. Philadelphia: University of Pennsylvania Press, 1981.

Kearns, Doris. *Lyndon Johnson & the American Dream*. New York: Harper & Row, 1976.

Oates, Stephen B. *With Malice Toward None: The Life of Abraham Lincoln*. New York: Harper & Row, 1977.

Steel, Ronald. *Walter Lippmann and the American Century*. Boston: Little, Brown, 1980.

Strouse, Jean. *Alice James: A Biography*. Boston: Houghton Mifflin, 1980.

Tuchman, Barbara. "Biography as Prism of History," in Marc Pachter, ed. *Telling Lives: The Biographer's Art*. Philadelphia: University of Pennsylvania Press, 1981.

Vandiver, Frank. "Biography as An Agent of Humanism," in James F. Veninga, ed., *The Biographer's Gift: Life Histories and Humanism*. College Station: Texas A&M University Press, 1983.

Ethnic History in Texas: The Road to Cultural Pluralism

Archie P. McDonald, executive director of the East Texas Historical Association, professor of history at Stephen F. Austin, and TCH board chair, invited me to provide the luncheon address at the Association's fall 1983 program. I was asked to speak on the development of ethnic history in Texas, but I wanted to do more than document significant developments in Texas studies. Of growing interest to me was the question of whether or not the explosion of new scholarship would ultimately lead to a more harmonious or a more divided state, to a more comprehensive history or to the unraveling of a history.

We will soon be celebrating the sesquicentennial of Texas's independence. There are many ways of thinking about these one hundred and fifty years of Texas history, and many perspectives that can be brought to bear. One fact, however, stands out: We have been a part of a bold experiment in the relationship between democracy and cultural pluralism. All states in the Union have participated in that experiment, but the Texas experience has been particularly rich and, to a great extent, serves as a microcosm of our national experience. Along the way, there have been some stunning successes and some overwhelming failures. As we approach the Texas sesquicentennial, we would do well to take stock of this experiment, and the role of the historian in it.

It is difficult to know where to begin but, for the purposes of this paper, let us begin with the clash of cultures that occurred at the point in time when this land became open in the early 1820s to Anglo settlement. We know much about the history of this period but, for a moment, leave aside the historical events and think with me about the tremendously divergent cultures that existed in this part of the New World. The first fifty years of Texas as a nation and then a state were shaped around cultural conflict, intense struggles involving Anglo, Spanish/Mexican, Native American, and African American cultures and societies. Each of these groups held their own unqiue perceptions about the way things are and the way things ought to be. Some, Native Americans for instance, sought, more or less, to live in harmony with nature and nature's resources, especially the land. Others, the Anglo in particular, sought to challenge nature, to subdue hostile and alien forces. The inheritors of the Spanish tradition thought that ultimate power on earth rested with the temporal instruments of God; others thought that temporal authority was derived exclusively from the people. One finds differing views and values on nearly all fundamental aspects of life—on money and wealth, on the nature of the family, on "public" and "private" property, on social and political governance, on male and female, on sex and marriage. Whether a descendant of a North Carolina white family, a slave brought by his owner from a Mississippi cotton plantation, a relative of a soldier who sought to put down the Texas rebellion, or a remnant of a once powerful Indian tribe, the people who lived in this land came from astoundingly different cultural traditions with different world views. The term "world view" implies a mythology—an overall structure to reality and experience composed of stories, legends and heroes that express commonly felt ideals and emotions. Each group, and their various subgroups, had differing mythologies, with each mythology having its own set of specific myths, symbols and images. A church, a stream, a man, a tree, a woman, a fence, might have very different meanings to people subscribing to different world views and mythologies.

What we see then, if one looks at nineteenth-century Texas, is a land very much alive with people of remarkably different histories, experiences, world views, and mythologies. Each group brought to this scene of cultural mixing and conflict something unique. I have no doubt that greed and power are forces that underlie the process of history or, to put it more directly, that conflicting myths do not alone result in revolution or slavery or the disappearances of whole races. But they have a lot to do with the historical process, and if greed is a powerful force—whether for land, free human labor, water, or whatever—there are values and mythological structures that support greed, permit slavery, and allow for genocide. Myth, of course, can play the opposite role—of opening up artificial, self protective boundaries, liberating slaves, creating governments by and for the people, or teaching classics to the Indians, as Sam Houston did. My initial point is this: Texas history cannot be fully understood without serious study of the world views and mythologies of those people who lived in this place at that time.

✦

The nineteenth-century clash of cultures between the Anglo, Spanish/Mexican, Indian, and African American was, of course, just a beginning. Some cultures were suppressed, indeed, eliminated, as in the case of some Indian tribes. Some became secondary cultures, shadow cultures, if you will, as in the case of the Texas Mexicans, or the freed blacks. White culture became diffuse as immigrants of differing ethnicity made their way to Texas—the Scotch Irish, for instance, or later, Jews, Italians, Poles, Germans, and many others. But the Anglo culture, supported by the original mythologies, world views and values, and reinforced by those European ethnic groups holding similar mythological structures, predominated. The traditional history of Texas flowed from that dominate culture and structure. A "sacred history" emerged, and the elements of that history are well known. The history flows from the Alamo and San Jacinto to the Republic to Annexation to the Confederacy to reconstruction, to industrialization, and it includes the subduing of the west, the building of towns, the work of the Rangers, the growth of the cattle industry, the building of railroads, the discovery of oil. Until fifty years ago, histories of Texas, as seen for instance in textbooks used in schools, were histories of the dominate culture and traditions. This history, for those who shared in it, was clear and well-defined, full of achievements and full of sorrows, but very understandable. Those Texans who belonged to the right tradition, those who were the inheritors of certain world views and myths, regardless of how much they had changed, had a history. To be sure, reality was a bit more complicated than that. There were, of course, plenty of blacks and Mexicans around, and most people had a vague memory of Indians once inhabiting the forests and the plains. But one didn't dwell too long on that, for the real history of Texas was there in the book and celebrated in homes, churches, schoolrooms, county court houses, and the state legislature.

But during the past fifty years, this sacred history has been slowly undermined by a growing body of historical works that document and interpret ethnic history and culture. One could cite innumerable examples—ranging from individual efforts of Texas scholars, like Américo Paredes' 1958 book, *With his Pistol in His Hand,* dealing with border culture, to Arnoldo de Leon's *They Called Them Greasers,* a just-released study of Anglo attitudes toward Mexicans in the nineteenth century. But they also include joint efforts and institutional publications, such as the series of books on Texas ethnic history published by the Institute for Texan Cultures. Along the way, there have been various studies of blacks, Jews, Italians, Germans, Czechs, remaining Indian tribes, and many others.

These studies in Texas ethnic history and culture have led to public recognition of cultural pluralism as a fact of Texas literature; that this is a state made up of very differing traditions, histories, and cultures. If the books are good, they are more than narrative histories; they provide information on an analysis of values, cultural traditions and myths of those groups. We have seen the rise of black, Mexican, and Indian studies in the curriculum of our public schools and of our universities. One must also note the growing number of films, novels, folklore studies, biographies, and poems dealing with minority cultures and experience.

◆

So the history of Texas is now far more complex than what it once was. There is no single, definitive, clear-cut history that can be passed from one generation to another. Thus, the writing of a history of Texas has become an extraordinarily difficult task. We have the obvious problem of what to include and what to leave out, but there is also the problem of how to frame Texas history, how to find the structure by which to tell the story. Do the well-worn demarcation points—the Alamo, annexation, the war between the states, the last cattle drive, Spindletop—really provide the framework by which to write a history of Texas? It is easier, I think, to write the history of Texas through the image of Texas as a melting pot than the image of Texas as a cultural mosaic. Can the Texas story still be told as history, or are we left with the possibility that it can be told only by way of art, a novel, for instance?

Beyond that point, however, we must recognize that this strange mix between a once-sacred and well-defined history and the diversity of histories and traditions and cultures that are now recognized, creates a kind of existential chaos. From the beginning, oral and then written history served a specific social purpose: to place individuals and cultures within a time and place, to explain the present by way of the past, and, most practically, to maintain institutions, values, and structures. That is, the telling of history served a religious and political purpose; religious in that it helped answer questions about the "why" of things; political in that it helped keep things together. One need only think of Hebraic history; there one finds a movement toward a common history, one that tells the story, explains things, and helps the individual know who and what he or she is. It is not surprising, therefore, that the preservers of Hebraic history held a religious office.

For all Texans, no single history can suffice. To understand what has happened to us by virtue of the growth of scholarship dealing with minority traditions and cultures, it is useful to use the Hebraic example. The Old Testament is a blending of a few differing traditions, stories, and interpretations, but a common story, a common history, nonetheless emerges, and, as the literature itself indicates, a strong effort was made to stamp out anything alien, anything that might erode that common tradition. But what would have happened if each of the twelve tribes of Israel had written their own history and, beyond that, if non-Jewish-but related cultures of Palestine had managed to weave their impure histories and traditions into the pure history and tradition?

Texas history is immeasurably enriched by a book like Professor Valentine Belfiglio's *The Italian Experience in Texas.* Our knowledge of Texas history is greatly expanded, and Italian Texans have found a history, a story to help place them in time and space. But the problem of course, is that there is no longer a single story, a unifying story, that adequately encompasses all. In the presence of so many stories, we tend to find our own: Mexican, African American, Czech, German, Anglo, East Texas, West Texas. We may find comfort in that, for we learn about our ancestors and we know how "our people" came to this moment in time. But we know that that history is only a partial one, and that others have their own very different histories.

Two particularly challenging problems emerge, one having to do with governance, the other with vulnerability. If each group claims only its own history, it is easy to say to hell with all the rest. In fact, with so many histories floating about, a certain relativity takes hold, and the power and influence of any particular history is greatly lessened. If one is black, the magnificent accomplishments of Stephen F. Austin's colonization efforts hold only negative meaning, for it can be seen as a part of a larger movement extending the evils of slavery further across the continent. If one is Indian, the only response to Mirabeau B. Lamar is one of revulsion. If one is Anglo, the border ballads about the life of the *vaquero* have little meaning. Put differently, without a common history, a common story, and common myths and symbols, public action of any kind becomes extraordinarily difficult. If you doubt that, think for a minute of the United Nations, and why establishing by consensus agreed upon goals and programs is nearly impossible. At its worst, one can foresee only impotence on the part of society and Texas government to shape a public agenda through consensus.

On the other hand, given this situation, we become vulnerable to that which promises to unite us. The history of the world is filled with false promises of unity, of short-cuts to the promised land of mutuality and shared interests. Because of the existential crisis, derived from many histories and no single history, it is tempting to find a way around the dilemma, to rally around some cause, person, process, myth, something that will make us forget our different traditions and histories, to give them up for the sake of unity.

There are some myths-in-the-making that deserve our close scrutiny, to determine whether they are productive and healthy myths that can unite us, or whether they are false myths, leading to false gods and down roads that we really don't want to go. One myth, which has its roots in the nineteenth century, is that of development. The myth of development is a myth because it is a recurring theme in our art, literature and experience that appeals greatly to our consciousness and seems to express our fondest dreams. It expresses our belief in the value of change and, as the saying goes, "progress is our most important product." That which goes by the name of development, therefore, seems good and right. Whether or not it is, of course, can only be determined by weighing the gains against the losses.

An allied myth is that of the value and beauty of a technological, information-based society. The dreamers are moving quickly these days, and before long the computer will dominate nearly everything we do. Central Texas, we are told, will one day make the California Silicone valley look like an experimental technological farm.

Note that these myths—the myth of development and the corollary myth of technology—have the potential of uniting all Texans—regardless of ethnicity—in common pursuit. I do not know if these myths are the key to our survival—they certainly would make for public consent and effective government in Austin—or the road to disaster. But they do have a way of making us forget our differences, our histories, our traditions. But, then, we must ask: Whose myths are these? From whose soil did they spring? Do we get sucked in, or do we not?

✦

Finally, we must ask: What should be the role of the historian of Texas given the nature of our times?

First, I think every effort needs to be made, where possible and practical, to relate the particular to the universal. That is, we need to make sure that an isolated event that is being studied, a particular period that is being analyzed, or a special person being interpreted, somehow relates to a much bigger picture of Texas history and culture. By relating the particular to the universal, we will be in a much better position to understand our differences, and the better we understand the differences, the better we are able to understand that which brings us together, that which transcends the differences, that which might allow us to see ourselves as a people united, as Texans.

Secondly, we need more historians who will write about these social and cultural problems, especially the problem of how historical knowledge is transmitted, and how historical knowledge helps shape public consciousness. A starting point might be joint sessions between professional historical societies and professional societies of those in other disciplines—philosophy, for instance. Collaborative work on the relationship between history and myth, on how a society transmits historical understanding, would be immensely valuable. I would like to see Texas chapters of the professional societies, including those of the psychiatric profession, exploring issues and subjects that are of interest to various humanities disciplines.

Thirdly, I think we could do more to help the public understand current issues of public interest by providing a broader and deeper historical perspective. We need more "writing outward," that is, writing to an educated public, rather than writing "up" towards one's imagined peers or simply "down" in a condescending way to mass audiences. We need to be public as well as academic historians, and we need to encourage placing historians in public contexts, not as archivists, but as scholars who can provide invaluable information that can contribute to the making of public policy.

Fourth, historians need to do what they have traditionally done: pursuing topics through research—in court houses, libraries, research centers—and, wherever possible, writing and publishing articles and books of depth and quality. I do not take this work for granted; the pressures and trends of our time do not guarantee the well-being of the history profession. But we know what our task is, whether it falls in a traditional or non-traditional area, and we know of its importance.

◆

Henry Adams, historian, was traveling in Europe in the early part of this century. He noted: "My idea of paradise is a perfect automobile going thirty miles an hour on a smooth road to a twelfth-century cathedral."

As the rate of technological development increases, we will need our twelfth-century cathedrals, and some of our cathedrals are the great works of history and literature. Historians are, in an important sense, the caretakers of these cathedrals. But historians are also the creators of these cathedrals, along with novelists, philosophers, artists, and others. Each of us has our own favorite historical works that we go back to from time to time and that we make sure our students read, not just because they provide a model of good scholarship, but because they impart to us the spirit and nature of a person, a time, an age, a culture, or a civilization. Over time, these great works of history become our cathedrals, created by historians and cared for by historians.

As I review the history of Texas history, I see many small cathedrals that are of immense importance to local parishioners and to various ethnic groups. As cathedrals, they provide a frame of reference, a sense of identity, a sense of worth.

I also see some medium-size cathedrals, belonging primarily to the Anglo tradition and, in some cases, reaching out to other traditions and experiences as well, cathedrals in which the primary movers of our society have been baptized and blessed.

I do not see large cathedrals, ones that encompass all traditions and cultures, that use the substance of those traditions and cultures in telling a story. We are still a very young state and perhaps it is too early, given our history and experience, to build such cathedrals. However much we may long for them, however much we may want a hymn that touches all hearts, however much we may desire symbols that speak to all, such cathedrals may not be built for many years. We need more time, in this cultural mosaic, to understand each other, to trust each other, to share with each other common experiences and endeavors, to know each other's histories, each other's hearts.

The definitive, perfect cathedral can never be built, for such a cathedral can only be a vision of that to which we aspire. Otherwise, we would be guilty of idolatry, of worshipping the material rather than the spiritual. But it is possible to have a vision of the perfect cathedral, and to build more beautiful, more encompassing, more universal cathedrals, to which, historically and spiritually, more and more traditions and people belong.

In the meantime, our task is as it always has been, to care for those cathedrals that already exist and, if we are lucky, to build a few new ones, however small, along the way. That, in itself, is no small task and, if done well, we will have made sure that the citizens of this state know what cathedrals are and, in so doing, we will have helped prepare the way for those more universal cathedrals that will be built when the time comes.

Works Cited

Belfiglio, Valentine J. *The Italian Experience in Texas*. Austin: Eakin Press, 1995 (re-issued).

De Leon, Arnoldo. *They Called them Greasers*. Austin: The University of Texas Press, 1983.

Paredes, Américo. *With His Pistol in His Hand: A Border Ballad*. Austin: The University of Texas Press, 1958.

1985

Windows to Understanding

This paper was given as the keynote address for the Annual Historic Preservation Conference sponsored by the Texas Historical Commission, May 3, 1985, in Fort Worth.

TCH has sought to relate its work to allied organizations, including the Texas Library Association (TLA), the Texas Association of Museums (TAM), and the Texas Historical Commission (THC). There have been many successful collaborations. For example, for many years the TCH provided funds to TAM to bring outstanding humanities scholars to speak at the Association's annual conference. Another example can be found in TCH's encouraging statewide and county historical associations to sponsor programs on local, state, and regional history. It has funded many such projects in the past twenty-five years. Most recently, TCH has entered into a cooperative venture with the TLA, led by TCH's senior program officer Monte Youngs and TLA's executive director Pat Smith, to stimulate more humanities programming in local libraries, using TCH's packaged programs.

◆ ◆ ◆

I welcome very much the opportunity to address this extraordinary association that represents all Texans who are active in preserving the magnificent heritage of our state.

I want to use this time to establish some connections between the Texas Historical Commission and the Texas Council for the Humanities, between historic preservation and the study of the humanities, between the act of preserving and the act of learning. In the ten years that I have served as executive director of the TCH, I have admired greatly the achievements of the Texas Historical Commission, and I have always felt that our missions were highly compatible. This is the first time, however, that I have had an opportunity to publicly express my understanding of the way each agency complements the work of the other.

There are some obvious political reasons as to why the making of connections among cultural agencies is a good thing to do. All of us have witnessed in recent years successful efforts to reduce federal appropriations for cultural activities, and many cultural programs have met with leaner appropriations at state and local levels. Likewise, all of us are part of a much broader sweep of recent economic and political history and theory. Particular consideration is being given to determining the most appropriate and necessary responsibilities of government at all levels, as well as determining what responsibilities might best be handled by the private sector. In such a climate, there is always the temptation for each agency to go its own way, to claim its own turf. In reality, however, our efforts will be preserved and strengthened if we are able to show how the various programs fit together, how the various agencies at federal, state, and local levels undergird the cultural life of this nation, and how the arts, humanities, historic preservation, libraries, and museums work together. More than ever, we need to explain ourselves to the public, and we must do so together and not in isolation.

Founded in 1973, the TCH works in collaboration with the National Endowment for the Humanities. Over the years, the TCH program has changed, but its primary mission has remained constant: to foster public understanding and appreciation of the humanities and to relate the disciplines of the humanities—history, literature, philosophy, religious studies, political theory, and related fields—to current public interests and issues.

We have organized the TCH program into three broad areas: grants, special projects, and *The Texas Humanist*, a bimonthly magazine. Through its grant program, the TCH awards funds—approximately $6 million since its beginning—to museums, libraries, colleges and universities, historical societies, public radio and television stations, for humanities projects. Through its special projects, the TCH implements the annual Texas Lecture and Symposium on the Humanities, sponsors occasional conferences, commissions research and original essays, publishes occasional books, and, for the Texas sesquicentennial, will sponsor fifty-two one minute episodes on Texas history and culture for commercial television stations across the state. Through *The Texas Humanist,* the TCH publishes for Texans a bimonthly magazine focusing on ideas, history and culture.

Unlike its sister cultural agencies, the Texas Commission on the Arts and the Texas Historical Commission, the TCH is a private, non-profit organization. Although primary funding comes from the NEH, it relies extensively on contributions from corporations and foundations. It does not receive state funding.

You will agree with me that our mission appears nebulous and certainly difficult. At times I have felt rather impatient with it, especially the first part of our mission statement that calls for fostering public appreciation and understanding of the humanities. It is possible to treat the humanities as if they were simply objects to be studied, like trees, for instance. There could be, I suppose, a Texas Council for Trees whose expressed purpose would be to acquaint citizens with the most important trees in our state. In that case, the staff of the Texas Council for Trees would be going about the state, organizing public programs that would equip citizens with skills needed to distinguish between live oak, pin oak, mulberry, Arizona ash, mesquite, cottonwood, and other species, and to know something about the life cycle, characteristics, and potential diseases of those species. Instead of *The Texas Humanist,* we would probably have *The Texas Forester.*

But the disciplines of the humanities cannot be treated as if they were objects, cut-off from the human spirit, separated from the creative impulse that brings us historical interpretation, philosophical analysis, novels, poetry, drama. Far from being remote and alien to the typical citizen, the humanities are closest to what it means to be human, in that the disciplines of the humanities are concerned with human experience and values. Our values (ethical, social, political, and so forth) are revealed through our history, literature, folklore and religious traditions.

Education in the humanities encourages the citizen to become an interpreter of his or her life, culture, and society. Formal humanities education begins in our public schools with instruction in English, history, foreign languages, government, and related subjects. For many, interest in the humanities does not end with high school or college education. When one reads a new biography, when one checks out a library book on an episode of American history, when one attends a museum exhibition, indeed, when one gets lost on a rainy weekend in a newly published novel, one demonstrates love for the humanities.

Where then do the concerns of those involved in historic preservation and those involved in public humanities programming overlap? What is it that unites us in common pursuit? I offer two answers, one general and one specific.

Undergirding both programs is a belief that we must not lose our common cultural inheritance. We are both entrusted with an obligation to provide current and future generations with knowledge of the past. There is similarity between the work of the preservationist and the work of the scholar of the humanities. The scholar most frequently tells a story of a person or a people in a particular time and place. Sometimes, it is a story of a people's literature, religion, folkway, or political system. The primary function of the humanities scholar, whether his or her work is carried out in the classroom, in publishing an article or a book, or in a public humanities program, is to retell in particular and universal ways the drama of human life. This work is nothing less than the preservation of our history and culture.

The historic preservationist is engaged in a similar activity. Our culture includes material objects, things built with our hands and the machines that aid us. To preserve and restore cultural products of the past—railroad stations, homes, farms, tools, entire villages—is to ensure the continuance of part of our culture, so that the story of the past can be known. Those of us who work in the humanities have come to see how important material culture is to the telling of history. In particular, historians have come to rely extensively on material artifacts in understanding and interpreting particular eras, places, groups and subgroups. I think especially of the kind of social, cultural and economic history that has been written in recent decades.

More specifically, historic preservation and humanities research and learning reflect a deep-seated, underlying belief that our lives are enriched and our prospects are brightened by remembering the past. We are acting in self-interest as much as we are acting in pleasure. It may be a nice thing to restore a nineteenth-century Fort Worth office building, and, when completed, we take delight in the architectural style and in the ambiance of a past era. But we know that much more is going on, for that structure provides an additional key to understanding the culture and history of a previous era, to contemplating the evolution of a city and a people, to knowing the links between past and present.

A recent experience has helped clarify for me the close relationship between preserving and understanding. Those of you who are avid preservationists know the difference between restoring and refurbishing a structure may smile at my example, but I'll proceed anyway, in order to make a point.

Not too long ago, my wife and I bought a house built in 1912—an old house by Texas standards. Until five years ago, that house was owned and lived in by one family spanning two generations. It is a fairly large home, located in Smithville, a small and essentially Southern town in Bastrop county just east of Austin. Adjoining the garage is a one bedroom apartment complete with water closet and half tub. We understand that for nearly forty years the family maid lived in this room, faithfully performing her duties as maid until the last member of the family died. During the past five years, the room had been used as storage for the new owners. When we toured the house with a realtor the room contained everything from saddles to branding irons to dilapidated furniture. When we moved into the house, all this was gone, and we began refurbishing the room.

Soon into the task, the history of the room became an overwhelming reality. At some point in cleaning and scrapping, we realized that nearly a whole life had been spent in this room. We sat where she sat, we heard the same creaks in the floor that she heard, and we looked out the same window that she looked out. Here a young woman passed into middle age, then old age. Here a woman, undoubtedly born of a family not too far removed from a slave society, received visitors, washed her hair, hung up her clothes, went to bed for 15,000 nights, dreamed as many dreams, and woke to as many mornings. Here she prayed, laughed, and cried. On one side of the room is a table that folds down from the wall. Here she probably read, and here she probably wrote a few notes now and then to friends and loved ones.

Our refurbishing is nearly complete, and we will use the room for a study. But it will never be entirely our room; it will always belong in some important way to this faithful servant. And when I sit at my desk and read, when I hover over the typewriter working on an article, I shall remember her, and when I do, I shall remember her world, a world undoubtedly shaped by limited citizenship and limited opportunity. I can almost hear her at times, softly whispering songs of sorrow, love and hope. Her world has become part of our world, and our lives are enriched because of it. Her life in that room deserves an historical marker of some kind, a small symbol to us and to those who will follow that a life was lived in that room. For us, she has become a window to understanding.

Why is cultural remembrance important? Why, in the end, is the work of the Texas Historical Commission and the Texas Council for the Humanities, and similar organizations across the country, vital to our society? Are our claims for their importance overblown? We don't provide many jobs, we don't add all that much to the economy, although there are those who seek to defend such programs on the basis of economic impact, and we don't have much to say about new sewers and streets, unless, of course, an historic structure is about to be demolished to make way for the new sewer line.

In answering these questions, the burden rests not so much with us as it does with those who say all this doesn't matter, that the only thing that matters is national defense, economic growth, and the pursuit of individual success. To those who say it doesn't matter, I would ask, Are you prepared for the United States to enter into the twenty-first century with citizens who have little knowledge of the past? Are you prepared for a society of cultural illiterates, a society suffering from historical amnesia, a society where the present and the future has no link to the past, a society inundated with information but without knowledge? Are you willing to have your children face vital political and social issues without an understanding of how life has until now been lived, without familiarity with the ideas, traditions, and beliefs that have sustained people in the best and worst of times?

Are we as a people ready to deal with international tensions, with the possibility of nuclear confrontation, with the struggle between capitalism and socialism, with the relationship between developed nations and nations of the third world, with the problems that derive from a high-tech society, including the problem of privacy, with pressing questions of medical technology, with dramatic shifts in the job market, without the understanding that comes to us through the study of history, literature, and philosophy, and without the understanding that comes to us through the preservation and interpretation of our material culture?

To ask these questions is to ask an even more basic question: What is it that citizens must know in order to live effectively within our democratic system? And two related questions: What parts of our communal history should be preserved, cultivated, interpreted, and made accessible to our fellow citizens? What must citizens understand in order to meet the challenges of the future?

This week we mark the anniversaries of two events that continue to cast long shadows. Ten years ago, Americans viewed their television sets with astonishment as network cameras captured the embarrassing, chaotic, unexpected flight of U.S. soldiers, embassy personnel, and a handful of South Vietnamese friends from Saigon as North Vietnam rolled to triumph. Forty years ago, Americans for the first time entered into the Nazi concentration camps, uncovering for the world the terror and madness of the Holocaust. The massive media coverage given in recent weeks to the fall of Vietnam, and the substantial media coverage given to President Reagan's trip to Bitburg, Germany, give evidence to our ongoing struggle to understand these events of world history. We are baffled by them, we are disgusted by them, we are alarmed by them. We want to recall them and yet we don't want to recall them. Our reaction to them tells us something very important.

We must care not only for the bright and shining moments of our history and culture, but also for the dark and tarnished moments when reason, justice, and understanding lost their way. A society that remembers only part of its history, that restores certain historically-worthy structures and not others, that publishes and reads books that tell only part of the story, is a society in trouble. It is as important for the citizens of tomorrow to see and to know a nineteenth-century East Texas sharecropper's home as it is to see and know a pristine East Texas Victorian house. Architecturally, one may outshine the other; culturally, one is just as important as the other.

To me, the most troublesome aspect about President Reagan's visit to the Bitburg cemetery where it was discovered some Nazi SS soldiers are buried, is the little thought that was apparently given to how such a visit could be planned and structured to acknowledge, rather than deny, this dark hour of Western civilization. We think of visits to cemeteries as honoring the dead, and so they usually are, but, in this case, coming close to those who helped perpetuate the Nazi horror—some would say too close—could possibly serve to remind the world that evil is never far away, waiting, as it were, to boil up again. We might recall that the Holocaust happened in a nation that treasured culture, that produced some of the best philosophers, poets, architects, and composers that the world has ever seen, a society in which the Protestant Reformation was born. And then we must ask why. How could this nightmare have happened? Evil must be remembered, not denied.

Clearly, our windows to understanding must be wider than that provided in 1930s Germany. Certainly, our vision must include the realities and experiences and values of those different from ourselves.

How then can we achieve personal and collective understanding that will contribute to wise and visionary citizens who can spot evil when it springs forth? Five factors seem especially important.

First, our youth must be given basic *tools of analysis*. Such tools come first through the study of language, through reading and writing. But they also come through other disciplines, including mathematics and the sciences. Students need to be able to reason, to understand arguments, to see assumptions.

Second, citizens of all ages need *texts* that manifest our cultural inheritance. The printed word bears enormous responsibility, but, as noted, the preservation of material culture has become increasingly important, along with, I should add, film. These cultural objects serve as texts as well, and those texts need to be preserved.

Third, citizens of all ages need *interpreters*—teachers trained to explain these texts. A society that cares about the past, that preserves the past, will ensure that there are an adequate number of teachers to interpret these texts for the public. A published text of worth that is not read, a restored building that is not used, a museum exhibit that draws few people—each fails in its mission. Our interpreters are found in a variety of settings—in schools and universities, in libraries, in museums, in historical societies, in the editorial departments of newspapers and magazines. Too often, our interpreters of culture are undervalued.

Fourth, we must encourage citizens to *imagine*. It is not enough to learn facts, to know dates, events, and people. We must use this information to get inside the lives of others, to feel what others felt, to experience what others experienced. Through the exercise of the imagination, we learn more deeply what it means to be human, to dream of new possibilities, to succeed and to fail, to feel compassion, to love, and to wonder. We must exercise this imagination toward the low as well as the high moments of civilization.

Fifth, we must nourish the ability of citizens to make *judgments*, to determine for themselves what is of value and what is not, what is exemplary action and what is not, what is right and what is wrong, what is decent and what is indecent, what is good and what is evil. One cannot judge adequately unless there is free exchange of ideas. Hence, our society must care for those structures whereby citizens have access to multiple interpretations of our cultural, political, intellectual, and religious heritage.

In looking at these five tasks, we see how the act of preserving and the act of learning are brought together. Historic preservation and the humanities provide windows to understanding. The humanities build and make use of that which has been preserved. If preservationists do their job well, and I speak here of the person whose life is devoted to documenting cultural traditions as well as the person who restores a building, humanities scholars will have ample opportunity for interpreting the richness of the human experience in all its variety and depth.

We must walk where others have walked in order to discover for ourselves new paths of hope. There is no short-cut. We must know and understand human history and culture. May your work, and our work, provide citizens of this state many windows to understanding.

Texas Myths:
Prospects for a
Shared Culture

A decade of reviewing grant requests from Texas organizations and institutions led me to the subject of Texas myths. An overwhelming number of grant applications by the early 1980s came from two related categories: (1) local and state history, and (2) ethnic history and culture. These projects reflected the profound geographic, cultural, and ethnic diversity of the state. As a way of illuminating Texas history, and as a way of digging deeper into the significance of this pluralism, the board of directors accepted my proposal to emphasize in 1984 Texas myths, the stories and heroes embodying the values of the various cultures and ethnic groups. Texas Humanist editor Marise McDermott helped write an NEH funding proposal, while special projects staff Robert O'Connor and Sherilyn Brandenstein implemented council-sponsored parts of the project.

We received an Exemplary Project Award from the NEH for this multifaceted project that included the following: a session at the 1984 meeting of the Texas State Historical Association entitled "The Texas Frontier: Formative Myths Behind the Nineteenth-Century Clash of Cultures;" the 1984 Texas Lecture and Symposium on the Humanities, honoring writer John Graves and involving a number of key Texas scholars; the commissioning of papers for publication in the book Texas Myths; *and publication of a special issue of* The Texas Humanist *magazine.*

The TCH also funded eight projects through a request for proposals. The Panhandle Plains Museum presented a film series, symposium, and exhibit, all examining the myth of Quivira. The Southwest Alternate Media Project of Houston presented twelve film programs examining cinematic treatments of myths about Texas with scholars' papers published in a special issue of Southwest Media Review. *Texas Woman's University in Denton presented a conference on how the arts, mass media, and cultural traditions have shaped mythical images of women. Texas A&M University's Department of Philosophy explored the "symbiotic relationship" between the land and the persons who live and work on it at a public symposium. The Institute for the Humanities at Salado hosted a weekend symposium entitled "Understanding Texas Myths: the Personal and the Collective Mythology." The Department of Literature and Languages of East Texas State University sponsored a series of lectures and discussions on ethnic myths in Texas. KERA-TV, Dallas, produced a one-hour video for broadcast on the themes of land and environment in Texas myth and folklore. Tarleton State University in Stephenville sponsored the production of two half-hour video programs on literary Texas.*

The essay below was written as an epilogue for the book, Texas Myths, *published by Texas A&M University Press, 1986.*

This volume tells of the remarkably different traditions, experiences, and world-views that can be found in Anglo, Mexican, Native American, and African American cultures of nineteenth-century Texas.

The concept "world-view" implies a mythology, a structuring of human experience through heroes, legends, and stories that express commonly felt ideals and emotions. Each Texas group, and its various subgroups, brought a different mythology to bear on its experience, and each mythology had its own set of specific symbols and images.

Yet one must acknowledge that modern scholarship, reflecting on diverse cultures worldwide, has emphasized the "monomyth," the strikingly similar themes that occur in the myths of different places and times. That is, if one looks beneath the specific outer "trappings" of a myth, one finds a core that is psychologically similar to the core of myths from other cultures. Explanations for this phenomenon of universality differ. Otto Rank emphasized the biological/psychological inheritance of humankind. Carl Jung found the common source of mythology in the collective unconscious. Joseph Campbell points to the primary structure of culture and of the human psyche.

It should be possible, therefore, to discover beneath particular myths elements that express human experience at its most fundamental level. Such a study, however, lies beyond the scope of the present work. Instead, the essays in this collection shed light on two preliminary tasks: the identification and interpretation of the formative myths of the peoples who settled in Texas, and an investigation of how these myths helped to shape the history of the state. Thus, they disclose the diversity of Texas myths—the extent to which Anglo-Texan myth was infused with Western European, Protestant myth; the Mexican-Texan myth with Spanish Catholicism, with strikingly different expressions of authority, family, devotion, and obligation; the African American myth with West African culture and religion and with American slave culture; the Native-American myth with unique notions of land and kinship. The writers have not sought to identify the core of human experience—the common memory, the primary relationships, the archetypal experiences that lie beneath these particular expressions of myth; that is a challenge that still lies ahead. As Joseph Campbell writes in *The Hero with a Thousand Faces*: "Myth is the secret opening through which the inexhaustible energies of the cosmos pour into human cultural manifestation. Religions, philosophies, arts, the social forms of primitive and historic man, prime discoveries in science and technology, the very dramas that blister sleep, boil up from the basic, magic ring of myth."

In this land that came to be known as Texas, they boiled up indeed. Although Indian and Spanish-Mexican culture had long flourished, it was the Anglo culture that emerged as the primary driving force behind the development of Texas. The Anglo-Texan experience was, of course, intimately related to the conquest of the New World, the settlement of European peoples on the Atlantic seaboard, the drive for political and economic self-determination, the American revolution, the westward movement, the development of an entire continent. Thus Anglo-Texans shared in the formative myths of their European-American ancestors, including the myth of America as the New Israel, America as a special place with a special people carrying out a divine commission expressed politically as Manifest Destiny and individually as the quest for life, liberty, and happiness.

When Anglo Texans finally got around to writing their history—perceived as *the* history of the state—the story was told as a sacred history, a story that shared elements of the more basic American myth and, behind that, European-Protestant myth. The historical narrative moved from the pilgrimage to the promised land to the establishment of the Republic to annexation to the Confederacy to reconstruction, to the growth of the cattle industry and industrialization, all documented by historians within the context of Manifest Destiny.

This traditional history, seen perhaps in its purest form in public school texts, was not a social history; it was the history of a people. It was a linear, patriarchal history, full of sacred moments and complete with heroes. The story of Texas took on epic proportions. The Anglo-Texan story is, therefore, part of a much bigger story, and the Anglo-Texan myth is part of a much bigger myth. It was a story fit to be told, a story of legendary dimensions, a story made for Hollywood. The American public, influenced deeply by formative American myths and, behind that, Western European Protestant myth, was enchanted by the mythic representations of its Texas cousins.

And so were Texans. One of this country's foremost scholars of myth, Mircea Eliade, tells us that myth is didactic, creating exemplary heroes for a whole society, heroes who embody particular values. Protectors of the sacred history and its heroes have never been in short supply in Texas, where transmitters of the Anglo-Texan myth helped the public know who they are, where they came from, and what they ought to do. The Alamo and San Jacinto became shrines, and museums were built to remind us of the lives and accomplishments of Texas heroes from cowboys to Rangers to oilmen.

An examination of the cultural landscape of present-day Texas indicates that the traditional Anglo myth is very much with us, and certain characteristics associated with heroic figures of that myth—individualism, courage, risk-taking, optimism—are valued by Texans. One sees this, for instance, in the increasingly prominent role of the developer. The Texas developer has taken on heroic proportions and he now stands alongside the cowboy, the cattle baron, the Ranger, and the wildcatter as a formative figure commanding attention and, frequently, admiration. In present-day Texas, nearly everything is perceived as worthy of development: timberland, farm land, barren land, improved land, urban centers, villages, lakeshores, seashores, and offshores, outer space, small businesses. Development for the sake of development, and the wealth that it brings, ensues. It is an extension of the older Anglo-American myth that "big is better" and "progress is our most important product."

The continuance of the Anglo myth is also reflected in the speed and intensity with which Texas has emerged not only as a high-tech center, but as the next "Silicon Valley" in the 300-mile stretch between Dallas and San Antonio. Is it Texas's manifest destiny to be the place where the fifth-generation computer is created and manufactured?

Finally, the continuing influence of the Anglo myth is found in the lives of ordinary Texans. Texans remain a self-reliant people, assured that anything and everything is possible. This is a place where dreams of accomplishment, power, and wealth come easily. The Anglo influence remains an all-important force, even if the historical origins of the myth are frequently forgotten.

✦

But powerful social, political, and literary developments in Texas in the last thirty years have led to increased recognition that the Anglo-Texan tradition is not the only one. Of course, in the lives of many ordinary people, it never was the complete story, or even the most important one. For blacks, Mexican Americans, Native Americans, and even newly-arrived immigrants from Eastern and Southern Europe and elsewhere, other histories, heroes, and myths dominated. Music, folklore, customs, family relationships, language, religious observances, preserved the traditions, values, and myths of Texas' subcultures. Internal and external factors prevented easy assimilation.

Extensive progress has been made in identifying, documenting, and disseminating these traditions. There has been a virtual explosion of studies in Mexican American, Native-American, African American, and women's history, as seen in the exhibits of the Institute of Texan Cultures, in titles of books published by the states presses, in hundreds of grants awarded in the past decade by the Texas Council for the Humanities for public programs focusing on ethnic history and culture, in entirely new departments in our colleges and universities devoted to these pursuits. This interest in minority and ethnic studies occurred simultaneously with dramatic social and political change that brought minorities further into "mainstream" (that is, Anglo) culture and society, change that stemmed from a desegregated and far more open society.

As a result, the Anglo-Texan story and myth are no longer the only public story and myth. The traditional history has been augmented by a growing body of historical and literary works that document, interpret, and bring to light the myths, world views, and histories of the diverse cultures that make up Texas. For example, historian Roberto Mario Salmón writes in *The Texas Humanist* (January 1985):

> Through a cultural osmosis, Mexican Americans in Texas
> represent the vision that drove Coronado. They are the
> ethnic, racial, and cultural blending of Indians, Mexi-

cans, and Spaniards. They are the northern frontier of
Nuevo Santander, later the Mexican State of Tampaulipas;
the turbulent national frontier between the United States
and Mexico; the political, social, economic, and cultural
frontier of a people battling against powerful forces to
make a more profound impact on their own destinies.

The point for us is that minority history and myth have slowly made
their way into public consciousness; Mexican vision stands alongside
Anglo vision as a formative influence in the lives of millions of Texans.

The emergence of minority history, culture, and myth into public
awareness has led to a Texas increasingly perceived as a cultural mosaic. Mexican, black, and Indian traditions have been reclaimed, and
many others as well—Polish, Czech, German, and Italian. In the 1960s
and 1970s, in particular, we tended to acknowledge our own traditions
and the world-views and myths from which they sprang. Cultural pluralism became an unofficial national policy, and Texas seemed to be a
case-study in living out that policy. Textbooks, for instance, were re-
written to include minority experience and perspectives, and the extent
to which Spanish should be taught in the public schools as both a
primary and secondary language became a critical public policy issue.

But, more recently, some scholars have argued that perhaps we
have gone too far down the road of cultural pluralism, and that insufficient effort is made to understand and to reclaim the dominant tradition
behind the development of Texas. Hence, T. R. Fehrenbach writes that
without the traditional Texas hero—flawed as he might be—Texans
will lose whatever cohesion they still have left. A similar point, but in a
broader context, is made by William McNeil in an essay on myth in
Foreign Affairs:

> Myth lies at the basis of human society. That is because
> myths are general statements about the world and its
> parts, and in particular about nations and other human
> in-groups, that are believed to be true and then acted
> on whenever circumstances suggest or require common
> response. That is mankind's substitute for instinct. It is
> the unique and characteristic human way of acting to-
> gether. A people without a full quiver of relevant agreed-
> upon statements, accepted in advance through education
> or less formalized acculturation, soon finds itself in deep
> trouble, for, in the absence of believable myths, coher-

ent public action becomes very difficult to improvise or sustain.

At a gut level, we know that McNeill is right—there must be a shared culture if society is to function. The challenge of the present time is that of forging a shared culture from the multiple, sometimes conflicting histories and traditions that have flourished in Texas.

The Anglo myth, as we have seen, is alive and well, but, more often than not, that myth is cut-off from its social, political, and cultural origins. When that happens, we are left with fragments that are perceived to be the whole myth—or worse still, Hollywood-created images that tell us what it is to be Texan. In the former case, we are left with certain values—intense competition, for instance—that are not balanced by other, now-forgotten values of the Anglo myth. Such a situation presents the danger of a society with a strong economy but a weak social fabric, a society bubbling with activity but without a clear sense of aims and purposes, a society of the strong that does not know what to do with the weak.

A symptom of this danger can be seen in the rash of teenage suicides that afflicted the affluent, suburban, high-tech communities of Plano, north of Dallas, and Clear Lake City, south of Houston, in 1984. In a period of ten months, eleven Plano teenagers took their own lives, and in a period of two months, six teenagers in Clear Lake City committed suicide. In both cases, psychologists, ministers, school officials, and parents were baffled, but some clues were offered: extreme competition, over-indulgence in material goods, drugs, parental pressure for academic excellence, family instability, and intense peer pressure. As one Clear Lake City student put it: "Popularity is based on what you wear and how much money you have. It's not who you are; it's what you are." We may be losing myths that can tell us who we are.

We are in need of remembrance. We must remember the forgotten elements of the Anglo-Texan myth—the spirit of adventure of Stephen F. Austin, the love of liberty of the defenders of the Alamo, the courage and fortitude of the frontier family. If we do not remember the whole myth, if we fail to understand the context and nature of its images, we are left with symbols distorted by time.

But we are also in need of synthesis. In addition to understanding more deeply the Anglo myth, we must open ourselves to the myths of other cultures—to appreciate, understand, and learn from those myths that have sustained generations of Native Americans, blacks, and Mexican Americans.

I think of the murals of Raúl Valdez. In Dallas, Houston, Del Rio, McAllen, and Austin, Valdez has sought to work through his own "cultural confusion" by painting color collages full of history and myth on expansive concrete walls. A recent Austin mural, *Moviminto*, displays in dramatic form the Chicago heritage. It is not enough to admire Valdez's work. If one is Mexican American, a tradition may have to be rediscovered. If one is not Mexican American, a history and myth must be learned. We must incorporate what we can.

The challenge of Texas is to sustain a society based on enduring myths of various traditions that give meaning and purpose to life. We need myths to live by, myths that support fairness, love, compassion, loyalty, and honor—myths that can give us the kind of grounding we need in a high-tech, competitive, commercial world. We would do well to remember that a vibrant outer life must be balanced by a strong inner life, by myths and symbols that speak of ultimate things, that place human experience in a broader, deeper context.

One important task of teachers and writers in the humanities is that of tending to our myths. If the primary purpose of education in the humanities is to orient the student into his or her cultural background *and* surroundings, myth cannot be overlooked, for it is through myth that we discover our spiritual homeland. Indeed, myth might be the starting point in humanities education—the teaching of legends, tales, and heroic characters.

Thus humanities teachers bear enormous responsibility in preserving our cultural heritage, in selecting what legends, stories, tales and heroic lives should be taught. Especially, those who write our histories, who must choose between events, personages, processes, and even cultures to tell a story, who must weave many fabrics into a completed and artistic whole, have an awesome responsibility, for they are, in a real sense, the makers of myth, and myth, as we have seen, holds a society together; out of myth flows life itself.

But the ultimate task of those who tend to our myths may be the discovery and clarification of how disparate and even conflicting myths tell us what it means to be human, to be born of mothers and fathers, to feel love and hate, to aspire and to fail, to dream, to be lonely, to achieve, to mourn, to be reborn, to die. At the deepest level, the task is to determine how all myths depict shared human experience.

Prospects for a shared culture in Texas do not rest simply on increased understanding of one's own myth and on the imaginative leap into other cultures, histories, and myths—although that is surely the starting point. In the end, prospects rest on our collective ability to see that the experience portrayed in a myth—alien as it might at first seem—is also everyone's experience. As we have seen, behind the Anglo-Texan myth lies European-American, primarily Protestant myth. Behind African American myth lies the culture and religions of West Africa. Behind Mexican-Texan myth lies a mix of Spanish Catholicism, Indian tradition, and Mexican culture. The religious symbolism and myth that undergird these varied traditions all stem from archetypal experiences that unite humankind, including the experience of rebirth and wholeness. It may not be *my* tradition, but it is a valid expression of my experience as well.

We must remember the many myths that have flourished in this remarkable place called Texas. We must remember the sad myths—those myths that speak, for instance, of greed and murder—as well as the happy myths, for such behavior is part of our collective experience, and understanding that behavior through myth helps us understand what it means to be human. Given the didactic function of myth, cross-cultural dialogue can help each group define for itself the best, most useful myths in its tradition.

Myths shed light on our individual and collective journeys; myths are the guardians of life. Joseph Campbell says it best in the *Hero with a Thousand Faces*:

> The imagery of myth can never be a direct presentation of the total secret of the human species, but only the function of an attitude, the reflex of a stance, a life pose, a way of playing the game. And where the rules or forms of such play are abandoned, mythology dissolves—and with mythology, life.

Works Cited

Campbell, Joseph. *The Hero with a Thousand Faces*. Princeton: Princeton University Press, revised edition, 1990.

Eliade, Micea. *The Sacred and the Profane*. Harcourt Brace, 1968. Also, *Myth of the Eternal Return*. Princeton: Princeton University Press, 1954.

Fehrenbach, T. R. "Texas Mythology: Now and Forever," in *Texas Myths*, Robert F. O'Connor, ed. College Station: Texas A&M University Press, 1986.

Scholarship and Citizenship in the Humanistic Tradition

The following essay was published in Contemporary Essays on Greek Ideas: the Kilgore Festschrift, *published by Baylor University Press, 1987. It was one of eighteen essays written to honor Baylor University professor of philosophy and department chairman, William J. Kilgore. An accomplished scholar and teacher in the history of philosophy, Latin American philosophy, and metaphysics, Kilgore made very important contributions in Texas, the United States, and abroad to scholarly and public understanding of academic freedom and responsibility. His understanding of the academic enterprise, which I first encountered as a student of his during my undergraduate studies, has inspired me in my pursuit of the public humanities. I focused my paper for this collection on the relationship between the scholar and society, and how the disciplines of the humanities can be used in public settings to elucidate complex public issues.*

✦ ✦ ✦

For nearly twenty-five hundred years, philosophy has held an indisputably important place in the Western humanistic tradition. The history of the discipline of philosophy, and the biographies of those people who have shaped the tradition, are worthy of study, for we learn much about the relationship between society and the scholar, between culture and the advancement of human knowledge.

It is often said that virtually all intellectual problems that have dominated the history of the philosophical tradition in the West have their origin in ancient philosophy. "In Socrates and his followers," argues Albert Avey, "we meet the formulators of great philosophies which have constituted the major traditions of Western Civilization." It is argued further that all later philosophical thought must reckon with the ancients, and that much of the philosophical inquiry of Western culture involves commentary upon and criticism of the Socratic, Platonic, Aristotelian, and Hellenistic movements of the Classical period.

For those who care deeply about the well-being of the philosophical pursuit, the ancient period is instructive for other reasons as well. The life, teachings, and death of Socrates continue to provide the preeminent historical focus for analysis of the relationship between the philosopher and society. Two particular problems in this relationship—one personal and the other environmental—are especially worthy of study.

The personal problem stems from the inevitable alienation that the philosopher experiences by holding true to the Socratic proposition that "the unexamined life is not to be lived." However much one may want to emphasize the constructive aspects of philosophical inquiry—the pursuit of truth, the passion for clarity of thought, the desire to find universal principles that assist in understanding life—it is likely that from time to time the public will perceive philosophical inquiry as potentially destructive and corrupting. As such, the philosopher as gadfly is personally vulnerable. The assertion that it is necessary to question, to doubt, to remove from one's thought that which is untenable, before one is able to arrive at beliefs worthy of human experience, is to place oneself at odds with those forces in society dedicated to the preservation of those traditions, ideas, and beliefs that form accepted knowledge and that provide intellectual support for existing values and institutions. Hence, the specter of alienation and vulnerability form the personal problem of the philosopher.

The environmental problem stems from the fact that the conditions of one's society and culture influence deeply the nature and shape of philosophical inquiry. Two aspects of this problem are especially important. First, the history of philosophy—and other humanities disciplines as well—tends to substantiate the notion that philosophy prospers through cultural, social, and political hard times. "That philosophy should be rather fanned than extinguished by times of decadence is not surprising," writes scholar Micheline Sauvage, "since it is precisely the unacceptable which sets the reflective conscience in motion." That is, philosophy tends to prosper under adverse environmental conditions. Ancient Greek philosophy prospered as Athens withered. Second, however much the philosopher may want to hold a steady course in his or her inquiry, it is inevitable that the social and political issues of the time weigh heavily on the philosopher both in terms of perception of the issues and in terms of the issues themselves. As vulnerable and potentially alienated the philosopher may be, he or she is very much a part of society and culture, and the conditions of the given society and culture influence deeply the identification and delineation of philosophical issues, including, on occasion, escape from those very conditions and issues that may be of deep concern to other scholars.

These personal and environmental problems can be seen in every era of the history of philosophy. But for many, these problems are particularly relevant today, for philosophy, like other humanities disciplines, has been influenced considerably by advances in the social sciences, and we know more today than ever before about the interplay between ideas and society, about the transmission and transformation of commonly-held concepts, values, and beliefs, and about the politics of culture. The result is that these personal and environmental problems—acute in the discipline of philosophy but very much a part of other humanities disciplines as well—have tended to be incorporated into the self-understanding of the contemporary American scholar.

This awareness of the tenuous relationship between the scholar and society, and the awareness of the potential impact of changing social, political, and cultural conditions on the work of the scholar, have led many to ask some fundamental questions about the well-being of the humanistic pursuit in this country, about the status of the humanities disciplines, about the study of philosophy, history, literature, and other disciplines that have been central to liberal learning.

Recent studies indicate that the humanities have lost considerable favor with the American public. A 1984 report by the National Endowment for the Humanities on the status of the humanities in higher education reflects on statistics compiled by other organizations. Two-thirds of academic deans at colleges and universities surveyed in 1983 by the American Council on Education "indicated that the most able entering undergraduates were turning away from the humanities to other fields, mainly professional and technical." The NEH report states that "this is not merely a rejection of a career in the humanities, but a rejection of the humanities themselves." An even more recent study by the Council, also referred to in the NEH report, states "that a student can obtain a bachelor's degree from seventy-five percent of all American colleges and universities without having studied European history, from seventy-two percent without having studied American literature or history." And the Modern Language Association reports that the percentage of colleges and universities requiring foreign language study for admission has dropped from thirty-five percent in 1966 to fourteen percent in 1983.

Data on declining humanities majors, also found in the NEH report, confirms the drift away from the humanities. From 1970 to 1982, when the number of bachelor's degrees in all fields increased by eleven percent, undergraduate degrees in English dropped by fifty-seven percent, philosophy by forty-one percent, history by sixty-two percent, and modern languages by forty-one percent.

To discover the reasons for this decline, one must begin with developments within the academy itself. First, there has been a tendency in this country for graduate schools to produce narrow specialists in the humanities whose primary goals lie in research in narrow fields. Second, as Robert Nisbet and other writers have pointed out, the curriculum has been marked by the expansion of secondary and sometimes trivial courses, especially in the humanities and the social sciences; consequently, there is loss of agreement on what kind of education an undergraduate education ought to bring. Third, academic administrators, giving in to the narrow research interests of the faculty, have too frequently adopted the practice of assigning graduate students to teach lower division courses, with the consequence that undergraduates not majoring in the humanities remain unexposed to the best scholars in the humanities.

But these academic factors insufficiently explain the drift away from the humanities. One must also look at broader cultural and social developments.

First, one can point to the near-obsessive interest of students in the 1980s in professional and career interests, and society's growing inability to understand the relationship between career education and the liberal arts. Edwin J. Delattie, President of St. Johns College, makes the point that a person gains the chance to learn what a career is through the liberal arts. Without the liberal arts, students are taught that a career is nothing more than "a succession of jobs" in which success is determined "by rate of promotion and rate of income." The liberal arts appear to be rather useless as the American dream is increasingly filled with materialistic content.

Second, one must remember the social and cultural impact of deep-seated American anti-intellectualism. Richard Hofstadter's 1962 landmark book, written in response to the political and intellectual conditions of the 1950s, documents the "common strain" of American anti-intellectualism which "is a resentment and suspicion of the life of the mind and of those who are considered to represent it; and a disposition constantly to minimize the value of that life." While Americans admire *intelligence*, which has practical aims, *intellect*, which "examines, ponders, wonders, theorizes, criticizes, imagines," is highly suspect and downright threatening. In finding the origins of this anti-intellectualism, Hofstadter turns first to American Protestantism. "The evangelical movement," says Hofstadter, "has been the most powerful carrier of . . . religious anti-intellectualism. . . ." This sentiment received stimulation from the revolt of the "common man" and the pressure of modernity and secularization. A host of new influences, ranging from Darwinism and Freudianism to urban lifestyles and to the exposure of new ideas through radio, newspapers, advertising, and film, led to pronounced efforts to stem the flood of personal and social subversion. Intellectuals were held responsible. Hofstadter quotes evangelist Billy Sunday: "Thousands of college graduates are going as fast as they can straight to hell. If I had a million dollars I'd give $999,999 to the church and $1 to education." And again: "When the Word of God says one thing and scholarship says another, scholarship can go to hell!"

Third, one must acknowledge that contemporary Protestant fundamentalist leaders, inheritors of American anti-intellectualism, have launched a full-scale attack on "secular humanism." While this movement displays a great deal of confusion over the terms "humanism," "humanistic," and "humanist," its impact is clear: continued deprecation of the life of the mind, of human reason, of the pursuit of truth. Now, for the first time in American history, religious fundamentalism has become a major political force. Since it is likely that an undergraduate student coming out of this major American tradition will encounter, through the study of literature, history, philosophy, anthropology and other disciplines, scholarship that says something different than a simplistic, literal understanding of the "Word of God," as Billy Sunday knew, it is better, it is frequently thought, to avoid these subjects altogether, to concentrate on a career, to pursue non-threatening fields in the sciences and the professions.

What, then, is the future of the humanistic enterprise, and, more specifically, what is the immediate future of philosophical studies? This essay began by noting that Socrates provides the preeminent historical focus for analysis of the relationship between the philosopher and society. The scholar who holds true to the Socratic proposition that "the unexamined life is not to be lived" may inevitably experience vulnerability and alienation, especially when the social and cultural environment is one which deprecates the life of the mind and the value of humanistic studies. Given these current conditions, what is it that scholars trained in philosophy and other humanities disciplines must remember about their work and the importance of this work to society?

✦

In answering this question, I offer four propositions as starting points.

First, there is a kind of knowledge available only through humanistic studies. In an essay dealing with the nature of this knowledge, Walter Kaufmann identifies five elements of historical knowledge that come through humanistic studies. The first is knowledge that certain things happened, certain events took place, certain individuals did this and created that—thereby leading to an awareness of human history and culture. The second is knowledge of the thought and work of the greatest people who have shaped our culture—knowledge of poets, thinkers, politicians, soldiers. The third is knowledge how those who have belonged to certain traditions—whether in painting, poetry, philosophy, or other disciplines—have undertaken their creative work. One learns a craft through study as well as by doing. The fourth is knowledge of quality gained through study of the best that has been thought and done. One gains a sense of perspective, and is better able to judge new developments in a variety of fields. The fifth is knowledge of personhood gained through the study of music, literature, art, philosophy, religion, and other fields of human endeavor. The social sciences and the sciences can give us only partial answers to the nature of personhood.

Put differently, we can say that humanistic studies are invaluable in helping to ensure a collective memory of the past, in helping to ensure a civilization that reflects upon itself, and in helping to ensure the stimulation of imagination—of what might be possible as society seeks the good, the true, and the beautiful.

Second, public learning takes place outside as well as inside the academy, and thus the humanities scholar is called upon to engage the public wherever found. Socrates exemplifies the noble ideal of the public humanist. Socrates was a teacher, but he rejected the most obvious temptation of the humanist, to associate exclusively with fellow intellectuals. Instead, he spoke to his fellow citizens and did so on their own turf, in the marketplace, on the battlefield, at athletic events, in homes, and, of course, in his prison cell, using language that citizens would understand.

Life-long learning holds a key place in contemporary society. Fundamental scientific, technological, and economic changes are occurring at such a fast pace that life-long learning becomes a necessity. While the humanist's primary responsibility is to the classroom and to the creation of new knowledge, he or she also has responsibility to participate fully in today's learning society, to demonstrate the importance of life-long learning in the humanities, and to help ensure that opportunities exist whereby adult learners can increase their knowledge in the humanities while expanding their knowledge in other fields. If humanistic studies are confined to the academy, the humanities will indeed seem to be of secondary importance to the public.

Third, humanistic learning—inside as well as outside the academy—is an essential public good and necessary for civic conversation. American society, shaped as it has been by the Enlightenment, accepts scientific research and advancement as a public good. But we struggle hard to convince ourselves that humanistic learning is also a public good. Without the public's familiarity with the historical knowledge gained through the humanities that Walter Kaufmann writes about, civic conversation will be disembodied. Only through the humanities can we integrate the different realms of human endeavor; only through the humanities can we retain a sense of historical continuity; and only through the humanities can we gain common knowledge and language—tools necessary for public discourse. Public dialogue—civic conversation—depends upon the diffusion of humanistic studies.

Fourth, civic conversation must include discussion of vital public issues, and humanities scholars are called upon from time to time to speak out on those issues. One must remember John Dewey's central concern that a free and democratic society is obligated to find the intellectual means whereby citizens participate in the analysis and resolution of vital public concerns.

There is a tendency among some contemporary scholars to shy away from public issues, to limit the function of humanistic education to the study of important traditions and texts, to forget that—as Hans-Georg Gadamer has shown—the humanistic act involves application as well as understanding and interpretation. In the tradition of civic humanism, the primary concern has been on contemporary issues of public life, not on exemplary figures or famous texts as things in themselves.

Although it is good to remember, for instance, that America's founding fathers were men steeped in humanistic learning, we must also recall that for these civic activists such learning served one primary purpose: to assist in understanding the new world about them. Their focus was on new departures—on the development of ideas and systems to meet new social, political, and economic conditions—not on restitution of old ideas, policies, and practices. One is again reminded of the Socratic tradition, that of maintaining a reverence for the past while focusing on the status of things as they are.

To recall these propositions is to position the scholarly community for the advancement of humanistic learning in a democratic society. But the last proposition is extraordinarily demanding and difficult, and our inability to remember the potential contribution of the humanist to public issues may be a contributing factor in the decline of confidence in ourselves as humanists and in the vitality of the humanities. Given the confusion and uncertainty concerning this matter, it is important to look deeper into the relationship between the "doing" of the humanities—the profession at work—and responsible action on the part of the scholar on important issues. To clarify the matter, I turn to the life and work of Erasmus of Rotterdam.

✦

Erasmus may seem to be far from the perfect example of the public humanist. Unlike some of his humanist colleagues of the sixteenth century, Erasmus detested controversy, shunned popularity, feared social conflict, and avoided immediate contact with the masses. Erasmus was not a Socrates. But because Erasmus was so very human, because it is easy for us to understand his personal struggles, because he has not been mythologized like Socrates, he provides an extraordinarily useful case study in the relationship between the humanist and public life.

Erasmus was born in 1466 of an illegitimate union, a fact that influenced deeply his personality and behavior throughout the course of his life. The stigma was made worse through the power of canon law; since his father was a priest, the sin involved was much greater than that between lay people. Erasmus continually struggled with feelings of rejection and alienation.

From the ages of four to twenty, Erasmus was educated in schools of the Brotherhood of the Common Life. Although highly critical in later life of the disciplinary methods used by the Brotherhood, the society was part of the *devotio moderna*, and he learned from the Brothers some of the early values of the humanist movement, including an emphasis on a religion of the heart as opposed to mere ceremonial observances of church laws, and an emphasis on piety and ethics over structure and theology. Perhaps most importantly, Erasmus was allowed to read secular literature.

At the age of eighteen, Erasmus joined an Augustinian monastery, but he found the environment unfriendly, non-academic, and terribly confining. He desired the outside world, the companionship of worldly humanists, and success through his writings. Seven years later, in 1493, Erasmus jumped at the opportunity to leave the monastery to become secretary to the Bishop of Cambrey, a task that proved to be a disappointment to him since he had little liking for the world of politics and ambition.

Two years later, in 1495, Erasmus received permission to continue his studies at the University of Paris. Here he gained deeper familiarity with the humanistic movement and, through that influence, came to hate the residue of medieval scholasticism that still prevailed at the University. Erasmus's experience in Paris pushed him toward the center of Renaissance humanism. He published some Latin poems and wrote the core of his later *Colloquies*.

In 1499, at the invitation of one of his Paris pupils whom he tutored, Lord Mountjoy, Erasmus journeyed to England. During this initial two-year stay, he came to know John Colet and Thomas More, studied at Oxford, and enjoyed the life of a rising humanist scholar. He returned to the continent in 1500 and, over the next number of years, was constantly on the move, pressed to find patrons to support his studies and writing. Private patrons or university professorships were the only viable ways—outside of tutoring—whereby a scholar without independent means could be free to pursue his work. In 1503 Erasmus published the *Enchiridion*, a statement of his platform for reform of the church, arguing that the only way to overcome abuse was through education—especially knowledge gained through the study of classical literature and scripture. Such knowledge involves the "philosophy of Christ" which leads one away from sacerdotal, ritualistic, institutional, dogmatic religion to a simple, pure, inner faith. For Erasmus, the duties of religion are reduced to the fundamental ethical requirements of knowing and mastering oneself.

Erasmus was in France, England, and then, from 1506–1509, in Italy, where he tutored the sons of an esteemed doctor destined for government business. When Henry VIII became King of England in 1509, Erasmus left again for the country he liked so well. For five years he received a yearly stipend from the Archbishop while teaching at Cambridge. He became more involved in the issues of his day, as seen, for instance, in the satire, *Julius*. Prompted by the war of 1513 between England and France, Erasmus claims that the root of the current struggle could be found in the warring attitude of Pope Julius. A strong pacifism emerges.

In 1514 Erasmus left England to go to Basel, one of the leading centers in publishing humanistic literature. He was hailed by the German humanists. He stayed several years to oversee the publishing of numerous books. From 1517 to 1521 Erasmus was in Louvain once again. Here, in his fifties and at the height of his career, he became a major force in the humanistic movement. Erasmus was convinced that the revival of letters would go hand in hand with a revitalization of Christian piety.

But Erasmus had only a short time to enjoy prestige and popularity, for, as a leading scholar of his age, he quickly became embroiled in the social and theological revolution that swept through much of Europe—a revolution so intense and powerful that even a shy and retiring man like Erasmus could not escape its claims. Before looking at this era, a few comments on Erasmus's life and accomplishments are in order.

One sees in Erasmus certain qualities and activities that are at the heart of the humanistic tradition. Although he turned down numerous professorships, preferring instead the life of wandering and professional non-committal, Erasmus was an educator. Much of his life was spent tutoring, and he was an educational theorist, expostulating on the existing educational system and offering ideas for reform. As a humanist, Erasmus loved great literature, particularly the gospels and classical Greek and Latin texts. He was deeply concerned with the issues of his day—war and peace, church abuses, social and political reform—and he believed strongly that the kind of education that one could gain through the study of great literature could lead to the sort of knowledge and the right kind of attitude required in order to resolve these issues. Humanistic literature provided the resources and the framework for the resolution of fundamentally important issues of public life, broadening one's horizons, deepening one's perspective, and making possible the kind of sentiment needed to see that the business of life can be conducted differently.

Erasmus was inadequately prepared for the conflict that befell him after 1517. The desire for tranquillity and security—needs that most scholars of the late twentieth-century can surely identify with—formed two of the basic characteristics of Erasmus's personality. According to historian Johan Huizinga, Erasmus felt a great need for friendship and concord, intensely disliking contention. Peace and harmony ranked above all other considerations, and they were, says Huizinga, the guiding principles of Erasmus's actions. "He always hoped and wanted," writes Huizinga, "to keep his pen unbloody, to attack no one, to provoke no one, even if he were attacked." From this perspective, one understands Erasmus's platform for reform. It involved no plans for disruption, no open revolt, no dramatic attempt to become militant. Rather, it was based on the conviction that quiet, thoughtful education through great literature would ensure reform. He believed that his program would accomplish the desired goals without serious conflict.

The same need for tranquillity and security encouraged in Erasmus a tendency to be aloof from the bitter struggles of the time. His style of life involved an aristocratic ideal. As Huizinga writes: "It is foolish to be interested in all that happens in the world; to pride oneself on one's knowledge of the market, of the King of England's plans, the news from Rome . . . the sensible old man . . . has an easy post of honor, a sage mediocrity, he judges no one and nothing and smiles on all the world. Quiet for oneself, surrounded by books—that is all things most desired."

But do not be mistaken. Erasmus could write persuasively, with the best of the Renaissance humanists, on the issues of the day. His passivity and aloofness must be seen as both a personality characteristic and as a humanistic attitude. From the latter perspective, it is the need for objectivity and distance that is paramount. Thus, when Erasmus writes on educational issues, ecclesiastical and political abuses, or international tension and conflict, he does so as a humanist rather than as an educational official, a politician, or a diplomat. His methods are those of the humanist and his resources are the texts of great literature.

Martin Luther, Augustinian monk, also appreciated great literature, at least as found in the Scripture. In his intellectual and spiritual development at Wittenberg, Luther gained familiarity with Erasmus's work, particularly his Greek New Testament, published in 1516. Luther looked upon Erasmus, as did many scholars, as one who was opposed to scholastic theology and the abuses of the church, and as one who sought to rediscover the purity of faith of the early church. Thus Luthur and his followers felt that Erasmus would be a sure supporter in their struggle against these abuses. Indeed, much of Erasmus's own platform for reform seemed similar to that of Luther's; in the *Enchiridion*, for instance, one discovers arguments that parallel closely those that appear in Luther's writings and correspondence during the period 1517 to

1520. As the Reformation emerged in Wittenberg and other German cities, Luther and his followers believed that Erasmus would join their ranks.

At first, in letters to Luther's associates, Erasmus gave mild support to the reformers. But by 1520 the heresy had spread throughout much of Germany, thereby causing great alarm among papal supporters and stimulating a flurry of writing. Because so many of Erasmus's views were identical to those of Luther and because Erasmus had shown himself through correspondence to be sympathetic to Luther, it was inevitable that Erasmus himself would come under attack by the conservatives as a sympathizer to the cause.

Erasmus, with an innate distaste for personal and societal conflict, sought to withdraw from the controversy. In 1521 he moved from Louvain, where Catholic conservatives were increasingly hostile to him, to the more protected city of Basel. For the next three years he tried to keep his distance and to concentrate on scholarship, reworking the *Colloquies* and expositing the Gospels.

But finally, in 1524, Erasmus felt compelled to enter more directly into the most public issue of his day. Under attack by supporters of both Pope Leo X and Martin Luther, he could no longer remain aloof. Erasmus had become a central figure in Renaissance humanism, and as a scholar devoted to communicating to a wide audience, he was obligated to speak. At a more personal level, Erasmus had become convinced that Luther was hurting the cause of learning by virtue of his dogmatic stance. He also feared that Luther's movement would lead to open violence through a popular rebellion that could engulf all of Europe. Furthermore, many Catholic conservatives believed that if Erasmus did not write against Luther, then certainly he must be for Luther. Erasmus feared that he would be blamed for instigating the entire revolt.

Erasmus published on September 1, 1524 in Basel *A Diatribe Concerning Free Will*, directed against Luther. Instead of dealing with secondary matters—the possible consequences of the revolt on the European economy, for instance—Erasmus was true to his humanistic calling and went to the heart of the matter, the fundamental philosophical and moral problem of whether or not the individual has free will.

To the late twentieth-century mind, it is difficult to imagine that a social and political problem as enormous as that of the Reformation might indeed center in a philosophical issue. We are insufficiently trained to discover the philosophical and ideological underpinnings of social, economic, and political developments and issues. Even humanities scholars seeking to understand and interpret the sixteenth-century Reformation tend to gravitate toward non-philosophical, non-ideological explanations—such as the price revolution caused by an influx of silver to Europe from the New World, the hatred of territorial princes to the political power of Rome, or the rising merchant class in the cities of Europe. Many factors contribute to major social and political revolutions, and a constellation of such factors, followed by a dramatic event that pulls the constellation closer together and into public consciousness, must occur. But what we tend to forget are the primary philosophical and moral views that underlie the positions taken and the events that unfold. In an age when the sciences have taken precedence over the humanities, the tendency is to concentrate on secondary factors.

But not with Erasmus. In his analysis of the revolution underway, he concluded that differing notions of the human will were responsible. Much of medieval Catholic thought and practice hinged on the belief that each person must act, and is free to act, to align himself with Christ, the church, and God. Salvation depended upon such acts. Luther, drawing upon his interpretation of Scripture, argued that there is nothing that the individual can do by himself to earn salvation. Human beings lack free will, and one is justified by faith alone, a faith that comes from the grace of God through Christ. Faith, for Luther, overcomes the limitations of the whole person—will and intellect.

By writing on the problem of determinism versus free will, Erasmus felt that he was going straight to the philosophical issue that separated the two men while, at the sane time, making clear his overall position *vis a vis* the reformers. Erasmus argues that free will, that power that allows the self to seek salvation and to live a moral life, is proved by the fact that without free will, repentance would be senseless and punishment of sin unjust.

Luther's response came in 1525 with the publishing of *The Bondage of the Will*. Luther argues that free will is a term that refers to God alone, for apart from God's grace man is unable to effect salvation. Natural man cannot choose the good.

Erasmus responded to Luther's essay in 1526 and 1527 with additional arguments backing up his position on free will. The published works were read widely, and Erasmus won the support of the papists. After these distasteful but morally obligatory episodes, Erasmus sought to return to a more solitary life. But in 1533, three years before his death, Erasmus wrote a book entitled, *On Bending the Peace of the Church and on Quieting Dissent*, in which he claimed that the best way to still the ecclesiastical and social schism was for everyone to practice a sound, heartfelt Christian morality. This book, much to Erasmus's surprise, engendered additional criticism from both sides.

For Erasmus, the problem of what attitude to take toward Luther was an essentially moral issue. He could either support or condemn Luther and the heretical movement. As much as he would have liked to, he could not remain silent, for he ranked as one of the most eminent thinkers of his age and as one of the great commentators on the public concerns of his time. But the way in which to respond became a consuming problem. How should the humanist act? For the first few years of the movement, he extended a carefully guarded sympathy toward Luther, then for several years he turned in the direction of cool aloofness, and then finally he condemned Luther and his followers.

In understanding the position taken, it is important to remember how different Erasmus's religious outlook and world view were from the general thought of the century. His basic creed was neither the supremacy of a dogmatic theological conviction nor the unqualified acceptance of the authority of an ecclesiastical or secular institution. Rather, it was a sentiment that stressed the perfectibility of the individual in the image of Christ through education. To achieve this goal, toleration is necessary. Thus during the early years of the Reformation, Erasmus stood quietly by, refusing to draw final conclusions. Erasmus realized that many centuries of conflict had been caused by men who had drawn such conclusions, and therefore he opposed this course, calling people instead to continue the search for wisdom, a different course that required the employment of an ethic that stressed toleration, simplicity, and love.

What can we learn from Erasmus that will assist us in understanding the humanist and his or her role in public life?

First, Erasmus was beholden to no one. The freedom to study, reflect, write and publish was dear to Erasmus. As noted, certain personality traits undoubtedly heightened the need and desire for freedom. At various times in his life, especially in his younger professional years, he had patrons who supported him. He did not like this arrangement, although he found it preferable to that of being under the thumb of a monastery, an order, or an official of the church. The drive for independence was so great that Erasmus refused numerous professorships that were offered to him. But he had to survive, and until sufficient financial resources were secured through his work, Erasmus adjusted to the necessity of patrons, tutoring positions, and occasional teaching assignments. What Erasmus teaches us is that scholarship and proper involvement in public life—where one speaks for the humanities and from the humanities—depends on considerable external and internal freedom, and that both the humanist and the humanities suffer if this freedom is compromised.

Second, Erasmus was tolerant throughout his professional life. Indeed, Renaissance humanists detested the intolerance of the preceding centuries. Humanistic learning implied the necessity for tolerance, for understanding that different views on important topics and issues could be held by reasonable people, and that open debate was required in order to resolve differences. Passionate, intolerant behavior on behalf of any cause was unbecoming to the true humanist. A certain psychological distance between the position held and the idea, movement, or event itself was required. Erasmus tended toward condemnation only upon the occasion of the intolerance of others.

Third, Erasmus thoroughly disliked narrowness in thought, exemplified in his day by scholasticism. But Erasmus was just as opposed to the dogmatic narrowness of the reformers. Whether Catholic or reformist, such ideological narrowness was inconsistent with the humanistic tradition. Obtaining knowledge and wisdom is a never-ending process, and well-defined systems said to be complete and definitive can only do damage to the human soul and intellect.

Fourth, Erasmus spoke out on the most vital issues of his day. Although he was a shy and reticent person, he believed that the humanist had a great deal to say on timely social, cultural, political, and educational issues. The true humanist could not hide from these issues. But he approached the issues not as an expert, but as a humanist, drawing especially on classical texts of the humanistic tradition. As such, Erasmus never pretended to be something other than what he was. If the issue could not be resolved, it was not his fault, for he had done his job as a humanist in clarifying and interpreting those issues.

Fifth, as he spoke out on the problems of his day, Erasmus went directly to the most important philosophical and moral issues at stake. He did not engage in an intellectual dance; he went to the heart of the matter. He did not show off, pretending to be knowledgeable in areas where he had little or no expertise. Instead, he did what was best and what was most important—analyzing and critiquing the ideological underpinnings of different positions taken on those problems. In so doing, Erasmus shows us one of the most valuable contributions of the humanist active in public life, that of pointing out the contexts and assumptions of positions held on vital issues.

Sixth, despite his reluctance, Erasmus, in the end, was morally obligated to take a position on the most important issue of his life time, the Protestant movement. It was inconceivable not to take a position. The humanist who cares, the humanist truly involved, cannot cut himself off at the point of analyzing the philosophical and moral assumptions of those who hold differing views on whatever issue is in question. The time comes when the humanist must go one step further, to move from understanding and interpretation to saying what he or she believes is the right course of action, the right way to resolve the issue. To argue otherwise is to deny that the humanist is a citizen too. Thus, Erasmus was led to condemn the Protestant Reformation.

Over the past four and one-half centuries, many scholars have attacked Erasmus for this position. Historian Preserved Smith writes: "Convinced as I am that the Reformation was fundamentally a progressive movement, the culmination of the Renaissance, and above all the logical outcome of the teachings of Erasmus himself, I cannot but regard his later rejection of it as a mistake in itself and as a misfortune to the cause of liberalism." In such a statement, one sees Smith's own ideological position, an obvious preference for progressivism, Protestantism, and liberalism, over medievalism, Catholicism, and conservativism. But to accuse Erasmus of making a "mistake" is to misunderstand Erasmus's religious sentiment and his philosophy. Behind Erasmus's appeal for Christians to move away from ritualistic and dogmatic-scholastic religion to the practice of biblical Christianity (Luther's platform as well), one finds the presupposition that the individual can through the power of his mind and will become a true follower of Christ (a view opposed to Luther's theology). What we find in Erasmus is that when a position is taken, as it was in regard to the Reformation, it flows from his scholarship and from his interpretation of the nature and background of the issue in question. But from the standpoint of this essay, the most important thing is that position-taking on vital concerns of public life is intrinsic to the humanistic enterprise.

✦

Erasmus teaches us a great deal about the relationship between scholarship and citizenship. By remembering the important elements of the humanistic endeavor, we clarify for both academic and public communities the role that the philosopher, and undoubtedly the historian or literary critic as well, can play in the process whereby society remembers the past, grapples with the present, and gives shape to the future.

Erasmus also deepens our understanding of the personal and environmental problems of the humanist as previously noted. We see how pressing social and political concerns influence the selection and delineation of subjects pursued by the scholar, and we gain deeper understanding of the personal vulnerability of the humanist, and of the potential alienation felt by the humanist as public concerns are addressed and as the Socratic principle that "the unexamined life is not to be lived" is reinforced through words and deeds. But, more importantly, we see that difficult social and cultural circumstances can lead to the renewal of the humanistic endeavor, to advances in human knowledge and public understanding.

But these are difficult times for the humanities, and many questions remain unanswered. Can the humanities community overcome the public's distrust of the humanist? Can Americans gain a new understanding of the value of humanistic thought? Can scholars transcend feelings of alienation and estrangement? Can scholars ignore those who would put limits on humanistic inquiry? Can the profession find new ways of discussing with the public the value of humanistic knowledge? Can today's humanists reclaim the Socratic and Erasmian ideals of discourse on the most important philosophical and moral questions underlying public concerns?

Undoubtedly, a correlation exists between the fact that the humanities, over the past several decades, have lost public favor, and the fact that, during the same period, scholarship has tended to become increasingly narrow, isolated, and removed from fundamental public concerns. The late Charles Frankel wrote: "When the study of human experience turns entirely inward upon itself, when it becomes the study of the study of human experience, and then the study of the study of that study, it does not achieve greater objectivity; it merely becomes thinner."

Renewal within the humanities profession may come by remembering the civic function of scholarship, and by recalling that political, cultural, and social concerns are as central to philosophy and other humanities disciplines as they are to the social sciences. Indeed, one of the most fruitful areas of study at the present time is the field of social and political philosophy. But other developments may also prove to be extraordinarily useful in understanding the relationship between the humanities, civic conversation, and the determination of societal ends— recent efforts that provide the basis for further work in the relationship between humanistic learning and citizenship, especially in the interdisciplinary field of the sociology of knowledge where certain traditional epistemological issues are dealt with in a broader, more public context.

It is clear that we as a nation cannot deal with such fundamental concerns as the relationship between developed and developing countries, war and peace, human rights, religious fundamentalism and political and military power, rapid technological advances, and the physical environment, without the benefit of humanistic studies. Humanities scholars have an obligation to reclaim the tradition of civic humanism, to explore with the public the philosophical, historical, and moral issues underlying these great public concerns. And the humanities, noted Charles Frankel, "have usually been at their best and most vital . . . when they have had a sense of engagement with issues of public concern."

An unexamined public life of a community, a nation, a civilization, is as unworthy to be lived as the unexamined life of an individual. By reclaiming the tradition of civic humanism as exemplified by Socrates and Erasmus, today's humanities scholars may provide the means for the survival and renewal of the humanities and, perhaps, of civilization itself.

Works Cited

Avey, Albert. *Handbook in the History of Philosophy.* New York: Barnes & Noble, 1961.

Bennett, William J. *To Reclaim a Legacy: A Report on the Humanities in Higher Education.* National Endowment for the Humanities, 1984.

Delattie, Edwin J. "Real Career Education Comes from the Liberal Arts." *The Chronicle of Higher Education,* January 5, 1983.

Godamer, Hans-Georg. *Truth and Method.* New York: Seabury Press, 1975.

Hofstadter, Richard. *Anti-intellectualism in American Life,* 1962. Reprint, New York: Alfred Knopf, 1970.

Huizinga, Johan. *Erasmus and the Age of Reformation,* 1924. Reprint, Princeton: Princeton University Press, 1984.

Kaufmann, Walter. "Is there a Kind of Knowledge Available Only Through Humanistic Study?" in William L. Blizek, ed. *The Humanities and Public Life.* Lincoln: Pied Publications, 1978.

Leuchtenburg, William E. "Charles Frankel: The Humanist as Citizen" in John Agresto and Peter Riesenberg, eds. *The Humanist as Citizen.* National Humanities Center, North Carolina, 1981.

Nisbet, Robert. *Prejudices: A Philosophical Dictionary.* Cambridge: Cambridge University Press, 1982.

Sauvage, Micheline. *Socrates and the Human Conscience.* New York: Harper & Brothers, 1960.

Smith, Preserved. *Erasmus: A Study of His Life, Ideals, and Place in History.* New York: Ungar, 1923.

1989

A Commencement Address

The following address was given for the graduates of the College of Liberal Arts of The University of Texas at Arlington, May 20, 1989, at the invitation of Dean Tom Porter, a former member of the TCH board of directors.

How pleased I am to be with you for this wonderful and inspiring occasion. In an era marked by rapid change, it is important that we nurture those civic occasions that bring us together, link us to the past, and call us to service in the future. Graduation is one such occasion. Through this public ceremony, with all its splendor and tradition, we are able to reaffirm our faith in the value of learning, in the meaning of accomplishment, in the triumph of achievement, and in the joy of claiming life's passages. So let us relish these moments together.

I would like to reflect on an important perspective set forth by our new president. George Bush has suggested that we need a "kinder, gentler" nation. Now I know that the president's observation has been the object of much curiosity and some jocularity. But I am captivated by this presidential plea, a plea that I see as a forthright assessment from a man who surely knows that we face awesome challenges as we enter the last decade of this century. I also want to explore this theme because all of you, as students of the liberal arts, have devoted extensive time to the study of society and culture.

Unfortunately, sometimes such study, due to the demands of preparing for a profession, fails to address issues related to the "big picture," that is, to broad assessment of our society and culture. My theme today is what you as liberal arts graduates can bring to the reassessment and hoped-for revitalization of contemporary American society and culture.

Most of you who are graduating today majored in the humanities, social sciences, or fine arts. I suspect that many of you were advised at one time or another during your university career to find another major, perhaps in engineering, accounting, or business, so that you would be assured of securing a high-paying job upon your graduation. If I were to ask those of you who were so advised to stand, few of you, I assume, would remain seated.

As you well know, higher education in the United States during the past twenty years has been marked by declining enrollments in the humanities, social sciences, and fine arts, and burgeoning enrollments in more professionally and vocationally identified disciplines. I am happy to tell you that recent statistics indicate that the tide is now turning, that there is much better sailing ahead for liberal arts graduates, for there is renewed interest in and esteem for the value of study in the humanities, the social sciences, and the arts.

Increasing numbers of your fellow Americans, including your future employers, are recognizing that broad education in the liberal arts may indeed be the best preparation for sustained professional growth over a lifetime.

But such education is also the best preparation that one can have for dealing imaginatively with the present realities of contemporary society and culture. Because of your familiarity with the currents of history, with the broad themes of literature, with the dynamics of culture, indeed, with the world of ideas, you are in a leadership position to foster constructive change.

In thinking about this plea for a kinder America, we discover some underlying assumptions. One assumption is that nations, like individuals, have personalities. Now that is a big claim, and there are those who are troubled by this personification of nations. Yet we know that there is a rich body of literature in the humanities that focuses on special traits of particular nations.

Whether we are students of this literature or not, we tend to associ-

ate traits of the human personality with national behavior and sentiment and, indeed, with government administrations. Who can doubt
that Nazi Germany was cruel and ruthless? Who can doubt that the
administration of General Noriega in Panama is morally corrupt? Who
can doubt that the Stalinist regime in the Soviet Union was repressive?
Who can doubt that the administration of President Arias in Costa Rica
is peaceful?

We think of nations much as we think of individuals. Some are old;
some are young. Some are disciplined; others are unrestrained. Some
are calm; others are in conflict. Some are strong; others are weak. Some
cherish learning and freedom of thought; others seek to control thought
through stifling philosophies and ideologies.

We also think of nations as having experiences that pattern our
own. The American Civil War, we say, was a trauma to the nation.
World War I, we are told, shocked the nation into realizing its relationship to allied nations. Franklin Roosevelt, in the midst of the Great
Depression, said we as a nation were paralyzed by fear, and told us that
we have nothing to fear but fear itself.

In one of the most unusual presidential addresses ever, Jimmy Carter,
on a Sunday evening in July, 1979, reflecting deeply on a national
paralysis of will, claimed that the nation was suffering from a crisis of
confidence. "We can see this crisis," he said, "in the growing doubt
about the meaning of our own lives and in the loss of a unity of purpose for our Nation." Whether his assessment was correct or not, it
surely was one that we didn't want to hear, and it just as surely was one
that marked the beginning of the end of his administration. Yet I suspect that we did not doubt that nations can be purposeful or purpose-
less, and that nations can evidence various amounts of confidence.

Thus President Bush's plea for a kinder, gentler nation should not
strike us as odd or inappropriate. But there is another assumption underlying this plea as well, the obvious one—the assumption that we as
a nation have not been as kind and as gentle as we should be, or,
indeed, as we are capable of being.

We have heard a few things from President Bush about the ways in
which we have not been so gentle and kind. For instance, Mr. Bush has
talked about excessive materialism, about the problem of ethics in government and professional life, and about inadequate attention paid by
our society to the very young.

Those observations are starting points, but we need clarity on this
matter. If the decade of the 1980s stands for the rebirth of American
confidence, overcoming the paralysis of will that Jimmy Carter unsuc-

cessfully sought to address, such confidence has come with a cost, and that cost is a nation that is less kind and gentle than it is capable of being. Here are a few sobering statistics gleaned from the press.

In the area of *housing and homelessness*, federal funding for subsidized housing is down by eighty-one percent. In New York City, the estimated waiting time for a public-housing vacancy is eighteen years. There are an estimated three million of our fellow citizens who this very night are homeless.

In the area of *welfare*, the Aid to Families with Dependent Children program reaches only sixty percent of eligible children living in poverty, compared with eighty-four percent fifteen years ago. In the majority of states, such aid for a family of three is less than half the poverty level. The Women, Infants and Children nutrition program reaches only fifty percent of the eligible poor.

In the area of *public health*, community health centers serve only five million of the twenty-five million poor who are eligible. The consequences in terms of human suffering are staggering. The United States, for instance, has the highest rate of infant mortality among developed nations.

In the area of *child care*, it is estimated that one out of every three girls and one out of every five boys born in this country will experience sexual abuse by the time she or he is eighteen.

In the area of *education*, Chapter I, the major federal education program to help disadvantaged primary and secondary school children, reached seventy-five out of one hundred eligible poor children in 1980; today it reaches only fifty-four out of one hundred. About 500,000 poor children have been dropped from the program.

Approximately twenty-five million Americans are functionally illiterate. The personal, social, and economic cost of this rate of illiteracy can hardly be measured. It is estimated that one out of three Texans is functionally illiterate. Almost two-thirds of adults in Texas with incomes below the poverty level are high-school dropouts. There is a strong correlation between illiteracy and drugs and crime. In Texas, ninety percent of the prison population dropped out of school. It costs $15,000 a year to keep a person in prison; it costs $3,800 a year to keep a child in school.

A recent report by the Mott Foundation, *America's Shame, America's Hope*, documents a national tragedy—the fact that we are not educating one-third of our children, young boys and girls who, by and large, are children of poverty. Here in Texas, it is estimated that thirty-four percent of black students and forty-five percent of Hispanic students do not graduate from high school.

It is important that we see these sobering realities of American life as challenges to our society and culture, not just challenges to federal, state, and local governments.

Widespread poverty, hunger, homelessness, inadequate health care, illiteracy, child abuse, crime and delinquency, represent a sad reality of American life, the dark shadow beneath our gleaming skyscrapers, our still-expanding economy, our technological prowess, our military strength, our renewed confidence, our principles of freedom and justice, our interstate highways and jumbo jets, our BMWs and designer jeans, our home computers and facsimile machines.

The plea for a more humane nation beckons us to face these challenges, to incorporate into the spirit of America a deeper passion to right wrongs, to reduce suffering, to empower all Americans with the knowledge and skills needed to be productive citizens. Without such passion, our nation is seriously flawed, a shallow and troubling image of the nation we can be.

But what will it take to enhance this American spirit, to incorporate into our sense of national purpose and destiny a kinder America?

It will take, first of all, a great deal of clear-headed thinking about the proper roles of the three major sectors of American society—government, non-profit, and private enterprise. We must ask tough questions about the relationships that exist among these three sectors, about the responsibilities of each sector, and about what needs to be done to put a presidential plea into public action. For nearly a decade, we have seen, for better or worse, the shrinkage of federal responsibility for addressing the social ills of our society, with the hope that state and local governments and the non-profit and private enterprise sectors, will have the desire and resources to tackle these difficult problems. In a serious and sustained way, we now must be about the task of re-evaluating what it is that each sector can contribute to producing policies and programs that address difficult national problems.

But it will take much more than that. The most serious challenge is that of revisioning American society as a community. Our nation has always had a difficult time forging a sense of community because of unique historical circumstances and because of our endearment to individual rights.

It was Alexis de Tocqueville who, in *Democracy in America*, identified individualism with the American character. Tocqueville believed that the success of democracy in the U.S. would depend upon the ability of certain structures—the family, churches, local politics, and so forth—to sustain connections between individuals and the wider community. Without such institutions, American individualism would be destructive.

One hundred and fifty years after Tocqueville, sociologist Robert Bellah and his colleagues, in *Habits of the Heart: Individualism and Commitment in American Life*, argue that individualism has marched inexorably throughout our history. "We are concerned," they write, "that this individualism may have grown cancerous—that it may be destroying those social integuments that Tocqueville saw as moderating its more destructive potentialities, that it may be threatening the survival of freedom itself." For Bellah, an excessive utilitarian individualism has dominated the American landscape, with the individual perceived as the only firm reality, with personal energies devoted to the "calculating pursuit of one's own material interests." In short, a vision of how the individual is related to the wider community is lost.

The predicament that Bellah describes has contributed to a nation not so kind and gentle, a nation which, while espousing the virtues of freedom and individual rights, has shown far too little concern for the disadvantaged and the downtrodden.

A sense of community to which all Americans belong is the prerequisite of a nation that evidences kindness and gentleness, for it is community that unites us in common purpose, that genuinely protects the rights of its members, that fosters tolerance, that overcomes prejudice, and that instills in its members empathy, that quality of the heart that allows us to relate authentically and constructively to others.

The surest path to this revisioning of community in America is that of civic conversation, public dialogue that focuses on our problems, our dreams, our fears, our aspirations. Ironically, at the very time when communication among Americans has never been easier, through technological wonders, civic conversation may be reaching an all-time low.

We have not found the means to replace many of those structures that fostered civic conversation in our earlier history—the New England town meeting, the neighborhood church and school, women's clubs in frontier towns, chautauquas, and countless other institutions and organizations, although, I add, many Americans were excluded from this conversation. Meanwhile, we have moved from a rural to an urban society. With incredible speed, we have progressed from an agricultural to an industrial and now to a post-industrial society. Our population has grown dramatically. Home and work are often separated. Many of us are employed by large and impersonal corporations. We deal with faceless bureaucracies. Most of us are cutoff from the land which, in the past, nourished our sense of community and belonging.

Complexity abounds. Chances are, the majority of you will change careers two or three times. You will be required, in meeting employment responsibilities, to retrain and to learn new technologies, new bodies of knowledge, new modes of analysis and thinking. If you are married or will be married, you and your spouse will undoubtedly both work, presenting you with what will seem to be an insurmountable task in balancing the needs of family life with professional obligations.

Public issues too have become more complex. Grave environmental issues, ethical issues related to new technologies, especially in the field of medicine, issues related to international relations, including issues stemming from the apparent ending of the Cold War, issues related to rampant violence and crime, all these issues and more—issues that demand the interest, understanding, and involvement of citizens—are very difficult to address in any meaningful public fashion.

The potential result, I fear, is what Bellah calls a "culture of separation" in which the individual is the only firm reality, preoccupied with self-interest and material gain. We lose sight of each other, only to wake up one morning to find that three million of our fellow Americans are homeless, that poverty is widespread and on the rise, that twenty-five million Americans cannot read and write, that our beloved nation is a major consumer of drugs and that we have one of the highest per capita prison populations in the world.

We are waking up now to that reality. As difficult as that may be, consciousness of our problems and our pain is the first step toward healing. President Bush's plea for a kinder nation is recognition, I think, that we have not done what we need to do to foster community. My challenge to you, then, is to invite all of you to accept the opportunities that are yours as citizens of the United States of America as we enter the last decade of this century, as we cast our eyes, our hopes, our dreams, on a new century and a new millennium.

A kinder, gentler nation will be possible only if we develop this sense of community to which all Americans belong regardless of race, gender, and class. The path to this sense of community can only come through civic conversation.

Conversation begins at home. It means honest talk. It means listening carefully. It means tolerance, but it also means honesty in expressing one's views and feelings. Such conversation needs to occur in our places of employment, in our schools, our churches, our civic organizations. It needs to take place in the public arena, with all of us demanding honest and thoughtful views of our public servants on difficult issues and concerns.

This conversation must be wide and deep. We must hear our many voices, Anglo American voices, African American voices, Hispanic American voices, Vietnamese American voices, Japanese American voices, Native-American voices.

And we need to hear from those who cannot speak. That takes listening of a special kind.

If we hear all these voices, if we engage in genuine public conversation, we may be on our way to a kinder and gentler nation, and to the restoration of the American dream in all of its dimensions.

Throughout the 1980s, we heard President Reagan, on many occasions, draw from the Puritan tradition to talk about America as the city on the hill, the beacon of hope to the nations of the world, a city where economic opportunity, prosperity, and freedom reign. But our new president has told us that, in this fine city, something is not quite right, we have fallen short in the virtues of kindness and gentleness.

Perhaps it is the peculiar and special responsibility of your generation to change the personality of the nation, to make this city on the hill a community where all Americans belong, a city that is not afraid of confronting its problems through open dialogue, a city where all voices are heard, a city that knows no divisions by class or race, a city where children do not live in fear of being abused, a city where everyone has a home and no one is without food and medical care. A city where the elderly live comfortably and have meaningful lives. A city where the physically and mentally impaired are loved, live in dignity, and contribute to society. A city where play is as important as work. A city that nourishes faith and commitment and love. Now *that* would be a shining city indeed.

As you leave behind your university work to pursue chosen careers and new responsibilities, you will find, as the years pass, the desperate need, in this demanding, competitive, and fast-paced world, to carve out of your busy schedule quiet times for intimacy, for personal renewal, for re-connecting yourself to your roots and to your loved ones.

As you do, remember that your nation needs the same thing—moments and occasions where we are intimate with each other, where we talk to each other about our fears and failures, our dreams and achievements, our rich cultural heritages, our kinship with each other and with the world community.

If you and your classmates contribute to this rebirth of community, to making this great nation a kinder and gentler city on the hill, you will form a new and perhaps the greatest generation of American patriots.

Let us pray that through your ideas, words, and deeds, through everything that your minds, hearts, and hands touch, this great city will be able to experience, and the wider world will be able to see, the promise of a new day in America.

Works Cited

America's Shame, America's Hope. A Report of the Mott Foundation, Flint Michigan, 1989.

Bellah, Robert, et al. *Habits of the Heart: Individualism and Commitment in American Life.* New York: Harper & Row, 1985

Tocqueville, Alexis de. *Democracy in America.* New York: Random House, 1945 (revised edition).

Making Connections: The Humanities, Culture, and Community (with James Quay)

James Quay, executive director of the California Council for the Humanities, and I were asked to provide "the big picture" for the Task Force on Scholarship and the Public Humanities, a joint endeavor of the American Council of Learned Societies (ACLS) and the Federation of State Humanities Councils. The Task Force was formed to find ways and means to broaden and improve scholarly participation in the public humanities. Directors of the various national humanities organizations associated with the ACLS, academic administrators, cultural leaders, and executive directors of a number of state councils participated in the conference, which was held at the Johnson Foundation's Wingspread Conference Center, Racine, Wisconsin, October 6–7, 1989. Additional support was provided by the Joyce Foundation and the Pew Charitable Trusts. This paper, along with a rapporteur's summary of the proceedings, was published by the ACLS, Occasional Paper No. 11, 1990.

While humanists normally ask their audiences to consider the past as prologue, we ask our audience to consider what's present as prologue. We ask you to imagine the conditions of American life in the twenty-first century and to describe a role for the humanities in terms of those conditions. In doing so, we ask you to see beyond the debates of the present hour, beyond the ACLS and the Federation, beyond the Helms amendment and the size of the NEH budget. From such a vantage point, we do not see an impending crisis in the humanities; rather we can confidently assert that so long as there is a human future, the humanities will be a part of it, for both the subject and audience of the humanities must endure as long as humans endure. What is less clear is the connection between those of us who are professional humanists and the rest of American society.

Twenty years ago, Robert Hutchins proposed one possible connection in a book entitled *The Learning Society*. By that term, Hutchins meant a society whose primary goal was the intellectual development of its citizens. Such a society, he thought, would offer opportunities for education to every man and woman at every stage of their adult life. For Hutchins, Athens was the model: "In Athens, education was not a segregated activity, conducted for certain hours, in certain places, at a certain time of life. It was the aim of society. The city educated the man. The Athenian was educated by the culture, by *paideia*."

Were he writing today, Hutchins might not be so eager to embrace Athens as a model for the Learning Society. Feminist scholarship, for example, has taught us to consider more carefully the condition of Athenian women before we champion Athenian society as a model. Writing in 1968, Hutchins believed that machines could do for every American what slaves had done for the Athenians and argued that growing affluence, a dissolving class structure, and an increase in leisure time would combine to make education every adult's birthright. Twenty years later, we must consider all three of Hutchins's assumptions questionable: Americans in 1987 reported they had eight hours *less* leisure time each week than a decade before; children of the lower and middle classes face the prospect of living standards *below* those of their parents; and the existence of a permanent underclass points to a hardening rather than a dissolving of class structure in this country.

The erosion of Hutchins's major assumptions is a caution to anyone projecting a future, but it does not invalidate his argument for a Learning Society. As a scholar and an administrator, Hutchins knew well enough how much the rate of change had accelerated in this century. He argued that the investment in education is usually justified by promises of increased personal and national prosperity, an educational system's products cannot be known for twenty-five years, and neither national or personal needs can be reliably predicted that far in advance. Therefore, Hutchins concluded, the Learning Society cannot simply offer a vocational training; it must offer an education, and the most practical education for people of any age is the most theoretical one, an education informed by the wisdom of the past, an education informed by the humanities.

Some Twenty-First Century Trends

Regardless of whether or not conditions in the twenty-first century *favor* the creation of a Learning Society in this country, we argue that future conditions will *require* that ours be a Learning Society. To begin, let us suggest a few of the influences which promise to affect American culture into the next century.

1. Migrations of people across national borders

Unless a change in U.S. government policy severely restricts immigration, this country—and other modern industrial nations—will continue to attract immigrants. Recent immigration has included large numbers of Southeast Asians and Central Americans, but the demographic composition of immigration to this country will likely change as we move past the year 2000. Regardless of the immigrants' country of origin, Americans will need to know more about people from cultures quite unlike their own. For political as well as for moral reasons, Xenophobia and racial tension are not acceptable alternatives. Public school curricula and textbooks will have to change and the leaders and workers in those institutions called upon to help the new immigrants settle in this country will have to be educated.

2. Continued Population Growth

This increase in population brings with it an increase in pressure on natural resources and land, igniting conflicts between the mandates of economic growth and the desire for environmental protection. Ethical questions regarding access to resources are bound to grow as pressure on those resources intensifies. In addition, the increasing population will shape political and social institutions. The formats and forums of public discourse in a large democracy continue to be shaped by the need of the country's aspiring leaders to reach large audiences. The dialogue and debates found in town meetings may be viable options for small New England towns, but increasingly it is the monologue of television ads and direct mail campaigns that defines the modern American election. At least since the nineteenth century, Americans have lived in an age of mass politics. Their democratic continuation demands both powerful media and citizen capacity to criticize them.

3. Continued Development and Deployment of Information Technologies

The amount of storage, delivery and retrieval of information will continue to grow. Philosopher Hubert Dreyfus has shown how the designs of the latest artificial intelligence machine influence theories of human knowing and human being. As computers become more widely available and more sophisticated, their languages and the conceptions upon which those languages are based will spread from the hacker subculture into popular culture. The sheer volume of information will continue to require that specialists master particular areas and that generalists discern large patterns. But Americans will need new ways to see forests through the trees, to turn information into knowledge, knowledge into wisdom. Computer technology and telecommunications may nourish networks while communities wither. Americans may find it easier to communicate with a like-minded colleague in a distant city than a contrary neighbor.

4. Media and Communications

The power of the media to shape culture is undisputed. Video cassette recorders have changed American viewing habits in the last ten years, and cable television has uncoupled Americans from broadcast networks. Media outlets multiply, but their ownership is concentrated into fewer hands. Some of us lament the superficial content of much broadcast programming, but also the fact that such programming is often the only common culture that many Americans can discuss.

Literacies Old and New

Looking at these four trends, we can discern the need for at least three new literacies in the twenty-first century—literacies informed by the humanities.

The first is a need for *multicultural literacy*—the need for Americans to understand more about inhabitants of and immigrants to this country and the many cultures from which they come. In a provocative essay, "How to Be A North American," philosopher Alasdair MacIntyre writes that every society enacts its own history as a more or less coherent dramatic narrative, inviting its citizens to participate in national life by considering themselves both as characters in that story and as authors of it. Members of a nation of immigrants must come to terms with *two* interdependent dramatic narratives: that of the American people and that of the particular ethnic group to which they belong. As MacIntyre says:

> If we do not recover and identify with the particularities of our own community—North American Indian,

347

Spanish Catholic, New England Protestant, European Jew, Irish, Black African, Japanese, and a host of others—then we shall lose what it is that we have to contribute to the common culture. We shall have nothing to bring, nothing to give. But if each of us dwells too much, or even exclusively, upon his or her own ethnic particularity, then we are in danger of fragmenting or even destroying the common life.

MacIntyre is mindful of the complexity of this task and recommends that Americans not only be told the stories of other peoples but also told the same stories from rival perspectives; for example, the story of the Little Big Horn from the perspective of the U.S. Army and the Lakota. One of the tasks of the scholar is to recover, analyze, and transmit these stories, including stories found in books that have never been called great and those never found in books at all—stories of women, of slaves, of working class people. If this task is limited to the confines of a single required college course, like Stanford University's Western Cultures course, for example, the breadth of MacIntyre's sophisticated task is reduced to a simplistic choice: *either* we preserve the common culture through a curriculum of great books *or* we expand the common culture through texts reflecting multicultural diversity.

MacIntyre knows that multicultural literacy is not accomplished in required courses but achieved over a lifetime. He recommends a program of adult reading that will require scholars to ask not only what books Americans should read at age twenty, but at age thirty, fifty, and seventy. Hutchins did not foresee the need for multicultural literacy, but in the twenty-first century, it is part of the mandate for a Learning Society.

A second literacy is *civic literacy*—the need of Americans to know about their government, its history and the political principles on which it is based. The need for this literacy is as old as American democracy itself. Since it was Thomas Jefferson who wrote so compellingly of the need for an educated citizenry if American democracy were to flourish, it is fitting that a student of Jefferson should restate Jefferson's argument today. In a 1987 report entitled *The Humanities and the American Promise*, Merrill Peterson wrote that the most important public mission of the humanities is improvement of the quality of civic discourse.

Peterson argues that in a democracy, with government deriving its authority from the will of the people, a primary index of civic vitality is the vigor and quality of public discussion and debate. Effective participation in this discussion is made possible not only by guarantees of political liberty, but also by the education of citizens in ways that strengthen and encourage their responsible involvement. All of the trends mentioned above have the potential to impair the participation of Americans in the democratic process. Young native-born Americans and immigrants from nations with quite different traditions need the civic education of which Peterson speaks. We have already mentioned ways in which a large population tends to turn civic discourse from dialogue to monologue. Wed to the broadcast media, the modern electoral process creates a new form of demagoguery—thirty-second sound bites and one-minute television spots. United with new information technology, electronic democracy turns to focus groups and instant polling. Americans in the twenty-first century will need heavy doses of two scholarly virtues—the faculty of critical reasoning and the time to reflect and discuss—if democratic culture is to prosper.

The third literacy is more difficult to label—we are going to call it *community literacy*—and here too we offer a suggestive text, Robert Bellah's recent lecture "The Humanities and the Survival of Community." For Bellah, communities are defined by common moral understandings and the necessity to reach workable compromises when agreement about those understandings fails, and he finds the humanities, as the disciplines most intimately concerned with cultural heritage, indispensable to thinking and discussion of common moral understandings.

Bellah and others see community as endangered in America. Let us illustrate the danger with a California example. In 1988, the Council sponsored a conference on "Cultures in Transition: Immigration in the Central Valley" in Fresno, a city of 300,000 in the largely agricultural San Joaquin Valley. A panel discussion of immigration included representatives from the Central Valley's latest immigrants: Cambodians, Vietnamese, and Laotians. Their stories were filled with the grief of leaving one's native land, the difficult adjustments to an alien culture, and the sometimes hostile reception from their new American neighbors, not to mention the generational tensions created by the fact that children adapt so much faster to the new culture than parents do.

A fourth panel member, a rabbi, seemed out of place at first but his topic was not—the difficulty of keeping his community together. For Jews in America, he said, community was threatened not by oppression but by freedom. Borrowing a phrase of Walter Lippmann's, the Jewish community was being eroded by "the acids of modernity." It was soon clear that those same acids were eroding all communities. Both broadcast television and contemporary mobility threaten the connections to place that bind communities together. Those connections can sometimes be constricting, and we know that the broadcast television's window to the world can be liberating and the opportunity to leave one's home can be exhilarating. But these days, we increasingly have the sense that our communal life is out of balance: we need less acid and more base. The threat of the acids of modernity may be the one thing that all ethnic communities share in common.

Public Service Scholarship

So far we have spent all our time talking about trends and literacies and nothing about scholarship and the public humanities, but we hope the connection is not difficult to see. All too often, the terms "scholarship" and "public humanities" stand in opposition, with scholarship considered the equivalent of "private" or "academic" humanities. We think it more useful and more accurate to consider scholarship and the public humanities not as two distinct spheres but as parts of a single process, the process of taking private insight, testing it, and turning it into public knowledge.

The humanities scholar is granted time for reflection and research, often supported by public funds. She uses this time to journey to and extend the borders of what is known, but even closeted in her office, with only a keyboard for company, she does not travel alone, for she takes with her methods and insights given to her by teachers and colleagues she respects. As many acknowledgments in scholarly books demonstrate, scholars read their manuscripts to spouses, to friends, to colleagues, to editors. They read them at professional gatherings and formal lectures. They reshape them based on the response they receive, and then they publish them. *Publication* is the goal.

From one point of view, this part of the process is working very well. An unprecedented number of scholars are doing research and publishing articles in an ever-increasing number of journals. The quantity of scholarly books published grows yearly. One of the reasons for the abundance is that it is driven by a reward system that demands published articles and books as proof of intellectual vitality and as justification for professional advancement. The process has its critics. In *Humanities in America*, Lynne Cheney observes that scholarly specialization has narrowed and deepened as the number of scholars has increased, and that "as specialization becomes ever narrower, the humanities tend to lose their significance and centrality." In *The Last Intel-*

lectuals, Russell Jacoby believes that the increase in the number of academically-oriented scholars has meant a loss in the number of publicly-oriented intellectuals, and Wayne Booth in an essay titled "The Scholar in Society" has confessed that "in every field but my own, I find myself ready to ask a simple and nasty question: 'Just how many scholars of that kind does a society *need?*'"

Privately, many scholars, including the authors of *Speaking for the Humanities*, concede and lament the obscurity of some scholarship, but they write that "the recommendation in *Humanities in America* that 'to counter the excess of specialization . . . those who fund, publish, and evaluate research should encourage work of general significance' ignores the fact that general significance only develops from specialized and particularized research." Fair enough. But how is this development to occur? The present system is geared to reward those who generate specialized and particularized research, but who rewards those who carry the knowledge the next step toward the public? Our contention is that the process of turning private insight to public knowledge breaks down at this point.

Wayne Booth notes that America has a history of chautauquas and lyceums and college lecture series and literary journalism, what he called *haute vulgarisation*. "The tradition is not dead," he wrote in 1981, "but I have the impression that it is pursued these days more vigorously among scientists than among humanists. Where is the Lewis Thomas of literary critics? Where is the *Scientific American* among our journals of literary study?"

The institutions dedicated to preserving this tradition are state humanities councils, historical societies, museums, and libraries, what Lynne Cheney calls "the parallel school." These institutions are funded by government agencies and user fees. They're doing better in some areas than others, but they're in place. We don't need a new set of institutions to complete the circuit. These institutions frequently bring scholarly knowledge to the public. The most direct way is to bring the scholar herself before a public audience. State humanities councils have been doing this for nearly twenty years now and have many successes to their credit, but there is something *ad hoc* about this process.

What we could use is a more systematic way of locating public questions and problems and a more systematic way of surveying the scholarly literature. We need more people in the middle to provide connections. We need scholars willing to survey scholarly literature and to relate their disciplines to timely public issues and concerns. We are not saying that we need to stop funding the kinds of scholarship being pursued today. What we are saying is that we need an additional kind of scholarship—public service scholarship—that is influenced by and for the benefit of the wider public.

This new scholarship is socially valuable and needs to be respected and rewarded as such. Each of the three scholars cited—MacIntyre, Peterson, and Bellah—brought to bear upon a present and future need his study of the past. The essays cited are examples of the kind of scholarship we advocate, scholarship that addresses important issues of public culture. Not every scholar can do this scholarship. Not every scholar needs to. But we think this work is as critical to building the Learning Society we need as the pioneering work done by the scholar at the margins.

Late last year, when the California Council was updating its scholars file, it sent out a brief questionnaire asking scholars why they participated in public humanities projects, and what benefit they had derived from such participation. Over 200 scholars have returned the questionnaire, and though the Council cannot claim that the percentages reported below are representative of the professoriate nationally, it does think the weighting of their responses is significant. The sample is not skewed in favor of scholars involved in public programs, incidentally; about half of the respondents had never participated in a public humanities program, though all would be willing to do so.

Of those who had, ninety-eight percent said their participation was an extension of their responsibilities as teachers, ninety-six percent said it was an extension of their responsibilities as scholars, and ninety-four percent said it was an extension of their responsibilities as citizens. Very few—less than one in six—saw participation as a distraction from either their scholarship or their teaching. Seventy-two percent said participation in public projects had influenced their scholarship positively and eighty-two percent said it had influenced their teaching positively. Not one respondent thought it influenced their teaching negatively. Yet three out of four scholars reported that their participation in humanities projects for the public had no influence on promotion and tenure decisions.

One might expect this to be true at institutions where a premium is put on research, but in this sample, the reverse was true. Sixty percent of professors at the University of California said it had not influenced their promotion; as did two-thirds of California State University professors, eighty percent of private college professors, and ninety-four percent at community colleges. We have two reactions to these statistics: dismay and admiration. Dismay that colleges and universities tend not to recognize in promotion and tenure decisions the service being performed by public-spirited professors, and admiration that so many scholars persist in lending their time and expertise to public humanities projects despite the lack of formal professional reward.

The alternative to making connections between scholars and the public is the perpetuation of mutual suspicion and hostility and the continuation of cultural polarization, the familiar split between "town" and "gown" and "low" and "high" culture. Those of us working with state humanities councils often find ourselves fighting two recalcitrant stereotypes: those of the remote, condescending pedant and the anti-intellectual citizen. Our task is to bring the scholar and citizen together on matters of mutual interest and concern. When we move beyond the stereotypes, when we initiate programs on important matters, we find plenty of room for creative interaction.

We all know where the public tends to get its information: broadcast media, mostly television, followed by newspapers and magazines. There may be other sources of information—one's coworkers, friends, parents. But where do Americans get their *knowledge?* Where do they find knowledge that integrates information into broader contexts of value, time, and place? In a Learning Society, scholars would help supply this knowledge.

And we all know the scholar's comfort with what A. Bartlett Giamatti called the "free and ordered space" of the university, with the principle of intellectual freedom, with the opportunity to pursue any thought deemed worth pursuing. But where do scholars go to test the importance of their ideas to the body politic? Where beside the classroom do they carry out their responsibility as scholar-citizens? In a Learning Society, the public would help provide this arena.

Culture and Monoculture

In *Habits of the Heart*, Robert Bellah wrote that "cultures are dramatic conversations about things that matter to their participants." By this definition, American culture is created in part when scholars publish their research before their colleagues. It is also created in part when the public's questions meet the scholars research and when the public's opinions meet the scholar's questions. If scholars are not encouraged and rewarded for interacting with the public, then the public will tend to get its knowledge primarily from broadcast media, while the scholar will tend to write without his fellow citizen in mind.

In academic circles, we currently hear debate about the relation of the dominant culture to minority cultures in the curriculum, but it is a mistake to define the dominant culture as the culture of dead European white males. The dominant culture is not the culture of Plato, Kant, Hume, and other luminaries of the Western tradition, but rather, the commercial consumer culture—the monoculture. It might be better called the anticulture, for it works to destroy all authentic culture by substituting stimulation for engagement, entertainment for reflection, and stars for heroes and private opinions for public dialogue. It invades our homes via television and radio, inhabiting space that could be occupied by books, stories of one's neighbors and family, and dialogue on important concerns. As Wendell Berry observed sadly in his essay, "The Work of Local Culture," most of his neighbors, who once spent their evenings talking to one another, "now sit until bedtime, watching TV, submitting every few minutes to a sales talk. The message of both the TV programs and the sales talks is that the watchers should spend whatever is necessary to be like everybody else."

Instead of multicultural literacy, the monoculture tends to give us representations of non-whites as tokens or exotics. Instead of civic literacy, the monoculture tends to give us radio and television talk shows on topics of momentary interest. Instead of community literacy, the monoculture tends to give us southern California lifestyle and disengaged voyeurism via satellite dish. Instead of engagement, the monoculture tends to gives us entertainment.

The monoculture is driven by the authority of demand, translated into ratings. Even when they appear to offer information or knowledge, Neil Postman has demonstrated, the media really offer us only amusement. They must deliver excitement and the best way to do this is through sex and violence. The images they offer have lovely surfaces but little depth. They offer debates—which can be as exciting as prizefights—but no dialogue—which requires time and trust. Our obligation as humanists, then, is to counter the negative aspects of the monoculture. The texts of the humanities, their tradition of critical reflection and dialogue, their ability to convey compelling stories and real issues, make possible the civic conversation upon which community depends. Without the connecting impulse of the humanities, the pursuit is crippled beyond repair.

Questions for the Cultural Conversation

If the threat is thus defined, the challenge to us is to foster an improved and expanded cultural conversation. The starting point is for us to listen to our fellow citizens, to take into account their deeply-felt questions and concerns, and to find ways to bring humanistic learning to bear on those questions and concerns. We must, as scholars concerned with culture, as proponents of public service scholarship, make our criticism of the monoculture part of the new civic conversation.

We emphasize again that not all scholars need to do this. Both the scholar's and the public's quest for knowledge extends beyond civic issues and concerns, beyond immediate and contemporary social and cultural problems. Public programs should explore the full range of human experience and thought, but we do need more public service scholarship that connects with the American public on deeply-held concerns. What direction might such scholarship take?

We have identified six major questions that we believe are of genuine concern to the public. We recognize that many scholars are currently at work on more manageable, more specialized aspects of these large questions. By offering them here in their stark public formulation, we hope to remind scholars that simple, direct, compelling, and often enduring questions are the starting point of their own inquiries, and to suggest that a return to such questions can be useful to the scholar as well as to the public.

Can the earth be saved?

Although the threat of nuclear annihilation is still with us, surprising developments in American-Soviet relations and in Eastern European politics have renewed public confidence in the human ability to control weapons of mass destruction. But as one threat to human survival lessens, another has emerged—that of preserving the environment so that life on this planet can continue. Growing public recognition of the seriousness of the problems we face have lead to some very recent significant national and international initiatives to preserve the environment. Such efforts most likely will intensify in the years ahead.

Some think that corrective action will be too little and too late. They predict water shortages, smog alerts in our major cities, power blackouts, more oil spills, the death of oceans, rivers, and lakes, the continued warming of the planet, nuclear waste dumped indiscriminately, the extinction of animal species at a staggering rate, and the collapse of entire civilizations. Others believe that, because we are aware of the challenge, we can act to prevent these catastrophes. If so, the cost will be extraordinarily high, not only in dollars but also in terms of personal and national sacrifice. We may have to accept controls over our natural resources in ways that we cannot now imagine, including water and energy fuels. Such controls may affect what we eat, how we live, how frequently we may be allowed to use remaining recreational land, how we move from one city to another, from home to work, the materials with which we build our homes and office buildings, how we stay warm in the winter and cool in the summer.

Environmental issues will dominate life in the twenty-first century. The interested public knows that we will be forced to respond to these issues, and to do that, we will need to fully understand them. Ultimately, these issues will be dealt with both privately, in how we live, and publicly, in the policies that we as a people encourage or discourage, pay for or don't pay for. Satisfactory resolution of the issues will depend upon increased citizen understanding of the cultural, economic, and historical forces that have contributed to our environmental crisis as well as upon increased citizen understanding of the ethical dimensions of the crisis and of proposed solutions. Issues of the environment should be a central concern of public service scholarship in the decade ahead.

What is America?

As we prepare for the challenges of the twenty-first century, we cannot underestimate the public's interest in the aims, purposes, and values of American civilization. Issues related to our national identity have been, of course, at the center of our cultural conversation since the founding of the Republic. But even as the rejection of communism in Eastern Europe is hailed as a vindication of "American" values, problems here at home are casting troubling shadows on those values.

Widespread use of drugs, violence on our streets and in our homes, the crisis confronting our courts and prison systems, make us ask: What's wrong with America?

Frequent outbursts of racial violence, continued evidence of racial prejudice, expressions of religious bigotry, raise serious questions about the American character.

Chronic poverty, hunger, and homelessness in our midst make us question how committed we are to the ideal of equal opportunity and how much compassion we have for our fellow citizens.

The continued growth of impenetrable bureaucracies in government and business cast long and troubling shadows over our notions of personal freedom and self-government.

The growth of minority populations and the weakening of traditional majority culture prevent the making of easy connections between those cultures that contributed to the founding of the Republic and those that will shape our lives in the next century.

These and many other characteristics of contemporary American society lead to provocative and challenging questions about the aims of American civilization and the future of the United States. The public wants to know what that nation stands for, what it values, what its goals are, and where it is headed. What is America, and what does it mean to be an American?

We see signs that Americans are eager to discuss substantive issues related to American identity and values. Last year, Frances Moore Lappe published *Rediscovering American Values,* a book in which alternating conservative and progressive voices debate their respective views of freedom and human value. Public response has encouraged the author to create "Project Public Life" to provide groups who want to continue the discussion of American values begun in the book with the means to do so. Teachers of the humanities can make invaluable contributions to such efforts through public service scholarship, helping the public understand more fully the historical and ethical dimensions of what are thought to be uniquely American values.

Can our system of education work?

Many voices of education reform, such as those heard at last year's President's Education Summit with the Governors, have based their arguments on the need to keep this nation economically competitive. Other proponents of reform, digging deeper, have argued that our society needs educated citizens who understand the world about them, citizens who are in touch with our nation's history and culture, citizens who can exercise their public responsibilities, citizens who can have the skills to deal with the tough public issues that confront the nation.

At state and local levels, citizen concern over our educational institutions often tends to focus on more immediate questions. Will our children receive from the public schools the kind of education that will ensure employment? Will we be able to send our children to college? Will skyrocketing costs coupled with diminishing financial aid mean that thousands of talented youngsters will be denied the opportunity to go to college? If so, what will happen to these young people, many of whom are members of minority groups? Will our children be adequately prepared for all the challenges that will come their way in the decades ahead?

Unfortunately, much of the present public debate surrounding education reform has failed to acknowledge the many accomplishments of public education in the twentieth century, including the opening of doors for minorities and the underprivileged. To ask the question "Can our education system work?" is, of course, to also ask about quality education—about the curriculum, textbooks, and the preparation of teachers and faculty. But, just as importantly, it is also to ask whether or not this nation is committed to ensuring access to quality education for all qualified students.

One of the most important education issues facing the nation is whether or not we build on this record of accomplishment or allow the doors of education to close on many students. We must ask tough questions about high minority dropout rates in our schools and colleges, about the adequacy of student financial aid through governmental and private sources, about the extent and effectiveness of remedial education and student counseling programs, and about funding priorities. Central to equal opportunity is an education system that allows all citizens to achieve their potential.

Education issues brought into the public arena demand the best insights of public service scholarship. The monoculture provides little insight into these difficult issues. Citizens need and want to learn more about the historical, cultural, political, and ethical dimensions of those issues facing American education.

Can we get along with other nations?

For most Americans, the world has indeed become the "global village" that Marshall McLuhan wrote about nearly two decades ago. Modern technology, especially television, breaks down insularity. As the world gets smaller, communication between peoples increases. International communication now takes place daily among tens of thousands of citizens, in board rooms, market places, museums, and libraries, through teleconferences, telephones, and fax machines.

Citizens sense that what happens in other nations can have a profound impact on their nation and their lives. They sense that the jobs that they and their children will have in the decades ahead will be increasingly tied to the development of a single world economy with closely linked worldwide economic institutions. Famine in Africa, the closing of borders in China, the opening of borders in Eastern Europe, the level of production of remaining oil in the Middle East, third-world default of loans from developed nations, free trade among nations of the European Economic Community—these and many other developments have important consequences for our economy here in the United States.

Likewise, citizens understand in new ways that political instability in one region of the world may have grave implications for international relations. They are aware of the potential impact of nationalistic fervor, of sweeping social and political revolutions. They know that Third-World nations can paralyze developed nations through terrorism and nuclear blackmail.

Citizens want to know what the prospects are. Will we be able to get along with other nations? What will the threats be?

Increased emphasis must be placed in our public service scholarship on understanding those nations and cultures whose futures bear so much on ours. Citizens want to know more about changes in the Soviet Union, about developments in Eastern Europe, about the history, culture, and problems of Central America, about the cultures and economic rise of nations in the Far East, about cultural and political conflict in Africa. We have an obligation to find new ways of expanding and enriching the public's understanding of other nations and cultures.

Can we control technology?

Some scholars of the history of science, including Jacques Ellul, have proposed that modern technology is literally driving culture. That thought has weaved its way into public consciousness with the result that citizens sense the extent to which technology may be controlling us rather than the other way around.

To argue that technology is driving culture is to acknowledge two basic facts: that we often simply do not know the long-term consequences of a particular technology until the technology is in place for many years, and that we deal with ethical implications only after the emplacement of particular technologies.

We are still coming to terms with the unforeseen effects of older technologies, including those technologies involving nuclear power. We are less clear about the impact of newer technologies, especially in biology and medicine. Implanted organs give life to many, but lead to shortages and could lead to black markets for donor organs. Drugs that expand the life span might provide years of happy retirement living, but raise serious questions about how society will pay for this increased longevity. The mass-administration of contraceptive agents might help to control the world's population explosion, but in the wrong hands, they could be used to subjugate whole nations and peoples.

Our challenge, wrote Willis S. Harman in 1976, is this: "Now that man has developed consummate skill in technology—the art of how to do things—can he develop equal ability to choose wisely which things are worth doing?"

Citizens are worried that these issues will be left to the experts. They are concerned by the growing gap between technological development and human values and the unforeseen consequences of technology on society and culture. As proponents of public service scholarship, we must encourage our fellow humanists to take on these issues and to connect with the public on the cultural and ethical dimensions of old and new technologies.

Can we be happy?

This question, which seems to hold a special place in the cultures of Western civilization, is as relevant for Americans today as it was at the beginning of the Republic. The times are different though, and the threats to personal happiness may be different from what they were before.

Our pursuit of happiness has in large part been shaped by that dominant trait of the American character, radical individualism and the accompanying quest for personal economic success.

Throughout our nation's history, this pursuit has been beyond the grasp of millions of citizens. If one were born black rather than white, female rather than male, and from the lower rather than the middle or upper class, the odds of achieving this success were long indeed. For those Americans of today who are trapped in poverty, who are unemployed or underemployed, lost in urban housing projects or rural settlements, often ill and frightened, the odds are just as overwhelming.

But even for those who achieve economically, those who find the American dream to be alive, happiness often appears elusive. Marriages dissolve and families break up. Stock markets crash. Freeways and blood vessels clog. Wives are battered and children are abused. Deals sour and bosses fire. In what, pray tell, does happiness consist?

Of course the founding fathers did not answer this question for us. The pursuit of happiness is open-ended and Americans, often discontented with the shallow images of success and power provided by the monoculture, are eager to know what happiness might be and what endeavors might contribute to personal fulfillment and accomplishment. Many of the symptoms of present-day unhappiness, from positive endeavors like self-help groups to negative developments like drug addiction, tell us that we feel hollow inside, that we want something more, that the pursuit of happiness at the dawn of the twenty-first century may necessitate dramatic and far-reaching changes in our culture.

Public service scholarship could make a significant contribution to the nation by helping the public understand this contemporary hollowness, by charting the history of our unhappiness, by documenting the cultural influences shaping our quests, by identifying and interpreting the happiness that we do find, by locating alternative understandings of happiness, by relating individual pursuits to collective pursuits. Once again an extraordinary opportunity exists for connecting scholarship with a genuine public concern.

Institutional Connections

But now we must ask a difficult question: How can a deeper, more inclusive cultural conversation that draws upon far more extensive public service scholarship take place And how can this take place against the background of the powerful monoculture?

Perhaps the long-sought revitalization of public schooling in the nation, as well as the refocusing of undergraduate education, will occur when we recognize more fully the connections that must be made between formal education and the need for new literacies and genuine cultural conversation. No single event could be of more importance to the furtherance of cultural conversation than the development and imple- mentation of curricula whose priorities are to familiarize students with the most important questions facing the nation, curricula that benefit from the riches of public service scholarship.

But that alone is not enough. If America is to be a Learning Society; if American cultures is to be a conversation about what matters, oppor- tunities for informal education must be created. For this reason, the strength and vitality of all those institutions that comprise the parallel school matter greatly.

The improvement of American cultural conversation is the most important task of the humanities community in the last decade of this century. The recognition of this task would have enormous impact on the life of the humanities, inside and outside of the academy. New interest in public service scholarship would lead to new institutional connections of great importance. While it is difficult to talk about spe- cific connections that would flow from the recognition of this task, we offer the following possibilities.

1. Public involvement in university life

Public participation in college and university life would be increased as new liaisons between the academy and the community are estab- lished. One can imagine advisory committees for newly organized pro- grams that include public representatives to discuss connections between our cultural conversation and undergraduate curricula and between our cultural conversation and reset in the humanities. One can imagine short-term and adjunct appointments to universities of persons in various professions and walks of life, individuals whose knowledge or experience lend depth and practicality to curricula. One can envision advisors for students from outside as well as inside the university.

2. Academic involvement in public life

With increasing interest expressed by the public and private sectors in this cultural conversation and the questions central to it, it is likely that humanities scholars would increasingly be called upon to provide valuable service outside the university. To respond to public questions, to stimulate discussion among employees, to offer perspectives and tentative answers, to address serious policy and ethical questions, to provide historical and cultural background, scholars would be brought in as consultants, writers, discussion leaders, critics. In doing so, the humanities community would be assuming a role that has been played for a number of decades now by the scientific community, although on entirely different kinds of issues and questions.

3. Interdisciplinary programs

The central questions focusing public service scholarship and enhancing our cultural conversation would become the driving force behind curricular development in our schools and universities. Since these questions cannot be formulated or answered in bits and pieces drawn from traditional disciplines, we envision the rise of new and far-reaching interdisciplinary courses and programs. Public school curricula as well as undergraduate curricula would be organized without much regard for traditional departmental lines. Courses connecting the humanities with science, literature with history, foreign languages with foreign culture study, technology with ethics, philosophy with sociology and psychology, would be primary characteristics of the new curriculum.

4. University-school collaboration.

Renewed recognition of the partnership that should exist between public school systems and institutions of higher education would occur. Hundreds of important experiments connecting colleges and universities with our public schools would follow. Many partnership models that already exist—scholars in the schools, university-sponsored summer seminars for school teachers, in-service school programs focusing on new scholarship—would be replicated throughout the nation.

5. Growth of the parallel school

With increased attention paid to the extent and quality of American cultural conversation, the institutions that comprise the parallel school would continue to grow. Museums and public libraries would begin to get a greater share of charitable dollars and tax support. With renewed interest in community, regional, and ethnic history, historical societies would prosper. The publishing industry would continue to grow as citizens read more and more. The media industry, responding to public pressure to provide more in-depth coverage, would increasingly turn to scholars for insight, expertise, and program planning. Scholars would develop new listening and research skills in understanding citizen concerns. State governments would recognize the vitally important role played by state humanities councils through new appropriations. Federal support for institutions comprising the parallel school would also grow as the Congress recognized the indispensable role played by the humanities in enriching our nation's cultural conversation through public service scholarship.

6. Growth of public humanities centers

One of the most remarkable developments in the humanities in the past decade has been the founding of public humanities centers and institutes. Leadership for these institutions has come from inside as well as outside the academy. The lectures, conferences, symposia, television documentaries, and publications already produced by these centers have reached large national audiences, as seen, for instance, in the work of the Institute for the Humanities at Salado, Texas, on the universal problem of evil. As new connections are made between the humanities, public service scholarship, and American cultural conversation, new centers would be established throughout the nation and increasing attention would be paid by existing centers to public issues.

7. Telecommunications

New communication technologies hold enormous potential as outlets for public service scholarship and as important resources for cultural conversation. In small high schools across the nation, in tiny villages and rural areas, students now can have access, through satellite television, to courses that would otherwise only be available only in large, affluent urban districts—courses in Russian literature, in technology and human values, in American women's history. A world-renown university professor of medical ethics can provide guest lectures to college classes thousands of miles away from his campus. Public libraries, through satellite television, can offer new programs that focus on the essential questions of our time for adult audiences. Conversations between instructor and students, already possible, will be common in the decade ahead. The growth of public service scholarship would lead to increasing use of these technologies on behalf of the humanities.

8. A new reward system

The weight given to traditional standards for university promotion —scholarship, teaching, public service—would change. Colleges and universities, including our major research institutions, would strive for more flexible systems that would recognize the differing contributions that scholars make to institutions, to the life of learning, and to the wider society. Increased recognition would be given for university curriculum development, for collaboration with public schools on curricular concerns, for undergraduate teaching, and, most certainly, for public service scholarship. One of the biggest inhibitors of public service scholarship is the way in which the promotion and tenure system frequently operates in American higher education. Scholars from major research universities with national stature should take the lead in promoting revision of the reward system.

Looking to the Twenty-First Century

In our comments, we have assumed that there is in this country an enduring connection between the health and vitality of democracy and the health and vitality of the humanities, a connection we would like to see strengthened by public service scholarship and a broader, deeper cultural conversation.

As we look to the twenty-first century, the great test of our democracy lies in enriching public conversation and extending participation in this conversation to all Americans. There are good reasons for optimism. The writers cited earlier, MacIntryre, Peterson, and Bellah, represent a growing number of scholars committed to public service scholarship.

We think of Américo Paredes's contribution to public understanding of the history and culture of Mexican Americans.

We think of John Hope Franklin's life-long quest to deepen public understanding of the history and culture of black Americans.

We think of Walter Capps' contribution to public understanding of the Vietnam War and of the young Americans who fought in that war.

We think of Carol Gilligan's remarkable effort to expand our understanding of ethics and morality.

We think of Riane Eisler's promising re-evaluation of the evolution of Western culture and the partnership model she proposes for meeting challenges of the twenty-first century.

We think too of the many scholars and film and television producers who have collaborated on such large-scale media projects as *The World of Ideas*, *Eyes on the Prize*, and *Ethics in America*.

And we think of the many scholars who participate in the conferences, symposia, exhibits, and local media programs sponsored annually in hundreds of communities throughout the nation by state humanities councils.

This optimism, however, should not keep us from seeing the primary challenge we face—that of strengthening and expanding connections between scholarship and the public.

As we wrestle with our public responsibilities as scholars, as we contemplate new and exciting ways whereby scholarship in the humanities can connect with enduring questions and timely issues, we will be reminded that public conversation on vital concerns, like any honest, personal conversation, can be difficult. We believe such difficulties are signs of vitality, not decline. If scholars in the twenty-first century can make the kinds of connections suggested here, scholars in the twenty-second century will never have to endure discussions about a crisis in the humanities. In a Learning Society, they'll simply be too busy.

Works Cited

A Nation at Risk: The Imperative for Education Reform. Washington, D.C. National Commission on Excellence in Education. U.S. Department of Education, 1983.

Bellah, Robert N., *et al. Habits of the Heart: Individualism and Commitment in American Life.* Berkeley: University of California Press, 1985.

Bellah, Robert N. *The Humanities and the Survival of Community.* San Francisco: California Council for the Humanities, 1989.

Berry, Wendell. *The Work of Local Culture: The 1988 Iowa Humanities Lecture.* Iowa City: Iowa Humanities Board, 1988.

Booth, Wayne, "The Scholar in Society," in *Introduction to Scholarship in Modern Languages and Literatures,* Joseph Gibaldi, ed. New York: Modern Language Association of America, 1981.

Capps, Walter. *The Unfinished War: Vietnam and the American Conscience.* Boston: Beacon Press, 1982.

Cheney, Lynne V. *Humanities in America: A Report to the President, the Congress, and the American People.* Washington D.C: National Endowment for the Humanities, 1988.

Dreyfus, Herbert. *What Computers Can't Do: A Critique of Artificial Reason.* New York: Harper & Row, 1979.

Eisler, Riane. *The Chalice & The Blade: Our History; Our Future.* San Francisco: Harper & Row, 1987.

Ellul, Jacques. *The Technological Society.* New York: Random House, Inc., 1967.

Franklin, John Hope. *From Slavery To Freedom: A History of Negro Americans.* New York: Knopf, 1980.

Gilligan, Carol. *In a Different Voice: Psychological Theory and Women's Development*. Cambridge: Harvard University Press, 1982.

Hutchins, Robert. *The Learning Society*. Chicago: University of Chicago Press, 1968

Lappe, Frances Moore. *Rediscovering America's Values*. New York. Ballantine Books, 1989.

Levine, George, *et al. Speaking for the Humanities*. New York: American Council of Learned Societies, 1989.

MacIntyre, Alasdair. *How to Be a North American*. Washington, D.C.: Federation of State Humanities Councils, 1988.

Paredes, Américo. *With a Pistol in His Hand: A Border Ballad and its Hero*. Austin: The University of Texas Press, 1958.

Peterson, Merrill D. *The Humanities and the American Promise*. Austin: Texas Council for the Humanities, 1987.

Postman, Neil. *Amusing Ourselves to Death: Public Discourse in the Age of Show Business*. Viking Press, 1986.

Jacoby, Russell. *The Last Intellectuals*. New York: Basic Books, 1987.

Woodruff, Paul and Harry Wilmer, eds. *Facing Evil: Light at the Core of Darkness*. LaSalle: Open Court Publishing Company, 1988.

ʼBuilding Community
in America

The following paper was given September 25, 1990, at a conference sponsored by the Mississippi Humanities Council: Mississippi 2000: A Governor's Conference on the Future of the State. Cora Norman, the executive director of the Council, asked that I focus my luncheon address on the theme of "building community," one of the key interests of the Texas Council for the Humanities.

The launching point for this talk was the Texas in the 21st Century project of the TCH, but the challenge of forging community in a state and nation of unprecedented pluralism had been a long-standing interest of the TCH. For example, in 1987 the TCH pursued the subject of community as its annual theme. The relationship between individualism and community in the American experience has been pursued relentlessly by philosophers, historians, and cultural critics, but a sense of urgency seemed to underlie the need to understand how these opposing forces can be creatively balanced and how we can counter, as Robert Bellah points out, a "culture of separation" with a "culture of coherence." In carrying out its 1987 special emphasis, the TCH recognized that there have been many factors at work that have tended to mitigate the potential disaster of excessive individualism. The history of Texas, like the history of the United states, is in a very important sense a story of community building. Thus through grant projects and through the

Council's own work, we sought to highlight the ideal of a wider community to which all citizens can belong by looking carefully at past and present expressions of community. Thus this address reflected the Council's past endeavors on this theme while highlighting the kind of public work that now needs to be done for community to blossom.

I have been asked to provide a broad perspective to your efforts to plan for the challenges of the twenty-first century by exploring the theme of building community.

I would like to focus my comments on the most important insight that emerged in our own project dealing with Texas in the twenty-first century. This was a three-year project that involved many components, including study groups, a statewide conference, and a series of five books. The overriding theme that emerged was that we as Texans could not meet present and future challenges without fostering a much stronger sense of community. No matter what area we were exploring—education, the economy, the environment, state government, mental health, and so forth—we reached one primary conclusion: critical issues in Texas could not be addressed responsibly and creatively without fostering a much stronger sense of community among all the citizens of the state.

We are not alone in arriving at this conclusion. Across the country, there seems to be growing recognition that community in America is threatened, as evidenced by an increasing number of conferences, symposia, articles, and books dealing with this subject.

I will talk primarily about community in its national context, although I hope that what I have to say will be relevant to what we can do in our individual towns and cities, as well as at the state level, to counter some dangerous trends that put in jeopardy all the good work that is going on in planning for the future.

Perhaps we can grasp the underlying problem best by looking elsewhere for a few moments, beyond our borders. The recent history of the Soviet Union provides us with a valuable lesson in regard to the close connection that exists between national identity and a strong sense of community. Today, the Union of Soviet Socialist Republics is in a state of dissolution. On the one hand, it has experienced the near total collapse of an ideology, a collapse that is having a dramatic affect on all areas of public life. On the other hand, simultaneously, it is experiencing the collapse of an empire as the various republics demand autonomy and as the numerous ethnic groups—with their remarkably differing histories, cultures, and values—assert themselves. One lesson that we can learn from this stunning process of dissolution is that a sense of community that works to pull the various peoples of a nation together cannot be instilled from the top down. Any such attempt ultimately is bound to fail.

This predicament of the Soviet Union has led one of our country's most astute observers of that country, Librarian of Congress James Billington, to suggest that a new Russian identity will need to be forged, an identity, he argues, that, if its evolution towards democracy is to be fulfilled, will only come when the authentic, pre-Stalinist Russian culture is allowed to blossom—the shared experiences of a people that successive Communist regimes sought to suffocate. Billington documents the progress being made: the rediscovery of morality in the works not only of Dostoevsky and Tolstoy but Pasternak and Solzhenitsyn as well; the development of scores of new voluntary organizations that are springing up across the continent; the recovery of lost regional history; the launching of an estimated four hundred to seven hundred new publications; the development of new encyclopedias of Russian history and culture; and an extraordinary religious reawakening among the people. For Billington, the developments seem to indicate that the people of the Soviet Union are now facing ahead on the "awesome challenge of trying to build democracy in a multicultural, continental context."

We too have faced, and continue to face, a similar challenge. For well over two hundred years, we as a nation have been about the task of building community among extraordinarily diverse peoples from all corners of the world. Our vision has been grand indeed, engraved for posterity on the Great Seal of the United States, *Novus Ordo Seclorum*—New Order of the Ages—and *E Pluribus Unum*—One Out of Many. And this sense of community which gave rise to our national identity and purpose has been grounded in the moral principles of freedom, equality, and self-government. True community, in a democratic culture, comes from the bottom up, from the beliefs and values of the citizens.

If the Soviet Union now looks to the United States for guidance on these matters, surely it in part must be because the challenges that we have faced in fostering this sense of community have been extraordinary ones. If we feel that our sense of community in America today is threatened, it might be good to remember just how difficult the road to full participation in the American community has been. We cannot forget that millions of Native Americans lost their history and culture and frequently their lives because of the conquering community's appetite for new land and new opportunity. We cannot forget that millions of other Americans, those of dark skin, were totally excluded from this community. We cannot forget that half of the remaining population could not participate in the government created by this community, could not exercise the right to vote, because they were born female. We cannot forget that millions more—those of Oriental and Hispanic ancestry, for example—held tenuous positions in this community and were often discriminated against.

But however difficult, the ideals upon which the nation was established, and the moral vision coming out of our own developing traditions—literary, legal, philosophical, religious, and so forth—were such to make possible an ever-widening circle of community, even though the challenge to extend to more and more Americans full participation in our national community remains very much with us.

But those who are writing about the problem of community in contemporary American society today are focusing on other sorts of problems that might not be as monumental or as dangerous as those that could only be solved on the battlefields, in the streets, and in the courts. But they are real problems just the same—powerful, demanding, complex. Where exactly, as we move toward the dawn of the twenty-first century, is community in America threatened?

The first threat involves an explosion of self-interest. In their 1985 book *Habits of the Heart*, sociologist Robert Bellah and his colleagues write extensively about the evolution of what they call "utilitarian individualism" in American society. Many observers of American democracy, including de Tocqueville, have noted that our experiment in democracy is fragile, that it is held together by certain structures—the family, churches, schools, local politics, and so forth—and that should these institutions lose their power, the connections that exist between individuals and the wider community would be lost. That is, American democracy is based in part on an unwavering recognition of individual rights, on the principle of liberty. Bellah claims that in the development of American history, individualism may have grown "cancerous," destroying our sense of how we are connected to, and responsible for, the wider society. Bellah recognizes how important this sense of individualism is, but he argues that if left unchecked, the individual is perceived as the only firm reality, with the consequence that more and more Americans live for themselves, neglectful of the wider needs of the community.

In the five years that have passed since the publication of *Habits of the Heart*, we have seen much that confirms what Bellah talked about. We already know how the decade of the 1980s most likely will be perceived by subsequent generations as an era of considerable economic prosperity that was accompanied by extensive greed, an era when materialism got the upper hand. The extraordinary scandals— surely symbolized in the Savings & Loan debacle—and the frequent flaunting of wealth and the peddling of influence for personal gain show how far down the road of utilitarian individualism we may have journeyed. One is reminded of what Bellah wrote in 1985: When the only thing that holds Americans together in the post-industrial, post-modern age is concern for the economy, "we have reached a kind of end of the line."

A second threat lies in our growing cynicism. Writers Donald Kanter and Philip Mirvis draw on a comprehensive national survey of American employees in their new book, *The Cynical Americans: Living and Working in an Age of Discontent and Disillusion*. According to the authors, "Some forty-three percent of the American populace fit the profile of the cynic, who sees selfishness and fakery at the core of human nature." They state: "The survey shows that cynics mistrust politicians and most authority figures, regard the average person as false-faced and uncaring, and conclude that you should basically look out for yourself. Cynical tendencies are growing into a consensus world view with implications for society, commerce, and the workplace." This latest survey only confirms data collected in recent years by others. National surveys indicate that in the last several decades we have witnessed growing mistrust on the part of the public toward those in positions of leadership. Confidence in the Supreme Court, in the Congress, in the Executive Branch, in state and local governments, in religion, in the press, have dropped dramatically. Confidence in business leadership has fallen from approximately a seventy percent level in the late 1960s to about fifteen percent today, according to Harris polls noted by Kanter and Mirvis.

Cynicism breeds alienation, a sense that one doesn't matter in the scheme of things, that one's actions don't count, that one is left to fend for oneself. The percentage of such people holding these feelings, according to Harris polls, has doubled from 1966 to today—from twenty-nine to sixty percent. Perhaps this is one explanation as to why the United States has the lowest rate of voter participation of all industrialized nations, with less than one-half of eligible voters bothering to cast their ballots in the last election. And perhaps it is related to the fact that the percentage of young adults who read newspapers has dropped from sixty-seven to twenty-four percent in the last twenty-five years.

A third threat lies in our growing inability to address collectively serious social problems. The statistics are overwhelming—I'll cite just a few:

• Regarding poverty: There are an estimated thirty-three million Americans who live in poverty. Approximately three million Americans are homeless.

• Regarding violence: The United States leads all industrialized nations in homicides. Sexual assault and the sexual abuse of children are reaching near epidemic proportions.

• Regarding public education: Nearly thirty percent of our students nationally do not finish high school. There are now over four million young Americans, age eighteen to thirty, who are dropouts.

Citing these and other statistics about our diminishing democratic health have become commonplace, but our familiarity with them must not keep us from dealing with their import. If we could think of the American community as an extended family, we would have to conclude that far too many of our relatives are suffering terribly. Far too many lack adequate health care; far too many have dropped out of school; far too many are illiterate; far too many have sought solace in alcohol and drugs; far too many possess uncontrollable rage and hate; far too many are in prison; far too many are sleeping on the streets; far too many have seemingly lost their way in life, unsure of themselves, not knowing what to do, not knowing where to go for help.

A family cannot be complete, a people cannot be whole, without concern for every member of the group. We cannot have a strong and vibrant sense of community in America unless we find new and far more effective ways of helping those who are struggling, those who have a difficult time helping themselves, those who need assurance that they belong, that they matter, that they too can contribute to the common good. Nor can we of a capitalist, democratic society be whole unless we sustain traditions of philanthropy and generosity, using wealth to benefit those in need.

Some Primary Tasks

To meet these contemporary challenges to our sense of community, we need to shore up the intellectual foundations of American culture. I'm sure that there is much that could be done in other spheres—economics and politics, for instance—but all too often we tend to neglect our inner life, the life of the mind and human spirit. So I offer my perspective on three important tasks designed to improve our sense of how we are connected to each other.

The first is the historical task. Nothing is more important to the development of community than shared knowledge of our past. The foundation of modern history can be found in the myths of primitive societies—sacred histories, grounded in metaphysics, which served to answer fundamental questions about where a people came from, about the meaning of life, about duties and responsibilities, good and evil, and right and wrong. It was not until the modern era that history as we know it today—secular history—was divested from an allegiance to mythic sacred history. Yet modern history functions in ways similar to the mythic sacred histories of earlier societies. The narratives that we tell about ourselves, about where we came from, about our past, about how we have come to be what we are, function as mythic texts for a community. From these narratives the identify of a people is formed. A community's character is defined, and a sense of belonging is fostered. Further, these narratives, and the values and world views that they promote, have a direct bearing on public policy, on how governments go about their business, on values held, on options perceived, on decisions made. So the kinds of narratives that we write and teach and work to sustain have as much impact on the future of the whole community as they do on the place of the individual within that community.

Given that, and given the challenges to community in America, it is easy to understand why the field of history is in so much turmoil these days. As we come to recognize the true multicultural makeup of the American community, as we contemplate the dramatic shift in demographics, we come to realize that any historical narrative that neglects, excludes, deprecates, or otherwise disestablishes members of the community, has a powerful negative impact. When this happens, the result is a community that is divisive at its core, and one consequence of this is that the public policies of such a community will also be divisive, failing to work toward the common good.

So the historical task at this time really involves two endeavors. The first is that of promoting better understanding among Americans of our multiple histories and cultural heritages. This is the road to shared experiences and values. This endeavor opens to us new worlds. This is an important means of authenticating the cultural backgrounds of all Americans. This is an exciting endeavor, one that needs to be undertaken not only in educational institutions but in our communities as well. Museums, public libraries, book clubs, and other organizations must continue to sponsor programs for the public that document and interpret the rich cultural mosaic that represents the American community.

The second endeavor is that of working these multiple stories, this new history, into the dramatic narratives that express our collective self-understanding. Our history books must strive for a new kind of synthesis, and this is true not only in regard to our national history but our state and city histories as well. Historians are called upon to find new threads that can be used to weave the various fabrics into new cloth.

The second task I shall call the moral task. This task focuses less on the past and more on the present. This is the task of taking stock, of exploring and evaluating how we as a community conduct the business of life. This is an exploration into public morality. We need a much better grasp of that which works to promote community as well as that which tends to undermine community. We need a better grasp of the hidden as well as the open values that the goals, public policies, and actions of our society seem to embrace.

It might be useful to think of the American community as an entity that shares certain characteristics with that of the individual, as a larger self composed of many individual selves. If so it should be possible, in carrying out this moral task, to explore the ethical implications of our

- economic self—how we produce, manage, and develop material wealth;
- religious self—how we sustain and practice spirituality;
- civic self—how we sustain and practice the art of self governance;
- learning self—how we ensure opportunities for the expansion of knowledge and skills and the gaining of wisdom;
- interactive self—how we work to sustain productive relationships with others;
- playful self—how we help ensure renewal of the spirit; and
- protective self—how we protect ourselves from those who would harm us, without destroying our integrity in the process.

I offer the language of the self because we often find it difficult to get to the core of our public life, to evaluate in serious ways how we as a nation, or state, or city, conduct ourselves. In doing so, it might be possible to step back from our immediate situations, from the very complexities of modern life, from the damaging effects of worn rhetoric and the frequent emptiness of the broadcast media, to ask very simple, very direct questions about our moral health.

The third task is the imaginative task. This task is more concerned with the future than the present or past, although it surely draws strength from creative voices of the past.

It is the imagination that allows us to resist the tendency to think that the way things are is the way things always have been and always will be. The imagination is the human capacity to see new possibilities. As such, it is the basis for hope.

It is possible for societies, like individuals, to go through periods where the imagination is in short supply. Samuel Coleridge, one of the great theorists of the imagination, when going through such a period in his own life, remarked that his imagination was "tired, down, flat and powerless," a condition with which many of us can surely identify. But we also know the exhilaration that comes when our own imaginative faculties are alive and well, creating images that motivate us, that instill in us a sense of purpose, something to work toward, images that we throw up on an imaginary screen, images that make us cry and laugh and love. History shows that societies too move back and forth between periods of flatness and dullness and periods of great creativity where a constantly dazzling array of images are offered to the public.

In America, there appears to be no shortage of the technological imagination, as evidenced by the astounding deployment of new technologies in recent decades. Nor is there a shortage of entrepreneurial imagination, the ability to envision entirely new industries, services, and markets. But I'm not sure that the same can be said for what noted legal theorist and native Texan Charles Black calls the humane imagination and, for that matter, what we might call the civic imagination.

The *humane imagination* is the capacity to imagine and continually re-imagine the inner personalities of others—their feelings, thoughts, desires, needs, and to imagine with growing truthfulness. This capacity is the foundation for human relations, for understanding other people.

Few of us are totally wanting in the humane imagination, and we exercise it with some regularity in regard to our families, friends, colleagues and associates. But when it comes to those who are different from us, those for instance who are of another race, those who are chronically poor, those who are unemployed, those who are people of lands and cultures very different from our own, our imagination is often found wanting.

The *civic imagination* allows us to grasp the social and political structures and forms that bring us together as a people. The history of community-building in America is surely the history of exceptional individuals who had enormous capacity to create images of new structures, new institutions, new alliances, that could serve the community, and out of that imagining came hospitals, libraries, women's clubs, civic organizations, labor groups, religious congregations, utopian experiments and, most recently, self-help movements and groups.

But like the humane imagination, the civic imagination is often in short supply, and we must do all we can to encourage this capacity in ourselves and in our fellow citizens. The "acids of modernity" tend to work against the cultivation of civic imagination. The values of our consumer culture, the emphasis placed on materialism, the impact of mass media, and many other conditions of contemporary life tend to discourage the exercise of civic imagination.

The behaviorists would tell us that our problem is one of incentives and rewards. There is no shortage of incentives or rewards for the exercise of technological and entrepreneurial imagination. But how do we provide incentives for the exercise of humane and civic imagination, and how do we reward those who make significant contributions on our behalf?

But incentives and rewards reflect our communal values, and thus I am inclined to believe that the problem is more one of education. Perhaps there is a corollary between the defects that we have in the exercise of humane and civic imagination and the status of the humanities in our public schools and colleges and universities. The seeds for this cultivation of the imagination in the child come from the parents, but, as the child gets older, school plays an increasingly important role. And it is through the humanities—humane letters, the arts of poetry, fiction and drama, as well as history and related fields—where the humane and civic imagination can be exercised. When the humanities suffer, when they are squeezed out of the curriculum, when they are thought of as less useful or practical than other subjects, we can be sure that we are inhibiting the development of humane and civic imagination in our children.

The development of this capacity is critical to the need that we have as individuals and as a society to recognize our inherent freedom. We want to be able to make decisions based on a wide range of options. It is the imagination that allows us to create images of how we want to be, how we want to get along with other people, how we want to organize our civic life, and if those images grow cold or shrink or disappear altogether, then our freedom has been greatly diminished.

The humane and civic imaginations light the fires that bring warmth to community.

Leadership

Taking on these three tasks—the historical task, the public morality task, the imaginative task— would help us deal constructively with the major challenges to community noted earlier. Robert Bellah tells us that "cultures are dramatic conversations about things that matter to their participants." Our history matters, how we conduct our public business matters, how we develop and exercise humane and civic imagination matters. And it will matter to more and more Americans if we can broaden and deepen the conversation.

The starting point is public education, and we must be willing to do whatever is necessary to ensure schools that prepare as many young citizens as possible for full and productive lives in the American community of the twenty-first century. But we must not stop there. We have a responsibility at national, state, and local levels to create opportunities whereby our fellow citizens can come to know each other, opportunities that will allow discussion on issues that matter to us, opportunities whereby our community is made whole.

But we need leadership at all levels if we are to become a true learning society. Across the country, we need city councils, mayors, governors, state legislators, and corporate leaders to say that these tasks are important, that the spiritual health of the American community, and of our local communities, is of fundamental importance to the future of the nation.

Perhaps the furtherance of a strong sense of community in America will come through initiatives undertaken at the local level in our various towns and cities. Public education remains essentially a local responsibility. The improvement of undergraduate education remains primarily the responsibility of local institutions. The furtherance of public conversation on things that matter can best be accomplished by marshalling the cultural resources of particular communities. In so doing, models of civic friendship, civic responsibility, and civic dialogue are created for other towns and cities, for entire states, and even for the nation.

I believe the prospect for developing a stronger, more healthy sense of community in America, as we move toward the twenty-first century, is good. The best kind of community protects and nourishes the best kind of individualism. And when we exercise humane imagination, when we exercise civic imagination, we are in reality protecting individual rights and furthering individual responsibility.

The successful resolution of tough public policy issues will undoubtedly stem from attitudes and values that put people at the center, whether the context is education, the environment, government services, or global interaction. All these issues will seem overwhelming unless there is a common denominator: shared communal interests, or quality of life for all members of the community. We would do well to remember a sentiment expressed by John Dewey: "What the best and wisest parent wants for its child, that must the community want for all its children."

Works Cited

Bellah, Robert N., et al, *Habits of the Heart: Individualism and Commitment in American Life*. New York: Harper & Row, 1985.

Billington, James H. "Russia: Historic Continuity or Radical Change," in *Texas Journal of Ideas, History and Culture*, Vol. 13, No. 1. Fall/Winter, 1990.

Black, Charles L., Jr. *The Humane Imagination in the Great Society*. Austin: Texas Council for the Humanities, 1984.

Kantner, Donald L. and Philip H. Mirvis. *The Cynical Americans: Living and Working in an Age of Discontent and Disillusion*. San Francisco: Jossey-Bass Publishers, 1989.

1997

The Humanities and the Civic Imagination

The following essay was originally written for the 1994 William Bennett Bean Symposium on the Humanities, sponsored by the Institute for the Medical Humanities at the University of Texas Medical Branch at Galveston. It was published in revised form in the collection of essays that Noëlle McAfee and I edited, Standing with the Public: The Humanities and Democratic Practice, *Kettering Foundation Press, 1997.*

In this essay I explore public service scholarship by looking carefully at the contribution that the TCH made over twenty years in an extraordinary intellectual and social project, that of documenting, interpreting, disseminating, and discussing the history and culture of Mexican Americans in Texas, thereby contributing to a broader and more comprehensive understanding of community. The essay offers thoughts on how the public role of the scholar might be reconstructed so that the humanities can contribute in even more successful ways to democratic culture. It underscores the important fact that the humanities have their origin in the community as well as in the academy.

✦ ✦ ✦

It is often claimed that the humanities in America are in trouble. Critics point to the fragmentation of academic disciplines, the over-specialization of scholars, the priority placed on research over teaching at many universities, an abundance of esoteric scholarship, and an apparent slippage in societal support. While these criticisms need to be taken seriously, this paper seeks to demonstrate that there are some creative dimensions in the humanities today that hold great promise for the disciplines of the humanities and, more importantly, for American society. These dimensions include the public humanities—scholarship and programs that respond to public needs and interests. This essay focuses on the relationship between the humanities and critical challenges facing the American people.

This public dimension to the humanities has emerged at a critical time in the life of the nation. Challenges and problems continue to grow in severity—the erosion of public confidence in basic institutions of American society, frequent political deadlock in federal and state legislative bodies, rampaging crime, inadequate public schools, ethnic and cultural fragmentation, abused and neglected children, and urban deterioration. Indeed, these challenges and problems, now brought into sharper focus as preoccupation with Cold War realities gives way to clearer perceptions of where we as a nation have been and where we are, have resulted in a dramatic flight into private spheres. For the privileged and the well-off, the private sphere is often dominated by professional goals and materialistic pursuits. For the poor and the oppressed, the private sphere all too often is dominated by life on the edge, a life enveloped in poverty, fear, loneliness, and despair.

Deeper and more humane visions of our society, of how we are connected one to another, are needed to counter the loss of public space and the expansion of private space. The privileged seem to have lost a notion of a civic republic; the poor and dispossessed seem out of touch with the ideals behind the dramatic social movements of the past. For both, disconnection and rootlessness take hold.

In his book *The Radical Renewal: The Politics of Ideas in Modern America*, Norman Birnbaum points out the critical need in American society for the rehabilitation of public life and the reconstitution of citizenship. Birnbaum joins an increasing number of concerned writers who recognize that old ways of thinking will not solve new kinds of problems. How can the struggle for survival give way to a nation made whole, a democracy of citizens committed to each other and to commonly shared goals and values? Without a sense of common ground, of an enlarged vision that transcends cultural, social, and political divisions, it is likely that the problems we now face will only grow in severity.

It is the thesis of this essay that the humanities have the capacity to help foster a communal vision that can revitalize American public life, and that the humanities in their contemporary public dimension offer some remarkable avenues for the exercise of this capacity.

The Humanities and Civic Imagination

For this vision to emerge, the nation needs a rebirth of civic imagination, the capacity to grasp the social and political structures and forms that can be used to invigorate our public life, bringing citizens together to deal with societal challenges and problems. The civic imagination arms us with ideals and values that counter the weight and sharpness of that which would pull us apart. It is the civic imagination that allows us to create images of how we want to be, how we want to get along with others, how we want to organize our civic life, what we want to value collectively, how we want to use our resources. The civic imagination promotes connections among citizens and with those organizations and institutions so essential to democratic culture.

Nothing could be more important to American society and to the humanities than for more scholars to acknowledge that the cultivation of the civic imagination has become an important public priority. America needs a "community of thought" to help nourish the civic imagination and to serve as midwife to the ideals and values that can strengthen society. Birnbaum maintains that a community of thought is not necessarily identical with a community of scholars. "The universities," he writes, "can hardly be regarded as the sole or privileged repositories of thought. In the most creative periods of American intellectual life, they were sometimes silent, sometimes connected to creative currents outside themselves." The community of thought most certainly includes scholars, but it also includes public intellectuals and educated and imaginative citizens in general. A community of thought is a precondition to finding common ground, discovering shared values, and forging public policy that represents the will and thought of the people. "What images of human possibility," asked philosopher Charles Frankel, "will American society put before its members?"

Despite challenges and problems in the humanities, there are plenty of reasons to hope that this task of cultivating the civic imagination will be taken seriously by more scholars.

There are small comforts from history: the inspiring societal visions offered by Renaissance and Enlightenment humanists, for example, or, closer to our time, the intellectual shapers of various nineteenth and twentieth century social movements, such as the abolitionist, suffragist, and civil rights movements, which remind us of the possible connections between humanistic ideas and social change.

And there are comforts from our own times. The core disciplines of the humanities continue to be taught and studied in many schools, colleges, and universities. While the humanities may have been marginalized in recent years in some institutions, they remain vibrant and appreciated disciplines in many others. This is an important point, because the teaching of the humanities in elementary, secondary, and postsecondary settings is central to the development of a community of thought and to the civic imagination. All other efforts are dependent upon this foundation.

Some contemporary models of the humanities engaged provide additional hope, such as the compelling visions of culture offered recently by feminist scholars, the documentation of local history, the application of the humanities to particular public issues, such as issues related to the environment, and the clarification and interpretation of issues of life and death offered by a small but growing number of scholars working in medical environments—models that are often relevant to challenges before us.

Important models of the humanities engaged in a more comprehensive and public fashion are offered by the state humanities councils, funded by the Congress through the National Endowment for the Humanities. Working under a Congressional mandate, state councils have encouraged and sponsored projects that bring together scholars and the public. Each year, more than three thousand projects are sponsored by councils operating in all fifty states, the territories, and the district of Columbia. Aside from these discreet projects, many councils have launched initiatives to heighten public awareness of the importance of the humanities to democratic culture. Undoubtedly, the state humanities program represents this nation's greatest experiment in a sustained effort to enrich American society and culture through the public humanities.

At the beginning of the state humanities program in the early 1970s, all councils had as their federally-mandated focus the sponsorship of public programs in which the humanities would clarify and interpret pressing public issues and concerns. This emphasis declined through the 1980s, giving way in many states to programs of more general cultural interest. This latter trend, first encouraged by the Congress itself when reauthorizing the NEH in 1976, was endorsed enthusiastically by NEH Chairs Bill Bennett and Lynne Cheney, who expressed skepticism about the usefulness of the humanities in addressing political, social, and economic issues. The humanities have much to contribute to the betterment of society, they argued, but primarily through the education of individual minds through the study of—and here they were fond of citing Matthew Arnold—the best that has been thought and said.

Those who believe that the humanities have much to contribute to the cultivation of the civic imagination and to the transformation of American society are pleased that the early state council effort to engage the humanities with important public issues is now being revitalized by NEH chair Sheldon Hackney. Hackney has made the expansion of public audiences for the humanities a top priority, and he has called upon state councils and other organizations and institutions to deepen and expand through the humanities national conversation on critical issues facing the American people, especially issues related to ethnic and cultural pluralism and American identity. For Hackney, the humanities provide important resources for public dialogue, and it is time, once again, to put these resources to work in the public arena.

In the twenty-five-year record of the state humanities councils, we find some important models of engagement enhancing the civic imagination that can guide future efforts.

State Councils and Public Service Scholarship

In thinking about the work of state humanities councils, it is useful to note that the legal structure of the councils provides the framework for such engagement. State councils are required by federal law to ensure that there is equal representation of academic and public sectors on their governing boards, so that all policy and funding decisions may be informed by public as well as scholarly interests.

In terms of practice, the state humanities program promotes what my colleague Jim Quay and I have called "public service scholarship." We have pointed out that the terms "scholarship" and "public humanities" all too often stand in opposition, with scholarship thought of as "private" or "academic" humanities, and the public humanities as the simple dissemination of humanistic learning to receptive but essentially passive out-of-school adults. It may be more useful to consider scholarship and the public humanities not as two distinct spheres but as parts of a single process. As such, the public realm can help initiate, direct, and shape humanistic scholarship.

However, the important role the state humanities councils have in the dissemination of the humanities should not be minimized. Indeed, in the last major planning document that the Texas Council for the

Humanities submitted to NEH, it drew from an inspiring passage in Henry David Thoreau's *Walden* to underscore its continuing commitment to provide communities throughout the state with programs that express this important but more limited understanding of the public humanities. In this passage, Thoreau indicted his town, Concord, for its gross neglect of the intellectual needs of its citizens. Thoreau complained about how little Concord did to enhance its own culture: "We have a comparatively decent system of common schools, schools for infants only; but excepting the half-starved Lyceum in the winter, and latterly the puny beginning of a library suggested by the State, no school for ourselves." He stated, "It is time that we . . . did not leave off our education when we begin to be men and women." Indeed, he argued, "It is time that villages were universities" and citizens "the fellows of those universities."

Thoreau offered readers his vision of a New World democracy composed of educated citizens. He contrasted the life of the European nobleman "of cultivated taste" who surrounds himself with art, science, and books with the intellectually Spartan existence of Concord. His plea was "to act collectively" to use the resources of the town to create an "uncommon school" that provides learning for all the citizens of the town. Instead of a having a society composed of a few well-learned nobleman surrounded by the dull-witted, ignorant masses, Thoreau envisioned—and pleaded for—a society where the common man became the enlightened citizen through access to life-long learning opportunities.

Thoreau wanted to unlock the treasure house of learning and wisdom. "Let the reports of all the learned societies come to us," he said, "and we will see if they know anything." After all, "shall the world be confined to one Paris or one Oxford forever?" He also asked: "Can we not hire some Abelard to lecture to us?" Here, indeed, is one model for the public humanities, scholars who speak to public audiences about their area of learning—their discipline, or perhaps their latest book or article.

Such activity is related to another endeavor, that of humanists writing for a broad public audience. While scholars are often criticized for writing only for a small group of peers, with publication in a professional journal the highest goal, there is a growing number of professional humanists, inside and outside the university, who consistently and with considerable success write for large public audiences. Examples that come to mind include Daniel Boorstein, Paul Kennedy, Jonathan Kozel, Patricia Limerick, and Robert Coles. A growing number of scholars have reached even larger audiences through television documentaries, such as those scholars who worked with Ken Burns in the production of the PBS series, *The Civil War*.

Thoreau and his public humanist descendants provide a valuable model of the public humanities, but it would be a mistake to let this model stand as the all-encompassing model promulgated by state humanities councils. As noted above, the term "public service scholarship" implies something more. If the Thoreau model were all we had—if this were the only model of the public humanities—we might see this work as an extension of teaching. By using the phrase "public service scholarship," an added dimension is implied, a dimension that stresses collaboration between the scholar and the public and that promotes a form of research and learning in which the public is contributing to and helping to shape the inquiry undertaken, as well as benefiting from it.

With deference to Thoreau and his model of the public humanities, I wish to argue that it is this more provocative understanding of the public humanities that needs to be understood and promoted, for it is this model which may hold the greatest capacity for the development of civic imagination.

Although the interested public might perhaps be fascinated by anything that Abelard's humanities descendants may have to say, it is far more likely that the public would prefer that these scholars tackle interests and issues that are of genuine concern to them, issues of fundamental importance to their very own city, town, and neighborhood, rather than any topic of these scholars' choosing. Further, they don't want these scholars just to ride in, display their humanistic pearls, and ride out. Rather, these scholars need to be good listeners, for the public wants to work with them in thinking through these concerns and issues. These citizens want to share their ideas with these scholars. And then they want these humanists to go about their scholarly endeavors, to analyze these issues and concerns, to conduct original research if that is appropriate, to collaborate with other scholars and resource persons whose fields and expertise might have something to offer, to find fresh and alternative ways of viewing these matters, and to test initial ideas not just with academic colleagues, but with them as well. And these citizens would like to work with these scholars in finding the best possible formats whereby others could learn of this work and help shape the next stage of this project which might involve endeavors to reach beyond their own immediate community.

If the state councils serve as a bridge between the academy and the community, as is often said, this larger concept of the public humani ties means that there is traffic—people and ideas—in both directions. It is easy enough to understand the movement of the scholar into the community. It is much more difficult to understand the movement of the public into the academy. The very thought of this public involvement tends to conjure up the worst fears of many academics, with images of new structures created by state legislatures or regents or trustees that provide expanded opportunities for meddling in internal university affairs quickly coming to mind. We should not let such fears divert us from finding and claiming appropriate ways whereby the public can interact with the scholarly community, ways whereby public issues can be placed on the agenda of higher education.

In commenting on the significance of the 1965 legislation establishing the National Endowment for the Humanities, Charles Frankel wrote that "Nothing has happened of greater importance in the history of American humanistic scholarship than the invitation of the government to scholars to think in a more public fashion and to think and teach with the presence of their fellow citizens in mind." Undoubtedly a true statement, but a fuller reading of the legislation leads to the conclusion that another kind of invitation was also extended, one that invited the public to reclaim the humanities as important resources for individuals and communities. What the federal government has done, in this sense, is to encourage the public to gain ownership of the humanities, to put the humanities to work on behalf of the public, to invite scholars to work side by side with them in addressing important public issues.

Public Humanities in Texas

How then has the public, through the work of state councils, responded to this invitation? And how have scholars responded to this expanded, more democratic, understanding of ownership? By looking at the work of one council, the Texas Council for the Humanities, we may be able to find some tentative answers.

One of the first things that needs to be said is that regional and local influences have undoubtedly weighed heavily in how these invitations have been received in different parts of the country. I suspect that the cultural, intellectual, and political diversity of the country have influenced deeply the nature and shape of public humanities endeavors undertaken by the councils. Thoreau's New England, Jefferson's Virginia, and Sam Houston's Texas all provide strikingly diverse heritages for the public humanities.

Texas doesn't seem to provide an abundance of fertile soil for the cultivation of the civic imagination through public service scholarship.

A state with a complex political, cultural, and economic history, it lacks a significant intellectual tradition. Texas is a society that has traditionally claimed the frontier ethic of its Anglo Texan origins. Deep in the Texas psyche—at least its majority part—is a preference for action over contemplation, autonomy over community, and opportunism over longer-range thinking.

As a result, the state humanities council in Texas has tilled some difficult soil, sowing public humanities seeds in an environment not always conducive to public deliberation. We wish this very special invitation from the federal government were taken more seriously, not only in neighborhoods and communities across the state but in the board rooms of corporations and in the halls of the Texas Legislature as well. Yet there is a record here worth looking at; indeed, a record that inspires. I limit my exploration to one of the long-standing concerns of the TCH, that having to do with the relationship between majority and minority cultures in Texas.

From the inception of the state humanities program in Texas in 1973, Texas's extraordinary ethnicity has been a matter of great interest and concern. Black and Hispanic members of the board of directors—public as well as academic—took the lead early on in making the case that the humanities had much to offer in broadening Texans' understanding of the state's diverse cultures, and that the state council could play a significant role in stimulating new scholarship and making that scholarship available to the public as an important step toward equal participation by all groups in the civic, cultural, and economic life of the state and nation.

Mexican American studies in Texas as a field by and large preceded African American studies and, to this day, the body of scholarship dealing with Texas Mexican American history and culture exceeds that of Texas African American history and culture. While it would be possible to document the state council's role in expanding public understanding of African American history and culture and women's history and culture, for the purposes of this essay, I wish to look at TCH's work focusing on Mexican American history and culture.

Historian David Montejano points out that in the history of Texas "Mexican-Anglo relations have traversed a difficult path, from the hatred and suspicion engendered by war to a form of reconciliation" present by the mid-1980s. According to Montejano, "the Texas Mexican community still lags far behind on all mainstream indicators in the areas of education, health, income, and political influence," yet there are a number of signs that indicate that an intense clash of cultures has abated, and that "a measure of integration for the Mexican American" has been achieved. In the Mexican American community, Montejano points to knowledge of English as well as Spanish, intermarriage, the development of a middle class, and the emergence of Mexican Americans as political actors in the state. In the wider community, one can certainly point to broader recognition of Mexican American history and culture and the potential benefits of a pluralistic society. Progress has occurred, and, as Montejano points out, this would not have happened without the political mobilization of the Mexican American community in the 1960s and 1970s, a period in which the Texas population of Mexican descent grew from seventeen to more than twenty-five percent.

By the time TCH made its first grant awards, Chicano activism was in full swing. The political party Raza Unida presented a candidate for governor in 1972 who received nearly a quarter of a million votes. Mexican American studies, as an emerging interdisciplinary field in the humanities, received its impetus not so much from the academy, which in many places showed little interest, if not outright resistance, but from the community. That is, the Mexican American community demanded that the history and culture of Mexican Americans be studied, written, published, taught, and disseminated, for without a public history, full participation in society was impossible. There were stories to be told. For an emerging number of Chicanos who had pursued graduate studies in the humanities, new opportunities arose for working with the public to document Mexican American history and culture, thus providing the scholarly and intellectual foundation for a broadly-based social and cultural movement as well as a more comprehensive understanding of the American Southwest.

This engagement of scholars with the community on matters of concern to the Mexican American population can be found in the earliest projects supported by the TCH. The Council worked with the Intercultural Development Research Association of San Antonio in sponsoring a series of public conferences in six communities that explored moral values underlying the system then in place to finance public education, and moral values of alternative systems. The project coincided with the birth of a profound twenty-year legal struggle to ensure a more equitable funding system that would not discriminate against financially poor school districts that tend to have heavy minority populations. In South Texas, Colonias Del Valle, Inc., of San Juan, located near the border, was awarded funds for a series of meetings over several months in which scholars and the public met to discuss the history and status of the Colonias and to ascertain the historical and cultural reasons why these unincorporated communities lacked basic municipal services, including water. The major organizer of this project, a community activist who believed that the humanities had something to offer in understanding the political, cultural, and ethical dimensions of this problem, was later elected to the Texas House of Representatives. The Alice Public Library, located in South Texas, sought to respond to the needs of its community by sponsoring with the TCH a workshop on special consumer problems that occur in bilingual/bicultural communities. Anglo and Hispanic scholars in linguistics, ethnic studies, business history, and ethics, participated. Scholars from Trinity University, the University of Texas at Austin, the University of Texas at San Antonio, Pan American University (now the University of Texas–Pan American), and Collegia de Mexico (Mexico City) worked with attorneys, government officials, social workers, and civil rights activists to sponsor a major public conference on "Immigration and the Mexican National," a two-day event that drew an audience of 500. Mexican American scholars at Corpus Christi State University (now Texas A&M University–Corpus Christi) responded to the community's interest in Chicano literature by organizing a major conference that drew twenty-six thousand people for fifty-one separate activities that took place over eight days. An anthology of Chicano literature was published as a result of the project. Some fifteen years later, the scholar who served as project director told this writer that no source other than the TCH responded favorably to requests for publication support, and that to his knowledge the Texas Council for the Humanities was the only funding source available in Texas at that time for the dissemination of this and other new scholarship in Mexican American studies.

Case Study: University of Houston Symposium

One of the more important early efforts to promote dialogue and advance public service scholarship was a public symposium sponsored by the new Mexican American Studies Program at the University of Houston (TCH Grant M79-526, awarded in March 1979, in the amount of $12,790). The organizers of this 1979 project, and the group that set the agenda for the symposium and the published papers that followed, included five Mexican American scholars from the University as well as a Mexican American United States Attorney, the executive director of the Association for the Advancement of Mexican Americans, and the deputy director of the Mayor's Office of Community Development, among several others.

Organizers established five objectives for the project: (1) to promote interest in and a greater knowledge of Mexican heritage in Texas; (2) to provide an opportunity for a group of humanities scholars to present the results of their research to the public and to receive public response to that scholarship; (3) to encourage Chicano scholars, in a special way, by providing them with a public forum; (4) to stimulate a dialogue between Mexican Americans and Anglos regarding the present and future aspirations of the people of Mexican heritage in Texas; and (5) to foster greater understanding of problems faced by Mexican Americans and to suggest recommendations for more responsive public policy. The last objective caught the eye of the U.S. Commissioner of Immigration and Naturalization, Leonel J. Castillo, who encouraged the TCH to support the project.

The major symposium presentations, published later under the title *Reflections on the Mexican Experience in Texas*, included an analysis of Chicano demographic trends and their significance, 1950–1970; Chicano labor history in the last half of the nineteenth century; an analysis of the political origin of the term "Chicano" and its usage; the experience of Mexicanos along the Texas-Mexican border during the period of the Mexican Revolution; trends in Chicano literature; Chicano culture as seen through music and dance; an analysis of the educational status of the Mexican American; and Chicano political strategies. Other scholars responded to these presentations, and most of these responses are published in the proceedings as well.

In reviewing this body of work, one is struck by the participants' engagement with critical issues facing the Mexican American population of Texas. In the preface to the proceedings, the editors note that "Mexican heritage, a basic component of Texas culture, has not always been considered an asset in Texas . . . public discussion is necessary in order to examine negative attitudes, and their causes, toward Texans of Mexican descent." The editors then state:

> This symposium, co-sponsored by the Mexican American Studies Program at the University of Houston Central Campus and the Texas [Council] for the Humanities, initiated what is hoped will be a continuing discussion leading toward better understanding of Mexican heritage and Texas culture. The Symposium stimulated the beginning of a dialogue between the Mexican American community and the Anglo American community regarding the present and future aspirations of the people of Mexican heritage in Texas. We hope this written record

of the Symposium will foster greater understanding of problems faced by the Mexican American people of Texas, and will suggest recommendations for more responsive public policy.

These scholars perceived their work as serious engagement with issues of contemporary public life. Examples of such engagement can be found in the published papers. One scholar, after a thorough presentation of demographic facts, observed that every available statistic indicates that, although progress is being made, "the Chicanos have a long road to travel before they achieve full participation in the mainstream of America." A commentator responded by pointing out that "unless educators begin to plan now for the influx of Mexican American students and their cultural and academic needs, the educational situation of Mexican Americans in Texas is going to get much worse before it gets better."

After providing a brilliant analysis of Chicano labor history in South Texas in the last half of the nineteenth century, another scholar observed:

> For those who have dominated the writing of Texas history, Chicanos do not merit a place in the chronicle of the state. Anglo historians cannot fathom a changing, evolving, and effervescent Tejano population taking the initiative in an effort to alleviate adversity. Yet . . . the South Texas Tejano community between 1848–1900 held its own before ambitious Anglo businessmen, cattlemen, and farmers bent on reducing them to powerlessness. In truth, Mexicans took their understanding of the white economic system and used it to wrest a living despite antagonistic circumstances.

In responding to this paper and the conclusions drawn, a noted scholar stated that "the author . . . fills a void in Texas history that never should have existed." Another scholar noted:

> This is an exciting time . . . to watch historians, most of whom are young Chicanos, broaden our understanding of the past to include a people who had been shoved off of the stage of history by writers whose sole interest was in the Anglo-American players. [These] historians

. . . are moving the minority players back onto the
stage, one by one, and we will all be the richer for
being exposed to the full cast of characters who shaped
the political, economic and social history of the state,
the region, and the nation.

Through this research, one is inescapably pulled into a broad cultural project. The research points to the obvious: the prevalence of
racism in our society; the negative consequences of stereotyping; the
need to document cultures that have been ignored by majority scholars; the need to legitimatize stories that were lost; the need to document contributions of Mexican Americans in Texas history and culture;
the need to address social wrongs; the need to ensure equality of opportunity; the need to organize politically; and so forth. Unabashedly,
the original proposal that brought TCH funding and co-sponsorship
noted that public policy implications would flow from the research
undertaken, a concern that was seen in a positive light by the TCH
board of directors.[1]

But the symposium itself was not a total success. The program was
held on the campus of the University of Houston, which limited public
attendance, and too many of the presentations involved the reading of
papers, rather than presenting shorter summaries that work better in
public settings. But, reflecting on the project sixteen years later, I draw
the conclusion that it was a significant event in authenticating new
scholarship on the Mexican experience in Texas, in fostering dialogue
between Mexican American and non-Mexican American scholars, in
expanding public involvement in and understanding of the interrelationship of majority and minority cultures, and in stimulating more research and projects that would grapple with the pluralistic heritage of
Texas. Through this public service scholarship, an important contribution was made to our civic imagination.

Allied Efforts

There have been more projects—well over one hundred during the
past fifteen years. Here are a few examples of continuing engagement.
The Mexican American Chamber of Commerce and the San Antonio
City Council asked the San Antonio Museum Association for more programming on Hispanic culture. With TCH funding, the result was a
1981 thirty-minute multi-media presentation, *Mil Colores*, which, after a
brief historical outline, documents the influence of Hispanics on San
Antonio and discusses some key issues such as bilingual education and

the development of Mexican American political organizations. As noted by a local newspaper, the key to the success of this project was a small group of San Antonio-based Hispanic scholars.

There have been efforts to document and expand the public understanding of the rich tradition of Hispanic theater. TCH worked with scholars to develop newspaper supplements disseminating new scholarship on the history of Mexican Americans in Texas. It has supported research and production costs for a one-hour dramatic film on the life and music of singer Lydia Mendoza. It has funded radio programs interpreting Mexican American literature and research and public programs on the unique architecture found in Texas' border cities. It has supported research and programs on the image of the Mexican American in American film and literature. It has financed research, lectures, readings, and discussions in five Texas towns on Mexican American women in literature and the arts. It has sponsored research and a symposium allowing Mexican, Anglo American, and Mexican American scholars to offer fresh interpretations of the Texas revolution. A number of projects that have sought to document the connections between the history and culture of Mexico and the history and culture of Texas Mexican Americans have been funded by TCH. It has supported many museum exhibitions that document and interpret Mexican American history and culture, from the specific, such as the meaning of the religious and secular observance *Día de los Muertos* to the general, such as the relatively unknown cultures of ancient West Mexico. And the TCH has helped many communities across the state document their local history, working with citizens to uncover this history and place these stories in a broader social and cultural framework and often in the context of regional, national, and international history.

Advisory committees for these projects have included public as well as academic representation. Some of the sponsors have been universities (especially in more recent years), but others have been local community organizations and institutions, such as Casa de Amigos in Midland, La Pena, Inc. in Austin, Guadalupe Cultural Arts Center in San Antonio, Institute for Intercultural Studies and Research in San Antonio, Southwest Center for Educational Television, and Houston Hispanic Forum, to name a few.

TCH itself has also stimulated this scholarship of engagement in a number of special ways. The March/April 1984 issue of *The Texas Humanist* was devoted to an exploration of "The Borderlands: Grappling with a Dual Heritage," with original essays by a number of leading scholars and writers. In 1986, TCH launched "The Mexican Legacy of

Texas" as its special emphasis topic for the year of the Texas Sesquicentennial. Funding from the NEH allowed TCH to combine its own work with work undertaken by grantees. Through a request for proposals, the TCH approved eleven grants for public programs dealing with various facets of this subject, with these programs held in Houston, Kingsville, Abilene, Edinburg, Harlingen, San Antonio, Austin, Brownsville, Dallas, Fort Worth, and College Station. TCH commissioned essays by leading Mexican American scholars, with presentations drawn from these essays given in a number of public settings. Excerpts of papers given at the 1986 Texas Lecture and Symposium on the Humanities were published in the Spring/Summer 1987 issue of *Texas Journal of Ideas, History and Culture*, the successor magazine to *The Texas Humanist*. One can also point to a new round of public service scholarship focusing on Mexican American history and culture as a component of TCH's 1992 special emphasis on "Encounter of Two Worlds," to mark the Columbian Quincentenary. Conferences, exhibits, lectures, and media programming all flowed from this initiative.

Much of this work has moved into the mainstream of humanistic scholarship, as seen for instance in the increasing number of titles of books published by university presses; for example, a collection of essays published under the title *Tejano Origins in Eighteenth-Century San Antonio* by the University of Texas Press. These essays stem from a TCH-funded symposium and exhibit focusing on community development and identity in a Spanish Borderlands region. In their acknowledgments, the editors state that the book "is evidence of the enthusiasm displayed during the last several years by many people interested in better understanding the relevance of the history of Spain and Mexico in the regions that now constitute the United States Southwest." They also note that "it was the enthusiastic support from San Antonio's community organizations which made the symposium a great success."

The dissemination of this scholarship has led to greater public awareness of Mexican American and Latino culture in general. For example, the Fall/Winter 1994 issue of *Texas Journal of Ideas, History and Culture*, devoted to a survey of Latino literature in the United States, offers a sixteen-page resource guide and selected bibliography for teachers, librarians, and general readers. Of the two hundred and fifty-six works cited, none were published before 1967, and only a handful were published before 1980.

This new scholarship has reached very large audiences throughout the United States through film and television. I think of Hector Galan's work, and the 1993 broadcast of *The Hunt for Pancho Villa* as part of

The American Experience series on PBS. Working with a talented group of scholars, Galan drew on old black-and-white photos, rare archival film, and oral histories to shed new light on an extraordinary period in the history of Mexico and the U.S. Southwest, and offered fresh perspectives on Villa as an agent of historical change.

In this model of engagement, the Mexican American community of Texas, and many others outside this community who were supportive of its efforts, asked something very special of the scholarly community—to document the history and culture of a people, to further prepare that people, and those from other cultures and traditions—including the dominant culture—for a cultural, political, and societal pluralism in which all groups stand on equal footing. In this intellectual and social project, a project still far from complete, the state humanities council appears on the scene as a catalyst, helping to bring the needs, interests, and insights of the public to the scholar and the growing knowledge and insight of the scholar to the public.

This model of the humanities engaged, which promotes dialogue among citizens of diverse backgrounds, what Cornel West calls "transracial communication," surely serves to cultivate the civic imagination, expanding public understanding of how peoples and cultures are bound together. "The essence of the humanities," states the Commission on the Humanities in its 1980 report, "is a spirit or an attitude toward humanity. They show how the individual is autonomous and at the same time bound, in the ligatures of language and history, to humankind across time and throughout the world." The humanities allow the individual to imagine the life of another, with the result that empathy is evoked. But bonding also occurs, as autonomy gives way to an enlarged sense of community. We cannot hope to build institutions and cultural structures that bring together the American people and that work to advance American society without an adequate and empathetic understanding of the histories, traditions, and experiences that bind us together. Nor can we deal with those forces that would pull us apart, leaving us to twist in the cold winds of ignorance and prejudice, without this understanding.

Reconstructing the Public Role of the Scholar

How shall we understand this model of scholarly engagement? It certainly offers a fresh and invigorating model that differs fundamentally from previous models of the scholarly profession which may still inspire but which now may be obsolete, models which have received considerable scrutiny in the last several years.

On the one hand, we have Allan Bloom (*The Closing of the American Mind*), who grieves over the loss of the traditional intellectual scholar who in his view has become the victim of all that is wrong with the modern university. The traditional scholar that Bloom wishes to resuscitate is one who stands above and outside the clash of cultures, outside competing economic and political interests, and yet one who has a vision of the good life, knowledge of the best that has been thought and said, an ideal of what it means to be an educated person, and one who, in this view, serves as the bearer of an intellectual tradition that ought to shape the moral development of individuals.

On the other hand, we have Russell Jacoby (*The Last Intellectuals*), for whom the problem is the opposite in that the challenge for the contemporary scholar is not the intrusion of the public on the university but the shrinkage of the public sphere within the university. The contemporary university scholar stands in contrast to the public intellectuals of the past, writers like Lewis Mumford, who knew how to write for a general, albeit well-educated, public audience on matters of public interest. These intellectuals, Jacoby argues, have vanished, giving way to the narrow, self-absorbed scholar whose work is read more and more by fewer and fewer people—mainly associates whose sub-specialties match his or her own (on this point Jacoby and Bloom agree). Jacoby notes that "Literature, history, and philosophy belong to the common stock of humanity; their importance resides partly in their accessibility to an educated reader." Intellectuals have become isolated academics, and in the process they have lost not only the ability to communicate with large audiences, but the ability to interact on contemporary social problems as well. The university, Jacoby maintains, is now cut off from the society and culture in which it exists.

Jacoby might be right in his assessment of the decline of public intellectuals in the Mumford tradition. And Bloom certainly is correct in pointing out that the day is over when, as Carl Boggs comments in his book *Intellectuals and the Crisis of Modernity*, "traditional intellectual work could be carried out in a relatively self-contained, autonomous university setting, when the contemplative life could flourish without the bothersome intrusions of social conflict."

What this model of engagement shows, I believe, is that there are many roles being played by today's scholars with which Bloom would surely disagree and with which Jacoby unfortunately seems ignorant. Boggs observes that while "Bloom and Jacoby each bemoan the passing of genuine intellectual activity in modern society, they have altogether different agendas in mind." Yet "if both embrace romanticized visions of an independent intelligentsia, they also agree that authentic rational inquiry has been marginalized within the public sphere, if not abolished completely." Boggs correctly points out that contemporary experience contradicts this assessment. Since the 1960s we have seen the rise of "a highly visible critical intelligentsia in the United States," and this, coupled with "the growth of a radical culture and intellectual subculture . . . suggests that the thesis of intellectual decline needs to be fully reconsidered."

The model of engagement that I have offered demonstrates how some scholars are responding to critical public issues of our time. It demonstrates, as Boggs maintains, that "older modes of understanding the role of intellectuals are obsolete, demanding fundamental new theories and concepts." As noted earlier, thousands of scholars from public and private colleges and universities participate each year in public projects supported by the state humanities councils, and of these there are a significant number who are exploring models of engagement that depart radically from the traditional public humanities model.

In understanding this development, I offer four components of this model of public service scholarship as seen in the work of those Texas scholars focused on Mexican American history and culture in public projects supported by TCH, elements that set this model off from the ones offered by Bloom and Jacoby.

First, these scholars seem to derive their intellectual interests and energy from the people with whom they have maintained or have established genuine conversation. They see themselves as inside, not above or outside, this community. The inspiration for their work comes as much from the people as it does from their own intellectual curiosity.

Second, these scholars see themselves as part of a community of scholars who are concerned with this particular history and culture—its past, present, and future—and they tend to be open to interdisciplinary and multidisciplinary collaboration.

Third, they believe that they are closing the gap between social and cultural life and politics. They recognize that their intellectual work can and should support a broad civic agenda, empowering citizens to exercise their rights and responsibilities as citizens.

Fourth, these scholars are carving out an expanded understanding of their profession, giving concrete expression to the idea of service, and offering alternative models for how the profession conducts its business and for the values that it holds.

This public service scholarship model gives hope that as the twentieth century closes we may see the reconstruction of the role of the scholar in American society. The key factor in this reconstruction will be the public, for the transformative power of the projects that express this model rests not in bringing scholars before the public, although that is surely a public good, but rather in bringing the interests, concerns, and ideas of the public to scholars. When that happens, when that connection is made, and when scholars respond with enthusiasm, those participating scholars inevitably will be about a magnificent task, that of working side by side with the public to enhance the civic imagination.

But this model of engagement remains overall a promise. This important work has only begun, and further development and refinement of the model is needed. Can the humanities community be motivated to connect with the public, to take on the cultivation of the civic imagination as a primary task? Where might these connections occur? And, if these connections are made, how might a rebirth of civic imagination lead to the rehabilitation of public life, the reconstruction of citizenship, and the transformation of society? How can we intellectually connect the humanities to primary public issues? How can we stimulate scholarship on issues and themes that weigh heavily on the public's mind? How and what will scholars learn from the public? And how can we develop a community of thinkers—citizens willing to use the humanities in public deliberation—upon whose shoulders such a project ultimately rests? Where exactly might the points of engagement be? And, most importantly, what will scholars and the public learn together, should serious engagement occur?

There is no shortage of issues that are of deep interest to the public and that call out for scholarly engagement. I offer one example—the consequences of exploding crime and violence in American society, a matter of deep concern to communities across the country. Increasing crime has led to an ever-expanding prison population, with 1,012,851 persons incarcerated in state and federal prisons as of June 1994, a figure that does not include an additional four hundred and forty thousand persons in local jails either awaiting trial or sentenced to short terms. In less than a decade, the United States prison population has doubled.

Texas is first in the nation in the rate of incarceration. According to state officials, in a few years only China and Russia will have more prison beds than Texas. Texas has underway the largest public works project undertaken by any state in the United States, a $1.3 billion effort to double its prison capacity, to a total of one hundred and forty-five thousand inmates. And officials see no end in sight; by the year 2000,

Texas will need more than two hundred thousand beds. The chairman of the Texas Board of Criminal Justice defends this extraordinary project, arguing that "We have no alternative, no other choice. . . . If there's any criticism, it's been that we're not building fast enough."

No other choice? What kind of investment in the state's future are the citizens of Texas making? Perhaps before embarking on this unprecedented prison-building project, more preliminary questions should have been asked—questions that beg for extended public deliberation. Why the crime explosion? Why are Americans almost five times more likely to be the victim of a violent crime in the 1990s than in 1960? Why did juvenile crime in the United States increase forty-seven percent from 1988 to 1992? Why are we such a violent society? What are we as a society doing wrong? What are the root causes of violence and crime? What do the demographics of the prison population tell us? And what do the horrific illiteracy and school dropout rates tell us as well? What values shape our response to crime and to issues of punishment and rehabilitation? What might we learn from other societies? What are the characteristics of those democratic nations that have low crime rates? And what does it mean when the prison budget is second only to public education in a state budget, when a prison budget explodes from $91 million a year in 1980 to a projected $3 billion a year twenty years later, and when we seem prepared to allocate an estimated $40,000 a year to maintain a prisoner for the next thirty years but argue endlessly over whether spending $5,000 a year on each public school student may be too much? Have we really explored all the alternatives? Upon what basis—what moral and political foundation—do we proceed to build more and more prisons, expending vast sums of scarce public funds, when it seems abundantly clear that the penal system is broken, that incarceration for the purposes of deterrence, punishment, and/or rehabilitation, no longer works? What values are operative in the public policy chosen? In public policies not chosen?

The Humanities and Communal Vision

As we look to the twenty-first century, the development of an educated and engaged citizenry has increasingly become a matter of personal and societal survival. If the humanities are to help cultivate the civic imagination, if this becomes a national project involving as many citizens as possible, then we know that more scholars in the humanities will need to allocate more time to interaction with the public and to critical issues facing society. These scholars will need to be good listeners, to hear with empathy the questions being asked by their fellow citizens. We need ongoing conversation between scholars and the public, not one-time programs. We need projects in communities across the nation that promote the kind of sustained dialogue and thinking that fosters the civic imagination and lifts scholars and their fellow citizens beyond the social, cultural, and political divisions of our time. We can hope that such projects will inspire people to rebuild a terribly weakened civic infrastructure. Scholars who participate in these projects have an opportunity to make an invaluable contribution to American democracy.

Within the university community itself, as public issues are taken more seriously, increasing energy will need to be focused on undergraduate teaching and especially on those courses that all undergraduates—regardless of majors and planned careers—should take, if we are to nourish intellectual leadership in the community. Undoubtedly, more attention will have to be paid to multidisciplinary approaches to inquiry and learning and to successful models for the stimulation of civic imagination, models of interaction and learning that might hold relevance for public programs. And, for this project to be successful over the long haul, graduate education in the humanities, the preparation of individuals for careers in the humanities, will need to focus increasingly on this project and on the relationship between scholarship and citizenship. In so doing, the humanities community, in replanting itself, may very well be preparing a very different kind of scholar for the twenty-first century.

Carl Boggs reminds us that "the intellectual realm has been viewed throughout history as a wellspring of creative innovation . . ." In its financial as well as moral support of the humanities, especially through state and federal appropriations, the public should request the engagement of the scholarly community. We Americans need a vision of a revitalized Republic, an engaged citizenry willing to ask tough questions about American identity, about what it is that we as a people value, about how we want to be and how we want to live, individually and collectively. The humanities, which have their foundation in the community as well as the academy, have much to offer in fostering this vision.

Works Cited

"A Conversation with Cornel West." *Humanities* 15 (March/April 1994).

Birnbaum, Norman. *The Radical Renewal: The Politics of Ideas in Modern America*. New York: Pantheon Books, 1988.

Black, Charles L., Jr. *The Humane Imagination*. Woodbridge, Connecticut: Ox Bow Press, 1986.

Bloom, Allan. *The Closing of the American Mind*. New York: Simon and Schuster, 1987.

Boggs, Carl. *Intellectuals and the Crisis of Modernity*. Albany: State University of New York Press, 1993.

Frankel, Charles. "Why the Humanities?" in *The Humanist as Citizen*, edited by John Agresto and Peter Riesenberg. Chapel Hill: National Humanities Center, 1981.

Hofstadter, Richard. *Anti-intellectualism in American Life*, 1962. Reprint, New York: Alfred Knopf, 1970.

Humanities in American Life: Report of the Commission on the Humanities. Berkeley: University of California Press, 1980.

Jacoby, Russell. *The Last Intellectuals*. New York: Basic Books, 1987.

Melville, Margarita B. and Hilda Castillo Phariss, eds. *Reflections on the Mexican Experience in Texas*. University of Houston: Mexican American Studies, Monograph No. 1, 1979.

Montejano, David. *Anglos and Mexicans in the Making of Texas, 1836-1986*. Austin: The University of Texas Press, 1987.

Poyo, Gerald E. and Gilberto M. Hinojosa, eds. *Tejano Origins in Eighteenth Century San Antonio*. Austin: The University of Texas Press, 1991.

Quay, James and James F. Veninga, "Making Connections: The Humanities, Culture, and Community," in the *Report of the National Task Force on Scholarship and the Public Humanities*. New York: American Council of Learned Societies, Occasional Paper No. 11, 1990.

[1] While encouraging sponsors of such projects to examine options to particular public policy issues and even to recommend among these options, the Texas Council for the Humanities, consistent with federal guidelines, prohibits partisan politics or the direct influencing of legislation. It also has consistently supported the idea that all programs need to be open to multiple perspectives and viewpoints.

Index

Schon, Donald, 246
School and College: Partnerships in Education (report), 161
schools, elementary and secondary, 44
secular humanism, 321
Select Committee on Education, 175, 250
Select Committee on Higher Education, 205–206, 209, 223–224
self governance, concept of, 149
Self-Rule: A Cultural History of American Democracy (Wiebe), 147–148
Serrano, Andres, 42, 115
sexual abuse, 338
Shakespeare (exhibit), 34
Shell Oil Companies Foundation, 10, 17
Sherman, Gene, 36
Shorris, Earl, 46
Skidmore College, Saratoga Springs, NY, 27
Smallwood, James, 168–169, 170, 172, 174
Smith, Denny, 128
Smith, Preserved, 332
Snow, C.P., 182
social ills
  dealing with, 356–357
  statistics on, 338
Social Studies Education Center, Southwest Texas State University, 22
South Plains Friends of the Humanities, 21
Southwest Alternate Media Project of Houston, 309
Southwest Center for Educational Television, 393
Southwest Center for Urban Research, 8
Southwest Institute for Research on Women, Tucson, Arizona, 27
Southwest Texas State University, 216, 243
Speaking for the Humanities (American Council of Learned Societies), 118, 130, 351

specialization, as a result of professionalism, 182
Spindletop, 28
"Splendors of Mexico" (exhibit), 10
standardized achievement tests, 175
standards for program, 79–80
Standing with the Public: The Humanities and Democratic Practice (Veninga and McAfee), 138, 379
State Board of Education
  corporate influence on, 177
  improvement of curriculum, 175
  and public school curriculum, 162–163
state government, 55–61
state humanities councils
  accountability, 55–61
  audits, 128
  board of directors, 4–6, 56
  budgets, 107–108
  Cheney as defender of, 111
  criticism of, 106–107
  defending appropriations for, 102–108
  goals, 73
  mission, 68–82
  models, 153–154
  role in exploring relationship between humanities and public life, 95–101
  role of in democracy, 146–156
State Preservation Board, 11
statistics on humanities projects, 352
Stearns, Peter, 260
Steel, Ronald, 13, 271, 279, 280
Steele, Shelby, 259
Strachey, Lytton, 275
Strouse, Jean, 13, 86, 271–273, 280
The Structural Transformation of the Public Sphere (Habermas), 137
Stuckey, Sterling, 14
The Study of the Future (Cornish), 196
subject based programs, 76–82
Sunday, Billy, 321
Supple, Jerome, 243
Symms, Steve, 128

DATE DUE

Printed
in USA

HIGHSMITH #45230